PHP in Action

Objects, Design, Agility

DAGFINN REIERSØL
MARCUS BAKER
CHRIS SHIFLETT

MANNING

Greenwich
(74° w. long.)

Manning Publications Co.   Copyeditor: Benjamin Berg
Sound View Court 3B   Typesetter: Tony Roberts
Greenwich, CT 06830   Cover designer: Leslie Haimes

ISBN 1-932394-75-3

Printed in the United States of America
1 2 3 4 5 6 7 8 9 10 – MAL – 11 10 09 08 07

brief contents

contents

preface

The story behind this book is personal. A few years ago, I came to the realization that what I had done in my professional life until then was not quite up to my own expectations. Though not dramatic enough to qualify as a midlife crisis, this realization got me thinking in new ways.

I was doing web programming in PHP at the time. I was in an isolated position in the company I was working for, so I decided to put my own work under the microscope. I asked myself, "How can I boost myself to a higher level of performance?" One idea that occurred to me was to review my own work at the end of every day. What did I do that was most successful? How could I do more of that? What was less successful? How could I do less of that?

The task that stood out like a sore thumb was debugging. It was obviously taking up a major part of my time, and anything that would make debugging more efficient or diminish the need for it should make me more productive. I looked around for ways to catch bugs earlier. I tried defensive programming, with limited success. Then I stumbled across agile processes and test-driven development, Extreme Programming, and refactoring. It seemed like what my colleagues and I had been doing for some years, only better. I took up the methodology first in my own, individual work. At this point, there was little recognition of it in the PHP community. I was early; I worked test-first with the very first alpha version of PHPUnit that appeared in March 2002.

The idea of writing this book occurred to me when I inherited some nasty PHP code from a fellow programmer. I realized that the code could be improved, refactored, in ways that I could describe systematically. This had to be useful to someone, I thought. And there was no book about agile processes and test-driven development in PHP.

Then, one event jump-started the project: I got fired from my job. (A few months later, I became a member of the board at the company I had been fired from, but that's an entirely different story.) It took about three years to finish the book. It was hard to get it into a shape that the reviewers were sufficiently enthusiastic about, and I had to rewrite most of it a couple of times. Marcus Baker and Chris Shiflett came into the process near the end. In the meantime, the marriage of PHP, agility, design patterns, and unit testing had become a mainstream subject. The most important official events in this process were the release of PHP 5 and the start of the Zend Framework project.

Among the many things I learned along the way is the importance of reading books yourself if you want to write one. I believe in the importance of deep understanding, not as knowing a lot of details, but as knowing each detail in depth. And I believe that comes from having a strong foundation and from being able to see one issue from several perspectives.

That has led me to repeatedly reexamine the basics. I keep asking seemingly stupid questions; in fact, I'm often mistaken for a beginner in web forums, even when discussing subjects I know well. And I believe that the deeper my own understanding is, the better I can explain the subject to others. I hope this quest will prove helpful to you too.

DAGFINN REIERSØL

acknowledgments

I wrote this book with a little help from my friends, and enemies.

To get the enemies out of the way first, I use that word to make a point; they are not bad people, nor are they out to get me (I hope). But there were a few who made my life a little more difficult, pushing me into doing things I would otherwise not have done and into raising own level of performance. And I am grateful to them for that, but I'll show my gratitude by *not* naming them.

On the friendly side, I thank my wife, Regine, and my daughter, Maria, for love, support, and challenge. I thank my son Jacob (now six years old) for his reckless enthusiasm and original wisdom, some of which is reflected in this book.

On a more practical level, the most important contributions have come from the co-authors: my good friend, Marcus Baker, whom I have never met; and Chris Shiflett, who took the time out of a busy schedule to produce an introduction to security.

Like many other Manning authors, I am deeply impressed with the Manning staff and their commitment to quality. They know and do what it takes to lift a book to a higher level of readability and interest. Maybe I'm just conceited, but I like the result so much that whenever I need to reread a chapter, I actually enjoy it!

The review process is exhausting but important. Publisher Marjan Bace, in particular, has a unique ability and determination to take the least-uplifting feedback, even when it's unspecific, and squeeze something useful out of it.

Thanks to these reviewers who took the time out of their busy schedules to read the manuscript at various stages of development: Richard Lynch, Andrew Grothe, Kieran Mathieson, Jochem Maas, Max Belushkin, Dan McCullough, Frank Jania, Jay Blanchard, Philip Hallstrom, Robin Vickery, David Hanson, Robbert van Andel, Jeremy Ashcraft, Anthony Topper, Wahid Sadik, Nick Heudecker, and Robert D. McGovern. Special thanks to Mark Monster who did an extra pass through the book just before it went to press, checking it for technical accuracy.

Another indirect contributor is my long-term friend and colleague, Per Einar Arnstad. The ideas from our creative discussions and interactions are part of the bedrock of my thinking about software, and his entrepreneurial spirit inspired me to take the risks necessary to make this work possible.

Thanks also to another colleague, Tarjei Huse, who gave me what may be the most intelligent overall feedback on the manuscript.

Finally, a special word of thanks to Kathrine Breistøl, who promised me the full proceeds from the return bottles in her kitchen if my financial situation were to become intolerable. I never had to ask her to round them up.

about this book

This book's purpose involves a kind of bigamy. It introduces state-of-the art object-oriented design principles, patterns, and techniques. Then it weds these to two different partners. The first partner is PHP, the programming language. The second partner is the PHP programmer's everyday work.

More specifically, this book is about handling and implementing these principles, patterns, and techniques in PHP with its specific syntax and characteristics. It is also about how to apply them to the specific and common challenges of web programming.

Who should read this book?

This book is for programmers who develop applications in PHP and want to learn modern object-oriented practices, principles, and techniques, and how to apply them to the everyday challenges of web programming.

It is not a beginner's book in PHP; it presupposes a minimum of familiarity with PHP—or experience in other programming languages—and with the basic ideas and challenges of web programming.

How this book is organized

The book is divided into four parts. Parts 1 and 2 introduce the principles, patterns, and techniques mentioned initially and demonstrate how they can be implemented in PHP. Part 1 introduces and develops the subjects of object-oriented programming and design. Part 2 deals with unit testing and refactoring.

Parts 3 and 4 apply the material from the first two parts to the everyday challenges of web programming. Part 3 is about the web interface, while part 4 deals with databases and data storage.

Part 1: Basic tools and concepts

Part 1 moves gradually, chapter by chapter, from the nuts and bolts of object-oriented programming in PHP to the more conceptual subject of object-oriented application design.

Chapter 1 introduces and discusses the pros and cons of PHP and agile practices.

Chapter 2 and *chapter 3* deal with the mechanics and syntax of object-oriented programming in PHP. Although objects and classes are ultimately inseparable subjects, chapter 2 focuses mostly on object features and chapter 3 on class features.

Chapter 4 discusses why objects and classes are a good idea, how they relate to the real world, and how we can tell the difference between good and bad object-oriented designs.

Chapter 5 is about the basic class relationships—inheritance, association, and composition—and the role of interfaces in program design.

Chapter 6 is where we start to go into object-oriented design in earnest. It deals with object-oriented principles that serve as general guidelines for design.

Chapter 7 introduces the subject of design patterns—recurrent solutions to common design problems—and describes some of the most common ones.

Chapter 8 shows how design principles and patterns work in the context of an extended example: date and time handling.

Part 2: Testing and refactoring

Part 2 focuses on testing and refactoring (improving the design of existing code) from two perspectives: as quality assurance, and as a learning process.

Chapter 9 introduces unit testing and test-driven development, using a database transaction class as an example.

Chapter 10 digs deeper into the realm of unit testing, showing how to set up tests properly and use mock objects and other fakes to make testing easier. It builds on the previous example by creating a contact manager on top of the transaction class.

Chapter 11 is about refactoring, with a particular focus on web applications. It deals with refactoring in the traditional object-oriented sense as well as techniques for getting poorly designed procedural code into a more manageable state.

Chapter 12 finishes the subject of testing by moving the searchlight from unit testing to web testing. Using the contact manager once again, it shows how to make sure the user interface is what the customer wanted and how to design the entire web application top-down.

Part 3: Building the web interface

Part 3 is about the defining feature of web programming: the web interface.

Chapter 13 explains the principles of separating HTML markup from program code, and describes how this can be done by using template engines and specific techniques.

Chapter 14 takes on the challenge of assembling web pages from many separate components and tells you how to implement the Composite View design pattern.

Chapter 15 introduces the subject of user interaction and the Model-View-Controller (MVC) design pattern.

Chapter 16 teaches you how to implement the web-specific variations on MVC, including Page Controller and Front Controller.

Chapter 17 deals in depth with server-side and client-side input validation and how to synchronize these.

Chapter 18 shows how to develop form handling, building on the PEAR package HTML_QuickForm.

Part 4: Databases and infrastructure

Part 4 deals with the subject of databases and data storage from an object-oriented point of view.

Chapter 19 tells two different stories. One is about how to handle database connections appropriately in an object-oriented application and how to deal with the configuration the database connection requires. The other is about database abstraction: how to make the code independent of the specifics of one database management system.

Chapter 20 is about the challenges posed by the fact that we have to use a completely separate programming language—SQL—to query the database. It shows how to encapsulate, hide, and generalize SQL code.

Chapter 21 assembles some of the pieces from the two previous chapters into complete design patterns for object-oriented data access.

Appendixes

Appendix A gives some specific information on testing and test tools that did not fit into the chapters on testing. Reference material on the essential parts of the SimpleTest and PHPUnit APIs is included.

Appendix B is an introduction to security in PHP.

How to use this book

The parts of this book are relatively independent. It should be possible to start reading any one of them without reading the earlier parts. Unless you already have a strong grasp of object-oriented programming and design, reading part 1 first is likely to make your understanding of part 3 and part 4 easier, deeper, and more complete. But the workings of all the examples in the later parts are explained in detail. The examples throw light on the concepts from part 1, but generally do not depend on them.

On the other hand, some of the chapters in each part depend heavily on each other. For example, it may be difficult to read the refactoring examples in chapter 11 without understanding the basics of unit testing as explained in chapters 9 and 10.

Source code

All source code in listings or in text is in a `fixed-width font like this` to separate it from ordinary text. Annotations accompany many of the listings, highlighting important concepts. In some cases, numbered bullets link to explanations that follow the listing.

Source code for all of the working examples in this book is available for download from www.manning.com/reiersol or www.manning.com/PHPinAction.

Author Online

Purchase of *PHP in Action* includes free access to a private web forum run by Manning Publications where you can make comments about the book, ask technical questions, and receive help from the authors and from other users. To access the forum and subscribe to it, point your web browser to www.manning.com/reiersol or www.manning.com/PHPinAction. This page provides information on how to get on the forum once you are registered, what kind of help is available, and the rules of conduct on the forum.

Manning's commitment to our readers is to provide a venue where a meaningful dialog between individual readers and between readers and the authors can take place. It is not a commitment to any specific amount of participation on the part of the authors, whose contribution to the AO remains voluntary (and unpaid). We suggest you try asking the authors some challenging questions, lest their interest stray!

The Author Online forum and the archives of previous discussions will be accessible from the publisher's website as long as the book is in print.

About the authors

DAGFINN REIERSØL has been designing and developing web applications, web content mining software, web programming tools, and text analysis programs, mostly in PHP, since 1997. He also has a long history as a technical writer of software manuals. He lives in Oslo, Norway.

MARCUS BAKER has been a software consultant for many years specializing in OO design and development as well as web application development and testing. He is also a columnist for *PHP Architecture Magazine* and lives in London, England.

CHRIS SHIFLETT is a PHP consultant and security expert as well as a leader in the PHP community. He is the founder of the PHP Security Consortium and the author of the *HTTP Developer's Handbook* and *Essential PHP Security*. He lives in Brooklyn, New York.

about the title

By combining introductions, overviews, and how-to examples, the *In Action* books are designed to help learning and remembering. According to research in cognitive science, the things people remember are things they discover during self-motivated exploration.

Although no one at Manning is a cognitive scientist, we are convinced that for learning to become permanent it must pass through stages of exploration, play, and, interestingly, re-telling of what is being learned. People understand and remember new things, which is to say they master them, only after actively exploring them. Humans learn in action. An essential part of an *In Action* guide is that it is example-driven. It encourages the reader to try things out, to play with new code, and explore new ideas.

There is another, more mundane, reason for the title of this book: our readers are busy. They use books to do a job or solve a problem. They need books that allow them to jump in and jump out easily and learn just what they want just when they want it. They need books that aid them in action. The books in this series are designed for such readers.

about the cover illustration

The figure on the cover of *PHP in Action* is a "Paysanne," or French peasant woman. The illustration is taken from the 1805 edition of Sylvain Maréchal's four-volume compendium of regional dress customs. This book was first published in Paris in 1788, one year before the French Revolution. Each drawing is colored by hand.

The diversity of the illustrations in Marechal's collection speaks vividly of the uniqueness and individuality of the world's towns and provinces just 200 years ago. This was a time when the dress codes of two regions separated by a few dozen miles identified people uniquely as belonging to one or the other. These drawings bring to life a sense of isolation and distance of that period and of every other historic period except our own hyperkinetic present.

Dress codes have changed since then and the diversity by region, so rich at the time, has faded away. It is now often hard to tell the inhabitant of one continent from another. Perhaps, trying to view it optimistically, we have traded a cultural and visual diversity for a more varied personal life. Or a more varied and interesting intellectual and technical life.

We at Manning celebrate the inventiveness, the initiative, and the fun of the computer business with book covers based on the rich diversity of regional life two centuries ago brought back to life by the pictures from this collection.

Tools and concepts

When you have a job to do, a natural way to start is to first find the tools you need. In the object-oriented world, the distinction between tools and concepts is blurry. There are tools to describe and implement conceptual relationships, and there are conceptual strategies that act as tools for the design process.

This first part of the book is about these tools and concepts; most of them belong to the category of object-oriented programming and application design. We will be applying these to the challenges of web programming in parts 3 and 4. We will look at the syntax of objects and classes in PHP, why and how these can be put to use, and how to use design patterns and object-oriented principles.

C H A P T E R　1

PHP and modern software development

A cartoon depicts a man in a business suit, apparently a doctor, talking on the telephone: "Yes, Mr. Jones, acupuncture may work for a while. Any quack treatment may work for a while. But only scientific medical practice can keep a person alive forever."[1]

This absurd and arrogant statement is obviously not likely to convince the patient. And yet, if we ignore the bizarre specifics, we can see that the fictitious doctor is at least addressing an important issue: the importance of keeping long-term goals in mind.

The long-term benefit of medical treatment is a long way from the subject matter of this book, but the long-term perspective in software development is another matter. Modern software engineering may not attempt to make software last forever, but long-term productivity is one of the key issues in the development of new technologies, principles, and methodologies. This is the reason why object-oriented programming is the *de facto* standard today: it is a way of making software easier to maintain and develop beyond the first version. Other buzzwords such as *design patterns* and *agile development* are also related to this.

---

[1]　This is quoted from memory. I saw this cartoon years ago in the office of a colleague and have not seen it since.

3

Version 5 of PHP (recursive acronym for PHP: Hypertext Processor) is, among other things, an attempt to make it easier to use these conceptual and methodological tools in PHP.

In this book, we start there and discover how that changes everything. We will cover three interrelated goals:

- *Explore and maximize usage of the toolkit.* We will use modern methods and tools to raise our development skills to a new level.
- *Provide full coverage.* We will be applying the toolkit to every facet of web programming, from the user interface to database interaction.
- *Keep it simple.* We will follow Albert Einstein's recommendation to keep everything as simple as possible, but no simpler.

Whatever your reasons for using PHP (they may be somewhat accidental, as they were for me), it's helpful to understand PHP's strong points and even more useful to know how to overcome its limitations. For this reason, we start this chapter by discussing some of the pros and cons of PHP itself. Then we introduce modern object-oriented and agile methods and see how they relate to PHP.

1.1   HOW PHP CAN HELP YOU

PHP has always been a language which is especially useful for web programming. It still is, and with PHP 5 (and PHP 6, which may be released by the time you read this), it has been brought up-to-date and established as a language that is fully compatible with modern object-oriented methods, practices, and principles. In the following sections, we will see why PHP has become so popular as a web programming language and how to deal with the limitations of the language.

1.1.1   Why PHP is so popular

There is no doubt that PHP is a popular web programming language, at least in the sense of being heavily used. Studying the URLs of pages you visit on the Web should be enough to demonstrate that. There has to be a reason for this popularity. Some commercial products may gain popularity through massive marketing efforts, but PHP clearly is not among them.

In this section, we will see how PHP encourages a pragmatic attitude and how convenient it is—being easy to use and deploy, having important security features built in, and supporting standard ways of doing basic things. Finally, we will note how PHP also works with "enterprise" design and technology, including commercial database management systems and layered or tiered architectures.

A pragmatic attitude

One thing I like about PHP is the attitude of the people who use it. PHP has always been a pragmatic solution to real problems. It's only natural that PHP programmers tend to be pragmatic rather than dogmatic, humble and open rather than conceited and pretentious. They like PHP, but they know that there is no perfect technology, no perfect programming language. Everything has its pros and cons, its advantages and disadvantages. PHP programmers tend not to start language wars. That's fortunate; often arrogance on behalf of a programming language—or any other software—is based in ignorance. You know all the things your favorite language can do, and you don't know how to do the same things in other languages. It's easy to assume that these things can't be done. But that's rather like assuming that your car is the only one in the universe that has air conditioning.

Finding faults with a programming language is easy. If it lacks a feature you desperately feel you need, you can use that as a reason to put it down. If it has a feature you think is totally unnecessary, you can frown upon that. PHP 4 had no visibility constraints such as private methods; this of course was a Bad Thing to programmers who were used to languages such as C++ and Java. PHP 5 has visibility constraints, and I'm sure there are others—who are accustomed to other languages that lack these features—who find this appalling.

The fact is you don't know how a feature or the lack of it works in real life until you've used it for a while. PHP has been criticized for having too many functions, in contrast to Perl, which has fewer. I've used both languages extensively, and I happen to prefer the way lots of functions are easily available in PHP. Someone else may feel differently, but the most important point is that the difference is much less dramatic than some people think. Language wars are too often fought over differences that may have a marginal impact on overall productivity.

Easy to use and deploy

PHP is easy to learn. The threshold for starting to make simple web pages with dynamic content is low. Anyone who is capable of creating an HTML page will also be able to add simple dynamic content to it using PHP.

Some will lament the fact that this will let you do (some) web programming even if you are not a properly educated software engineer. But this is the way the world works. A large part of basic software development has been about empowering users who are not computer experts, allowing them to do more and more tasks that were previously reserved for the technical gurus. In the 1960s, you couldn't even use a computer without the aid of a technical expert. That changed as interactive terminals, PCs, and office software appeared. The invention of the electronic spreadsheet made it possible for end users to do calculations that previously required a programmer. And today, most applications allow a fairly wide range of customization without programming. Search engines provide easy ways to specify a search without using Boolean expressions. These are just some examples of tasks that used to require programming skills, but no longer do.

Another, more relevant objection to PHP's low threshold of entry is the fact that it can make things seem too easy. It may foster a false impression that complex web applications using databases with complex dynamic user interfaces can be created and maintained with just basic knowledge. But web applications are like any other software: developing and maintaining large systems with complex logic and processing requires knowledge of design principles, development methodology, and programming practices. That is why books like this one exist.

Yet the simplicity of PHP for the most basic web pages—coupled with improvements that make it easier to create complex object-oriented designs—allows it to serve a continuum of needs from the simplest, humblest web sites that may have a hit counter and one simple form, to complex, highly interactive, high-volume, high-availability sites.

Another factor that makes PHP convenient is availability. PHP is free software; it often comes installed on Linux platforms. About 60 percent of web servers run Apache, and the PHP Apache module is installed on about half of them. Nearly all hosting services offer PHP, and it's usually cheap. So PHP is widely available, and once it's available, adding new PHP web pages is as easy as with plain HTML.

In addition, PHP programming does not require an IDE or similar development aids. There are IDEs available for PHP, but any simple text editor will do if nothing fancy is available.

"Inherently safe" features

There has been a lot of focus on the security of PHP applications in recent years. Making sure a web application is secure requires real commitment on the part of the programmer, whether the platform is PHP or something else. Many security aspects will be addressed in this book.

In spite of the difficulty of securing an application, security may be part of the reason for PHP's success. On the operating system level, the way PHP is usually packaged and installed makes it relatively secure even when little effort and expertise is spent on security. When PHP is run as an Apache module, PHP scripts are protected and restrained by Apache. Typically, they cannot use the file system except for web files—the ones that are visible to users anyway—and PHP-specific include files. The scripts typically run as a user with very limited access to files on the server, and are unable to crash Apache itself.

Web application standards

Years ago, I used to say that web programming in PHP was like going on a package tour: being able to order flight and hotel reservations and even activities in one easy bundle. In a word, convenient. Perl web programming was more like having to order the hotel and the flight for yourself, while Java web programming could be likened to getting the airplane parts by mail-order-kit and having to build it yourself.

I hasten to add that this is no longer a fair description, especially in the case of Java. Although the initial cost is still higher than in PHP, you no longer have to build your own class to do something as relatively simple as encoding and decoding HTML entities. PHP web programming is still every bit as convenient as it was, though.

When I say *standards*, I'm not referring directly to the recommendations put out by the World Wide Web Consortium (W3C). I mean built-in basic infrastructure for developing web applications. This is part of the reason why PHP is so easy to use for simple web applications. Among other things, PHP has the following built into the language:

- A way of mixing HTML and dynamic content.
- Session handling.
- Readily available functions for all common tasks in web programming—as well as many uncommon ones. The typical ones include functions to handle HTTP, URLs, regular expressions, database, and XML.

For simple web programming, there is little need in PHP to get and install extra packages or to build your own infrastructure beyond what's already present.

Beyond simple convenience, there is another, not widely recognized, benefit of built-in web programming infrastructure: it makes communication easier. If everybody knows the same basic mechanisms, we can assume this knowledge when explaining more advanced concepts. Session handling, for instance, can be taken for granted with no separate explanations required, so it becomes easier to focus on the advanced subjects. Books such as this one benefit from that fact.

Encourages use of modern principles and patterns

It may be an exaggeration to say that PHP 5 is a giant leap for programmer-kind, but for PHP programmers, it represents an opportunity to use modern object-oriented programming techniques without twisting their brains into knots (unnecessary knots, anyway, such as those caused by the awkward object reference model in PHP 4).

References really are the one impediment when using techniques such as design patterns in PHP 4. Advanced object-oriented designs tend to require the ability to pass an object around without creating copies of it. It's essential that more than one object is able to hold a reference to the same object, and that changes in the referenced object are seen by the other objects. All of this is possible in PHP 4, but cumbersome. In PHP 5, it becomes as easy as in most other object-oriented languages.

PHP 5 has many other object-oriented enhancements as well, but none of them are strictly necessary to take advantage of the advances in object-oriented design.

Connects both to MySQL and other databases

One of the strengths of PHP is how easy it is to use MySQL and PHP together; there are approximately 40 books that have both "PHP" and "MySQL" in the title.

But PHP also connects to other open-source databases such as PostgreSQL and to commercial ones such as Oracle, DB2, Microsoft SQL server, and many others.

This is no surprise to PHP developers. But it's worth pointing out, since so-called enterprise applications typically use commercially available database management systems, and it's important to recognize that this does not preclude the use of PHP.

Works in layered architectures

Layered or tiered architectures are another mainstay of enterprise systems. As Martin Fowler points out in his book *Patterns of Enterprise Application Architecture* [P of EAA], the word *tier* usually implies a physical separation: the layers are not just separated conceptually and syntactically, but they are also running on different machines.

Either way, PHP is an option for parts of the system or all of it. This book will explore how to build all the parts of a web application using a layered architecture in PHP. There are other possibilities as well: for example, PHP can be used as a presentation layer for a J2EE-based application. PHP will play along with most other relevant technologies and communication protocols.

We have seen some of the reasons why PHP is a successful web programming language. But what about its limitations and weaknesses? We need to know something about those, too.

1.1.2 Overcoming PHP's limitations

Does PHP have limitations and weaknesses? Of course. As I've already admitted, there is no perfect programming language.

It's harder to decide exactly what those limitations are. They can only be judged by comparing PHP to other programming languages, and you can't do a fair comparison without extensive real-world experience of both or all the languages you are comparing

One anti-PHP web page makes the following claim: "PHP works best when you forget everything you've ever learned about good programming practices. Unfortunately, that still doesn't mean that good practice is expendable. Your code will still bite." This book attempts to prove otherwise—to show exactly how good programming practices can be used effectively in PHP.

We will look at some of the criticisms of PHP and ask what can be done about them. What follows is a list of some possible or potential weaknesses and how they will be addressed in this book.

Lacks type safety

There is a never-ending discussion between programmers: some prefer statically typed languages such as C, C++, Java and many others. Others prefer dynamically typed languages such as PHP, Perl, Smalltalk, Python, and Ruby.

Static typing means that the compiler checks the types of variables before the program runs. To make this possible, the programmer must tell the compiler which variables are supposed to belong to which types. In Java, you have to explicitly name the types of all instance variables, temporary variables, return values, and method arguments. In PHP, a dynamically typed language, no such declarations are necessary.

The idea of static typing is that it provides *type safety.* It's harder to introduce the wrong content into a variable because the content is likely to be of the wrong type, and in a statically typed language, the compiler will catch that during compilation. So some bugs in a program will be caught at compile time.

This is undeniably an advantage. The never-ending discussion concerns the question of whether this advantage outweighs the advantages and the convenience of dynamic typing. Are the bugs that are caught by static typing frequent and important ones? Are they bugs that would be caught early on anyway? Will statically typed languages make the code more verbose, thus making bugs harder to spot?

Whatever your position on this issue, there are ways to improve the situation. The compiler or interpreter is the first line of defense even in a dynamically typed language. The second line of defense is unit tests: testing the program in bits and pieces. Later in this chapter, we will see how unit testing is not necessarily a chore, but potentially a way to make programming less stressful and more pleasant.

The emphasis on unit testing has led some software gurus, such as Robert C. Martin, to move away from the idea that static typing is essential and to become more favorably inclined toward dynamically typed languages. This is based on the argument that type errors can be intercepted by the unit tests even when the compiler is not able to identify them.

Furthermore, object orientation in itself increases type safety. Objects tend to fail if you try to treat them as something they're not, and that makes problems come to the surface earlier, making it easier to diagnose them. We will discuss this further in chapter 4.

Lacks namespaces

Although this may be remedied in version 6, PHP lacks a namespace feature that would make it easier to define large-scale structure and prevent name conflicts between classes. This is a real deficiency in my opinion, especially for large projects and library software. But even then, it may be more of an annoyance than an insurmountable obstacle. In chapter 8, we will discuss some ways around this.

Performance and scalability issues

Critiques of PHP frequently point out specific problems that are believed to limit the performance of PHP applications.

The best comment to this is the "cranky, snarky" one from George Schlossnagle: "Technical details aside, I think PHP can be made to scale because so many people think that it can't."

Performance, like security, depends on skill and work more than on the programming language you're using. If you believe that using a specific programming language, or even a set of software tools, will guarantee performance and scalability, you will likely fail to achieve it.

Good program design—as outlined in this book—helps you when you need high performance by making it easier to implement generic optimization strategies, such as caching cleanly and without being overwhelmed by complexity.

Security loopholes

As mentioned, PHP has some security advantages. It also has some weaknesses, especially if you use older versions and features such as `register_globals`.

The only way to achieve security in web applications is to understand security and follow practices that protect against specific threats. There is an introduction to security in appendix B, and secure practices are discussed throughout this book.

Security loopholes are often caused by bugs. The frequency of bugs and other defects can be drastically reduced by good program design and agile practices such as unit testing and refactoring. We will get an overview of these practices in the following section.

1.2   LANGUAGES, PRINCIPLES, AND PATTERNS

The evolution of software engineering and methodology since 1990 has transformed *object-oriented* from buzzword to household word (in programmer households, that is). During this time, there have also been some conceptual innovations and shifts in the object-oriented paradigm. *Design patterns* have become widely popular. The idea of using objects to model real-world entities has been modified or deemphasized. And the concepts of *agile development* have become acceptable even in polite society. PHP 5 is an attempt to incorporate some of these ideas into PHP.

In this section, we will get an overview of the most important ideas in agile development and object-oriented design. We will introduce design patterns, refactoring, and unit testing, take a look at how and why they work and how they fit together, and begin to see how they can be implemented in PHP.

1.2.1   Agile methodologies: from hacking to happiness

You can hack your way to success. Just start coding with no thought for the morrow, pushing eagerly ahead along the path of least resistance. It can work; that is a provable fact and worth keeping in mind. I've seen several commercially successful programming projects with little methodology, structure, or systematic design effort.

That does not mean that I recommend it. In fact, this book is largely about how *not* to develop applications this way. Yes, you can cook spaghetti code in large batches; you can duplicate everything every time you need a variation on a feature. You can avoid planning ahead, so you understand nothing in the first place and then write code that is a complete mess, so you won't understand anything afterward either. And this may work for a while. Muddling through may be effective here as in other areas of life. But, eventually, you will run into trouble.

If you choose to hack, you can typically get a lot of features done quickly in the beginning, but as your application grows in complexity, you will be slowed down by hard-to-find bugs and the need to maintain duplicated code.

The traditional alternative is typically to emphasize up-front design. The idea is that you need to plan well ahead and design everything in a relatively detailed manner before you start to code. And if you're good at doing the design, the resemblance between what you do and what the customer needs will be sufficient to get you through to the first release without major problems. But along the way, you will probably have yielded to the temptation to make some changes that weren't planned, but make the software more palatable to the users. The fact is that user requirements change, and this tends to corrupt pretty designs. As programming guru Martin Fowler puts it: "Over time the code will be modified, and the integrity of the system, its structure according to that design, slowly fades. The code slowly sinks from engineering to hacking." [Fowler Refactoring]

The problem is illustrated by the so-called cost-of-change curve. With time, it becomes increasingly time-consuming and costly to change the software. The problem is often illustrated in an approximate manner by something like an exponential curve, as in figure 1.1.

The way that agile methodologies such as Extreme Programming (XP) attempt to solve this problem is by doing less up-front design, making sure it is always possible to

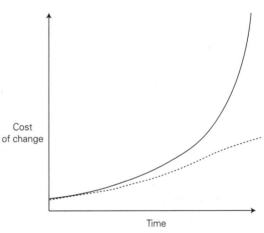

Figure 1.1 The cost-of-change curve. If the higher one is typical, agile methods are an attempt to flatten or at least lower it, as suggested by the dotted curve.

make design changes, and constantly improving the structure of the code using a set of systematic procedures known as *refactoring*.

While such a lightweight, or agile, methodology may be considered a sort of compromise between a heavy methodology and no methodology at all, it does not compromise on the quality of code or design.

Another idea that's of central importance in XP is developing software incrementally and delivering frequent releases to the customer. Developing an application without feedback from users is only slightly less dangerous than driving a car blindfolded. Unlike driving, it won't injure you physically, but you can easily end up with a product no one wants to use.

The idea is that specifying the user interface up front is insufficient. Users need to try the "look and feel" of an application. You can draw pictures of the interface, but that exposes the users to only the look, not the feel. So in agile development, it's important to get an actual application up and running as quickly as possible.

This is not a book on methodology. There are endless discussions on the merits of agile methodologies and the various practices involved, but they are beyond the scope of this book. Although some of what I will present in this book may be placed in the category of agile practices, I believe that most of it falls comfortably within the realm of consensus. Whatever your methodological preferences, they should not determine this book's usefulness to you (or lack of it).

Our recipe for success is to combine the best methodology with the best software tools, and our main software tool is PHP. So let's look next at how PHP 5 relates to the methodology.

1.2.2 PHP 5 and software trends

Version 5 of PHP can be seen as the expression of at least two different trends in modern software engineering: the object-oriented trend and the simplicity trend.

The object-oriented trend has carried with it a number of innovations, including several object-oriented languages, design patterns, and various rules and principles. The new features of PHP 5 are specifically designed to allow PHP programmers to be a part of this trend.

On the other hand, and especially in agile development, there has been a realization that problems aren't solved simply by throwing ever more complex object-oriented constructs at them, and that complexity should be kept at a minimum. PHP helps with this, too, owing to the convenience and simplicity of PHP for basic web programming tasks, and the fact that the new object-oriented features are mostly optional.

1.2.3 The evolving discipline of object-oriented programming

When object-oriented programming started to take over the world, it was generally considered a way to model the real world. Since the real world contains objects and actions, object-oriented languages seemed appropriate. And it seemed natural to model relationships between concepts as relationships between classes. Class inheritance is supposed to model an "is-a" relationship, so since a news article is a document, the NewsArticle class should inherit from the Document class as shown in the UML class diagram in figure 1.2.

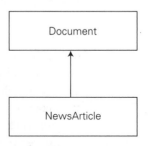

Figure 1.2
The "is-a" relationship

But the emphasis has shifted from modeling the real world to decoupling between software components. Programs are easier to maintain if you have "plug and play": if you can use standardized components easily, replace one class with another without disturbing the rest of the system, and add new features with as little change to existing code as possible. *Decoupling* refers to the fact that there is less dependency, less commitment, so to speak, between parts of the program.

And decoupling does not necessarily, or even most of the time, imply modeling the real world. It is mostly related to the mechanical interaction in the software itself—and to the user requirements it satisfies—rather than to its theoretical and conceptual relationship to the rest of the world.

A conceptual inheritance relationship implemented in software helps decoupling to some extent. But often the way to decoupling is to isolate parts of the behavior of a class into a separate component. Just for the sake of the discussion, let's assume that the only difference between a news article and other documents is in the way summaries are handled. We could have a separate summary component that's used by the document class, as shown in figure 1.3. Ignoring the fact that there is now a new "is-a" relationship, the key fact expressed by the diagram is the ability of the Document class to use either of the document-specific summary classes interchangeably. The summary is separately pluggable. What we've done to get here is analyze the "is-a" relationship to find what behaviors are actually relevant in the particular case.

We will return to this issue repeatedly in later chapters, particularly chapters 5 and 6.

There is an area of overlap between real-world modeling and decoupling. It has to do with *abstraction*. Abstraction is a natural part of modeling the real world; in fact, it's a necessary part. In object-oriented programming, a class such as Document is an abstraction since it represents any number of concrete instances—any number of actual documents. Abstraction is also a way to achieve decoupling, since a component that is defined by an abstract interface can easily be replaced by another component with the same interface.

In programming, abstraction is often expressed by abstract classes and interfaces. In PHP, these were introduced in version 5. Whether they are actually necessary to abstract design is a question we will begin to answer in chapter 2.

1.2.4 Design patterns

Software design patterns started to become generally known after the book *Design Patterns*, by the so-called "Gang of Four" [Gang of Four], was published in 1995. It represents the trend away from a strong emphasis on real-world modeling, since the design patterns are primarily vehicles for decoupling: enabling parts of the software to vary independently of each other.

Since then, there has been a virtual explosion in more-or-less complex design patterns. Today, there are so many available that simply finding the one you need for a

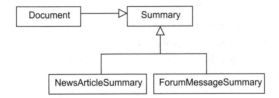

Figure 1.3
By analyzing the "is-a" relationship, we can focus on the behavior that is important.

particular purpose may be a time-consuming task. This book will focus mostly on the patterns that are most relevant to web programming and to the web programmer's everyday tasks.

The interest in design patterns has started to become serious in the PHP community only in the last few years. PHP developers haven't had much of a culture for this kind of thing, but nowadays you can easily find examples of design patterns in PHP.

1.2.5 Refactoring

Refactoring means improving the design of existing code. You're not adding features, just moving, splitting, merging, deleting, and renaming. It is a way of keeping code supple so that it stays easy to maintain and add features even as it grows in complexity.

Without refactoring, it's easy to get into a one-way street that leads eventually to the death of the program. The poorer the structure of the code, the more you may have to resort to what some colleagues of mine used to call "approximate programming." As I understand the expression, it refers to the fact that if you don't understand your own code, you can still make changes by acting on hunches and trying them out until you find something that works. Unfortunately, approximate programming muddles the code even further and makes the job still harder the next time around. Frequently, you'll end up needing to reimplement the whole thing.

There are known and unknown species of refactoring. Martin Fowler and others have done us the service of cataloging a number of refactorings found in the field. Fowler's book *Refactoring* [Fowler Refactoring] has specific, step-by-step instructions on how to do each of them.

Automated tests are the key to refactoring. They make it possible to test the code between each small step in refactoring. Doing this kind of repeated testing manually would be far too time-consuming. So if you have no automated tests, you will put off testing until you are finished refactoring. When you finally start testing, you will likely find— or fail to find, depending on your thoroughness—several bugs. And likely there will be one or more bugs that are hard to find because you don't know where they are located.

When you have sufficient automated tests set up, you can refactor one small step at a time. You move or change some code and then you test. If a test fails, you know the problem is somewhere in the part of the program you just changed. You know approximately where the bug is, and you can locate it quickly.

For effective unit testing, you need a test framework. The best known unit testing frameworks for PHP are PHPUnit and SimpleTest. In this book, we will be using SimpleTest for the most part, but appendix A has the basics of the PHPUnit API.

At this writing, there are no refactoring tools for PHP. We have to edit the code manually. Chapter 11 of this book introduces some of the techniques that are useful in typical web applications. In addition, refactoring PHP 5 is very similar to Java. The techniques in Martin Fowler's classic book *Refactoring* [Fowler Refactoring] are not hard to apply in PHP.

1.2.6 Unit testing and test-driven development

"It tastes *healthy!*" my daughter objected when I tried to get her to take her medicine at age three. Software testing is similar. It's supposed to be good for you, to improve the quality of your programs and indirectly your success, your paycheck, and your quality of life in general. In spite of this, testing is not generally considered a pleasant or high-status activity. Kent Beck, who is one of the pioneers of agile development and the creator of Extreme Programming, calls it "the ugly stepchild of software development." So maybe it just tastes too healthy.

That's how it's always been, anyway. But in recent years, testing has had a surge in popularity. Programmers are getting "test infected," or you might say, addicted. Some are even claiming that it's fun: "Test-driven development is a lot more fun than writing tests after the code seems to be working. Give it a try!" (http://junit.sourceforge.net/doc/faq/faq.htm#best).

The buzzword is *test-driven development* (TDD) or *test-first development*. But how does it work? How *can* it work? How can you test something that doesn't even exist? Why would any sane individual want to try it?

Part of the answer is that test-driven development is one of the sanest things you can do. It makes your programs work better, and it feels much better.

That automated testing would make programs work better because they have fewer bugs is at least logical. But why should test-driven development feel better? Why is it more fun?

It feels better because it's less stressful and more satisfying than most other ways to program. You spend less time searching for bugs and more time programming. That is one source of stress eliminated. You get fewer complaints from dissatisfied users/customers. You get the freedom to play with and change the structure of your code. That means you can learn more. I recently read that brain researchers had found that learning has some of the same effects on the brain that cocaine does. (I assume they weren't referring to harmful effects, or the educational system would be in deep trouble.)

TDD also helps you produce code of higher quality, code that you can read with satisfaction and say, "This is pretty good."

Writing the tests before the code might seem like putting the cart before the horse, but if you think about it, it's perfectly reasonable. It's a way of getting more mileage from the tests. They do some good even if you develop them afterwards, but you miss part of the value.

Why? Because the tests are a help from the very first time the code is running and even before that. If you develop a function and then write a test afterward, you have no benefit of having an automated test during the early stages of debugging. Figure 1.4 shows how this works.

In contrast, TDD lets you benefit from the tests while implementing the feature being tested, and even before implementation, as shown in figure 1.5.

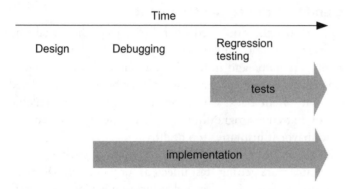

Figure 1.4 In traditional testing, the tests are helpful only after the features have been implemented.

If you have a test ready from the start, the need for debugging tools is slight. The tests help you see what the code is doing, and help you pinpoint the location of a bug when it first appears.

All of this could be achieved, as well, by writing the function to be tested and then the test immediately afterward, before actually running the function. But there is one more important advantage to writing tests first: it helps design, too. A unit test is client code for the function or method (usually) you want to develop. When writing client code first, you'll see what sequence of calls and what parameters are needed and a convenient way to structure them for actual use.

None of this means that you should test more than is necessary to make the program work. The agile principle is to test anything that might fail. Some pieces of code are so simple that in practice they don't fail. It's no fun writing pointless tests. On the other hand, it's easy to underestimate the likelihood of bugs.

When I recommend the test-first approach, don't take my word for it. Try it and see how it works. But you have to try it properly or you won't get the full benefit. You

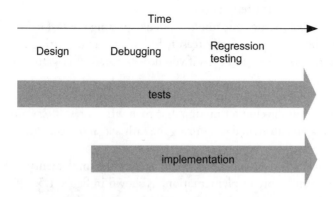

Figure 1.5 In test-driven development, the tests are doing useful work much earlier.

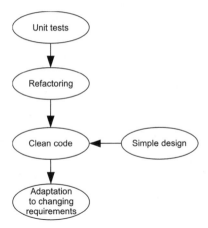

Figure 1.6
How some essential elements of agile development depend on each other.

have to actually write the tests first and then the code. If you've been programming for a while, this could mean breaking some ingrained habits; I certainly had to do that.

Unit testing is a prerequisite for the rest of the agile practices. Figure 1.6 shows how it interacts with some of the other practices.

Unit testing makes refactoring practicable. Refactoring and simple design enable us to achieve clean, maintainable code. And maintainable code is necessary if we want to be able to adapt to changing requirements.

Test-driven development will be covered in chapters 9, 10, and 12. For a deeper treatment, try Kent Beck's book *Test-Driven Development by Example*. [Beck].

1.3 SUMMARY

PHP is a popular web programming language that is ready to meet today's design principles and practices. PHP 5 came at the right time; while keeping the convenience of earlier versions of PHP 4, it enables us to go further in implementing advanced object-oriented designs. To help us achieve this, we will use agile methods, object-oriented principles, design patterns, refactoring, and unit testing.

In the next chapter, we will start exploring how object-oriented programming works in PHP. We will look at the basics and some features that were introduced in PHP 5, including exceptions, object references, and the ability to intercept method calls.

CHAPTER 2

Objects in PHP

It's been said that most programming languages are at their best *before* they are implemented. That may be true for languages that were designed according to ambitious specifications, but PHP is definitely not one of those. Its humble beginnings are illustrated by the original meaning of the acronym PHP: *Personal Home Page*. It started out as a simple way to add dynamic content to HTML pages and grew into a more and more complete programming language. Object orientation was not originally part of the language, but has gradually grown in importance. Version 5 has moved PHP into the mainstream of object-oriented languages. It provides most of the features programmers expect in an object-oriented language, while maintaining dynamic typing and still letting us choose our programming style.

That's why PHP 5 is an important tool in your toolkit. It eases the burden of writing object-oriented code, allowing you to focus more on getting the design right and implementing it, instead of struggling to satisfy the demands of the language.

PHP 5 also has other object-oriented features that were not available in PHP 4. Most of them are features that have existed for a long time in Java and some other object-oriented languages. The result is that PHP 5 code can be more Java-like than PHP 4 code. But using the new features is mostly optional, so you're not forced into a more Java-like programming style if you're used to the PHP style and want to keep it.

This chapter and the next one are closely related; together they cover the object-oriented features of PHP. While the next chapter is about the features that are strongly tied to the concept of a class, this one treats the basic features that are relatively independent of class structure. (In fact, these features might have been available even in procedural PHP, but aren't.)

We'll start this chapter by going over the basics of objects; then we'll look at one of the most useful of the features introduced in PHP 5: exception handling. After that, we'll make sure we understand the most important feature of the PHP 5 object model: the fact that objects are treated by reference. This makes object handling much more natural and eliminates the need to use the rather cumbersome references mechanism in PHP 4. Finally, we'll look at how to magically manipulate method calls using one of the more advanced features that were introduced in PHP 5.

2.1 OBJECT FUNDAMENTALS

There are two keys to understanding how objects and classes work. One is knowing the mechanics of writing a class and using the language constructs that support object-oriented programming.

The other, more difficult, and advanced topic is understanding how to make objects interact in a way that achieves the main aim of object-oriented programming: maintainable code—that is, object-oriented design, which we will be looking at in the rest of this book.

This chapter and the next focus on using the object-oriented language features of PHP 5, without going too deeply into design considerations. This sequence might seem lopsided, since it's customary to start with the theory and then show how to practice it. The idea here is to start with just a little theory and get some practice to solidify it before moving on to more advanced ideas.

In this section, we'll do an overview of some of the basic mechanics of PHP objects. We'll think a little bit about what classes and objects are, do a simple "Hello world" example, look at how we create objects, and introduce the notion of class inheritance. But before we start, a short explanatory comment on why we want to compare PHP to Java.

2.1.1 Why we're comparing PHP to Java

This chapter and the next one contain a lot of comparisons between PHP 5 features and the corresponding ones in Java. The reasons for this are practical; there are no value judgments implied. There is no intent to make a contest between the two languages or to imply that Java is the only or best alternative to PHP.

Rather, the idea is to learn something from the comparison and to make sure we get the details right. Most of the new object-oriented syntax in PHP is Java-like. Since many of the differences are subtle, it's easy to confuse the two. For example, the `interface` construct is almost identical in the two languages. But in PHP, unlike Java, the constructor can be specified in the interface just like the other methods.

Comparing two similar programming languages highlights and clarifies the specific details of each. And since Java is undeniably an extremely popular language, many developers are likely to be using both languages and switching between them. There are PHP developers who program Java occasionally or frequently, and some readers are likely to be programmers who are new to PHP but have some Java experience.

2.1.2   Objects and classes

The basic mechanical aspects objects and classes are documented in the PHP manual, but we will run through them briefly and hopefully get a slightly different and fresh perspective.

According to the manual, a class is "a collection of variables and functions working with these variables." That may be as close as we can get in a short sentence, although it's entirely possible to have a class without variables. The functions are called *methods* in proper object-oriented terminology.

You might say that a class is like a house. The methods are rooms and the class declaration represents the outer walls of the house. Different activities take place in different rooms: cooking in the kitchen, sleeping in the bedroom. Similarly, each method in a class does one specific job.

The walls make sense because they protect the code inside the house from disturbing the code outside and vice versa. If all variables are global, you can never change the way a variable is used without the risk of creating a bug in some other part of the program. Functions in PHP help protect variables by making them local to the function. Classes extend this concept further by introducing variables that belong to an object so that they can be used in multiple methods without being global. The fancy name for this is *encapsulation*.

2.1.3   Hello world

Let's try a simple example. It is hard to find object-oriented examples that are both simple and realistic. So let's make up a scenario: you are required to create a web application that outputs "Hello world!" Unfortunately, the competition has a fully buzzword-compliant, object-oriented "hello world" application, and marketing absolutely need the words "object-oriented" on the feature list. So you make a class that generates HTML code for a "hello world" message.

```
class HelloWorld {
    public $world = 'World';

    function getHtml() {
        return "<html><body>".
            "Hello, ".$this->world."!".
            "</body></html>";

    }
}
```

To use this class, you would do something like this:

```
$greetings = new HelloWorld;  // Create the object
echo $greetings->getHtml(); // Display the greeting message
```

The class generates the HTML document by concatenating constant strings and inserting the name it has stored in the variable $name. This variable is called an *instance variable*. An instance variable belongs to the object and is available as $this->world in any method inside the class.

Set the variable as you define it. The public keyword declares the variable and makes it globally available. Using public variables is not necessarily good practice in PHP 5, but it keeps things simple as we're experimenting.

To use the instance variable in the getHtml() method, refer to it as $this->world.

This variable is only used in one method, but instance variables become really useful only when they're used in more than one method.

2.1.4   Constructors: creating and initializing objects

The "hello world" application is a resounding success, and management and marketing applaud your efforts. Unfortunately, a couple of days later, your boss comes back to you and tells you that the program is not compatible with the company's motto, "universal excellence." Everybody knows that "universal" means anywhere in the universe; clearly the application must be able to say hello to any planet or other astronomical object. (The ones that have a high profile, anyway.) Besides, the company has an anti-discrimination policy that makes Earth chauvinism unacceptable.

You object that "world" can apply to any world, not just this one. But the boss insists. Well then, you'll just have to make it possible to specify the planet's name when creating the object:

```
$greetings = new HelloWorld('Epsilon Eridani II');
echo $greetings->getHtml();
```

The new keyword creates a new instance of the class. In addition, it runs a method called a *constructor* that we can use to initialize and configure the object. In PHP 5, constructors are named construct().

So now we can use the constructor to set the user name:

```
class HelloWorld {
    public $world;

    function __construct($world) {
        $this->world = $world;
    }

    function getHtml() {
        return "<html><body>".
            "Hello ".$this->world."!".
            "</body></html>";
    }
}
```

Instance variables make it possible for different methods to share variables even if they are not global. So if you have a legacy PHP application that uses global variables liberally, a useful trick is to turn them into instance variables in a class. A bulletin board system might have a display_messages() function with the following global variable declaration:

```
global $db, $strings, $mode;
```

$db is an object representing the database connection, $strings is a collection of language-independent strings, and $mode is a display mode (threaded or non-threaded).

Let's pretend we want to refactor this application. One possibility is to make these belong to a class instead—say, MessageView. Then the variables would be instance variables instead:

```
class MessageView {
    public $db;
    public $strings;
    public $mode;

    function __construct($db, $strings, $mode) {
        $this->db = $db;
        $this->strings = $strings;
        $this->mode = $mode;
    }

    function display_messages() {
        $result = $this->db->query('SELECT * FROM messages');
        //etc...
    }
}
```

This example also illustrates how an instance variable can contain another object, in this case an object representing the database connection. In PHP 5, this means that the object contains a *reference* to the other object. Object references will be explained later in this chapter.

Figure 2.1 shows how the previous example can be represented as a UML class diagram. The MessageView class has three instance variables. $strings and $mode are represented as attributes. (Since UML is a notation that's supposed to be independent of programming language, we're leaving the dollar signs out). Since $db is an object, and probably a somewhat-complex one, it's shown as a separate class.

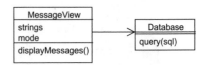

Figure 2.1 UML class diagram of the MessageView class with attributes, and the related Database class

2.1.5   Inheritance and the extends keyword

Conceptually, inheritance in object-oriented programming is a way to express relationships between categories. Technically, inheritance is a way a class can get all or some of the features of another class cheaply. (The alternative is to create an instance of the other class and use that, but that is significantly more work.)

A class inherits the features of another class by simply adding the `extends` keyword to the class declaration. Let's see what happens if we make an empty class that extends another:

```
class NewsArticle extends Document {
}
```

There is now what is called a *parent-child relationship* between the two classes. The NewsArticle class is the child; the Document class is the parent. The practical result of what we have done is that the NewsArticle class works exactly like the Document class. If we had copied and pasted the entire Document class and changed its name, that would have had the same effect. The difference is not in how the code works, but in the fact that we don't have to duplicate the code. We are reusing the Document class, and that's a good idea.

Figure 2.2 shows (as in chapter 1) how this relationship can be represented as a UML class diagram.

This is good, except for the obvious fact that we usually don't need two classes that work exactly the same way. It makes

Figure 2.2
Simple UML class diagram of the parent-child relationship between Document and NewsArticle

more sense if the child class contains some implementation. We can add new methods and data or we can *override* methods. For example, the NewsArticle class may have variables, say `$newsSource` or `$byline`, that are not present in the Document class.

Let's continue with our previous example. Again, this is not very realistic, but let's pretend we want a class that is more general: one which can represent any HTML document, not just the ones containing greeting messages. So we start by putting the basic HTML document into place:

```
class HtmlDocument {

    function getHtml() {
        return "<html><body>".$this->getContent().
            "</body></html>";
    }

    function getContent() { return ''; }
}
```

The `getHtml()` method inserts the result from the `getContent()` method between start and end tags for the HTML document and returns the result.

`getContent()` is fairly pointless, since it returns an empty string. But Html-Document is just our parent class. We can add a child class that does something more like what we did before:

```
class HelloWorld extends HtmlDocument {
    public $world;
    function __construct($world ) {
        $this->name = $world ;
    }

    function getContent() {
        return "Hello, ".$this->world."!";
    }
}
```

The `getContent()` method in the HelloWorld class now overrides the `getContent()` method in its parent class. And the `getHtml()` method works as if we had copied it from the HtmlDocument class to the HelloWorld class. So this class does the same job as our previous HelloWorld class, but the `getHtml()` method is now in the parent class. That means we can make another class that extends the HtmlDocument class and puts something else inside the document.

2.1.6   Inheriting constructors

Inheritance is not just a privilege of ordinary methods. Constructors can benefit from it, too. Some of the work that goes into constructing an object may be common to similar classes, and some may be different.

A new style of constructor was introduced in PHP 5 that makes this easier. Instead of using a constructor with the same name as the class, we can use the special method name `__construct()`:

```
class Document {
    protected $title;
    protected $text;
    function __construct($title,$text) {
        $this->title = $title;
        $this->text = $text;
    }
}
```

This makes it slightly easier to inherit constructor behavior than with the old-style constructors:

```
class NewsArticle extends Document{
    private $introduction;
    function __construct($title,$text,$introduction) {
        parent::__construct($title,$text);
        $this->introduction = $introduction;
    }
}
```

`parent::construct` calls the constructor from the Document class.

Another question entirely is how useful it is to inherit constructor behavior. Doing too much of it may make refactoring harder. In this example, it might be better to move all the construction into the child class and duplicate it in the other child classes to make the code more readable and easier to change. That tiny amount of duplication is not likely to hurt anyone.

Until now, we've been studying how objects work in normal circumstances. Earlier, we noted how a class is like a house with rooms. Now we want to know what to do if there's a fire. We want to be able to get out quickly but safely. To make this possible, object-oriented languages (including PHP from version 5) use a feature called *exceptions*.

2.2 EXCEPTION HANDLING

The simple way to handle an error in PHP 4 was to `die()` on error. Martin Fowler calls this "the software equivalent of committing suicide if you miss a flight," but adds that "if the cost of a program crash is small and the user is tolerant, stopping a program is fine."

In PHP 5, as in many other languages, we have an alternative to suicide: throwing an exception. This is the software equivalent of throwing yourself from a window in a house or building and hoping someone catches you in a net before you hit the ground. If we don't handle the exception by using `catch` at some point in the code that calls this class (directly or indirectly), the program will stop and print a message with a call stack trace. So the immediate effect is approximately the same as `die()`, but if we decide later that we want to handle the error, we can do that more easily.

The mechanics of using exceptions are one thing; using them wisely and judiciously is another. This section will not show all the ins and outs of exceptions; rather it will concentrate on showing reasonable ways to use exceptions and on the aspects of PHP 5 exception handling that are most useful for supporting this.

More details on the technical aspects of PHP 5 exceptions are available in the online PHP manual and elsewhere. For an excellent in-depth discussion of how to use exceptions, you may want to look at the chapter on reliable collaborations in the book *Object Design* by Rebecca Wirfs-Brock and Alan McKean [Wirfs-Brock].

In this section, we'll start out by finding out how exceptions work. Then we'll consider how and when it's appropriate to use exceptions and when it might be better to use good, old-fashioned return codes. We'll see how to create our own exception classes, and try our best to find out how to replace built-in PHP errors with exceptions. Finally, we'll see how to avoid over-using exceptions.

2.2.1 How exceptions work

The programming language construct known as the *exception* is a way to communicate error or exception conditions between different parts of the program—without going through the normal channels, so to speak. For example, we might have the name of the database the application is using in an environment variable called DB_NAME. Without exception handling, we could let a method retrieve that name as follows:

```php
public function getDatabaseName() {
    if (!array_key_exists('DB_NAME',$_ENV))
        die("Environment variable DB_NAME is not set");
    return $_ENV['DB_NAME'];
}
```

This, then, is the suicide version, using `die()` rather than `exit` to make the parallel clear, although the two have exactly the same effect. But using an exception instead is really very simple:

```php
public function getDatabaseName() {
    if (!array_key_exists('DB_NAME',$_ENV))
        throw new Exception(
        "Environment variable DB_NAME is not set");
    return $_ENV['DB_NAME'];
}
```

If we do nothing to catch the exception, this has the same effect as `die()`: it stops the application. It does one additional thing, though: it prints a stack trace which may be useful for debugging. You can get a stack trace without using exceptions by using the functions `debug_backtrace()` and `debug_print_backtrace()`. But throwing an exception is an even simpler way to do it.

```
Fatal error: Uncaught exception 'Exception' with message
'Environment variable DB_NAME is not set' in /path/exception.php:6
Stack trace:
#0 /path/exception.php(6): Config::getDatabaseName()
#1 /path/exception.php(12): Config->getDatabaseName()
#2 {main}
  thrown in /path/exception.php on line 6
```

If we don't want the users to see the technical error report (and in general we don't for security reasons), we're in a much better position having used exceptions rather than `die()`. If we've used `die()` in several places, we may have to find all the occurrences and change each one. If we've used exceptions, all we need to do is catch them at some convenient place, such as the top level of the application. For example, we could log the message and redirect the user to a page that just says an error has occurred:

```php
$config = new Config;
try {
    $config->getDatabaseName();
}
catch(Exception $e) {
    $logger->log($e->getMessage());
    header("Location: unrecoverable.php");
}
```

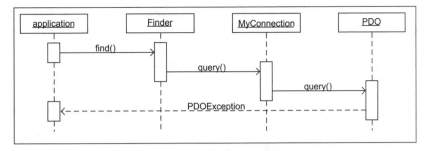

Figure 2.3 UML sequence diagram of program flow with an exception

Figure 2.3 is a UML sequence diagram that shows how exceptions work. The details of the diagram—class and method names—are unimportant. The essence is this: when the PDO object throws an exception, instead of returning to MyConnection, it bypasses both MyConnection and Finder, since neither of these have try and catch blocks. But the application catches the exception and handles it.

If you turn the diagram 90 degrees counterclockwise, it will be oriented to match the building analogy: The message flow climbs the stairs, passing the floors one by one, jumps out of the window on the PDO floor, and is caught in the net set up at the ground floor—the application.

There is one important advantage that exceptions share with die(): they interrupt further processing. The reason this is useful is that typically, when an exception is thrown, the rest of what happens in the current method is meaningless. A modest example is the getDatabaseName() method we just saw: returning the database name from the function is pointless since there is no database name to return. None of the PHP program is executed between the time when the exception is thrown and the time when the exception is caught.

2.2.2 Exceptions versus return codes—when to use which

The syntactical meaning of a programming language keyword is often different from the conceptual meaning of the word. This is also true in the case of exceptions. The word "exception" means something that happens rarely. In software design, there is a distinction between errors and exceptions. An *error* is typically something that's fatal or crippling to the program's ability to do its job; an *exception* is a situation that is uncommon, but recoverable.

In actual practice, exceptions (in the syntactical sense) are most useful for handling errors such as the one we saw. If the database name is not available and the application is totally dependent on it, the ability of exceptions to prevent further processing at that point is appropriate and useful. Trying to perform SQL queries with a nonexistent database and trying to process nonexistent data is only likely to generate further errors that are potentially confusing.

Error-handling code can be counterproductive: if you get too much of it, it will make the program less readable and make it harder to spot bugs.

If we have good unit test coverage (and we will see how to achieve that painlessly in the chapters on testing—chapters 9, 10, and 12), error handling is mostly needed on the boundaries of our application: its interfaces with other systems and the rest of the world. Even if your software is populated exclusively with well-behaved objects, you need to patrol the borders.

One border is represented by resources that are provided by the operating system, files, networking, and databases. You may know this already, but let's summarize some typical errors in a PHP web application:

- Errors from incorrect configuration information such as the password needed to connect to a database.
- SQL or XML syntax errors.
- Crucial files that can't be read.

But we may also need to patrol the other border: the one facing other software that is using our software. Security checks and validation of user input will typically occur at higher levels of the application; the response is more likely to be a direct message back to the user rather than an exception. But what if we are creating some low-level library software that is used by others? Checking the inputs—and making sure there are no absurd values—may save a lot of debugging time.

One possible example is a package that supplies statistical information on the data in a database. Typically, the clients of this library will need to provide the start and end times of the time interval for the statistics. What if the start time, or the end time, or both, are NULL, 0, or some other inappropriate value? If they are both zero and we are interpreting these as January 1, 1970, we will most likely return an empty data set.

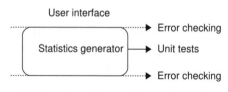

Figure 2.4 "Patrolling the borders": checking for errors and invalid input at the interfaces.

And finding out why the data set is empty may take a lot of fruitless searching.

Figure 2.4 shows how this might work. Assuming that we're responsible for only the statistics generator, we want to make sure it has test coverage and that we check for errors and invalid input at the interfaces.

So much for errors. For exceptions in the conceptual sense, for rare but recoverable situations, it may often be more useful to use ordinary conditional logic and return codes to recover from the error immediately, rather than throwing an exception. There are several ways to do this. The best way is usually to have the calling class ask the class it is calling for information that will allow the calling class to decide whether there is an exceptional situation in the first place. Another is to return an error code. Yet another is to simply ignore the problem. For example, if one out of a set of files to be processed is missing, the end user may prefer an incomplete result over an error message.

2.2.3   Creating your own exception classes

The Exception class is built into PHP itself and is always available. By creating child classes that extend the Exception class, we can define our own exception types. It can be as simple as this:

```
class ConfigurationException extends Exception {}
```

As we have seen before, a class that extends another class but contains no implementation works exactly the same as the original class. So why would we want to do it? Because exceptions are slightly different from ordinary classes. To distinguish different types of exception, it's customary to use different classes. And since the catch clause allows you to specify the exception class, you can use this to catch different exceptions in different places. For example, if you use one exception class for the failure to connect to a database and another for SQL syntax errors, the two can be caught in different places in the code.

On the other hand, it is a bad idea to make large exception class hierarchies. Wirfs-Brock and McKean recommend a maximum of five to seven different exception classes for the simple reason that it's hard to remember too many classes. Instead, you can use error codes to distinguish different subtypes within an exception class. A readable and safe way to do that is to use the ability of the Exception class to store the error code along with class constants. If we want a ConfigException with the ability to report both database connection errors and SQL syntax errors, we can define the Exception class as follows:

```
class ConfigException extends Exception {
    const SQL_SYNTAX_ERROR = 1;
    const DB_CONNECTION_ERROR = 2;
}
```

When we throw the exception, we can specify both the error message and the error code, since these are accepted by the constructor for the Exception class.

```
throw new ConfigException(
    "Could not connect to database $dbname",
    ConfigException::DB_CONNECTION_ERROR);
```

And when catching the exception, we can test for the error code and act accordingly:

```
catch(ConfigException $e) {
    switch ($e->getCode()) {
    case ConfigException::DB_CONNECTION_ERROR:
        echo "Connection error\n";
        break;
    case ConfigException::SQL_SYNTAX_ERROR:
        echo "SQL error\n";
```

```
        break;
    }
}
```

In real life, obviously, we would do something more sophisticated than just echoing a string.

But what if we want to handle only one of our exception subtypes here, and handle the other type somewhere else? It's simple: we can rethrow it so it can be caught by a different method or object:

```
case ConfigException::SQL_SYNTAX_ERROR:
    throw $e;
    break;
```

It's a good idea to name exception classes based on what went wrong rather than where it occurred. The ConfigException class in the previous examples is intended to convey the idea that they are exceptions that are typically caused by misconfiguration or bugs in the application.

2.2.4 Replacing built-in PHP fatal errors with exceptions

Once we're using exceptions, it's a bit irritating that errors from PHP are reported as PHP 4-style errors rather than as exceptions. But it is possible to build a bridge from the old error-handling system to the new. Although this will not catch all errors (fatal runtime errors such as calling a nonexistent method on an object will not be reported), it will make error handling more consistent.

The first things we need are an exception class to distinguish the PHP errors from other exceptions and a simple error handler to receive a PHP error and throw an exception instead:

```
class ErrorFromPHPException extends Exception {}

function PHPErrorHandler($errno, $errstr, $errfile, $errline) {
    throw new ErrorFromPHPException($errstr,$errno);
}
```

Now we can set the error handler. If we proceed to try to open a nonexistent file, we will get an exception instead of the old-fashioned error:

```
$oldHandler = set_error_handler('PHPErrorHandler');
fopen('/tmp/non-existent','r');
```

And if for some reason we want to return to the ordinary way of handling these errors, we can do this:

```
set_error_handler($oldHandler);
```

2.2.5 Don't overdo exceptions

We want to avoid cluttering our code with too much error handling, and exceptions help us do that, since the catch statements can be fewer than error handling conditionals that have to test the return codes from every method call. But even with exceptions, there is no reason to check for every conceivable problem. As Wirfs-Brock and McKean say:

> *Defensive collaborations—designing objects to take precautions before and after calling on a collaborator—are expensive and error-prone. Not every object should be tasked with these responsibilities.*

Fortunately, PHP never *forces* you to check anything.

Exception handling is one of the most important of the new features that were introduced in PHP 5. An even more important change was the new way of handling object references. This change is crucial in enabling object-oriented design.

2.3 OBJECT REFERENCES IN *PHP 4* AND *PHP 5*

When the police are looking for a wanted criminal or a missing person, it helps to have a photograph of the individual. A good photograph can make it easy to recognize a person, but it only shows how he looked at a particular instant. People change clothes, put on or remove makeup, cut or change their hair, shave, grow beards, put on sunglasses, even undergo plastic surgery. Sooner or later (sooner if it's a criminal working hard to avoid recognition) it becomes hard to recognize the person from the photograph.

Even more obvious and fundamental is the fact that doing something to the photograph won't affect the person. Putting the picture in a jail cell is futile. Unless you believe in voodoo, you have to live with the fact that the image and the person are physically separate. So there are limits to what you can do if you have only the photograph available. It's nothing like having the person present.

PHP 4 object handling is similar. PHP 4 creates a copy of an object every time you use an assignment or return an object from a function or method. So you get a "snapshot" that looks deceptively like the original, but is actually a different object and doesn't reflect or cause changes in the original. This creates some of the same problems as a photograph. In object-oriented programming, an object typically represents an entity, real or abstract, that cannot simply be changed by proxy. Changing *a copy of* a document won't help if the original is the one that's saved to the database. Changing an object representing the title of an HTML page won't help if the original is the one that's shown in the browser.

But unlike a photograph, a copy of an object has all the bulk and weight of the original. If the original object contains two megabytes of data, the copy does, too, so now you have four megabytes in all. So copying objects make the program consume more memory than necessary.

That's why PHP 4-style object handling is universally recognized as a Bad Thing. It seemed like a good idea at the time it was implemented, but it wasn't. The people who developed PHP did not passionately desire that kind of object behavior. It just happened to be easier given the way PHP had been implemented. Object orientation was not used a lot in PHP at the time. But as it turned out, object-oriented programming in PHP became quite popular. It eventually became obvious that the PHP way of handling objects was a liability. So it became an urgent priority to change the default behavior of objects in PHP to use references instead of copies. This has happened with PHP 5. Object orientation in PHP 5 now works the same way as in most other object-oriented languages.

PHP 4 has references, too, but they are different from the object references in most object-oriented languages. They can be used—and have been used—for object-oriented programming in PHP 4. But it's hard to understand how they work, and they sometimes do things you might not expect them to do. Their behavior is counterintuitive. PHP 5 objects, on the other hand, behave most of the time in a way that's useful and natural. Trying to use references in PHP 4 tends to cause headaches. In PHP 5, you can usually ignore the fact that the objects you pass around are actually references and focus your attention on making the code work.

This section starts out by explaining how object references work and what happened when "normal" object-oriented references were introduced with PHP 5. Then we found out why they are more useful than the earlier type of reference. They aren't always, though, and we'll take a closer look at that aspect as well.

2.3.1 How object references work

In PHP 4, when you create an object and assign it to another variable, the entire object and all its content is copied. In PHP 5, the variable contains a reference to the object, and only the reference is copied. The following example will have different effects in the two versions:

```
$user = new User;
$user->email = 'lou@example.com';
$sameuser = $user;
$user->email = 'barefoot@example.com';
```

In PHP 4, $sameuser->email is lou@example.com. In PHP 5, it has changed to barefoot@example.com.

That's because in PHP 5, there is only one object. $user and $sameuser are both references to the same object.

If you know references in PHP 4, you will realize that you can do this:

```
$user = new User;
$sameuser = &$user;
$user->email = 'someoneelse@example.com';
```

Now the same thing happens in PHP 4 and PHP 5. $sameuser->email changes.

But there is a difference. As the manual will tell you, the & operator produces a symbol table alias, which is a different name for the same content. That is not the same thing as a reference. The preceding code means that $user and $sameuser have the same content. In the PHP 5 object reference example, we copy the content of the variable, which just happens to be an object reference. With the PHP 4-style reference, we just give the same content a different name.

Most of the time, PHP 5 references are superior to the PHP 4 aliases. But there are uses for aliases, too. For example, if you have a large data structure that is not object-oriented (normally, I would not recommend that, but there's a lot of legacy code in the world), using an alias can still save you from copying all that content, just like in PHP 4.

2.3.2 The advantages of object references

As I've mentioned, object references help improve performance by preventing objects from being copied and consuming excessive memory space. In PHP 4 applications, many efforts were made to avoid this overhead by explicitly copying objects by reference. This makes sense if you have a lot of objects or if they are very large. (Try dumping a PEAR DB object and you will see what I mean by large objects. On the other hand, if you keep your design simple, it will help keep your objects smaller, too.) In PHP 5, these efforts are no longer necessary.

But having objects represented by references also has advantages for object-oriented design. It makes it easier to build and manipulate complex object structures. You put one object $dog inside object $doghouse, and then you modify the object $dog and you want that to be reflected on the inside of $doghouse. GUIs typically have this kind of complex structure. In web programming, we work with HTML documents, but let's say we are representing the elements in an HTML document as objects. We might do something like this:

```
$checkbox = new Checkbox;
$form = new Form;
$document = new Document;
$document->add($form);
$form->add($checkbox);
```

Now what happens if we change one of the inner elements?

```
$checkbox->setChecked();
```

In PHP 4, this is practically useless, since the checkbox inside the form inside the document won't change. In PHP 5, it will change, and when we generate the HTML code from the Document object, it will have a checked checkbox. This is obviously what we want, and it illustrates what I mean when I say that the behavior of PHP 5 objects is mostly intuitive, useful, and natural.

2.3.3 When references are not so useful

Object references may be wonderfully intuitive most of the time, but at other times we actively want objects to be copied rather than passed around by reference. This is the case with the kinds of objects known as *value objects*. If we represent dates, money amounts, and the like as objects, it will be more natural to copy them, because they have no identity.

To copy objects in PHP 5, use the `clone` keyword. We will deal with this in detail in later chapters.

After references, we will deal with one more feature that was introduced in PHP 5: the ability to intercept method calls and transform them before they are executed.

2.4 INTERCEPTING METHOD CALLS AND CLASS INSTANTIATION

In PHP 5, a feature was introduced called *overloadable method calls*. In practice, the feature allows us to intercept, re-route, and redefine method calls. It's like stealing someone's mail and opening it. Then we can send it to someone else, change the contents, or even throw it into the wastebasket. This means that we can change the usual way methods respond and even respond to nonexistent methods.

We will start this section by clarifying the official term *overloadable method calls* and how it relates to the idea of intercepting method calls. Then we'll see a couple of examples of how this can be used: Java-style method overloading, and a general logging mechanism for method calls. Finally, we'll take a peek at a related subject: how to use the autoload feature to control what happens when a class is instantiated.

2.4.1 What is "method overloading"?

"Method overloading" may be a slightly confusing term, since it means something specific in other languages. In Java and C++, method overloading means writing different methods that have the same name, but different numbers or types of arguments, and which method is executed depends on what arguments you supply. This is particularly useful in statically typed languages (such as Java and C++). Without method overloading, you might need two differently-named methods just to handle arguments of different types (for example, a date specified as a string or a numerical timestamp).

Overloadable method calls in PHP 5 are more general. You can overload method calls, but you have to define the overloading yourself. It works like this: if you try to call a method that's not defined, PHP 5 will call a method called `__call()` instead. Then you can do whatever you want with the "failed" method call. You can execute another method, possibly on another object, or you can give an error message that's different from the usual one. You can even do nothing; that will cause PHP to disregard failed method calls instead of generating a fatal error. That could be useful occasionally, but in general, be careful with anything that reduces the level of error checking and allows bugs to go unnoticed.

This behavior is not method overloading, but it does allow you to define method overloading, so it does make method calls *overloadable*.

The term *overloading* means that the same element (in this case, a method name) can have different meanings depending on context. And, since `__call()` lets us check the context and respond according to it, method overloading is one of the things we can do with it.

2.4.2 Java-style method overloading in PHP

Sometimes it's convenient to be able to call the same method with a variable number of arguments. PHP makes this possible through its ability to define optional arguments with default values. But sometimes, you need the method to have significantly different behaviors depending on the argument list. In languages that don't have method overloading, this means adding conditional logic to the beginning of the method. If you can use method overloading instead, you can skip the conditional logic and the code will be cleaner.

It's possible to implement this kind of method overloading using __call() in PHP 5. Let's look at an example. We're assuming that we will reuse the overloading behavior, so let's put it in an abstract parent class:

```php
abstract class OverloadableObject {
    function __call($name,$args) {
        $method = $name."_".count($args);
        if (!method_exists($this,$method)) {
            throw new Exception("Call to undefined method ".
                    get_class($this)."::$method");
        }
        return call_user_func_array(array($this,$method),$args);
    }
}
```

Most of the behavior of this class is defined by the one line in bold. If an undefined method is called, the __call() method generates a new method name consisting of the original method and the number of arguments, separated by an underscore character. Then it calls the method with the newly generated name, passing the original arguments along.

Now if we want to make an overloaded method called multiply that can be called with one or two arguments and will multiply them in either case, we make two methods called multiply_2 and multiply_3, respectively:

```php
class Multiplier extends OverloadableObject {
    function multiply_2($one,$two) {
        return $one * $two;
    }
    function multiply_3($one,$two,$three) {
        return $one * $two * $three;
    }
}
```

To use this, we just call the multiply method with two or three arguments:

```php
$multi = new Multiplier;
echo $multi->multiply(5,6)."\n";
echo $multi->multiply(5,6,3)."\n";
```

This is still not quite the same as method overloading in Java and C++, since we're only checking the number of arguments, not their types. However, we could use type information as well.

On the other hand, as we've seen, having the behavior depend on argument types is less important in PHP than in statically typed languages.

We've looked at how overloadable method calls work. For an example of how they can be put to use, let's see how they can be used to log method calls.

2.4.3 A near aspect-oriented experience: logging method calls

Aspect-oriented programming is a relatively new-fangled way of doing some things that are not entirely elegant in plain object-oriented programming. For instance, consider the problem of logging the start and finish of all method calls in an application. To do this in plain OOP, we have to add code to every single method. We can work to make this additional code minimal, but it will certainly add substantial clutter to our classes.

Logging is typically the kind of problem addressed by aspect-oriented programming. These problems, called *crosscutting concerns*, touch different modules or subsystems and are hard to isolate in separate classes. Another example would be checking whether the current user is authorized to use the method.

Aspect-oriented programming is typically done by defining *aspects*—class-like constructs that are inserted into the code during a code-generation process. Here, we will do something much simpler and more primitive using __call() in PHP 5. We use the PEAR Log class and control the logging process from the __call() method in a parent class, as shown in listing 2.1.

> **Listing 2.1 Parent class for classes in which we want to log method calls**

```
class LoggingClass {
    function __call($method,$args) {
        $method = "_$method";
        if (!method_exists($this,$method))
            throw new Exception("Call to undefined method "
                    .get_class($this)."::$method");
        $log  = Log::singleton('file', '/tmp/user.log',
                'Methods', NULL, LOG_INFO);
        $log->log("Just starting method $method");
        $return = call_user_func_array(array($this,$method),$args);
        $log->log("Just finished method $method");
        return $return;
    }
}
```

This is similar to our method overloading example, in that the actual method has a slightly different name than the name we call from the client code. The method we call from the client code doesn't exist, so __call() intercepts it, logs the beginning, calls the real method, and logs the end.

To use it, we need to extend LoggingClass and give the methods names that start with an underscore. (There's no compelling reason why it has to be an underscore; you can use anything that makes the names unique.) Listing 2.2 is a simplified class for handling dates and times:

Listing 2.2   DateAndTime class with methods that can be logged

```
class DateAndTime extends LoggingClass {
    private $timestamp;

    function __construct($timestamp=FALSE) {
        $this->init($timestamp);
    }

    protected function _init($timestamp) {
        $this->timestamp = $timestamp ? $timestamp : time();
    }

    function getTimestamp() { return $this->timestamp; }

    protected function _before(DateAndTime $other) {
        return $this->timestamp < $other->getTimestamp();
    }
}
```

The init() and before() methods will be logged; the getTimestamp() method won't, since the name doesn't start with an underscore character. I've added the init() method to allow the construction of the object to be logged as well. The __call() method is not normally triggered during construction. That's not surprising, since a class is not required to have a constructor.

The loggable methods are declared protected. That means they cannot be called from client code except through the __call() mechanism. They are protected rather than private because the __call() method is in a parent class.

Now let's try the class and see what happens. We make two different DateAndTime objects and then compare them:

```
$now = new DateAndTime;
$nexthour = new DateAndTime(time() + 3600);
print_r(array($now,$nexthour));
if ( $now->before($nexthour) ) {
    echo "OK\n";
}
```

The method calls are logged like this:

```
May 04 15:20:08 Methods [info] Just starting method _init
May 04 15:20:08 Methods [info] Just finished method _init
May 04 15:20:08 Methods [info] Just starting method _init
May 04 15:20:08 Methods [info] Just finished method _init
May 04 15:20:08 Methods [info] Just starting method _before
```

```
May 04 15:20:08 Methods [info] Just finished method _before
```

It's far from aspect-oriented programming (AOP) in a specialized AOP language. And in practice, if you want to log method calls, you may be looking for a profiling tool. There seems to be a potential for useful applications, though.

Overloadable method calls are a kind of magic that lets us define what will happen whenever a method—any method—is called. Autoloading classes is a similar concept: we can define what happens whenever we try to use an undefined class—any undefined class.

2.4.4   Autoloading classes

To use a class in PHP 4, you have to `include` or `require` the file that contains the class. PHP 5 has a way to avoid this by automating the process of loading classes. You can define a function called `__autoload()` that will be run each time you try to instantiate a class that is not defined. That function can then include the appropriate class file. Listing 2.3 shows an example that is slightly more sophisticated than the standard example.

Listing 2.3   Autoloading class files

```
function __autoload($className) {
    include_once __autoloadFilename($className);
}

function __autoloadFilename($className) {
    return str_replace('_','/',$className).".php";
}
```

The `__autoloadFilename()` function generates the name of the file to include. (There is a separate function for this just so it would be easier to test. We can run a test on the `__autoloadFilename()` function and check that its return value is correct. Checking that a file has been included is more difficult than just checking the return value.)

The `str_replace` function replaces all underscores with slashes. So if the class name is HTML_Form, the `__autoload()` function will include the file HTML/Form.php. This makes it easy to sort classes into different directories in the PEAR standard way.

If you have very small classes (there are some of them in this book), you might find it convenient to keep more than one class in a file. You can combine that with autoloading by making a link in the file system. Say you have a Template class and a Redirect class and they are both in a file called Template.php. In Linux or UNIX, you could do this:

```
ln -s Template.php Redirect.php
```

Now if you use the Redirect class, the `__autoload()` function will include the Redirect.php file, which happens to be a link to Template.php, which in turn contains the Redirect class.

2.5   SUMMARY

Object-oriented programming in PHP is a natural way to work, especially with the enhancements that were introduced in version 5. Some features are common to nearly all object-oriented languages. You can define classes that allow you to create objects with the behavior you want; you can use constructors to control what happens when the object is created; and you can use inheritance to create variations on a class. Exceptions provide more flexible and readable error handling.

Being able to handle objects by reference makes life much easier in PHP 5 than in PHP 4, particularly when dealing with complex object-oriented structures. The ability to call a method on the result of a method call is convenient in the same circumstances.

The ability to intercept method calls and access instance variables allows us to solve several different problems in a more elegant way. We can make the first step in the direction of aspect-oriented programming, using overloading to insert code before or after all method calls (or a selection of them) without having to duplicate all that code.

We are moving gradually from programming syntax toward application design. In the next chapter, we will take a look at some PHP features that act as tools for object-oriented design. Among them are visibility restrictions, class methods, abstract classes, and interfaces.

C H A P T E R   3

Using PHP classes effectively

From stone axes to passenger airlines, objects—real, tangible ones—are ubiquitous in technology. From that perspective, it's hardly surprising that software technology has come to depend on virtual objects. Classes, on the other hand, are something else. Naming, putting things into categories or classes, is inherent in natural language, but talking *about* categories of things and the process of naming is foreign to physical technology. Classes come out of philosophy and mathematics, starting with the ancient Greeks.

The combination of the two is extraordinarily powerful. In modern technology, abstract physics and mathematics are applied to the down-to-earth activity of making stuff. Object-oriented programming repeats this pattern: the conceptual abstraction of classes and the nuts-and-bolts workings of individual objects come together, creating a synergy.

Then again, classes and objects have both a hands-on, syntactical expression in the language and conceptual, abstract, and semantic meanings. In this chapter, we will focus on how to use classes and especially on the new features introduced in PHP 5.

We start by studying visibility restrictions: how we can improve encapsulation by not letting everything inside the class be accessible from the outside. Then we study how to use the class as a container for methods, variables, and constants that belong to the class itself rather than an object instance. We move on to another restrictive feature: abstract classes and methods, which can help structure class inheritance. Then we see how class type hints work, and finally we look at the workings and the role of interfaces in PHP.

3.1 VISIBILITY: PRIVATE AND PROTECTED METHODS AND VARIABLES

A central principle of object orientation is *encapsulation*. An object bundles together data and behavior that belong naturally together. Action can take place inside the object with no need for the rest of the world to be concerned with it. In the previous chapter, we compared a class to a house. Encapsulation is like having food in the refrigerator so you won't have to go out every time you want to eat. Or, perhaps more appropriately, when we're programming, most of the time we don't have to worry about what goes on inside the walls of the house. We don't have to feed the class from outside. If the food is data stored in instance variables, the methods of the class can eat it with no extra help from us.

To support encapsulation, many object-oriented languages have features that help us control the *visibility* of what's inside the object. Methods and variables inside the objects can be made invisible outside the object by declaring them `private`. A somewhat less restrictive way to do it is to make them `protected`.

PHP 5 has private and protected functions and member variables. Actually, they are private and protected *methods*, not functions, since they are always inside a class, but the syntax to define a method uses the keyword `function`, just as in PHP 4.

Private methods and variables are available only from within the same class. Protected methods and variables are available from within the same class and from parent and child (or more precisely, ancestor and descendant) classes.

A method is marked as public, private, or protected by adding a keyword before the word `function`:

```
public function getEmail() {}
protected function doLoad() {}
private function matchString($string) {}
```

Visibility restrictions are used differently for methods and instance variables (and class variables), although the syntax is similar. In this section, we discuss methods first and then variables. We look at why and how to use private and protected methods, then we discuss why it's recommended to keep all instance variables private. We try out using interception instead of accessor methods. Finally (and ironically), we introduce the concept of final classes and methods.

3.1.1   How visible do we want our methods to be?

Features to modify visibility are often absent or inconspicuous in dynamically typed languages; this is logical, since these languages tend to let programmers do whatever seems convenient without too many artificial boundaries. On the other hand, the ability to control the visibility of methods and instance variables can be seen as a natural extension of the ability to restrict the scope of an ordinary variable in procedural code.

Restricting the visibility of instance variables is generally no problem, since we can always provide a method to access them. But restricting the visibility of methods carries the risk of getting too restrictive. It depends on who will be using the methods. It may be tempting to use them to make sure your class is used in a specific way, that only the "official" API of a class is being used.

The problem is that it's fiendishly difficult to know ahead of time what methods will be useful when you, and especially someone else, start reusing a class.

We will be using private and protected methods in the examples in this book, but the underlying assumption is that a private or protected method can be made public at any time.

One way to think of private and protected methods is as a kind of documentation, an aid to readability. They make it easier to see how the methods are being used, and prevent you from using them incorrectly by mistake. But they don't necessarily dictate how they *should* be used in the future.

Visibility is slightly different in PHP 5 and in Java. Java has a package concept that affects visibility. By default, a method or instance variable is visible to any class in the same package. Protected methods and variables are available to child and descendant classes and to other classes in the same package.

By contrast, in PHP 5, default visibility is public; this makes it possible to program in PHP 5 in the same way as in PHP 4. If we do not indicate visibility, everything is publicly visible, as in PHP 4. PHP 5 also lacks Java's ability to make classes private and protected.

These differences are summarized in table 3.1.

Table 3.1   Visibility modifiers in PHP 5 versus Java

	PHP 5	Java
Private and protected classes		✓
Default visibility	Public	Package
protected means	Available only to child/descendant classes and parent/ancestor classes	Available to descendants and classes in the same package[a]

a. In Java, officially only the descendants can use a protected method, not the ancestors. How this works in practice is complex and beyond the scope of a PHP book. In PHP, however, an object belonging to a parent class can freely call any method defined in a child class.

We've discussed the reason to use visibility restrictions for methods. Assuming then that we want to use them, when and how specifically would we apply them? We will deal with private methods first and then protected ones.

3.1.2 When to use private methods

Private methods are often utility methods that are used repeatedly in a class (but not in any other class) or methods that are used only in one place. It might seem odd to have a separate method for something that happens in only one place, but the reason for this is typically readability: putting a chunk of code into a separate method that has an intention-revealing name.

Listing 3.1 is a simplified example of user validation. An administrator has edited an existing user account and submitted the form. If the administrator has not changed the user name, he or she is updating the existing user account. That's OK. It's also OK for the administrator to create a new user account by changing the user name, but the name must not clash with an existing user account, or that account will be overwritten or duplicated. To make the code more readable, there is a separate method to test for each of these situations in which the form submission will be accepted (nameUnchanged() and nameNotInDB()).

Listing 3.1 UserValidator class using private methods for readability

```php
class UserValidator {
    function validateFullUser($user) {
        if ($this->nameUnchanged($user) ||
                $this->nameNotInDB()) return TRUE;
        return FALSE;
    }

    private function nameUnchanged($user) {
        return $_POST['username'] == $user->getUsername();
    }

    private function nameNotInDB() {
        // Query the database, return TRUE if there is no user
        // with a name corresponding to $_POST['username'])
    }
}
```

$user is a User object representing the existing user that's being edited; in other words, the object whose properties were displayed in the form.

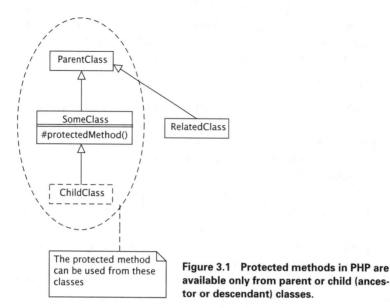

The protected method can be used from these classes

Figure 3.1 Protected methods in PHP are available only from parent or child (ancestor or descendant) classes.

3.1.3 When to use protected methods

Protected methods in PHP are available from within the same class and from ancestor or descendant classes—that is, when the class using the method inherits from the class that contains the method or vice versa, as illustrated in figure 3.1.

Opportunities for using protected methods appear when a child class uses a method from a parent class. It's also useful in the opposite case, when the parent class uses a method in the child class. This is slightly harder to wrap your mind around, but it's important nevertheless.

For an example of how this works, see the section on abstract classes and methods later in the chapter.

3.1.4 Keeping your instance variables private or protected

Technically, the `private` and `protected` keywords work exactly the same way with methods and instance variables. But in practice, there is a difference between variables and methods, since you can use a method to get a variable, but not the other way around.[1] This means that it's always feasible to keep member variables private or protected as long as you provide methods to get and set the value of the variable:

```
class Document {
    private $title;

    //...
    //...
```

---

[1] Unless, that is, you use the so-called overloadable property access feature, which we will discuss shortly.

```
function getTitle { return $this->title; }
function setTitle($arg) { $this->title = $arg }
}
```

That way you're not preventing anyone from doing anything, you're just controlling the *way* they do it. That's why it's hardly ever a problem to keep member variables private. And since it's not a problem, it is generally considered good practice, at least in languages that have no way to intercept the access to an instance variable so that its meaning can change if necessary.

3.1.5 Accessors for private and protected variables

As mentioned, a private member variable is one that can only be directly accessed from inside the class. In general, the ideal is for the variable to be used only inside the class. If you can avoid using it from outside, that's a sign that you're following the "tell, don't ask" principle.

If you do need to access the value from outside the class, you use accessors—also known as *getter* and *setter* methods—to get and set the value. Any object bigot will tell you that this is the only way to do it: member variables should never be public.

But finding a satisfying reason why it should be so is not necessarily easy. Not exposing the variable at all is a good idea, but when you do need to expose it, why do you have to use accessors? Some of the reasoning is not fully convincing. Some will tell you, for example, that if you have a zip code variable, it might need to be validated before it is set. So it's a good idea to make the variable private and have a setter method, setZipCode(), that takes care of validating it first. That way no one can set it to an invalid value. Something like this:

```
class Address {
    private zipCode;
    function setZipCode($zip) {
        // Do some validation
        $this->zipCode = $zip;
    }
}
```

That's convincing for the particular case of a zip code. But frequently, we just need to store the value as it is. So why should we have to use accessors when there's no processing needed? Of course, it might be needed in the future. But we don't know that.

So what if we just keep the variable public until the time we need to do additional processing? What happens is that all the occurrences of the variable have to be changed to accessor calls. The only problem with this is that we have no way to be sure where the variable has been used. We may not find all of them, and the ones we missed may show up as troublesome bugs. That is why it's better to use accessors from the very beginning: that is, from the time you actually need to access the variable. There is no reason to add accessors for all variables, and there is no reason to add a setter method for a variable that can be read-only. Normally, getters and setters should serve current requirements, not hypothetical future ones.

Using accessors has been common even in PHP 4. You can treat a variable as if it were private and make all accesses from outside the class go through accessors. PHP 5 makes life a little bit easier if you do use public variables and then want to make them private. Once you declare the variable private, PHP 5 will scream whenever you run some code that tries to use it from outside the class. So you're better off than in PHP 4, which might fail in more subtle ways. And in PHP 5, there is another possibility: you can use overloading to turn what looks like a variable access from the outside into an accessor call. So for example, when you run

```
$email = $message->text;
```

PHP will execute

```
$message->getText();
```

instead.

In the next section, we will see how to do this.

3.1.6 The best of both worlds? Using interception to control variables

PHP 5 has the ability to intercept and redefine property accesses.[2]

> **NOTE** We're using the term *property access* since it is the term used in the PHP manual. Property access is normally a way to get and set what we have been calling *instance variables*. In the PHP manual, these are referred to as *members* or *member variables*. For the purposes of this book, you can safely treat these terms as synonymous, along with the UML term *attribute*.

We can use this to make something that looks like a plain instance variable but is actually controlled by methods. If you define methods called __get() and __set(), PHP will run one of these methods when you try to access an undefined member variable. Let's see how this works with a text variable in a Document class. The simple version looks like this:

```
class Document {
    public $text;
}
```

We want to make client work the same way as before, while internally we control the accesses from accessor methods. Listing 3.2 shows how to do this.

---

[2] In the official documentation, this is called *overloading*, though this doesn't quite fit the standard definition of overloading. But it's not entirely unreasonable to use the term *overloadable*, since we can use it to implement something similar to Java-style method overloading.

Listing 3.2   Making property accesses execute accessor methods

```
class Document {
    private $_text;

    private function __get($name) {
        $method = 'get'.$name;
        return $this->$method();
    }

    private function __set($name,$value) {
        $method = 'set'.$name;
        return $this->$method($value);
    }

    function getText() { return $this->_text; }
    function setText($text) { $this->_text = $text; }
}
```

We've changed the name of the variable from $text to $_text and added methods called __get() and __set(). Now if we try to get it by its original name ($text = $document->text), PHP 5 will execute __get('text'). This method generates a call to getText(), which returns the value of the renamed member variable. Trying to set the variable will execute setText().

Figure 3.2 is a UML sequence diagram that shows this process.

Now we can use $document->text as if it were an ordinary public instance variable, but behind the scenes, we are calling getText() and setText(). We can add additional processing to these without having to change any client code.

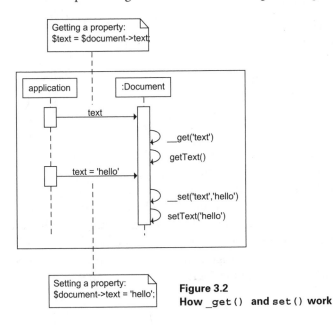

Figure 3.2
How __get() and set() work

It may be surprising that the __get() and __set() methods are private. This only means that we cannot call them directly:

```
$text = $document->__get('text');
```

However, it is possible to use them to intercept instance variable accesses.

This capability raises the question of whether it might be a good idea to use this approach for all member variable access. It *is* convenient and highly readable. And it's done routinely in some programming languages that have built-in support for similar variable handling. But at the time of this writing, it must be considered experimental in PHP. Using it across the board would mean deriving all classes from a class that has __get() and __set() methods like the ones shown. Also, it affects what kind of error messages you get. It's difficult at this point to assess all possible side effects of such a practice. So in this book, we will be using "old-fashioned" getters and setters.

3.1.7 Final classes and methods

The final keyword allows you to prevent child classes from extending a class by overriding a class or method. Here is a simple example of the restriction imposed by a final class:

```
final class AccessControl { }
class MyAccessControl extends AccessControl { }
```

This produces the following error message:

```
class bar may not inherit from final class (AccessControl)...
```

A final method is a method you're not allowed to override in a child class. A final method might look like this:

```
class AccessControl {
    public final function encryptPassword(){}
}
```

Now the following is forbidden:

```
class MyAccessControl extends AccessControl {
    public function encryptPassword() {}
}
```

When are final classes and methods useful? This is not an easy question to answer. Most books on object-oriented design simply ignore final.

There is some difference of opinion on this issue. Some say that you should use final to prevent bad design: if you think that inheriting from a class (or overriding a method) would be a bad idea, make it final. Others question whether this is realistically possible, since it involves trying to guess ahead of time what extensions to a class are needed. The previous examples suggest that there could be situations in which genuine security considerations would make it wise to use final.

One possible and more specific use of `final` is when a method or class is marked as deprecated. If a method or class is not really supposed to be used at all, it seems reasonable to prevent one use of it—overriding or extending it.

In Java, `final` is also used in a different meaning—to define class constants. PHP 5 uses `const` instead. The similarities and differences between PHP and Java are summarized in table 3.2.

Table 3.2 The `final` keyword in PHP 5 versus Java

	Java	PHP 5
`final` classes cannot be extended by child classes	✓	✓
`final` methods cannot be overridden by child classes	✓	✓
Syntax for class constants	`static final`	`const`

We've discussed visibility restrictions as applied to methods and variables in object instances. But methods and instance variables can also belong to the class itself. We will dig deeper into that topic in the next section.

3.2   THE CLASS WITHOUT OBJECTS: CLASS METHODS, VARIABLES, AND CONSTANTS

A class provides a virtual home for the object instances belonging to the class. It can also store information that is independent of the instances. For example, if we have a Product class and we create the Product instances from a table in a database, the name of the table logically belongs to the class rather than to any specific instance. And we may need to do something before we've actually created any instance. For example, the data needed to create an instance might need to be read from a database. This behavior, reading from the database, is related to the class but cannot be done by an instance of the class. One possible home for this behavior is in a class method: one that can be called using just the class name rather than a variable representing an instance:

```
$product = Product::find($productCode);
```

We use the double colon (`::`) whenever we want to access a method, variable, or constant belonging to a class rather than an object.

There is always an alternative. Instead of using class methods, variables, and constants, we could create another class (or classes) whose instances would provide the information and behavior belonging to the class. For example:

```
$finder = new ProductFinder;
$product = $finder->find($productCode);
```

This could be more flexible, but it's also more complex: there is an additional class and an additional line of client code. There are always pros and cons.

In this section, we will deal with class methods and when they're useful, class variables, and class constants. Since class constants have rather restrictive limitations, we'll also see how to deal with those by using methods and variables instead.

3.2.1 Class (static) methods

Class methods are methods that are not run on a specific object instance. They're defined in the class, but they work just like plain functions, except that you have to use the class name when you call them.

The keyword for class methods and variables is `static`. This terminology is derived from C++ and Java and is in common use. So although "class method" may be more appropriate and descriptive, *static method* is a customary term. In PHP, the typical static method is defined using `static function` or `static public function`:

```
static public function encryptPassword($password) {}
```

Let's say we have a User class that has an `insert()` method to save the user object in the database. It also has an `encryptPassword()` method that takes an unencrypted password as an argument and returns an encrypted password. So to create a new user object and save it in the database, you would do this:

```
$user = new User(/* Arguments including user name, etc. */);
$user->insert();
```

And to encrypt a password, you would do this:

```
$password = User::encryptPassword($password);
```

Inside the User class, we can use `self` to refer to the class:

```
$password = self::encryptPassword($password);
```

This has exactly the same effect as a plain function:

```
$password = encryptPassword($password);
```

The function itself could be identical, but in one case it's inside a class definition; in the other case it's not.

If you have a set of procedural functions that seem to belong together, you can put them in a class just for the sake of sorting. What you have then is actually a function library; the fact that you're using the *class* keyword to define it doesn't really make it object-oriented, since you're not instantiating any objects.

You can have class methods in PHP 4, but you can't declare them as such. In PHP 5, you can declare them using the `static` keyword:

```
static public function encryptPassword($password) {
    return md5($password);
}
```

The `static` keyword is similar to `private` and `protected` in that they document the intended use of the method and prevent you from using it incorrectly by mistake. If a method is defined as static, you can't do anything useful with the `$this` variable. So you should not try to do something like this:

```
static public function encryptPassword($password) {
    return $this->format(md5($password));
}
```

If you do, PHP 5 will generate a fatal error.

3.2.2 When to use class methods

There are several uses for class methods. Some of the more common ones are

- Creation methods and factory methods
- Finder methods
- Procedural code
- Replacements for constants

Creation methods and factory methods are methods that create and return object instances. They're frequently used when ordinary creation using new becomes insufficient.

Finder methods—to find an object in a database or other storage—may be considered a special case of creation methods, since they return a new object instance.

Some things can be done just as effectively with a snippet of procedural code as with an object-oriented method. Simple calculations and conversions are examples of this. Sometimes it's relevant to put procedural code into a class instead of using plain functions. The reason for keeping it in a class may be to avoid name collisions with other functions or because it belongs in class that is otherwise based on instance methods.

The fact that static methods can be used for all these things does not prove that they should always be used. Static methods have the advantage of simplicity, but they are hard to replace on the fly. If a method belongs to an object instance, it's potentially pluggable. We can replace the object instance with a different one to change the behavior significantly without changing either the client code or the original class. Let's re-examine our earlier Finder example:

```
$finder = new ProductFinder;
$product = $finder->find($productCode);
```

If we replace the product finder with another class (for example, we might want to get the product information from a web service instead), both the old ProductFinder class and the second line in the example can remain the same; the finder is pluggable. On the other hand, using the static method:

```
$product = Product::find($productCode);
```

Here, the behavior is built into the Product class, and there is no way to change it without changing that line of code. That's not much of a problem if it occurs only once, but if the class name is used repeatedly, it's another matter.

This problem may become particularly acute in unit testing: we may want to replace the `find()` method with another, fake one, that returns fixed test data instead of actual data from the database.

3.2.3 Class variables

Class variables are variables that belong to a class. To define one, you use the keyword `static` as with class methods:

```
class Person {
    static private $DBTABLE = 'Persons';
}
```

The table name is now available to all instances and is always the same for all instances. We can access it by using the `self` keyword:

```
$select = "SELECT * FROM ".self::$DBTABLE;
```

In this example, we declared the variable private, so it can't be accessed from outside the class. But if we make it public, we can refer to it like this:

```
$select = "SELECT * FROM ".Person::$DBTABLE;
```

But when is it appropriate to use a class variable? In this particular case, we might have used a class constant instead. Or we might have used an instance variable and initialized it the same way. That way all instances would have had the table name available. We could still have used it in instance methods inside the class:

```
$select = "SELECT * FROM ".$this->$DBTABLE;
```

But it would be unavailable to class methods, and it would be unavailable outside the class without first creating an instance of the Person class.

What all this means is that one of the typical uses for class variables—and class constants—is this kind of data: table names, SQL fragments, other pieces of syntax (regular expression fragments, `printf()` formats, `strftime()` format, and so forth).

Yet another way to look at it is to consider the fact that having lots of global variables in a program is a bad idea. If you do have them, one easy way to improve the situation (not necessarily the ideal, but everything is relative) is simply to collect them in one or more classes by replacing them with public class variables. So for a configuration class:

```
class Config {
    public static $DBPASSWORD = 'secret';
    public static $DBUSER = 'developer';
    public static $DBHOST = 'localhost';
    //...
}
```

Now we can connect to a MySQL server by doing this:

```
mysqli_connect(Config::$DBHOST, Config::$DBUSER,
               Config::$DBPASSWORD);
```

I have deliberately capitalized the names of the variables to emphasize their similarity to global variables and constants.

3.2.4 Class constants

Class constants are similar to class variables, but there are a few key differences:

- As the name indicates, they cannot be changed.
- They are always public.
- There are restrictions on what you can put into them.
- Although the way you use them is similar, the way you define them is completely different.

Instead of the `static` keyword, class constants are defined using the `const` keyword:

```
class Person {
    const DBTABLE = 'Persons';
}
```

Now we can access the constant using `self::DBTABLE` inside the class and `Person::DBTABLE` outside it.

In this case, the constant may seem to have all the advantages when compared to a variable. The table name won't change as we run the program, so there seems to be no reason to use a variable. And constants can't be accidentally overwritten.

But there is one reason why we might want to use a variable anyway: for testing. We might want to use a test table for testing; replacing the class variable at the beginning of the test is an easy way to achieve that. On the other hand, the fact that a constant cannot be changed can be good for security, since it will never be altered for malicious purposes.

Class constants are especially useful for enumerations. If a variable can have only a fixed set of values, you can code all the fixed values as constants and make sure the variable is always set to one of these.

Let us take a very simple authorization system as an example. The authorization system has three fixed roles or categories of user: regular, webmaster, and administrator.

We could represent the roles as simple strings. We would have a `$role` variable whose value could be either "regular," "webmaster," or "administrator." So to check that the current user has the privileges of an administrator, we might do something like this:

```
<?php if ($role == 'amdinistrator'): ?>
  <a href="edit.php">Edit</a>
<?php endif; ?>
```

The only problem is that the word "administrator" is misspelled, so the test won't work. It's a bug, but it can be avoided by using constants. In PHP 4, all constants are global, so we would have to give them names like ROLE_ADMINISTRATOR. In PHP 5 there's a tidier way to do it, called *class constants*:

```
class Role {
    const REGULAR = 1;
    const WEBMASTER = 2;
    const ADMINISTRATOR = 3;
    //...
}
```

Now we can do this instead:

```
<?php if ($role == Role::ADMINISTRATOR): ?>
```

We won't get away with any misspellings here; using an undefined class constant is a fatal error.

Compared to global constants, this is easier to figure out, not least because we know where the constant is defined (inside the Role class) just by looking at it.

But using class constants from the outside of a class is not necessarily the best way to do it. Leaving the work of testing the role to an object could be better.

```
<?php if ($role->isAdministrator()): ?>
```

This hides more information from the client code. It is an example of a principle called "tell, don't ask." In general, it's better to let an object work on its own data rather than asking for the data and processing it.

In the second example, we were using the constant from outside the Role class. If we were to use it inside the class to decide the *behavior* of the object, we could start considering another option: using inheritance to differentiate the behavior of the different user categories. So we would have subclasses of Role that might be called AdministratorRole, WebmasterRole, and RegularRole.

3.2.5 The limitations of constants in PHP

Class constants are fine as long as they're willing to do our bidding, but their limitations tend to show up early. The value of a constant can be set only when it's defined, and it cannot be defined inside methods in a class. You can only assign plain values to a constant; there is no way to assign an object to it. You can't even use string concatenation when defining a constant.

> **NOTE** As with most syntactical limitations, there is always the possibility that these will have changed by the time you read this.

And as mentioned, there is no way to replace the constant for test purposes.

For all of these reasons, we need to know what to do when we need to replace a class constant.

Using class variables instead of constants

The simplest and most obvious replacement for a class constant is a class variable, typically a public one. Since variables can be changed after they're defined, we can do so inside a method or function, giving us the opportunity to assign to it an object or the result of any kind of processing. But making sure it happens is slightly tricky. We can do this in the constructor for the object, but then the variable will not be available until we have created the first instance of the class. Of course, we might just create one right after the class declaration, if possible. Or simpler, we could have a class method to initialize class variables and run that. If we are using two different MySQL databases `rbac` and `cms`, we might make a connection to each one available like this:

```
class Connections {
    public static $RBAC;
    public static $CMS;

    public function init() {
        self::$RBAC =
            new mysqli('localhost','user','password','rbac');
        self::$CMS =
            new mysqli('localhost','user','password','cms');
    }
}
Connections::init();
```

This might seem ugly and cumbersome, but at least it works. But now we might as well make the variables private and add static accessor methods:

```
public static function getRbac() { return self::$RBAC; }
public static function getCms() { return self::$CMS; }
```

Using methods instead of constants

A read-only class method is often a perfectly valid replacement for a constant. In addition, they can be made to look almost identical. You can replace `Person::DBTABLE` with `Person::DBTABLE()`:

```
public static function DBTABLE() { return 'Persons'; }
```

It's simple and even works in PHP 4. Inside a method, we are not restricted in what we can do. For instance, if we want to reuse a long SQL statement that can be more easily formatted by using concatenation, we can do this:

```
class UserMapper {
    public static function sqlSelect($id) {
        "SELECT user_id,email,password,firstname,lastname,".
        "username,role+0 as roleID FROM Users WHERE id = $id";
    }
}
```

Class variables and constants were introduced in PHP 5; class methods were possible even in PHP 4, although there was no formal way to declare them or to prevent a class method from being used as an instance method. A similar situation exists with abstract classes and methods. In PHP 4, an ordinary class could function as an abstract class by using it as a parent class and never instantiating it. With PHP 5, it became possible to declare a class abstract.

3.3 ABSTRACT CLASSES AND METHODS (FUNCTIONS)

Abstract classes, another feature introduced in PHP 5, have a conceptual and a practical aspect, which we will deal with in greater depth later. Since this chapter is about the practical aspect, let us see what an abstract class actually does. We'll look at the basic workings of abstract classes and methods and then see how they can be applied to a class from the "Hello world" example in the previous chapter.

3.3.1 What are abstract classes and methods?

Making a class abstract is as simple as using `abstract class` instead of just `class`. When we do that, we are no longer allowed to instantiate the class. So you should not do this:

```
abstract class Foo {}
$foo = new Foo;
```

If you do, you will get this message:

```
Cannot instantiate abstract class Foo
```

So what's the point of having an abstract class? It's useful because another class, which is not abstract—in other words, a concrete class—can inherit from it.

An abstract method is really just a declaration of a method signature that can be used by child classes.

```
abstract protected function createAdapter(DomElement $element);
```

This so-called method does nothing; it just sits there pretending to be important. It's really just a method signature. But it's called a method in spite of that.

Technically, the relationship between abstract methods and abstract classes is that if you declare a method abstract, the class containing it must also be declared abstract. In other words, a concrete class cannot have abstract methods, but an abstract class can have concrete methods, as in the example in the next section.

3.3.2 Using abstract classes

In our inheritance example in the previous chapter, we had an HtmlDocument class and a "Hello world" child class. If you use the HtmlDocument class on its own, it will output an empty HTML page. So there's little point in using it except indirectly by way of its children. In other words, there will be no harm in declaring it abstract. While we're at it, we might as well declare the getContent() method abstract.

```
abstract class HtmlDocument {
    public function getHtml() {
        return "<html><body>".$this->getContent().
            "</body></html>";
    }

    abstract public function getContent();
}
```

The abstract method does nothing except force child classes to implement the get-Content() method. We had no use for the previous behavior of this method—returning an empty string—since all we get out of that is an empty HTML document, which is not the most exciting thing you can view in a browser. Instead, we are expecting all child classes to implement this method with a method that returns some text.

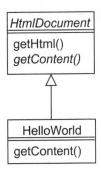

Figure 3.3
An abstract class with a concrete child class

In a UML class diagram, this can be expressed as in figure 3.3. The abstract Html-Document class and its abstract getContent() method are shown in italics.

What have we achieved by doing this? We've prevented two possible mistakes: instantiating the HtmlDocument class itself, and forgetting to implement the get-Content() method in a child class. In addition, we've made the code a little clearer. abstract class tells someone who is reading it for the first time that there are child classes of HtmlDocument. The intention of the class—to be a parent class with no independent job to do—is clearer.

One purpose of abstract classes is to support class type hints that are not overly specific. We will take a close look at type hinting in the following section.

3.4   CLASS TYPE HINTS

If you order pizza and get an encyclopedia delivered instead, you stay hungry. Worse yet, it's a sign that you have the wrong phone number and didn't communicate well with the people who took your order. Or perhaps the delivery person had the wrong address.

Similarly, if a method or function gets the wrong kind of input, it's often a symptom that there's a serious bug present. A function that does mathematical calculations will not work with strings or PEAR DB objects. And if you are passing PEAR DB objects to it, most likely you've made a mistake; they were supposed to be somewhere else and may be in short supply there.

Statically typed languages force you to specify the type of every single argument to every single method. Considering the fact that problems with input values are relatively infrequent, this may seem like overkill. On the other hand, one bug can cause lots of trouble. So some programmers have tried to implement various workarounds for type checking in dynamically typed languages. However, these tend to be incomplete and cumbersome.

Let's check out how type hints work, and then we'll discuss when they're useful.

3.4.1   How type hints work

PHP 5 has a solution that is incomplete, but not cumbersome. PHP can check the types of method arguments for you so you don't have to write explicit conditional code to do it. As of this writing, this is true only if the arguments are objects or arrays.

As mentioned, statically typed languages such as Java require you to specify the type of each argument to a method. A Java method will start something like this:

```
public void addDocument(Document document) {
```

void is the return type. In this case, it means that the method won't return anything, and Document means that the single argument has to be a Document object or an object belonging to a subclass of Document.

PHP 5 lets you do something similar with any argument that happens to be an object or an array. So you can say this:

```
public function addDocument(Document $document) {}
```

Unlike Java, PHP 5 won't tell you that you made a mistake until you run the code. The previous is equivalent to:

```
public function addDocument($document) {
    if (!($document instanceof Document)) {
        die("Argument 1 must be an instance of Document");
    }
}
```

So if NewsArticle is a subclass of Document, you can pass a NewsArticle object to the method, but not a plain string or a User object.

The good news about type hinting is that you get an earlier warning that you've made a mistake. Without type hinting, you won't get an error message until you try to use the object or value inappropriately, by calling the wrong method on it, for instance.

3.4.2   When to use type hints

Checking that the arguments to methods are valid can increase reliability and make debugging easier by catching errors earlier than they otherwise would have been. But this is a double-edged sword: If you add error-checking code where it's not necessary, it clutters your code and makes it less readable. This, in turn, can cause the code to become *less* reliable, since it makes bugs and security holes harder to find amid all the error checking. So in general, it's better to avoid too much checking unless the interface is one that you know may be used incorrectly. Good test coverage reduces the need for checking. On the other hand, if you're writing a class that's supposed to be used by people you may not even know, checking argument types is more relevant.

Type hints involve little code and enhance readability rather than diminish it. In well-factored, object-oriented code with lots of small classes, the hardest thing to understand may be the interaction between classes, and knowing the types of arguments makes it easier to unravel the relationships. (The alternative is to use comments.) But the real downside of type hints is dependency. Every type hint is a dependency on whatever class or interface the hint refers to. Therefore, although type hints may make it easier to find bugs, they also make the code harder to change. If you change the name of a class, you may need to change all the type hints for that class. For example, we might have a class called Date, and do a lot of this kind of thing:

```
$this->setDate(Date $date);
```

Now if we change the name of the Date class to DateMidnight, we will have to change all those type hints. Programmers who are used to dealing with this kind of thing in Java may tell you that you should type hint on an interface to avoid this, but finding out what interface you need is far from trivial.

Type hints are more likely to be useful in constructors than in other methods. Frequently, a constructor accepts an object as an argument, stores the object in an instance variable, and uses it later. A lot may happen between the time it's inserted and the time the object is used; by checking the type when it's passed into the constructor, we can get a possible error report much earlier, and it may be easier to find the bug.

PHP 5 type hints let you check only objects and arrays, not plain data types. Unless you write rather sophisticated object-oriented code, most method arguments are likely to be plain strings and numbers that are not "hintable."[3]

On the other hand, we could use type hints for plain data types by simply wrapping the data item in a class. We could even create String and Integer classes that have no purpose except to signal the type of the contents.

More useful, probably, would be to introduce a specialized class whose name indicated the meaning of the data item. Consider a typical query() method for a database connection object. We might use it like this:

```
$db->query('SELECT * FROM Log');
```

If we wanted to do something to prevent the possibility of passing some irrelevant string or number to this method, we *could* introduce a type hint requiring an Sql-Statement object:

```
class DbConnection {
public function query(SqlStatement $sql) {}
}
```

The SqlStatement object could be created from the string in a simple way:

```
$db->query(new SqlStatement('SELECT * FROM Log'));
```

In its simplest form, the SqlStatement object would be just a simple wrapper for the string. And to make it useful in more than this specific case, we could have a general wrapper class and extend it to create the SqlStatement class:

---

[3] Type hinting for arrays was new in PHP 5.1. Additional changes may have happened by the time you read this.

```
abstract class StringHolder {
    protected $string;

    public function __construct($string) {
        $this->string = $string;
    }

    public function getString() {
        return $this->string;
    }
}

class SqlStatement extends StringHolder {}
```

I am not advocating this approach; I'm simply pointing out the possibility. It would clearly be overkill for general use, but there may be circumstances in which type checking is important enough to make this particular kind of complexity worth the trouble.

Using type hints can be troublesome if you're tied to using a specific class name, since changing the class name requires you to change all the type hints. One way to get more freedom in using type hints is to use interfaces.

3.5 INTERFACES

The word *interface* has a semantic meaning and—in some programming languages— a syntactic one as well.

In object-oriented programming, the word *interface* typically means the set of messages an object can respond to—the set of operations it can perform. It's the very small and restricted language the object understands.

In the syntactic sense, interfaces are a way to formally declare this tiny language. And you can define what classes of objects respond to that particular tiny language. If you fail to give the designated objects the ability to understand the language, the compiler will complain.

Your average dynamically typed language has no interface construct. Interestingly, PHP 5 does. But how useful are they really, and for what purposes? Let's investigate. We'll start by seeing how interfaces work and discuss whether they are needed at all in PHP. Then we'll see a couple uses for interfaces: making design clearer, and improving type hints. Finally, we'll see how interfaces in PHP differ from interfaces in Java.

3.5.1 What is an interface?

Technically, an interface is a class-like construct that declares a number of methods. In fact, it's similar to an abstract class that has only abstract methods:[4]

---

[4] The template interfaces and classes that are used as examples in this chapter are web templates. The idea will be familiar to most PHP programmers but not to some who are more familiar with other languages. If it seems confusing, chapter 13 provides an introduction to the subject.

```
interface Template {
    public function __construct($path);
    public function execute();
    public function set($name,$value);
    public function getContext();
}
```

A class based on this interface can be declared using the `implements` keyword:

```
class SmartyTemplate implements Template {}
```

All this means is that the SmartyTemplate class must have all the methods in the interface, and the method signatures have to be the same. So `set()` needs to have two arguments.

The difference between this and an abstract class that has only abstract methods is that a class can only `extend` one other class, but it can `implement` more than one interface:

```
class DateRange extends     Range
                implements TransposableRange, ComparableRange {}
```

3.5.2   Do we need interfaces in PHP?

Do we even need interfaces in PHP, or are they just useless, pretentious, performance-hampering formalities? Do they have about as much concrete, practical value as wearing a tuxedo while programming?

Well, let's take the performance issue first. Interfaces will not affect performance much unless we put the interface in a separate file. Opening a file always takes time. So we need to be aware of that.

What interfaces do, in a practical sense, is next to nothing. In fact, if we are not using class type hints and our code is correct, interfaces have zero effect on how the code executes. Interfaces are primarily a way of making things explicit and of preventing some mistakes.

But although interfaces are not strictly necessary, they may have some value. They make some of our design more explicit and they can prevent some stupid mistakes. But at this writing, interfaces have existed in PHP for too short a time to make firm judgments as to when they will be useful and when they won't. What we can do is to explore some possible advantages and disadvantages, some insights and some pitfalls.

3.5.3   Using interfaces to make design clearer

An interface is practically the same thing as an abstract class with no implemented methods, except that a class can have only one parent class, but implement any number of interfaces.

Dynamically typed languages have traditionally not had abstract classes and interfaces. This makes practical sense, but conceptually speaking, it leaves something to be desired.

Nearly every modern programming language has classes and inheritance. So you can have classes that have part of their implementation in common and inherit this from their parent. Typically, such classes have both this practical relationship—the common implementation—and a conceptual relationship. For instance, if we have a Document class that is the parent of the Message class and the NewsArticle class, these are clearly related conceptually. If you remove the common implementation (there are usually different ways to do this), the conceptual relationship remains. It seems reasonable for a language to allow us to express this relationship even if there is no common implementation.

If abstract classes—even with no concrete methods—and interfaces are used to express similarities between classes and the way they work, it makes these conceptual or design aspects explicit, and that may make it easier to understand how the code is structured.

3.5.4 Using interfaces to improve class type hints

Just as with parent classes, interfaces can be used for class type hints. That means that the following method will accept an object belonging to a class that implements the Template interface or that extends a class called Template:

```
public function display(Template $template) {}
```

If a type hint is too specific, it may be too restrictive. For example, the `display()` method might be able to use objects that are not Templates. For example, it might be able to accept a Redirect object that would do an HTTP redirect instead of generating HTML code as templates habitually do. It can be useful to have some freedom in how restrictive the type hint becomes. A class cannot extend more than one class, but interfaces are unlimited; this allows us to express abstract relationships that fall outside the inheritance hierarchies. To express the similarity between a Redirect object and a template object—the fact that they are interchangeable in some contexts—we can use an interface called something like Response:

```
interface Response {
    public function execute();
    public function display();
}
```

A specific template class might extend a template class and implement the Response interface:

```
class FormTemplate extends Template implements Response {}
```

Figure 3.4 shows this situation. In the traditional UML notation, the `implements` and `extends` relationships are both shown with the same kind of arrow, representing generalization. The structure shown is atypical; normally, the Template class would implement the Response interface. But the dual inheritance shown might be useful in some situations; for example, if you were unable to change the Template class or if the FormTemplate class (but not other template classes) were needed in some context requiring the Response interface.

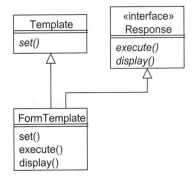

Figure 3.4 A class that extends a class and implements a template interface

In PHP, we have a lot of control of the degree of restrictiveness for type hints. At one extreme, we can simply leave them out, and unless the object we pass into the method is incompatible in practice, we will hear no complaints. At the other extreme, we can base the type hint on an interface or a parent class that has type hints itself.

The least restrictive way of using them without skipping them altogether is to use an interface that has no methods whatsoever—an interface that communicates a certain aspect or quality of a data type. We could have defined the Response interface like this:

```
interface Response {}
```

In Java programming, this kind of interface is sometimes called a *tag interface*. But there is an important difference between Java and PHP: when you name an interface as the type of a method argument in Java, the compiler will not allow you to call methods on that object that are not defined in the interface. The PHP type hint is just a simple check that the object is in fact of the correct type; you can call any method, however inappropriate, on the argument later:

```
public function display(Template $template) {
    $template->nonExistentMethod();
}
```

Of course, this method will fail as soon as PHP tries to execute `nonExistent-Method()`, but the type hint has nothing to do with that. There is no direct relationship between the type hint and the method call. There is only a weak and indirect one, since we can be sure to avoid this kind of error if we make sure not to use any methods that are not defined in the Template interface.

Anyway, since there is no such checking in PHP, we can always use a tag interface in place of a "real" one.

3.5.5 Interfaces in PHP 5 versus Java

One notable difference between Java and PHP interfaces has already been mentioned: PHP type hints don't restrict what methods you are allowed to call. Beyond that, there are some small differences in how interfaces work in Java and PHP.

One difference is the fact that a class in PHP is not allowed to implement two different interfaces if they both contain the same method. Java does not have this restriction. This restriction in PHP seems unnecessary, and I suspect that it may change in later releases of PHP 5.

Unlike Java, PHP 5 allows you to include the constructor in the interface. As we will see later, it's typically not useful to define the constructor as part of the interface, since the signature of the constructor is often what needs to vary between similar classes. But you can do it, and there may be situations in which it would be useful.

There are also a couple similarities that might not be obvious. In both Java and PHP, an interface can extend another interface using the `extends` keyword. And in both, you can add the `abstract` keyword to methods in interface, but it's not required, since all method declarations in an interface are abstract anyway.

Table 3.3 summarizes these differences and similarities.

Table 3.3 Comparing the interface construct in PHP 5 and Java

	PHP 5	Java
Overlapping methods		✓
Constructor in interface	✓	
Interface can extend interface	✓	✓
`abstract` keyword is optional	✓	✓

3.6 SUMMARY

Basic object-oriented programming provides a two-level organization: classes and methods in which data and different chunks of code that belong together can live together. Inheritance is an easy way for classes to share code. Visibility restrictions define what is visible outside the class and what is not.

Private and protected methods and variables help make object-oriented code more readable and help encapsulate the contents of an object. Interfaces, abstract classes, and type hints are not strictly necessary in PHP, but they can give us more room to express types and abstractions.

These features are intended to make it easier to develop complex structure and design. In the coming chapters, we will go beyond the syntactical and mechanical aspects and study techniques and principles that support the thinking that's necessary to achieve good object-oriented design.

C H A P T E R   4

Understanding objects and classes

If you want to confess a crime, you can say, "*I shot the sheriff.*"

If you want to write an academic paper about it, you express the same thing differently, something like this: "*The shooting of the sheriff was carried out by the present author.*"

The key difference between the two is that a verb becomes a noun; the verb form of *shoot* in the first one is replaced with the noun *shooting* in the second one. Experts on good writing style will tell you that the best one is the first, plainer way of putting it. It's more immediate and easier to read; it gets your point across with less fooling around. And they are right, of course. Anyone can confirm that just by reading the two sentences.

But there is another point that is not apparent from the example. The noun form, *shooting*, does make the sentence harder to read. On the other hand, it lends itself to expressing more abstract ideas. For example, we could say, "shootings are a leading cause of death among sheriffs." Epidemiologists and statisticians say this kind of thing all the time. Trying to rephrase it using the verb *shoot* may be possible, but probably awkward.

So when we're expressing a simple, concrete message, the verb is the best choice, but if the message is more abstract, the noun may be the best or even the only choice.

The process of making a noun out of a verb is called *nominalization*. It's interesting that the word "nominalization" is itself a nominalization. Linguists also need to express abstract ideas.

How relevant is this to object-oriented programming? An object-oriented programming language has nouns (objects) and verbs (messages or methods). I believe that one reason why object-oriented programming is so successful is that it can express abstractions easily and in a way that's natural to us. And abstractions cover more ground, so to speak, than concrete concepts. Code that uses abstractions can be more reusable than code that uses concrete implementations.

But there is a danger. In much the same way that the academic way to say "I shot the sheriff" is just pretentious and wasteful, you can also overuse abstraction in object-oriented programming. It's sometimes called *speculative generality*. And just as with natural language, overly abstract programs are harder to read and understand than the ones that use only as much abstraction as is necessary and appropriate.

How much is necessary and appropriate? That is one of the matters we will be exploring further in this chapter. We'll start by discussing the purpose of object orientation and how objects can help us. Then we start on the road toward object-oriented design by asking about difference between good and bad design. Finally, we'll discuss the relationship between software objects and the real world.

4.1   WHY OBJECTS AND CLASSES ARE A GOOD IDEA

The relative merits of object-oriented versus procedural code are sometimes debated even by gurus of object-oriented programming. Object orientation is a good idea, but not always. Except in the hypothetical scenario in chapter 2, there is no reason to make "Hello world" more complex than this basic PHP script:

```
echo "Hello world!\n";
```

In Java, you have to write a class to do something as simple as outputting "Hello world"; in PHP, you're free to ignore object-oriented programming for as long as you wish. (In practice, you can do that in Java and similar languages as well, since you're free to write a class that contains only procedural chunks of code, or even one long procedural method. That's not object-oriented in any meaningful sense of the word, and it's really the equivalent of plain PHP scripts and functions.)

The extra code that goes into writing a class just to output "Hello world" is wasted. It's unnecessary baggage. But object orientation wasn't invented to solve simple problems; its usefulness lies in making it easier to grasp and solve complex problems.

Somewhere between the "Hello world" example and the vast enterprise application lies a threshold at which object-oriented programming becomes more effective than procedural programming in the long term. I say "in the long term" because the main benefit of OOP is in making applications easier to maintain. Even if it takes slightly more effort initially, it can pay off in less work when you add new features and fix bugs.

I tend to think that the threshold is low. I find that writing classes helps me even when the program is relatively small and simple. Object-oriented programming makes it easier to decompose the program into parts, and since you have to name the parts—the classes—it's easier to see what those parts are doing. You can do that with plain functions for a while, but as the functions multiply, it becomes harder to keep track of all of them.

But in the end, you have to find that out for yourself. If you find that the procedural design is simpler and easier to understand and that making it object-oriented complicates it unnecessarily, keep the procedural design. Don't make it object-oriented just because it looks impressive.

This is a general point that we will return to. For example, there's no point in applying advanced object-oriented techniques such as design patterns unless they actually improve the design.

To find out when object-oriented programming is a good idea and when it isn't, we need to understand the specific reasons why it helps.

4.1.1 Classes help you organize

Classes have one benefit that is not hard to understand: if you have lots of functions in your program, you can get lost trying to keep track of them and making sure there are no duplicate names. The simplest way to use classes is to put procedural functions inside them, which means that in practice you're using them as containers, somewhat in the same way that files are organized into directories or folders.

That organization is further reinforced when you make your code still more object-oriented: You can organize data and the methods to handle that data in the same class. And, instead of having global variables, you can have instance variables belonging to an object, so the variables are available when they are needed and only then.

4.1.2 You can tell objects to do things

In his book *The Seven Habits of Highly Effective People*, Stephen Covey explains the concept of delegating responsibility when dealing with people. He tells the story of how his seven-year-old son volunteered to take care of the yard. To instruct his son on how to do it, Covey said: "Green and clean is what we want. Now how you get [the lawn] green is up to you. You're free to do it any way you want, except paint it."

This captures the essence of what, in object-oriented programming, is called encapsulation. You send a message to an object, saying in effect "do this," and the object does the job for you. You don't have to think about how it does the job nor what it needs to be able do the job. Because the object has built-in behavior, data, and perhaps access to other objects, you can use it without worrying about how it's implemented.

4.1.3 Polymorphism

Another important aspect of this is known as *polymorphism*. Different objects can be programmed to do the same job in different ways, and you don't have to know or care about the difference except when you're programming those objects themselves.

I have a son and a daughter. If I ask them to get dressed, they will dress differently. My son won't put on a dress; my daughter might. This has partly to do with the classes—Boy and Girl—that they belong to. It also has to do with the fact that they're *configured* differently. They have different clothes in their respective closets—or lying around on the floor. In other words, they have different wardrobes. If we represent this as a UML class diagram, we have the situation in figure 4.1.

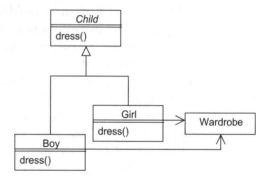

Figure 4.1 UML class diagram of pseudo-real Boy and Girl classes

If you're unfamiliar with UML, it might look as if they have the same Wardrobe. But what the diagram expresses is that both Boys and Girls use an object of class Wardrobe. But since they are different *instances* of the Wardrobe class, the two Wardrobes may contain different objects—items of clothing.

In the diagram, Child is a *generalization* of Boy and Girl. As mentioned in chapter 2, in statically typed languages such as Java, this has to be represented explicitly as a parent class or an interface. In dynamically typed languages such as PHP, this is not necessary (although it is possible in PHP 5). All we need is for two classes to implement the `dress()` method, and we're in business: we can mix objects belonging to the two classes freely, calling `dress()` without knowing which class the object belongs to:

```
$kids = array(new Boy, new Girl); // Twins!
foreach ($kids as $kid) {
    $kid->dress();
}
```

This phenomenon has come to be known as *duck typing*. Wikipedia says, "Initially used in the context of dynamic typing by Dave Thomas in the Ruby community, its premise is that *if it walks like a duck, and talks like a duck, then it might as well be a duck*. One can also say that the language ducks the issue of typing." A less likely interpretation is the idea that it doesn't matter whether a duck or a human being is typing the program code.

4.1.4 Objects make code easier to read

In my early days of hacking, I could write a program or a script, only to return a month later and have no idea what the code was doing. I knew the programming language, and I knew I had written the program myself, yet it was like trying to read the Epic of Gilgamesh from the original clay tablets in Sumerian cuneiform script.

Eventually, that changed. After I learned object-oriented programming, the problem was much diminished. Nowadays, my code may not always be self-explanatory, but understanding what it does is a lot easier.

Interestingly, some people I know claim that object-oriented programs are harder to read and understand than non-object-oriented ones. I think that is a misunderstanding. What they may be referring to is the fact that more general and more abstract code can be harder to read. It is usually possible, and sometimes tempting, but not always wise, to make object-oriented code general and abstract. Object orientation helps readability by letting you name concepts, hide confusing details, make code read more like natural language, keep related data together, and avoid overly complex conditional expressions.

Naming concepts

As we just said, abstract code can be hard to read. On the other hand, it may help readability as well. Later, we'll discuss the principles of when and how to use abstraction in a way that's meaningful and appropriate to the situation you're in. Sometimes using more abstraction is an appropriate way to make code more flexible and maintainable. So it can be a tradeoff: you're gaining something (flexibility) and losing something (readability and simplicity). If it's a good, intuitive abstraction, it may increase readability.

Typically, such abstractions will be domain concepts, concepts that are meaningful to the users of the system. For instance, the concept of *pricing* is a relatively abstract one, but one that most business users readily understand. On the other hand, if the abstraction is a somewhat vague technical one that's made up for the occasion, it's not likely to make the code easier to read.

Established technical concepts are more similar to business domain concepts. For example, when generating SQL, concepts representing parts of the SQL syntax (expressions, functions, clauses) will help make the code readable. If the job is very simple, it may be overkill to represent these as classes, but if you want to generate complex SQL statements, it's highly relevant.

Hiding confusing details

Another perspective of the same issue is that you can hide confusing details inside a class. That may not make them less confusing in themselves, but it keeps them separate so you can study them without having to deal with other confusing details (that may be conceptually unrelated) at the same time.

Making code read like English prose

Programs are harder to read than the average mystery novel or newspaper article. Plain English (or any other natural language we might happen to know) is inherently easy to understand because we're built to understand natural languages and have been practicing the skill since infancy. No matter how much of a geek you are, programs will always be harder to read than plain text. But we can take advantage of our built-in abilities by making program code read more like plain English. Helping us is the fact that object-oriented code has nouns (objects) and verbs (methods) just like natural languages. Making code nearly as readable as ordinary prose is a tall order; it's rarely achieved, and it's not always necessary or even desirable. But we can take some steps in that direction.

For an example, we will look at part of a design to generate an event calendar display. The event calendar display is capable of showing simultaneous events side by side. To achieve this, we represent the columns and the events as objects, as well as the overall CalendarView. The overall structure is illustrated in figure 4.2.

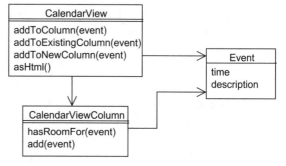

Since the point here is readable code, we'll look at the code for the part of the CalendarView class that takes care of adding a new event to the calendar. This operation is represented by the `addToColumn()` method, as shown in listing 4.1.

Figure 4.2 Calendar View classes to generate a calendar with simultaneous events side by side

Listing 4.1 Using method names to make code easier to read

```php
class CalendarView {
    public function addToColumn(Event $event) {                    ❶ Add an event
        if ($this->addToExistingColumn($event)) return;              to a column
        $this->addToNewColumn($event);
    }

    private function addToExistingColumn($event) {                 ❷ If possible,
        foreach (array_keys($this->columns) as $key) {               use an
            if ($this->columns[$key]->hasRoomFor($event)) {          existing
                $this->columns[$key]->add($event);                   column
                return TRUE;
            }
        }
        return FALSE;        ❸ Return FALSE if that fails
    }

    private function addToNewColumn($event) {                      ❹ Create and
        $column = new CalendarViewColumn($this->hours);              use a new
        $column->add($event);                                       column
        $this->columns[] = $column;
    }
}
```

❶ The `addToColumn()` method tries to add an event to an existing column using `addToExistingColumn()`. If that succeeds, it returns. If not, it adds the event to a new column using `addToNewColumn()`.

❷ The `addToExistingColumn()` method tries to add the event to one of the existing columns, trying them one by one. It adds the event to the first column it finds that has room for the event—in other words, the first column that has no events that overlap the new one. If the new event doesn't clash with any of the existing events in the column, the method succeeds, returns TRUE, and we're done. If not, it returns FALSE, and we continue.

❸ When we've looped through all the columns without being able to add the event, we return FALSE.

❹ `addToNewColumn()` creates a new column, adds the event to it, and adds the column to the CalendarView object.

This way of programming has several clear advantages:

- We can use object and method naming to do much of the job that would otherwise have to be done with comments. In contrast to comments, method and class names are part of the code itself, and are less likely to get out of sync. It's easy to forget to change a comment when you're working on the code; since method and class names are in the code, their presence is much more obvious. That is not to say that code should not be commented. But in well-factored code, having comments *inside* a method is usually unnecessary. Comments before the method to explain what it does is a different matter.

- We can subdivide the code into relatively small, intention-revealing methods. In procedural code, chunking this small would tend to become unmanageable owing to the large number of functions required.

- We can hide details. For example, the `hasRoomFor()` method probably has some kind of loop to check whether the new event conflicts with an existing event, but that need not concern us when reading this class. We could hide this with a procedural function as well, but using classes makes it much easier to sort out what details should be hidden at any given time.

Bundling data

Another basic, but important, way object orientation helps readability is that related data can be bundled together and treated as a unit. To some extent, this can be achieved using data structures based on PHP arrays, but objects have an edge here too.

Let's try a simple example. One we will be exploring later is time intervals or date ranges. Let us say we have two time intervals. One represents the whole month of June; the other represents just one day, June 10. In procedural code, we have to represent the start and end points of the intervals as separate variables. So to find out if one (the month of June) contains the other (June 10), we have to compare each of these separately:

```
if ($startjune < $startjune10 && $endjune > $endjune10) echo "OK";
```

In real code, the variables would probably have more general names than in this example, so it would be harder to see what was going on. You have to do some thinking (I do, anyway) to see that we're actually trying to test whether one interval contains the other.

It would help a little bit to make a function called `contains()` and pass the start and end points to that function. But we still have four variables and we have to remember the sequence of the function arguments.

Still easier would be to use arrays to represent the intervals, letting the arrays contain the start and end points. Something like this:

```
if (contains($june, $june10)) echo "OK\n";
```

Now we are starting to give the procedural code some of the properties of object-oriented code. We package data together and perform operations on the packages. An object-oriented solution also does that, but gives us a few additional benefits: the data package gets a class name (such as DateRange) that tells us something about what it's doing, the behavior (`contains`) has a logical home inside the class, and the object-oriented syntax adds yet another dimension to readability:

```
if ($june->contains($june10)) echo "OK\n";
```

Let's see how a class to create these objects might be implemented.

```
class DateRange {
    private $start;
    private $end;

    public function __construct($start,$end) {
        $this->start = $start;
        $this->end = $end;
    }

    public function contains($other) {
        return $this->start < $other->getStart()
            && $this->end > $other->getEnd();
    }

    public function getStart() { return $this->start; }
    public function getEnd() { return $this->end; }
}
```

This class is artificially simplistic, although it is real, working code. In practice, it can be preferable to use objects to represent the start and end times as well. As it is, the class assumes that the `$start` and `$end` variables can be compared using the standard operators. They could be UNIX timestamps or for that matter ISO format date and time specifications such as 2005-06-10 00:00:00. In chapter 8, we will look at more realistic date range or time interval classes.

Simplifying conditional expressions

In principle, an if-then-else statement is an idea that's obvious to anyone who speaks English. In practice, the logic of an if-then-else or switch construct is often hard to follow. The statements are often nested, the logical expressions complex. Sometimes, the legs of the conditional are so long that it's hard to see where they start and end.

Classes and objects make it easier to do decision-making in ways that are less confusing. We can extract methods to make intentions clearer, and we can use polymorphism instead of the conditional statements.

There are several classic refactorings that help us simplify conditionals. We will discuss them further in chapter 11.

Some of the tricks to improve readability—such as extracting code with recognizable intent into separate methods—are also helpful in achieving another important goal: eliminating duplicated code.

4.1.5 Classes help eliminate duplication

The most important way to eliminate duplication is to extract similar code into separate functions or methods. This means that most duplication can be eliminated by just using non-object-oriented functions.

In principle, that is. In practice and if the code is sufficiently complex, removing most or all duplication will force us to divide the code into much smaller chunks. Keeping lots of small procedural functions organized so that we know what happens where will be a major hurdle. The conditional logic to control what happens when is likely to grow complex. Sharing data between the functions will also be difficult and error-prone when there is no middle ground between local variables inside a function and completely global variables. And the global variables will be harder to control—it will be harder to avoid name conflicts when you have single global values strewn around your code than it would if those globals were organized into a few global objects.

> **NOTE** Even global objects should be used with caution and are often a warning sign, but a global object is clearly superior to keeping the same information in a sprinkling of single global variables.

The practical effect of this is that in complex procedural code, we are more likely to keep some duplication to keep it more readable and organized.

Having code well-organized also helps in spotting duplication. For example, if you have two similarly named methods in two different classes, that may well indicate duplicate code.

Object-oriented syntax hides more complexity and so helps eliminate more modest cases of duplication. In the DateRange example, we encapsulated the process of checking whether one range contained the other. In procedural code, we would have been more likely to duplicate the conditional expression, since a function to do just the conditional test would be relatively hard to use.

4.1.6 You can reuse objects and classes

Code reuse is too old and well-known by now to be considered a buzzword. Reuse is more like peace, prosperity, and freedom. Everyone wants it and lots of people like to talk about it, but the results aren't always up to expectations. On the other hand, there's always some of it going on. Even when we use the built-in functions in PHP, we are reusing some C++ code that may have been written by Zendians.

> **NOTE** The term Zendians refers to creatures from the planet Zend, or alternatively, to employees of Zend Technologies.

There's reuse on a small scale, as when you use the same class or method two or more times in your program, and then there's reuse on a large scale, as with libraries and PEAR packages.

Reuse on a small scale is perhaps most frequently the result of removing duplication, of extracting some duplicated code into a separate function or method. Then that function or method will be used at least twice, and that could be considered reuse.

Large-scale reuse is different, and attempts at it are often less successful. In principle, it seems like a good idea to use available libraries whenever we can. But there are reasons why it's often less work to write something yourself than to download some code. You can get a package that is large and monolithic, but maybe you need only part of what it does. And that package may depend on another package or some infrastructure that you don't really need. If the API of the package is not exactly what you need, you may find yourself either making your own design less than optimal or having to write adapter classes (this pattern is described in detail in chapter 7) to make your own software and the borrowed software work together properly.

And sometimes the API of the code you're trying to reuse is just obnoxious. I once tried to use a class that required me to set several cryptically named constants before I could get it to work. There was no documentation, of course.

If you do it yourself instead, you can end up with a more lightweight application that contains a smaller amount of code because you're only catering to your own needs, not to the needs of hundreds of other users.

The classical concept that is most used when discussing reuse is *coupling*. Simply put, this means that the code is like Lego blocks. Lego blocks have loose coupling: you can pull them apart and put them together in a different configuration.

The problem with applying this to programming is that it's impossible: classes can never be as interchangeable as Lego blocks. A class may sometimes be replaced with another class, but it's never possible to mix and match any class with any other class. The reason is that all Lego blocks have the same interface; object classes can never have exactly the same interface, although classes that have similar responsibilities can.

In object-oriented programming and design, we try to minimize coupling by reducing the number of dependencies between them. This is a complex subject that we will keep returning to.

It's easy to try too hard to achieve reusable code. It's important not to have too-high ambitions at first and not to introduce a lot of complexity to try to achieve reuse.

4.1.7 Change things without affecting everything

Another effect of low coupling between classes is that if you change one class, other parts of the system are less likely to be affected. In other words, there is less risk that fixing one bug will cause three new ones to appear.

The extreme example of the opposite would be the liberal use of global variables that is common in legacy PHP applications. You change the value of a variable and you have no idea what effect it might have in a different part of the application.

Global variables are generally considered harmful to your program's health, at least when used in excess. They tend to make code less modular and more cryptic. In one of the worst examples I've seen, I was trying to understand some PHP code written by a colleague. This code was in an include file. Unfortunately, it used global variables that were also used and modified in a different include file. It was impossible to figure out what the code was doing without looking at both files. But just looking at the first file, there was no easy way to know which variables were global, that they were used in another file, or which file that was.

Problems like this obviously make code hard to maintain. You may have enough self-discipline to keep globals from getting out of hand, but then you may also have to trust others to be equally disciplined. The safest way is to keep all or nearly all code in functions or classes.

4.1.8 Objects provide type safety

As mentioned in chapter 1, PHP is a dynamically typed language. It lets you work without telling the compiler which variables are strings and which are numbers. There are heated debates on static versus dynamic typing. It is clear that both approaches have pros and cons. The main selling point of statically typed languages is that the compiler catches some errors that *might* otherwise go unnoticed. Here, I just want to make the point that object-oriented code in a dynamically typed language is more type safe than procedural code.

PHP 5, while still a dynamically typed language, makes a concession to the idea of type safety by introducing type hints. But object-oriented programming in and of itself increases type safety. It achieves this by making it harder to use data in unintended ways and contexts.

Take date and time handling as an example. In procedural PHP code, it's convenient to represent a date and time as a UNIX timestamp—in other words, the number of seconds since January 1, 1970. This is easy to do since the built-in PHP functions are typically able to work with this representation.

But there is a potential for error. For example, we can do date and time arithmetic by just adding or subtracting an appropriate number of seconds:

```
$hourago = $now - 3600;
```

What happens if $now does not contain what we think it contains? $now may be a string, perhaps a formatted date string. That will cause both times to end up around January 1, 1970. The error may not become apparent before it hits the application's user interface. Or worse yet, the time value might be used for something else, like statistics, and it might be hard to trace the problem back to its origin.

If instead we do this in a typical object-oriented way, the time values will be represented as objects. To subtract the hour, we make a method call on the object. So we will do something like this:

```
$hourago = $now->addHours(-1);
```

If $now is a string, this line of code fails spectacularly. The failure happens earlier, and the problem is easier to debug than in the previous example.

So far in this chapter, we've seen a number of benefits from using object-oriented techniques. In order to realize those benefits, we need to apply those techniques with skill. The word "skill" comes from an Old Norse word meaning to distinguish. How can we distinguish between good and bad design?

4.2 CRITERIA FOR GOOD DESIGN

You can't possibly learn to sing in tune if you're tone-deaf. That's because singing is a process based on feedback. Just as when you're driving a car, you sense where you are and adjust your behavior according to your position.

The process of learning object-oriented design is similar. You need the ability to know the difference for yourself, to see, hear, or smell the difference between good and bad code. Most of the time, the world of programming is far too complex for final hard-and-fast rules.

Therefore, the first key to learning is to *compare* different solutions to the same problem. There are several ways to achieve this. When you refactor, it happens almost automatically, and it's one of the reasons why refactoring is so useful.

In the same vein, it's a good idea to consider possible alternative designs. This is not generally emphasized in books on software development, but it's a piece of advice you'll find in books that deal with problem-solving in general. Take the time to think about several different options; don't close any doors until you're able to explicitly list the pros and cons of each solution.

Too often, developers choose an algorithm or a design just because someone had an idea and fell in love with it or because no one even considered looking for alternatives.

Perhaps the strongest reason to consider alternatives is the possibility of discovering a simpler, less time-consuming way of doing the same thing. You can save hours or days of work, perhaps even weeks or months, by taking a little extra time to think about it. My favorite experience of this is from when I was responsible for keeping a Java program running at all times. The Java Virtual Machine at that time was prone to fatal crashes. Therefore, I wrote a script that would run periodically, check whether the Java program was running in a process, and restart it if necessary.

Then one day I realized the monitoring setup was superfluous. All I needed was to wrap the program startup in a simple shell script containing an infinite loop:

```
while true; do
    ./thatsuicidaljavaprogram
done
```

Now whenever the program crashed, control returned to the loop in the shell script, which restarted the program immediately. I had achieved the same thing with much simpler means; in fact, it was better, since restart was immediate.

In this case, the improvement was obvious. But in less clear-cut cases, you need a yardstick in order to evaluate the merits of different alternative designs. King Solomon asked God for the ability to discern between good and evil in order to govern his people. Our need is more humble: we just need some criteria to distinguish a good design from a bad one so that we can govern our software.

Oddly, none of the object-oriented books on my shelf have a chapter or section heading on that. The closest thing I found was an inverse treatment, "Design smells— the odors of rotting software" in the book *Agile Software Development* by Robert C. Martin, also known as Uncle Bob [Uncle Bob].

Here is a shortened version of his list.

1 Rigidity—hard to change
2 Fragility—easy to break
3 Immobility—hard to disentangle into reusable components
4 Viscosity—hard to do things right
5 Needless complexity
6 Needless repetition
7 Opacity—hard to read and understand

So the criteria for good design could be the opposites of these:

1 Flexibility—easy to change
2 Robustness—hard to break
3 Mobility—easy to disentangle into reusable components
4 Fluidity—easy to do things right
5 Simplicity
6 Once and only once
7 Transparency—easy to read and understand

These criteria differ in how easy they are to apply. The last criterion is the easiest; if you don't understand what your own code is doing when you read it, you're in trouble. And although some subtle forms of duplication may be hard to spot, it's usually easy.

The three last criteria are "static"; they do not involve or imply changing the code. The rest of them are about difficulties in modification. It's a bit paradoxical: how do you know how easy it is to change until you've actually changed it? And after you've changed it, it's not the same design anymore, so how do you know whether the new design is easy or hard to change? This means the rest of the criteria are harder to evaluate.

But experience helps. So does considering possible modifications to the design. And so do the object-oriented principles that we will study in chapter 6.

We will go into more detail on a few of these criteria here, although some are better considered from the background of the object-oriented principles.

4.2.1 Don't confuse the end with the means

One thing OO novices often do is confuse a design technique with a design criterion. I've seen people say things like "Does this design conform to the Model-View-Controller design pattern (MVC)?" Whether a design is an example of the MVC design pattern may be an interesting question in itself, but the answer to that question does not determine the quality of the design. To decide on its quality, we need to use the criteria listed previously (or something similar). Is it easy to understand, easy to change, and simple? Does it avoid duplicated code? If applying a design pattern makes it better according to those criteria, it is a good idea to apply the design pattern. If applying the design pattern makes the design more complex and harder to understand, it may be a bad idea to use it. If the design pattern gives you more flexibility at the expense of readability or simplicity, it is a dubious tradeoff. We need to consider what kind of flexibility we are getting and whether we realistically need that flexibility.

4.2.2 Transparency

There is a simple way to know how easy a design—and the code that embodies it—is to read and understand: just observe your own reactions when you look at it. Even a short time after you've written the code, you may find that some parts are less obvious than others.

But this is somewhat subjective. Obviously, people with different backgrounds will differ in what they find easy to understand. If you're familiar with a certain design pattern and are able to recognize it, you will find designs that incorporate it easy to understand. Someone who has never heard of the pattern may have more trouble with it. But mostly, transparency comes from naming methods, classes, and variables in a way that reveals their intention.

A design that's easy to understand helps satisfy most of the other criteria as well. The software should be easy to change, easy to reuse. It should be easy to do things right. And everything is easier when you understand what your code does.

4.2.3 Simple design

A fish has no legs, despite the fact that it might evolve into a land animal in a few hundred million years. It doesn't need legs. At least not yet.

A fish with legs has a lessened chance of survival in the ocean. Even more importantly, it's not an effective land animal, either. It can't even breathe air. Nor can it eat grass, catch mice, or go to the supermarket to buy bread. You have to redesign the entire animal to get it to work on land. But that's not the kind of thing you think of when you add the legs.

The typical scenario is something like the following. We say, "Oh, it might need legs; let's just build them. It's a small job, anyway." And we're almost right about the job. It takes only a bit longer to implement than we expected. But since the legs weren't necessary, we might forget about the whole thing. Then a few months later, we need to make some other changes. As it turns out, it didn't need legs; it needed thicker scales, but if we want to keep the leg feature, the scales and the legs have to interact properly. But now we're not sure exactly how the leg code works, and although we don't think it's in use, we're afraid to delete it because our test coverage is not complete enough to make us confident that the fish won't simply die. So we spend two to three times more work than necessary on the scales, and now the code is getting really ugly because we've been trying to combine a part of it we still don't understand completely with another, new part, and have to do some nasty tricks to make it work.

That's what we want to avoid by keeping design as simple as possible. In agile development, it's also known as YAGNI (you aren't going to need it). This is more specific than general principles advocating simplicity such as KISS (Keep It Simple, Stupid) or Zend Technology's phrase "extreme simplicity." The YAGNI mindset is a sort of intelligent procrastination: putting off doing a job until you're reasonably sure it's necessary. It means we might not put legs on a fish until it's washed up on the beach and desperately needs those legs to survive. The idea is that more often than not, you are unable to predict exactly what you'll need—or rather, what your users will need—a few months or weeks or even days down the road. So if you write a lot of code to serve those future needs, you end up doing extra work and having more code to debug and maintain, all to no avail.

Figure 4.3 is an example of a design that looks suspiciously like it's trying to satisfy too-ambitious requirements. Configuration files are typically read-only, and yet there is a class and a `save()` method that allow us to write to the file. It may be that whoever created this hypothetical design just found it more logical to make the design more "complete" by adding the ability to write back to the file, found the challenge interesting, or believed that it might become useful in a few months time in an administrator interface.

In other words, imagined future needs inspire programmers to make designs more complex than necessary. A slightly more sophisticated way of doing the same thing is to not actually implement future requirements ahead of time, but to make the system more

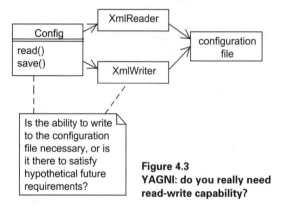

Figure 4.3
**YAGNI: do you really need
read-write capability?**

flexible or general so that it will be easier to implement future requirements once they materialize. Unfortunately, predicting what kind of flexibility you'll need is also hard.

If we can achieve flexibility at a low cost in complexity, we're OK. Otherwise, it may be better to keep the design a little more rigid and specialized for the sake of keeping it simple.

4.2.4   Once and only once

> *Number one in the stink parade is duplicated code. If you see the same
> code structure in more than one place, you can be sure that your program
> will be better if you find a way to unify them [Fowler Refactoring].*

According to Fowler, the two main objectives of refactoring are to remove duplication and make code easier to read and understand.

In general, we want to avoid duplication because it makes code harder to maintain. When we change duplicated code, it's easy to neglect to change all the copies, either because we forget or because we think it's unnecessary. Then one or more of the following happens:

- The program becomes harder to understand because the two copies are similar but not quite the same, and it's not obvious how or why they're different.

- We try to fix a bug, but we're not changing the code that is actually causing the problem. Instead, we change a duplicate of it. So the fix doesn't work, and if we're not even aware of the duplication, we may have no idea why. This is frustrating. At this point it's tempting to get drunk or bang your head against the wall. Unfortunately, neither of these procedures is considered good software engineering practice.

- We try to fix a bug, but we haven't changed all the places where the problem exists. So the bug is still there, but the frequency is lower. In other words, there is now a bug that does less mischief but is harder to find. However, by Murphy's law the bug will be very noticeable to some customers that use the program in a slightly different way than the people who test it, and instead of reporting it, they just give up on the entire application and go somewhere else.

In other words, on the whole, duplication is harmful to the quality of the product and impedes long-term progress.

On the other hand and in general, duplicated HTML code is another matter. The reason is that we might be leaving the layout work to professional web designers. To them, it's frequently useful to work with whole web pages, even though they might have some duplicated elements. Duplicated PHP code is something else. It's a form of evil and depravity, and our job is to root it out.

One common cause of rampant duplication is what is known as copy-and-paste programming. The following scenario illustrates the problem.

There is a web application that's tailored to a specific client. It even has the same layout as the client's web site, including the client's logo. Suddenly another client needs the same application—by yesterday, of course. The application now needs a new layout and perhaps one or two small variations on the existing features, such as an additional search criterion.

What do you do? If the application is like a lot of PHP applications, the HTML markup for the client-specific layout may be intermixed freely with the PHP code. You can change the layout by changing the markup; it's not that difficult. But having two different layouts and switching between them easily is not within the realm of possibility with this kind of structure.

So you copy everything. You take the whole directory with all the files and start hacking the copy. Typically, you won't even check to see whether there are any files that could be used for both clients. You would have to move it to some other directory containing common code, and who knows what might happen to the first client's application then? You don't have time to test the original application, so it's best to keep it unchanged. Of course, you know this is not good programming practice, but to do it right will take too much time, so you have to put off doing it right.

When you've done this 15 times, you have a set of 16 applications that do approximately the same thing but in slightly different ways. You can forget about adding a new feature that will work in all of them. Instead, you will have to add the feature to one of them—most likely the client that has the biggest bank account or screams the loudest. And if another client needs the same feature, you will have to do a separate, but similar, job implementing the same feature again.

You can get away with it. Even PHP "gurus" have done it. One PHP book actually has two chapters listing what is basically the same code in slightly different versions. But doing this with real code *will* slow your progress.

On the other hand, copying and pasting is not necessarily a bad idea *if* you take the time to remove duplication afterward. If you first copy and then alter the copy, you can compare the two and find out what's similar. Then you can extract the similarities into separate functions, classes, or (in the case of HTML markup) templates. This may be easier said than done, but we will deal with the process in more detail in later chapters.

Object-oriented designs can be complex, consisting of many interrelated classes. We have been approaching the subject from the most general angle possible, looking for universal criteria for design quality. If we take a similarly general approach at the level of single objects, what can we say beyond the syntactical aspects we've already dealt with? How do we think about objects in a way that will help us to do useful work? Should they be reflections of real-world objects, or are there more useful ways of putting them to work?

4.3 WHAT ARE OBJECTS, ANYWAY?

Software objects are both intuitive and mysterious. They're intuitive because of the similarity to the way we think and talk about the world, using nouns and verbs. But they're also mysterious, since the parallel is slippery. Most software objects, particularly in simple web applications, don't represent real-world objects. But frequently, we do need to represent real-world objects in software, so how do we do that?

In this section, we'll examine the limitations of the idea that objects should be reflections of real-world objects. Then we'll look at the basics of how to implement objects that are from the real world, or at least represent concepts that are meaningful to the user of the software.

4.3.1 Objects come from the unreal world

One popular PHP programming book admonishes us to "try to think of [objects in programming] as real world objects with real world behaviors."

The word "try" implies that we might fail to do this; that's an appropriate warning. We might fail, and we might be better off failing than succeeding. Software objects sometimes represent real-world objects. And these objects occasionally have some of the same behaviors as their real-world counterparts, but mostly they don't.

Object-oriented programming started with a language called Simula. As the name indicates, it was designed for simulation applications. Simulated objects do represent real objects, and the simulated objects would have some of the same behaviors as real objects. If you simulate road traffic, there would probably be Car object with the ability to move from point A to point B.

But object-oriented business applications are not simulations. To the untrained eye, they might seem like a random jumble of objects, most of which have little to do with the business. Some of the objects do represent real-world entities, some are objects that communicate between other objects and services, some objects communicate with the user, and some control program flow.

The objects that represent real-world objects are examples of domain objects or business objects. Domain objects may represent something concrete and physical such as a Person or something abstract such as Pricing. Domain objects are the objects that are relevant to the subject matter of an application. In an e-commerce system, for instance, people, products, prices, and pricing policies may be among the objects.

But even the objects that represent something tangible and physical don't necessarily behave the way their physical counterparts do. A Person class in a business application is highly unlikely to have methods named `eat()`, `sleep()`, or `work()`. Even the application-relevant behaviors, such as `buy`, might not be represented. A physical CD player might be represented in an online product catalog, but there is no `play()` method on the object representing the CD. It's just not relevant. On the other hand, an object representing the guts of a virtual CD player (the kind that you probably have on your PC) is likely to have a `play()` method. The object from the product catalog *represents* a CD player; the virtual CD player *simulates* the action of a real CD player. Figure 4.4 illustrates how different these are.

Figure 4.4 is a UML object diagram. Instead of classes, it shows object instances. The notation for the top line is <u>instance name:class name</u>. CD Player 1 is an instance of the CdPlayer class; CD Player 2 is an instance of the Product class.

Virtual objects may also have behaviors physical objects lack. A Document object might have an `addText()` method. A physical document—a piece of paper with or without marks on it—cannot add text to itself: someone has to do it. In the days when a typewriter was one of the most ubiquitous pieces of office equipment, there were also typists—people who specialized in typing text on sheets of paper. And, if you had a typist available, you might be able to tell the typist to add the text to the document. So you might think of the Document object as a document with a built-in typist.

If we were dead set on making our objects as similar as possible to the real world (albeit an old-fashioned real world), we might create a Typist class, perhaps even a Typewriter class. Then we would have to go through those classes to add text to the document. The simple reason why we don't do that is that it's unnecessary. The final criterion of a successful program is how it works, both as a program and as documentation of its own design. Any correspondence with the real world is only of interest if it improves the code.

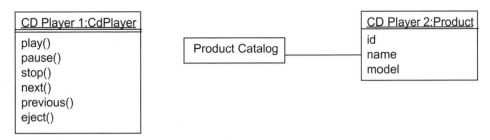

Figure 4.4   A CD player as simulation and as a product in an online product catalog

4.3.2 Domain object basics

But representing domain objects *is* one of the advantages of object-oriented programming. In simple web applications, the domain objects have a tendency to be dumb data holders, and representing them as associative arrays in PHP may sometimes be just as well. In other words, a Document object is not much of an object if it just contains a title and a text body and all it does is take those two data items in and spit them out on command.

```
class Document {
    public $title;
    public $body;
}
```

This is basically just a glorified version of an associative array that has the keys `title` and `body`.

You might make want to add accessors (`setTitle()`, `setBody()`, `getTitle()`, `getBody()`) and make the variables private. That gives us a bit more flexibility; we've encapsulated the process to get and set the variables. If we change the way it's done, clients (the classes or programs that use this class) won't know the difference. We don't want the outside world accessing the insides of the object any more than necessary.

Now the question is, do we even need the accessors? In the typical web application, we need to read the title and the body in order to display them on a page. We also need some way of setting them when we get the data from the database. If we set them when we create the object (in the constructor), we can avoid setting them by mistake. So we can do this:

```
class Document {
    private $title;
    private $body;

    public function __construct($title,$body) {
        $this->title = $title;
        $this->body = $body;
    }

    function getTitle() { return $this->title; }
    function getBody() { return $this->body; }

}
```

But the object is still just a dumb data holder. It does express something of the purpose of the Document object, though. A plain array tells us nothing about what it contains, except if we look at wherever the values are being set. So the class is documentation of how we intend to use this particular data structure. On the other hand, if it just mirrors the database table, it might seem unnecessary.

It's a slightly different story if we need to generate a summary from the text. Now it might be a good idea to let that be a method in the Document class. The example extracts everything up to and including the first period.

```
class Document...
    function getSummary() {
        preg_match('/^.*?\./',$this->body,$m);
        return array_shift($m);
    }
}
```

This is the kind of small adjustment to the data that might give objects value even in simple applications. Another example is outputting a date in different formats.

But the real benefits of using domain objects are realized when they embody business rules or business logic. For example, an e-commerce system might need to calculate prices using discounts based on varying criteria, including the kind of product, the season, and the type of customer.

Domain objects are also useful for expressing complex relationships. An example might be a tree structure such as a discussion forum with expandable/collapsible threads.

A moderately simple web application might have relatively little use for advanced domain objects. But the rest of the application can still benefit from using objects. Both database access and user interaction can gain from using object-oriented techniques. These objects have even less of a resemblance to "real" objects. Some of them might represent fragments of what the user sees in the application, but often the objects are "engines" that process, organize, or move data around. Template engines (described in detail in chapter 13) are an interesting example. In the section on the Adapter design pattern in chapter 7, we will see the difference between the objects used by two popular PHP template engines: Smarty and PHPTAL. PHPTAL objects represent something almost "real" (or at least familiar to anyone with experience of PHP web programming), a template containing HTML markup. A Smarty object, on the other hand, is an engine that can process any template. You feed the Smarty object a template and it generates the HTML output. Other types of objects that are commonly used in web programming are controllers and filters to process and interpret user input and objects that transform and move data into and out of a database.

4.4   SUMMARY

Object orientation helps make complex programs more manageable and maintainable by providing lots of options in the structure and organization of a program, by making program code easier to understand, by breaking the program into manageable chunks, and by encapsulating operations and data.

But skill and insight is required to make this happen. We need to understand how to do it and why. We need to know the difference between good and bad design even when there are no absolute rules that apply.

In general, objects and classes do not represent real-world objects and categories. Some do, but the correspondence is always imperfect and ruled ultimately by the user's requirements of the software rather than by a need to represent reality faithfully.

In the next chapter, we will familiarize ourselves with the basic relationships between classes—primarily class inheritance and object composition—and consider how they can be used optimally in object design.

CHAPTER 5

Understanding class relationships

Not long ago, I was watching a television talk show featuring actor Sven Nordin, who plays the Norwegian version of the solo theatrical performance *Defending the Caveman*. Nordin convincingly demonstrated the art of banging your head on a hard surface, although he did admit that it was a painful procedure.

A medical expert who was also present remarked dryly that "he shouldn't be doing that."

Obviously. It's easy to understand how that kind of abuse might be bad for your brain. On the other hand, it might be a vicious cycle: the more you rattle your brain, the less you understand how bad it is.

Throwing books at yourself may be marginally better. Just watch out for ideas that are too obvious; they may knock you temporarily unconscious.

An idea that is too obvious is the traditional view of inheritance in object-oriented programming. For example, an eagle is a bird. Thus the Eagle class must be a child class of Bird. Well, not always. Let's study it a bit more closely. First, we'll consider traditional class inheritance. For contrast, we'll take a look at the alternative, which is often called *object composition*. Then we'll discuss interfaces and how they work in object-oriented design. Finally, we'll see how all this comes together in the now-classic principle of favoring object composition over class inheritance.

5.1   INHERITANCE

Inheritance is a lucrative concept if you marry rich or peddle a commercial object-oriented language. Most object-oriented languages, including PHP, support inheritance. It means that a class can get automatic access to all the features of another class. Inheritance is important to understand, but relatively hard to apply. When exactly is it a good idea to use it? When is it better to avoid it? We will be investigating this issue in this chapter and later.

Traditionally, different languages refer to the inheritance relationship in different terms. Depending on the context, a class inherits from a "parent" class, a "superclass," or a "base" class. PHP uses the keyword "parent," so "parent" and "child" might be the most appropriate terms in PHP, but it's a good idea to know the other terms. For instance, there is a standard refactoring called *Extract Superclass* that we will be looking at shortly.

In this section, we start with the concept of inheritance and see the benefits and limitations of using it to guide our thinking about object design. Then, to illustrate the idea of inheritance and get a feel for how it relates to real code, we'll do a refactoring exercise, using inheritance to eliminated duplication.

5.1.1   Inheritance as a thinking tool

Inheritance is an eminently logical concept. Since we structure real-world objects into categories and subcategories, why not do the same with software? All eagles are birds, so Eagle is a subclass of Bird.

Eagles have characteristics and behaviors that are typical of birds in general (such as feathers or flying). They also have characteristics and behaviors that are not shared by all birds, such as a preference for foods such as rats or fish. In software, this is expressed by an inheritance relationship: objects in the Eagle class get all the behaviors, methods, and data that are built into the Bird class. In addition, the specific eagle behaviors can be implemented in the Eagle class itself.

Although the inheritance relationship between classes is an attempt to model the real world, the use of the word "inheritance" doesn't correspond to its meaning in real life. A real eagle inherits its characteristics from mommy eagle and daddy eagle, not from an abstract "Bird." "Parent class" expresses the fact that Bird is the "conceptual parent" of Eagle. But inheritance between classes does create a hierarchical relationship that resembles a family tree.

The theoretical idea behind inheritance is that it expresses an "is-a" relationship. An eagle *is a* bird. Similarly, a news article *is a* document. So, by this token, a NewsArticle class should have a parent called Document.

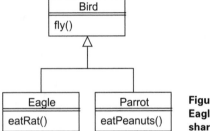

Figure 5.1
Eagles and parrots are both birds; they
share some behaviors and differ in others.

The practical rationale for using inheritance is code reuse. The Document class can contain code that is common to both news articles and discussion forum messages, while a NewsArticle class and a DiscussionMessage class contain code that is specific to these two kinds of documents.

Figure 5.1 is a pseudo-real class diagram of a Bird class hierarchy. It illustrates the theoretical idea of class inheritance. Some behaviors and properties are common to birds, some differ; the class diagram illustrates this relationship. It also gives a clue to some of the problems in applying the theory. What about flightless birds? Do they need to be a child class of bird, and do ostriches, penguins and kiwis need to be represented by child classes of the flightless bird class?

The simple answer, as far as software is concerned, is that we model only what's required. The user requirements determine what needs to be represented. If we're not concerned with flightless birds, it's fine for the Bird class to have a `fly()` method.

5.1.2 Refactoring to inheritance

It's not necessarily easy to use inheritance in an appropriate way. The *is a* relationship may be a good clue, but try searching for the `extends` keyword in the code for some PEAR packages, and you may start to wonder. The classes generally inherit from the PEAR class. For example, you might see:

```
class Mail extends PEAR
```

So does this mean that a Mail object *is a* PEAR? What is a PEAR, anyway? It's a "PHP Extension and Application Repository." No, the Mail object probably is not an extension and application repository.

On the other hand, the Mail object may be considered a "PEAR-compatible object" or some such. So you could consider this a trivial naming problem. When you see `extends PEAR`, you just have to read it as `extends PearCompatibleObject`. It's confusing, though, and confusion is the greatest obstacle to writing clean, well-designed code. That's why naming is not trivial.

My own understanding of inheritance improved a lot after I started refactoring. Typically, the opportunity to use inheritance arises when two classes have a lot in common and you can do the refactoring known as *Extract Superclass*.

Let's try it. As an example, we will use two classes that have parallel responsibilities, but in different contexts. We have a NewsFinder class for finding news articles in a database and a UserFinder class for finding users. The NewsFinder class is shown in listing 5.1. It's simplistic in having only one method, but nevertheless similar to a real-world example.

Listing 5.1 NewsFinder class for getting news articles from a database

```
require_once 'DB.php';
class NewsFinder {
    private $db;

    public function __construct() {                      Use PEAR DB ❶
        $this->db = DB::Connect(
            'mysql://user:password@localhost/webdatabase');
        if (DB::isError($this->db)) {                    ❷ Simple
            throw new Exception($this->db->getMessage());    error
        }                                                    handling
    }

    public function findAll() {          ❸  Example method
        $result = $this->db->query(
            "SELECT headline,introduction,text,".        ❹ Execute
            "author,unix_timestamp(created) as created,".   SQL
            "news_id ".
            "FROM News");
        if (DB::isError($result)) {
            throw new Exception(
                $result->getMessage()."\n".$query."\n");
        }
        while ($row = $result->fetchRow(DB_FETCHMODE_ASSOC)) {  ❺ Return
            $news[] = $row;                                        result
        }                                                         as array
        return $news;
    }

    public function setConnection($connection) {
        $this->db = $connection;
    }
}
```

❶ We use the PEAR DB package for this example. We store the DB object representing the database connection in an instance variable in the NewsFinder object. This is a simple and straightforward object-oriented way of handling database connections, but only one possibility of several. This will be discussed more fully in chapter 19.

For the sake of simplicity, there is no way in this example to configure the data source URL (the string starting with `mysql`). In practice, there usually will be.

❷ The error handling is similarly simple, using an unspecified type of exception. We're not introducing anything that there's no obvious use for.

❸ The `findAll()` method is just an example of what this class might do. It might have any number of other methods, but one is sufficient to illustrate the refactoring.

❹ The PEAR DB object has a `query()` method that executes an SQL query and returns a PEAR_Result object.

❺ Again keeping it simple, we collect the results from the DB_Result object as an array of associative arrays representing the rows.

The other Finder class is a UserFinder. The similarity to the NewsFinder class is fairly obvious. It might actually be less obvious if there were more methods, since these might be methods such as `findByLastName()` that would be relevant only for users. Listing 5.2 shows the UserFinder class.

Listing 5.2   UserFinder class, similar to the NewsFinder class

```php
class UserFinder {
    private $db;

    public function __construct() {
        $this->db = DB::Connect(
                'mysql://user:password@localhost/webdatabase');
        if (DB::isError($this->db)) {
            throw new Exception($this->db->getMessage());
        }
    }

    public function findAll() {
        $result = $this->db->query(
                "SELECT user_id, email, password, name ".
                "FROM Users");
        if (DB::isError($result)) {
            throw new Exception(
                $result->getMessage()."\n".$query."\n");
        }
        while ($row = $result->fetchRow(DB_FETCHMODE_ASSOC)) {
            $users[] = $row;
        }
        return $users;
    }

    public function setConnection($connection) {
        $this->db = $connection;
    }
}
```

The only parts of this class that differ from the NewsFinder class are the ones shown in bold. In the real world, duplication is frequently less clear-cut than in this case. In any case, it pays to look closely at what's similar and what's different. To make it easy, I've marked the differences in bold text. The constructor is the same in these two classes. The findAll() method has two differences: the SQL statement and the naming of the array that's returned.

Figure 5.2 is a simple UML class diagram of the two classes. Although the diagram alone doesn't prove that there is duplicated code (the two findAll() methods might be completely different), it does sum up the situation.

UserFinder		NewsFinder
findAll()		findAll()

Figure 5.2   Two very similar Finder classes

If we want to eliminate the duplication, we can extract a parent class that will be common to these two.

Extracting the DatabaseClient class

But what would be a good name for this parent class? A good name needs to say something about what these two classes have in common. We could call it Finder. Alternatively, since the common code we have extracted does database access, a good name might be DatabaseClient. Since naming is important, let's test this by appealing to the principle that inheritance expresses an *is-a* relationship. Is the NewsFinder a database client? Yes, clearly. And so is the UserFinder.

The constructor is easy to move into the DatabaseClient class. But what about the duplicated code in the findAll() method? We'll need to first extract a method to execute a query and return the result.

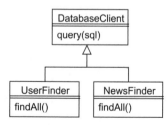

Now let's look at the refactored result. Figure 5.3 shows the result in UML. The query() method contains the code that was common to the findAll() methods in the two original classes.

Now let's see how this works in actual code. Listing 5.3 is the DatabaseClient class.

Figure 5.3   Extracting the common code from the findAll() methods into a query() method in a parent class

```
class DatabaseClient {
    protected $db;

    public function __construct() {
        $this->db = DB::Connect(
                'mysql://user:password@localhost/webdatabase');
        if (DB::isError($this->db)) {
            throw new Exception($this->db->getMessage());
        }
    }

    public function query($sql) {
        $result = $this->db->query($sql);
        if (DB::isError($result)) {
            throw new Exception(
                $result->getMessage()."\n".$query."\n");
        }
        return $result;
    }
}
```

Although we're seeing the final result here, in practice it's always a good idea to do this kind of refactoring one step at a time, running unit tests after each change. The sequence of steps in this case is

1 Create the DatabaseClient class.

2 Change declarations of the two finder classes, adding extends DatabaseClient to each of them.

3 Move the constructor from one of the finder classes to DatabaseClient.

4 Delete the constructor in the other finder class.

5 Extract a query() method in both of the finder classes.

6 Move the query() method from one of the classes into the DatabaseClient class.

7 Delete the query() method in the other finder class.

The simplified UserFinder class

The UserFinder class is now simpler and easier to read and understand (see listing 5.4). Database connection and error handling is conceptually different from manipulating data using SQL, so it's not surprising that sorting them into different classes helps.

Listing 5.4   UserFinder: the class uncluttered by database basics

```
class UserFinder extends DatabaseClient {

    public function findAll() {
        $result = $this->query(
                "SELECT user_id, email, password, name ".
                "FROM Users");
        while ($row = $result->fetchRow(DB_FETCHMODE_ASSOC)) {
            $users[] = $row;
        }
        return $users;
    }

}
```

The NewsFinder class will be similar, and there is still a bit of duplication due to the similar way the array is built from the DB_Result object. By renaming the array that's called $users in the UserFinder, we could extract four more common lines of code. The reason we haven't done so is because in a realistic case, we would want to wait and see what happens first, since in practice it would be more complicated: some methods will return single rows and some multiple rows, so it's better to have information on that before proceeding.

We have studied some of the ins and outs of inheritance. The alternative is object composition. Before moving on to interfaces and the idea of favoring composition over inheritance, we will take a look at how object composition works.

5.2   OBJECT COMPOSITION

In UML, there are a number of distinctions that express various ways that objects can relate by calling and referring to each other without inheritance: dependency, association, aggregation, composition. I'm lumping all of these under the heading of "composition," to clarify the contrast between all of these relationships on the one hand, and inheritance on the other, which corresponds approximately to the usage in the "Gang of Four" book *[Design Patterns]* as well. Conceptually, the principle is simple: one object "has" or "uses" another object or class. Technically, the greatest difference is between different ways of getting and maintaining the other object. One possibility is to hold the other object in an instance variable. The UML categories of association, aggregation, and composition refer to this type of strategy. Or the object can be used locally in a single method; the UML category for that is called *dependency.*

Table 5.1 lists some of the possibilities. It focuses more on differences that are expressed in code and less on theoretical, semantic distinctions. It's a good idea to know these possibilities and to be able to choose and compare them when programming.

Besides *Extract Method* and *Extract Superclass*, another common refactoring is called *Extract Class.* You take parts of one class, typically a few methods and the data those

Table 5.1   Ways an object can access another object

Main strategy	Getting the other object
Creating the other object in the constructor Getting the other object as an argument to the constructor	Creating the other object in the constructor Getting the other object as an argument to the constructor
Using the other object only when it's needed (dependency)	Getting the object as a method argument Creating the object on the fly Calling a static (class) method

methods use, and make a new class out of it. And invariably, the old class will have to use the new one, since that's the only way to make the client code work as before.

There are at least two reasons for extracting a class which is not a parent class. One is if a class is getting too large and seems to be doing several different jobs, perhaps even unrelated ones. Another is as an alternative to *Extract Superclass*. Referring back to the previous refactoring example, a parent class is not the only place to extract database-related code. More likely, we will want to extract it to a class that can be called from the class it's extracted from.

There are cases in which even the method names of a class suggest that there might be another class hiding within it. The PEAR Net_URL package has the following methods (code inside methods not shown):

```
class Net_URL {
    function Net_URL($url = null, $useBrackets = true) {}
    function getURL() {}
    function addQueryString($name,$value,$preencoded = false) {}
    function removeQueryString($name) {}
    function addRawQueryString($querystring) {}
    function getQueryString() {}
    function _parseRawQuerystring($querystring) {}
    function resolvePath($path) {}
}
```

For some reason, most of the methods seem to manipulate the query string of a URL. So it's tempting to extract a query string class. But we have too little information to decide that issue. It will have to look like an improvement when you see the result in code. The most likely process would be to extract some more methods at first and then the class later.

But just to try it out see how it works, let's assume that we want extract the query string class (Net_URL_QueryString probably). What is clear is that *Extract Superclass* is not an option, since it's not the case that a URL *is a* query string.

If we were to do an *Extract Class*, there would be a member variable in the Net_URL object containing the query string object. And typically, the query string-related methods in the Net_URL class would be implemented as calls to the query string object. We'll use the method addQueryString() as an example. This method would have been more descriptively named if it were called addVaria-

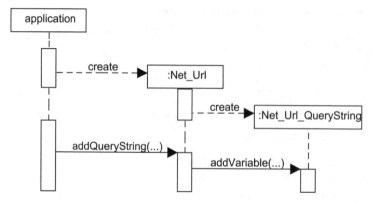

Figure 5.4   Sequence diagram of how Net_Url might work if we extract a Net_Url_Querystring class from it

bleToQueryString(). Keeping the somewhat confusing name, we could let the method call an addVariable() method on the query string object. Figure 5.4 shows how this might work. The URL object creates the query string object when it's created. Later, it delegates query string-related work to the query string object.

Here is a fragment of the (hypothetical) refactored code, using the same mechanics as the illustration:

```
class Net_URL {
    private $querystring;

    public function __construct($url = null, $useBrackets = true)
    {
        $this->querystring = Net_URL_Querystring::parse($url);
        // Construct the rest of the URL
    }
    public function addQueryString($name,$value,$preencoded = false)
    {
        $this->querystring->addVariable($name,$value,$preencoded);
    }
}
```

The constructor of the existing, non-refactored, Net_URL class accepts a URL string as an argument. We're keeping that and changing the body of the constructor so the query string object can construct itself. In other words, we've extracted the parts of the constructor that parse the query string parts of the URL and put that in a factory method in the Net_URL_QueryString class.

5.3   INTERFACES

An interface is a job description for one or more classes. In chapter 3, we saw an example:

```
interface Template {
```

```
public function __construct($path);
public function execute();
public function set($name,$value);
public function getContext();
}
```

What this means is that any class that `implements` the interface must have all the methods named in this interface description, and the arguments must be the same as well. The class does the job specified in the interface, but the interface gives no indication as to how it does the job, since an interface cannot contain any code that's actually executed at runtime.

In this section, we'll look at how interfaces can be used to think about object-oriented design. Since interfaces, unlike classes, allow multiple inheritance, we'll also examine that idea and its ramifications.

5.3.1 The interface as a thinking tool

If a parent class has no behavior, no code that actually does anything, it might as well be defined as an interface. If it does have behavior that can be inherited by child classes, it does something more than what an interface does: it allows behavior to be inherited. An interface can't do that.

Except for multiple inheritance, it might seem that interfaces are just a hobbled form of parent classes. Is there a point except for multiple inheritance? Well, the syntactical construct is not important, but the idea behind it is. The idea of interfaces is an essential part of modern object-oriented design.

Interfaces make visible a difference that is not apparent in most traditional object-oriented languages: the difference between *implementation inheritance* and *interface inheritance*. The `extends` keyword signals that both are present: child classes inherit both the interface (the job description) and a certain amount of behavior and data from their parents. Implementation inheritance is the sharing of behavior and data, and that is the workhorse of traditional object-oriented programming. Interface inheritance, signaled by the `implements` keyword, means inheriting just the method signatures.

As we have seen, inheritance is traditionally defined as expressing an "is-a" relationship. An eagle *is a* bird. A news article *is a* document. In other words, one is a subcategory of the other.

Similarly, you could say that interface inheritance expresses a "does" relationship. It expresses the fact that the class implementing the interface can respond to all the messages defined in the interface, so it can do the behaviors that are represented by the names of the method calls. A web template interface, for instance, may include method signatures to set variables and to generate HTML from the template. That implies that any class implementing the template interface is able to do all these things, but it implies nothing about *how* it does them.

So again, interfaces in the formal sense may seem rather pointless, because they *do* so little. This is particularly true in dynamically typed languages such as PHP. By making a template interface, all we do is constrain ourselves. We *must* implement those particular methods when we write a class that implements the interface.

The reasoning behind interfaces has more to do with principles than with implementation. It's a good thing to avoid using too much implementation inheritance. The clearest example of this is multiple inheritance.

5.3.2 Single and multiple inheritance

Year ago, I was on a tour of a Danish castle. We were told the story of a nobleman of a few centuries ago who had a problem: the money in the family had been stretched too thin because it had to be divided among a flock of numerous siblings. He solved the problem in a pragmatic way by marrying rich women no less than three times. That is multiple inheritance, although not quite what is meant by the term in object-oriented programming. But if we think of all the objects this nobleman must have owned, and consider the challenge of tracing each of these back to its original owner several generations earlier, we are getting a hint of why modern object gurus are skeptical of multiple inheritance.

Like Java, PHP doesn't allow multiple inheritance—multiple-implementation inheritance, that is, meaning that a class can inherit behavior from more than one parent class.

This is not because multiple inheritance doesn't make sense. Quite the contrary; multiple inheritance is a perfectly natural concept. Nearly all of us have (or had at one time) two parents. In the realm of concepts, parents are even more plentiful. An eagle is both bird and predator; it has some behavior characteristic of birds (flying) and some characteristic of predators (eating other animals).

So multiple inheritance is eminently logical. But it causes complications in practical programming, in somewhat the same way that people find it hard to wear multiple "hats." You have a role to play in a social setting. You may be both a programmer and an accomplished amateur mountain climber. At work, you're a programmer. Trying to express the role of mountain climber while you're at work is likely to be difficult.

When any class can inherit behavior from multiple parent classes, it's a far-from-trivial task to find out what class a particular behavior is inherited from. This gets even worse when more than one parent has the same behavior. Which behavior is the one you inherit? With single-implementation inheritance, at least you can search sequentially upward through the hierarchy.

Anyway, this is why the designers of some modern programming languages have decided that multiple inheritance is a Bad Thing and disallowed it. So you could see interfaces as a sort of "poor man's multiple inheritance." I thought so when I first bumped into them.

But again, the problem is that you can't simply replace true multiple inheritance with interfaces, since as I mentioned, interfaces *do* very little. If we have a class that would naturally inherit behavior from two other classes, what do we do? We don't want to just inherit the interface and reimplement the behavior; that would cause duplication.

The answer is simple, but not always easy to implement. You have to extract at least one of those behaviors into a separate class and let both classes that need the behavior use that class rather than inherit the behavior.

But there is a further twist to this story, and this is where we really start getting into modern object-oriented design. Even single implementation inheritance turns out to be easy to use to excess. The thing is, avoiding implementation inheritance forces us to focus on alternative ways of reusing code. As the so-called Gang of Four say in their book *Design Patterns* [Gang of Four], we should "favor object composition over class inheritance." This frequently leads to a design that is more flexible. It may also be easier to understand.

5.4 FAVORING COMPOSITION OVER INHERITANCE

When the Gang of Four tell us to favor object composition over class inheritance, they point out that inheritance and composition are alternative ways to solve the same problems. There is nothing you can do with inheritance that you can't do with composition, and frequently the result is more flexible and more logical. The main advantage of using inheritance is simplicity and convenience—in some situations.

We want the ability to refactor—to improve the design by moving chunks of code around. In many cases, this will force us to create components that are independent of an existing inheritance hierarchy and therefore easier to use from anywhere inside or outside the hierarchy.

Before using inheritance, it's reasonable to demand that the theoretical requirement for an "is-a" relationship between child and parent class is satisfied. But this is a necessary, not a sufficient, condition when implementation inheritance is concerned. Even when there is a logical "is-a" relationship, it may be useful to use composition rather than inheritance.

The issue is one that will recur in the following chapters. Many of the principles and patterns discussed in chapters 5 and 6 tend to push design away from heavy reliance on inheritance. In this section, we'll focus on a two points: keeping the names of parent classes meaningful and keeping inheritance hierarchies relatively shallow.

5.4.1 Avoiding vaguely named parent classes

One frequent and less than optimal use of inheritance is to let a parent class contain utility methods that are needed by several different classes. If you come across a file called Common.php, that is a typical symptom. Several PEAR packages have one or more "Common" classes. The problem with this approach is that the class name doesn't express its actual responsibilities and that there is no "is-a" relationship between the parent class and the child classes.

The cure for this ailment is to extract meaningfully-named classes from the "Common" class. This is not necessarily difficult. Frequently, the names of the methods contain keywords that are highly suggestive of classes that might be extracted.

Looking at some of the currently-available PEAR packages, this is easy to see. In HTML_Common, the word "attribute" keeps recurring. In PEAR_Common, "package" seems to be a frequent concept. In Pager_Common, the words "link" and "page" stand out.

> **NOTE** This superficial analysis of these PEAR classes is only intended to illustrate my point. To find out what changes would actually work, deeper analysis is required.

5.4.2 Avoiding deep inheritance hierarchies

Another problem we may encounter if we use inheritance freely is that of deep inheritance hierarchies.

A deep inheritance hierarchy is a sign that we've neglected to decompose the problem in a useful way, or that we have an overly theoretical design that contains representations of concepts that are not actually needed.

Figure 5.5 is a class diagram of a possible design that uses a lot of levels. There may be more classes in the hierarchy—for example, other children of HtmlElement—but to simplify, we're looking at just one child per parent.

At first blush, this may seem rather reasonable. There are "is-a" relationships between each level—or so it may seem. When we edit an HTML document, we may think of an HTML element as a string. But studying this design more closely, we see that both HtmlString and HtmlForm have a `validate()` method. This probably means something different in the two cases. We want to validate the HTML string to make sure it's syntactically correct. Validating the form probably means validating the user's input in the form.

More likely, we want to represent the HTML string and its parsed abstract representation in different classes that are not hierarchically related.

The design leaves us little room to refactor. The choice of which class to put each method in seems to follow from the logic of the design. This might seem like a good thing, but in real life, it's better to have alternatives to choose from. To some extent, we may be able to move the methods up and down the hierarchy, but for the most part, they're stuck where they are—unless, of course, we extract them into classes outside the hierarchy. Once we start doing that, one or more of the levels are likely to turn out to be superfluous.

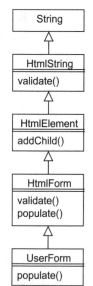

Figure 5.5 A possible design using a deep inheritance hierarchy

This is a hypothetical design that exists in UML only and has no implementation nor well-defined requirements. Changing it is much like guesswork, but figure 5.6 illustrates roughly how an alternative might look if we tried to reduce the depth of the inheritance hierarchy. It is conceptually different; there is a new class name, HtmlParser. This is typical of what happens when we refactor this kind of structure.

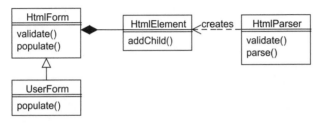

Figure 5.6 A similar design with a shallower inheritance hierarchy

5.5 SUMMARY

All the basic relationships between objects have both theoretical and practical aspects. Theoretically speaking, inheritance expresses an "is-a" relationship. In practice, it is also a way to reuse code. Object composition can express semantic relationships such as "has-a" or "uses," but can also be an alternative path to reusing parts of an implementation.

Interfaces are a way to represent what objects *do* in a more abstract way. They represent inheritance without code reuse. That may make them seem like a pointless formality, but they can also be helpful by making us focus on object composition as an alternative way of achieving reuse.

One of our major goals is to have pluggable, movable, reusable components. Favoring composition over inheritance is a major step in achieving this. In the following chapters, we will look at how to do this specifically and how to add additional flexibility without too much complexity.

C H A P T E R   6

Object-oriented principles

Once there was a large, heavy, complex web application with lots of modules, bells and whistles, or even timpani and trumpets. It was reasonably successful, but needed to be adapted to a new customer's needs. The customer needed something with fewer features but with a specific look and feel. The look and feel was well defined: There was an HTML file containing all the styling and layout that was needed.

The existing application had flexibility built in so that a web designer could change the layout templates to create a completely new layout. Everything was based on CSS and XSLT, so all it should take, in theory at least, was to copy all the style sheets and modify them. Unfortunately, that was not what was needed for this particular new customer. The task required tweaking existing features, removing some, and squeezing it into the layout that had been specified. Partly because of the size of the application, and the fact that the new required layout was simpler, it was easier to discard the old templates and use the HTML file as a starting point for new templates. So as far as the new requirements were concerned, the work that had been put into making it flexible was mostly wasted.

If you've been developing web applications, chances are you've seen this kind of thing. An application is supposed to be flexible, but when it meets the real world, it turns out that the flexibility that was planned is not the flexibility that's needed, and the apparatus needed to provide the flexibility is itself so complex that it makes the job of changing the application harder.

What we need is a free lunch, if there is such a thing. It would be great to be able to achieve flexibility without having to write a lot of extra code to prepare for future requirements.

Principles and design patterns have fancy names and academic-sounding descriptions, but ultimately it's all just practical advice. It's like the advice to a use screwdriver rather than a kitchen knife to insert screws, except that the principles and patterns are more complex than a screwdriver. It's all approximate, there are no absolutes, and there are lots of exceptions.

It should be possible for you to test all this practical advice in your own experience; to try it and see how it works. Applying these principles and patterns is mostly similar in PHP and other languages. This is even more so since PHP 5 was released, since version 5 has made it easier to construct complex object-oriented designs. However, there are some differences, particularly between dynamically and statically typed languages. We will discuss some of those as we move along. Often, PHP allows or encourages simpler, more straightforward ways of coding. We want to keep that in mind, and make sure we always know what—if anything—we gain by using an object-oriented design over a simple procedural script.

Robert C. Martin summarizes most of the principles in his book *Agile Software Development: Principles, Patterns and Practice* [Uncle Bob]. In this section, we will take a closer look at some of them and how they apply specifically to PHP.

We will be focusing on a selection of the most important ones: the *open-closed principle*, which teaches us how to add new features as new classes rather than by changing everything; the *single-responsibility principle*, which allows us to avoid changing too much at a time; and the *dependency-inversion principle*, to make it easier to reuse high-level modules. But first, we will take a closer look at the relationship between principles and patterns.

6.1   PRINCIPLES AND PATTERNS

Design patterns and object-oriented principles may be considered an attempt to provide the free lunch mentioned earlier. Design patterns are an attempt to give a systematic account of successful solutions to problems that are known to recur in program design. It's easy to overuse them, in which case you might get an expensive lunch, but when properly used they can provide flexibility without making the code much more complex. Sometimes they can even make the program simpler. We'll explore several design patterns in chapter 7.

Object-oriented principles are less like solutions and more like criteria or guidelines, heuristics that give a rough idea of how easy a design will be to maintain and a starting point for making it better.

The word *principle* can mean a lot of things to different people, but in our context it means something less detailed and more general than "how-to" type of information. Design patterns are excellent tools, and they are more specific than the object-oriented principles. The difficulty with patterns is not so much the "how-to" as the "when-to": knowing which situations call for the different patterns is a higher art form. We need to understand what we're doing and why we're doing it. The object-oriented principles will help us do that.

It's like learning a physical skill. If you want to play tennis, trying to hit the ball across the net would seem to be a good general guideline at first. Unless you're able to do that, more specific, detailed, and complex instructions are not likely to be helpful.

The principles we will be looking at come from different sources and are conceptually very different as well, but they have one thing in common: they all have three-letter abbreviations. And they are ways to make a design satisfy some of the success criteria given earlier: flexibility, robustness, mobility and fluidity.

6.1.1 Architectural principles or patterns

In addition to the typical design patterns and principles that often apply to the interaction between a few objects and classes, there are some principles or patterns that guide the architecture as a whole. The book *Pattern-Oriented Software Architecture* [POSA] defines these as architectural patterns rather than design patterns. Two of these will be covered in this book: layers (later in this chapter) and Model-View-Controller (in chapter 15). But calling them patterns tends to make some view them restrictively, as rigid rules rather than guidelines. It may be more useful to see them as overall concepts, paradigms, or sorting principles.

And it may be more important to understand and to keep them in mind than to apply them rigorously. A typical scenario is a web application that starts out extremely simple. Introducing layers or MVC may seem like overkill and probably is. But as the application grows, sooner or later the need to start sorting and separating arises, or the application will evolve into what is known as a Big Ball of Mud.

At that point, knowing some architectural principles such as layering will be extremely helpful in aiding the decisions about how to sort and separate. But before we can apply the principles usefully, we need to learn them in practice.

6.1.2 Learning OO principles

The ideas in this chapter may seem somewhat theoretical. To really learn the principles, it's necessary to use them in practice. There are many examples of them in this book. Above all, the practices of test-driven development and refactoring (as described in part 2 of this book) are extremely helpful in gaining experience and an intuitive sense of where to go next. As noted in chapter 4, we need to have some criteria for distinguishing a good design from a poor one. And two of these—readability and duplication—are relatively easy to evaluate. The others, such as flexibility and robustness, are harder to keep track of. Programmers who are trying to learn object-oriented design often ask how to make a design more flexible without understanding that flexibility may come at a cost. This is the "free lunch" issue mentioned earlier. The OO principles are a way of approaching the need for flexibility, robustness, mobility, and fluidity in a way that tends to keep the cost down, although we always need to consider the pros and cons.

The first and perhaps most important of the principles we will discuss is called the *open-closed principle*.

6.2 THE OPEN-CLOSED PRINCIPLE (OCP)

The open-closed principle tells us that a class or other software entity should be "open to extension, closed to modification."

What does that mean? The idea is that if the class or function has the flexibility you need, it's unnecessary to change the code to make it work differently. It's "closed" in the sense that you don't *need* to change it, not necessarily that you *cannot* change it. And it's "closed" *because* it's open. It's like the tree that bends in the storm instead of breaking.

In this section, we will first gain a basic understanding of the OCP by studying a trivial example. Then we'll look at a slightly more realistic case. Finally, we'll find out how relevant the OCP is in PHP compared to other programming languages.

6.2.1 OCP for beginners

In its simplest form, the OCP is trivial. For example, take this small scrap of code:

```php
function hello() {
    echo "Hello, Dolly!\n";
}
```

This is a unit (a function in this case) that's "open to modification" (that is, something that may *have to* be changed) because any change in requirements will force you to change it. If you want to output "Hello, Murphy" instead, you have to change the function.

To see how the OCP works, let's try instead:

```php
function hello($name) {
    echo "Hello, ".$name."!";
}
```

Now, the function is "closed to modification" if the name changes because there is a degree of freedom. On the other hand, there are other kinds of freedom that are not present. If you want to say "Good evening" instead of "Hello," you have to change the code.

Take the first bullet

So when and how does the OCP get interesting? It becomes more interesting—or at least less obvious—in two ways depending on two different questions:

- What degrees of freedom do we want? In other words, *when* do we want to apply the OCP, and to *which* aspects of our design?

- How can we do it with more complex code, such as a whole class, and with more complex variations in behavior? In other words, *how* can it be implemented in a realistic situation?

The difficulty with the first question—when to apply the principle—is that if we apply it indiscriminately, we might be tempted to prepare for all sorts of hypothetical future changes by introducing unnecessary complexity. Uncle Bob has a compromise between this and doing nothing about it: we want to "take the first bullet." If a certain kind of change happens, and we're not prepared, that's OK. But after that, we want to be prepared for similar changes in the future.

So if we're echoing "Hello, Dolly" and we need to be able to echo "Hello, Murphy," we want to make the change so that we can replace the name with *any* name. We don't want to restrict ourselves to those two names. Again, it's trivial in this case. Any amateur programmer will do the only sensible thing when it's as simple as using a variable. But with more complex behavior than inserting a name, it may take some work to figure out how to do it.

6.2.2 Replacing cases with classes

So how does it work in the real world?

If we have a PHP class that specializes in inserting news articles into a database and we want to make it insert topics into a topic list instead, we will have to do something more than replace a string with a variable.

Let's say we use a conditional statement to test whether we are dealing with a topic or a news article, as shown in listing 6.1.

Listing 6.1 Using a `switch` statement to distinguish news from topics when saving them to a database

```
public function insert($type,$data) {
    switch ($type) {
        case 'News':
            $sql = "INSERT INTO News (headline,body) VALUES('".
                $data['headline']."','".$data['body']."')";
            break;
        case 'Topics':
            $sql = "INSERT INTO Topics (name) VALUES('".
                $data['name']."')";
            break;
    }
    // Insert into the database
}
```

CHAPTER 6 OBJECT-ORIENTED PRINCIPLES

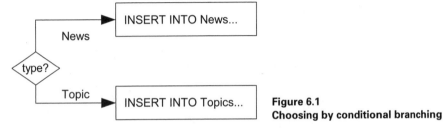

Figure 6.1
Choosing by conditional branching

A simple flowchart illustrates the structure of this approach (see figure 6.1).

Here we are not conforming to the OCP, because if we need to insert something else—such as a product or a person—into the database, we will have to change that `switch` statement, adding one more case to it. If we make a mistake, the existing code may malfunction. For example, accidentally deleting the first `break` statements would cause immediate disaster.

The obvious way to satisfy the OCP is to do the refactoring called *Replace Conditional with Polymorphism*. Instead of testing `$type` to find out what to do, we can have several different kinds of classes of objects that are programmed with different courses of action, as in listing 6.2.

Listing 6.2   Using separate classes instead of the `switch` statement

```php
abstract class Inserter {
    abstract public function insert($data);
}

class TopicInserter extends Inserter {
    public function insert($data) {
        $sql = "INSERT INTO Topics (name) VALUES('".
            $data['name']."')";
        // Insert into database
    }
}

class NewsInserter extends Inserter {
    public function insert($data) {
        $sql = "INSERT INTO News (headline,body) VALUES('".
            $data['headline']."','".$data['body']."')";
        // Insert into database
    }
}
```

This will allow us to write something like this:

```php
$inserter = new NewsInserter;
$inserter->insert(array('headline' => 'Man bites dog'));
```

Figure 6.2 is a UML class diagram showing this simple design.

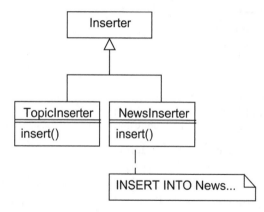

Figure 6.2
Inserter class hierarchy; the branches of the conditional statement have become separate classes

There are two significant and separate aspects that have changed between listing 6.1 and listing 6.2:

- Readability. You may or may not find the refactored solution more readable than the original, but they do read very differently, and as a general rule, eliminating conditional statements often increases readability.

- OCP. The other aspect is the open-closed principle (OCP). After replacing the different cases with different classes, we can add another case without changing the existing code at all. We can make a ProductInserter that will insert rows into a product table.

This is still a simplistic example—typically, a class like this would at least have methods to update and delete data as well—but it illustrates the principle, and we will return to it later.

The OCP has mostly been discussed in the context of languages such as Java and C++. Is the OCP as relevant in PHP as in Java and other statically typed languages? We'll discuss that next.

6.2.3 How relevant is the OCP in PHP?

There is one problem that is less relevant in PHP than in statically typed languages: recompilation. In a language that needs separate compilation before you can run the program, you need less compilation if a change affects as few classes as possible. This is not a problem in PHP.

But there is a more important reason for the OCP, and it is as relevant in PHP as in other languages. If a new requirement forces a change in different places, it is harder to see exactly where and how to make the change, and there are more places where bugs might be introduced.

For example, as mentioned in the earlier Inserter example, changing the `switch` statement could make the existing code (for inserting news articles or topics) malfunction. Adding another class is unlikely to have this effect.

While the OCP is about "closing" some classes so we won't have to change them, the single-responsibility principle does something similar from a different perspective. If we sort different responsibilities into different classes, there is less likelihood that changes to existing features will affect more than one class. We'll look at this principle next.

6.3   THE SINGLE-RESPONSIBILITY PRINCIPLE (SRP)

Don't be too good at too many things. Ignorance is not necessarily bliss, but you risk overextending yourself.

A few hundred years ago, it was common for one person to be an expert in what would now be considered widely divergent fields of study. In our day and age, keeping up with new developments can be hard enough even in a narrowly specialized subject. If you wanted to devour all news about computing, for instance, you would probably be busy more than 25 hours a day.

Similarly, a class that tries to do everything will have to change frequently because some responsibility it has needs to be updated.

So if a class has fewer responsibilities, it will be able to survive longer without being subjected to changes. The single-responsibility principle, as formulated by Uncle Bob, states: *A class should have only one reason to change.*

Examples of the opposite are easy to find. The most obvious may be the haphazard mixtures of HTML markup, PHP code, and SQL queries that characterize many web applications. If you have a PHP script that may change because someone wants a new color for the main heading, because a table in the database was changed, or because it needs to be secured against malicious attacks, it becomes fragile. A change in any one of these features—page styling, database layout, or security—can potentially break the other features. Typically, we will want each of these features in a separate class or classes.

Also, it's easier to reuse a class that contains just what you need and nothing more. Would you use a package containing 10,000-plus lines of code just to do something simple such as checking the validity of an email address? Probably not. Just picking the right class or function out of the package, and figuring out how to use it, may cost more work than implementing a new one.

But what exactly is a single reason to change? It would be absurd to interpret that to mean that there is one and only one user requirement that would cause it to change. There has to be a certain *kind* of requirement that will cause changes. For example, the Inserter class shown earlier will tend to change only for reasons related to database storage.

In other words, the Inserter deals with *object persistence*, which we will go into in more depth in later chapters. Sometimes a class will contain both domain logic or business logic—related to what the object actually does—and persistence logic—related to how the object is stored.

For example, let's say we have an object representing an event in an event calendar. All events are supposed to start and end on the hour, so the Event class has a method called `round()` that adjusts the start and end times to satisfy this condition. In addition, the class has a `save()` method to store the event in a database.

The two methods may change for completely unrelated reasons. The `round()` method might have to change because we want to round to the nearest half hour rather than the nearest hour. The `save()` method might change when the DBMS is replaced with a different one.

Like all these principles, the SRP is not a hard and fast rule. Violating the principle does little harm in simple cases, and in fact some of Martin Fowler's enterprise patterns—such as Row Data Gateway—do mix these responsibilities [P of EAA].

In the following subsections, we'll explore the SRP in practice. We will see how a kind of class that is common in PHP—the template engine—typically mixes several responsibilities. Then, as an experiment, we'll tease the responsibilities apart, creating one class for each of them. Finally, we'll sum up, checking out how successful the experiment was.

6.3.1 Mixed responsibilities: the template engine

For an example, we'll explore a kind of class that often has mixed responsibilities. It's a component that is well known in PHP web programming: the template engine. Template engines typically have the following abilities:

- Storing a set of variables
- Reading a template file
- Combining the first two to generate output

These could be considered three separate responsibilities.

NOTE   The ins and outs of templates engines are discussed in chapter 13.

Let's explore how to separate these responsibilities. To do that, we'll mix them first in a simple template engine class. The class is simplistic; it does only the minimal work it needs to do to support a template engine API. But it illustrates the basic mechanics.

To make sure we understand what we're doing, here is the plain PHP way to do what a template engine does using `include`. We set one or more variables, include a PHP file, and the variables can be displayed by using `echo` in the included file.

```
$hello ='Hello, world!';
include 'Test.php';
```

To replace this, we can create a template engine that uses PHP as a template language. You can construct a template, specifying a template file name, set variables using a `set()` method, and get the result as HTML using the `asHtml()` method. Using this template engine, we can do this instead of the `include`:

```
$template = new Template('test.php');
$template->set('hello','Hello, world!');
echo $template->asHtml();
```

You might think that the point of a template engine is to use a template language other than PHP. Nonetheless, there are some advantages to a template engine based on PHP templates:

- We have precise control of which variables are available to the test.php file. Since plain includes can use any variables that are available at the include point, the include files have a nasty way of becoming dependent on variables that are not apparent from reading the code. That makes it hard to move the include statement. It's stuck where it is, more or less.

- We have more control over the HTML result; we can post-process it and pass it around if we need to.

- The PHP-based template engine could be used as a halfway measure toward a "real" template engine. One possible scenario is if we're sure we want to use a template engine, but haven't decided which one. Or possibly we want something in the initial stages of a project that is extremely easy to install and deploy.

- We have made it explicit in the code that test.php is a template, presumably containing mostly HTML code.

Listing 6.3 shows the template engine class.

Listing 6.3 Simplest-possible template engine using PHP as a template language

```
class Template {
    private $vars;
    private $file;

    public function __construct($file) {          ❶
        $this->file = $file;
    }

    public function set($var,$value) {            ❷
        $this->vars[$var] = $value;
    }

    public function asHtml() {
        extract($this->vars);          ❸
        ob_start();                                ❹
        include $this->file;
        $string = ob_get_contents();
        ob_end_clean();
        return $string;          ❺
    }
}
```

❶ The constructor accepts a filename and stores it in an instance variable.

② The `set()` method accepts a variable name and a value and stores the name/value pair in an array belonging to the object.

③ To generate the HTML output, we need to make the variables available to the PHP code in the template. Extracting our array of variables is a simple way to achieve that.

④ `ob_start()` turns on output buffering. In plainer language, `ob_start()` tells PHP to store the data it would normally send to the browser.

The file we now include generates just that kind of data; normally it would be output, but instead PHP holds onto it. Now we use the `ob_get_contents()` function to get the suppressed output. Unless we turn output buffering off again, there will never be any output at all. `ob_end_clean()` turns output buffering off without sending any output.

⑤ Finally, we return the generated HTML output without sending it to the browser.

Figure 6.3 is a simple class diagram of this one class.

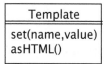

Figure 6.3   Class diagram of the simplest-possible template engine

Now that we've seen how the responsibilities can be mixed, let's move on and see how they can be implemented in separate classes. This separation may be overkill for a class this small, but we'll do it as an interesting experiment.

6.3.2   An experiment: separating the responsibilities

As mentioned, the template engine can be seen as having three separate responsibilities:

- Storing variables
- Reading a template file
- Processing the template; combining the variables and the contents of the file

The template engine in listing 6.3 might be too simple to warrant separating these into different classes, but let's try it and see how it works. We will separate the variable handling and the file handling into two separate classes and leave the processing in the Template class. Figure 6.4 shows how this may be done.

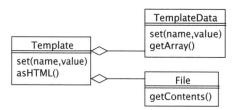

Figure 6.4   Class diagram of a simple template engine with responsibilities sorted into three separate classes.

Starting with the File class, listing 6.4 shows how it may be implemented. It is ridiculously simple; it is simply an object wrapper around the `file_get_contents()` function.

Listing 6.4   Extracting a separate class to handle the template file

```
class File {
    public function __construct($name) {
        $this->name = $name;
    }
    function getContents() {
        return file_get_contents($this->name);
    }
}
```

The TemplateData class, which handles the template variables (see listing 6.5), is almost equally simple. We can use it to set a variable and to get all of them as an array. We want an array since we want to use the `extract()` function to transform it into separate variables.

Listing 6.5   Extracting a separate class to handle the template variables

```
class TemplateData {
    private $vars;
    public function set($var,$value) {
        $this->vars[$var] = $value;
    }
    public function getArray() {
        return $this->vars;
    }
}
```

Using these two classes, we can now implement the Template class as shown in listing 6.6.

Listing 6.6   The Template class that uses the extracted classes

```
class Template {
    private $data;
    private $file;

    public function __construct($file) {
        $this->file = new File($file);      ❶ Instantiate the
        $this->data = new TemplateData;         extracted classes
    }

    public function set($var,$value) {
```

```
        $this->data->set($var,$value);
    }

    private function processTemplate() {
        extract($this->data->getArray());
        $string = $this->file->getContents();
        eval('?>'.$string);
    }

    public function asHtml() {
        ob_start();
        $this->processTemplate();
        $string = ob_get_contents();
        ob_end_clean();
        return $string;
    }
}
```

❷ A separate method for template processing

❸ Variables from the Template-Data object

❹ eval() instead of include processing

❺ Buffer output to get the result

❶ We start off by instantiating both of the extracted classes. Seeing objects being created in the constructor, we might wonder whether it would be a good idea to pass them in instead, but let's leave that for now.

❷ To separate the mechanics of output buffering from the template processing proper, we have a separate method to process the template.

❸ As before, we extract the array to get separate variables, but now the variables come from the TemplateData object.

❹ Since we are separating file handling from template processing, we can no longer use `include` to do both of these in one operation. Instead, we let the File object get the file contents and run `eval()` to process the template.

   `eval()` needs the PHP end tag (`?>`). `eval()` expects straight PHP code with no PHP tags around it. But since `$string` is the contents of the included PHP template file, it will contain HTML markup or PHP sections surrounded by PHP tags.

❺ The `asHtml()` method now primarily contains mainly output buffering code.

6.3.3   Was the experiment successful?

The reason we did the experiment—dividing up the Template class to separate the responsibilities—was to see where it went, to learn something, and from that perspective it was a success. But apart from that, is the version with three classes better than the single class? On the face of it, no: the Template class has hardly changed at all; all we've done is wrap basic PHP functionality in two classes.

   So right now, it's fairly meaningless. But it may become more meaningful later, if either file handling or variable handling becomes more complex. For example, if we want to search a set of directories to find the template, we can do that without changing anything except the File class. Or if variables can be represented as complex paths representing array elements and method calls (as they can with some template engines), we might be able to do that by changing just the TemplateData class.

NOTE   We actually gave up the ability to search directories when we stopped using `include`, since `include` searches PHP's `include_path`. But it's probably more useful to have one or more directories for templates only.

If the separation into three classes was a success, a possible next step would be to assemble the Template object from components. For instance, we might want to be able to do this:

```
$template = new Template(new File, new TemplateData);
```

That would make the components pluggable and replaceable rather than just independently changeable. We can accommodate choice as well as change. For example, this kind of construction lets us replace the File object with a different object that gets the template text from a database.

That is the OCP. The Template object is open to extension by replacing one of the components. So we see that the single-responsibility principle paves the way for the open-closed principle.

In the next section, we'll talk about how the dependency-inversion principle (DIP), the last of the three principles we'll discuss in this chapter, can help us make our high-level modules reusable.

6.4   THE DEPENDENCY-INVERSION PRINCIPLE (DIP)

Try mentioning the dependency-inversion principle in the comp.object newsgroup. The likely result is a thread with hundreds of replies and rampant disagreement on several points. What, if anything, does "inversion" really mean? Is the DIP a recent innovation, or was it invented by Plato around 400 BC?

Fortunately, answering these questions is not crucial to understanding and using the principle. However, the Plato angle is an interesting one. On the subject of abstraction, Plato did some of the earliest and most influential thinking in history. Plato believed that abstractions are *real*; that they have an existence independent of concrete examples and the world of the senses. The simplified form of the dependency-inversion principle says "depend on abstractions."

The Gang of Four says that you should "program to an interface, not an implementation." But what does "depend on abstractions" mean? It means that you're more likely to survive as an omnivore. A tiger does not thrive on lettuce; a cow that needs to go hunting or fishing is in trouble. In other words, these animals depend on specific foods, rather than on food in general.

The more omnivorous you can make the modules at the top of your software food chain, the better. It makes them reusable in other contexts.

The principle is easy to understand if we look at UML diagrams. In figure 6.5, the client depends on the concrete class Week.

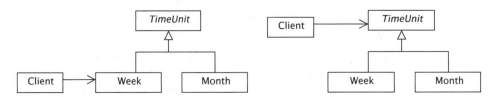

Figure 6.5 Client depends on the concrete class Week

Figure 6.6 Moving the dependency to a more abstract level

In figure 6.6, the client depends on the TimeUnit class (or interface) instead. This means that the client is not chained to one specific class. Instead, the client can use any class that extends or implements TimeUnit. So this design gives us much more flexibility.

But what does this mean in practice, and how does it relate to the way dependencies are handled in statically typed languages? We will explore these in the next two subsections.

6.4.1   What is a dependency?

The idea of a dependency looks great in UML; it seems clear and convincing. Anyone can see the arrow in the diagram. But it gets murkier once we try to implement it in actual code. What does "dependency" actually mean? What does the arrow represent? It implies that if a class is changed, the one that depends on it may also have to be changed. But what causes this dependency? How is it manifested? And is it the same in different programming languages? In fact, is it meaningful at all in PHP?

It *is* different—and harder to pin down—in PHP than in statically typed languages such as Java. But there is a dependency, and the idea of changing that dependency is not meaningless. So, we need to understand what a "dependency" is. The short version of it is that if class A uses class B, class A depends on class B.

But again, what exactly does that mean? Let's look at an example of a Calendar class that has the ability to generate a calendar for a specific month. There is a generate() method that takes the start time of the month in question and calculates calendar data for that month. It starts by creating a Month object representing the month and calling a method on the Month object to get the weeks in that month.

```
class Calendar {
    public function generate($starttime) {
        $month = new Month($starttime)
        $weeks = $month->getWeeks();
        // etc.
    }
}
```

In the example, the Calendar class *depends* on the Month class. There are two reasons, both shown in bold. We have to use the name of the Month class when we instantiate it. So if we want to replace the Month object with something different, we have to do something else.

The other reason why the Calendar class depends on the Month class is that it uses one of the methods in the month class: getWeeks(). This method is one that no other class is likely to have, making the dependency even stronger.

For a slightly different scenario, let's say the generate() method takes the Month object as an argument:

```
class Calendar {
    public function generate(Month $month) {
        $weeks = $month->getWeeks();
    }
}
```

Now we've moved the first dependency somewhere else; the creation of the Month object happens before it's introduced into the generate() method. But we've also introduced another, similar dependency by using a type hint. The type hint makes sure that the generate() method will only accept Month objects; that gives us more safety and less flexibility. The good news is that if we replace the Month object with another class of object by mistake, we are likely to hear about it. The bad news is that we can't replace it if we need to do so. Apparently, we've done nothing to weaken the dependency.

As long as we are calling the getWeeks() method, it will not be weakened very much even if we drop the type hint. Since the getWeeks() method is unique to the Month class, it is just as strong a test for the correct class as the type hint is. Using the type hint just causes the failure to happen a little bit earlier.

If the method were named more generically, it would be different:

```
    public function generate(Month $month) {
        $weeks = $month->divide();
    }
```

When we call the method divide() instead of getWeeks(), the type hint is more restrictive than the method call. There might be other classes that have a divide() method, but the type hint will stop any attempt to pass an instance of one of those other classes.

Whether passing a different object is likely to happen by mistake or on purpose is an interesting question. Most likely, the classes that have a divide() method are related. A Week class might have a divide() method that returns the days in the week. If we want the method to accept either one as an argument, we can skip the type hint (and make the variable names more generic as well):

```
    public function generate($unit) {
        $parts = $unit->divide();
    }
```

The alternative to leaving out the type hint is to make sure both the Week and Month classes have a common parent class or implement a common interface. This is where TimeUnit comes in:

```
public function generate(TimeUnit $unit) {
    $parts = $unit->divide();
}
```

Now the code works as before as long as we pass Week or Month objects, but if we pass an object that is not a TimeUnit, it will fail.

Even after doing these adjustments, there is still the issue of using the concrete class name when constructing the object. This is an issue in statically typed languages as well (in fact, it's a stronger issue because changes tend to require recompilation). The standard way of solving that is to hide object creation in a special class called a *factory*. The DIP violation is still there, but it can be contained and limited to certain classes. The simpler alternative is to just replace the class name with a variable. But this is much less flexible, since it requires the constructors' signatures to be the same.

6.4.2   Inserting an interface

A popular practice in statically typed languages is to add an interface to decouple classes from each other. Since the type name keeps recurring in the code in such languages, changing the type name from the name of a concrete class to an interface makes it possible to change the class and use a different one without changing the client code. So instead of using a concrete class called Date, if you let Date implement an interface called IDate, you can make the code depend on IDate instead of Date.

Since PHP 5 has an interface construct, does this make sense in PHP 5 as well? It might not seem that way. In PHP 5, assuming we are not using type hints, an interface has no practical consequences. So pretending it's there is the same in practice as actually having it there. We can always make a different class that conforms to the interface we haven't formally defined, and substitute that for the existing class.

But to make this work—to avoid having to change the client—the methods in the first class must represent what we need in the other class. If we're using a getWeeks() method, that's a dependency on one specific, concrete class. That implies that the interface must not contain that method. That's why defining an interface may be a good idea if we use it as an opportunity to think abstractly. If the interface is genuinely more abstract, in the sense of using more abstract or generic concepts, we've gained some flexibility that comes from that abstraction.

Another factor to consider is the likelihood of class name conflicts in PHP. This will be dealt with in more detail in the chapter 8.

So far in this chapter, we have been dealing with (object-oriented) principles in a relatively general, abstract sense. These are useful in practically any design regardless of its high-level structure. In addition, there are architectural principles (sometimes called architectural patterns) that serve as guidelines for the overall design of the application. The most common of these principles is the idea of *layers*. Layering is more specific than the object-oriented principles we have seen so far.

6.5 LAYERED DESIGNS

The idea of "layered" or "tiered" systems seems to be a common and natural way of thinking when constructing software. Functions, methods, or objects tend to have a pecking order: Function A pecks (calls) function B more often than function B pecks function A, which puts function B lower in the pecking order than function A. And when you have lots of cases like that, organizing code into layers is an almost obvious way to sort everything. It is as if you have all these components floating around and you need to catch them and put them on different shelves so it's easier to organize and remember.

In strict layered architectures, objects on each layer can only access objects on the next lower layer. Network protocols work this way, but in business software, layers tend to be allowed to use any lower layer but not higher layers.

I will be using the words "tier" and "layer" the way Martin Fowler does, reserving "tier" for layers that are physically separated.

This section will focus on a specific form of layering, the typical three-layer architecture for business applications. First we will do an overview of this architecture, and then we will discuss whether web applications really need these three layers—the Domain layer, in particular.

6.5.1 The "three-tier" model and its siblings

A layered design is somewhat like a hierarchical business or military organization. The pecking order is expressed by giving every component in the system a "rank," telling the components at a lower level to "do this, do that."

The typical three-layer architecture is shown in table 6.1.

The Presentation layer is the part of the application that talks to the user. In server-side web applications, this is done by generating HTML code and interpreting the HTTP requests sent back by the browser.

The Domain layer is the part of the application whose purpose is directly related to the core purpose of the application. For example, an e-commerce application will have to deal with domain concepts such as customers, products, shopping carts, prices,

Table 6.1 The three-layer architecture using Martin Fowler's naming conventions

Layer	Purpose
Presentation	The user interface and user interaction parts of the application, primarily the HTML page.
Domain	The "business logic."
Data Source	Stores and retrieves data in a database or other storage. In its simplest form, this is a thin shell of PHP code around SQL statements, providing a non-SQL interface to the data.

discounts, orders, and so on. The logic that is related to these domain concepts is the domain logic or business logic. For instance, a price may have to be calculated using discounts based on the customer, the product, the season, and other factors.

The Data Source layer supplies the services needed to keep information in permanent storage. Typically, the permanent storage is a relational database, but it may be stored in flat files or even using other, more exotic mechanisms.

Figure 6.7 illustrates how this might work in an event calendar application. The Presentation layer has classes to generate the calendar display. (Some code is shown in chapter 4, listing 4.1.) The Domain layer has a class to represent a calendar event and some classes to handle date and time logic. Finally, the Data Source layer has an EventMapper class for storing events in a database.

It's common to have a fairly loose approach to layering. The clearest example may be the Active Record pattern (see chapter 21), in which business logic and data storage logic is mixed into one class. Also, there is no rule that says you always need three layers. Sometimes two seems to be sufficient; sometimes one or more layer

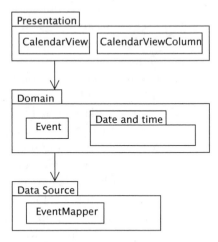

Figure 6.7 A three-layer event calendar application.

is divided into sublayers. A two-layer architecture may consist of a Data Source layer communicating directly with the Presentation layer. In fact, web applications often need so little logic between Data Source and Presentation that we may legitimately ask whether there is a need for a Domain layer at all.

6.5.2   Can a web application have a Domain layer?

Many web applications have little specific business logic. Their purpose is often to display some data from a database, (possibly) let the user edit it, and save it back to the database. This makes it little more than a user interface to a database table. This kind of application is frequently summarized by the acronym CRUD: Create, Read, Update, and Delete operations are all that are needed. Representing this data as individual objects is always possible but usually not strictly necessary. The plain PHP way, representing the database rows as associative arrays, is one alternative. In this context, it is possible to use some variation of the *Record Set* design pattern, representing a set of rows as one object.

This is more of a two-layer architecture, in which a pure data representation can interact with data-aware user interface controls without the need for a separate Domain layer.

Figure 6.8 shows how this works. We join data from database tables using SQL and then the resulting record set can be passed to *widgets* that know how to display a record set. A simplistic example would be an object that would be capable of generating an HTML table from the record set:

```
$table = new TableWidget($recordset);
echo $table->asHtml();
```

The only way to know when you need something like this, or something like a domain layer, is to try it out and learn from experience. Having some kind of domain object representation gives you a flexibility that may be useful if the need for complex business rules arises. On the other hand, agile principles tell us that having complexity that is not needed for current requirements may just mean carrying useless luggage.

Books on object-oriented software often focus on the Domain layer as the place that has the complex logic and is therefore the most natural place to use object techniques. However, in web applications, often other parts of the program have the most complex logic, and object-oriented techniques are helpful in dealing with this complexity. Some common examples of complexity in web programming are

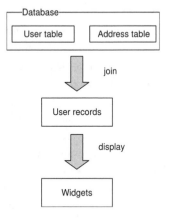

Figure 6.8   RecordSet principle

- Date and time handling , especially when dealing with calendars
- E-commerce features such as shopping carts and checkout
- User interaction and page navigation
- Input validation
- Presentation logic, such as the logic needed to create an event calendar that can display simultaneous events side by side
- Complex relationships between objects, such as the hierarchical structure of a threaded online forum
- Flexible storage involving different database management systems or even distributed software components

All of these examples are complex enough to definitely benefit from using object-oriented techniques.

6.6   SUMMARY

Object-oriented design is not easy. Fortunately, nowadays we have some guidelines to help us move in the right direction. Object-oriented principles aid our thinking about which designs are better than others, and why.

The open-closed principle helps us add new features outside an existing class instead of having to fiddle with all of them every time.

The single-responsibility principle also helps us avoid changing too many classes by improving cohesion: if one class has one responsibility, it has only one reason to change, and will not be touched by new requirements as frequently as otherwise.

The dependency-inversion principle is a way of making as many components as possible reusable by letting high-level components depend on abstractions rather than specific implementation details. Although the way it works is different in PHP than in statically typed languages, it is perfectly applicable to PHP.

Layered designs are fundamental and useful in most business applications. They help implement the single-responsibility principle by a high-level separation of concerns so that most changes need to affect only one layer.

As mentioned in the beginning of this chapter, design patterns are more specific than principles. Design patterns provide ways to solve specific, recurring design problems. In the following chapter, we will familiarize ourselves with some of the most common patterns, including Strategy, Adapter, Decorator, Null Object, Iterator, and Composite.

Design patterns

Not long ago, I was trying to get my son, age five, to ski. It started well: he saw his older sister skiing down a mild slope, and immediately became eager to show us how easily he could do the same thing.

He couldn't, though. He insisted on putting his skis on in the middle of the slope, and immediately fell flat on his back. I told him it was a nice try, but he disagreed. He had simply lost all interest. I suggested we go lower where it was less challenging. Instead he insisted on going to the top. I humored him and we went up. He had one look down the slope and said, "It's scary."

Of course it was scary. Of course he refused to try it.

I finally persuaded him to do it at the very bottom where the surface was almost flat. Better than nothing, I told myself.

Afterward, I started to ponder the cognitive limitations of a five-year-old. At that age, a child is capable of learning the skill. He's OK with the "how," but the "why" is beyond his ken. The idea that it will be more fun later if he takes the time to practice is meaningless to him. So is the concept that there is some middle ground between scary (the fear of falling) and boring (trudging across a flat field of snow as if wearing snowshoes).

This may seem like an odd introduction to design patterns, but the thing is, "why" is an important question when applying patterns. You can learn how to implement them, but if you don't know what good they are and in what situations to apply them, you may well do more harm than good by using them.

Much of the literature on software design nowadays focuses on design patterns. Design patterns are an attempt to make the principles of good object-oriented design more explicit. Patterns are defined as "a recurrent solution to a problem." But using them is not as simple as following a cookbook recipe. Applying a pattern can be daunting, since the description in a book is usually somewhat abstract and you have to figure out how exactly to use it in a situation that is different from the example given in the book.

As we've already hinted, an even greater challenge is discovering when you have the problem that the pattern is supposed to solve. Unless your requirement is extremely similar to an example you've seen, it's seldom obvious. And there are lots of situations in which you can use a design pattern but would be better off not doing it because you don't need the extra flexibility that the pattern provides. For instance, the book *Design Patterns* [Gang of Four] describes a pattern called *Command*, which involves creating an object-oriented class for each type of command in your program. So if you have an Edit command, you write a class called `EditCommand` and when you want to run the command, you instantiate the class and run a method that does whatever the command is supposed to do:

```
$editcommand = new EditCommand;
$editcommand->execute();
```

But why? You don't need a separate class just to execute a command. A simple function will do. (Even in strict object-oriented languages such as Java, you don't need a class for each command, just a method.)

Then what's the point? According to the book, the intent of the Command pattern is to encapsulate a request as an object so that you can "parameterize clients with different requests, queue or log requests, and support undoable operations." There are other suggestions as well for when the Command pattern is applicable. But if you don't need to do *any* of those things, creating command objects probably won't do you any good. Unless using the pattern actually results in code that is simpler, has less duplication, or is easier to understand, it may be better to steer clear of it.

Martin Fowler says, "I like to say that patterns are 'half baked,' meaning that you always have to figure out how to apply it to your circumstances. Every time I use a pattern I tweak it a little here and there." The converse is also often the case. If I've developed a design, partly by designing it first and partly by refactoring it, I often find that it can be described by a pattern, or several patterns, without matching any of them exactly.

The problem with many applications of design patterns is that the designers haven't taken the time to compare the design with one without the pattern or with one that uses a different pattern.

In this chapter, we will look at some of the more basic design patterns, primarily from the book *Design Patterns* [Gang of Four]. The selection of patterns is necessarily somewhat arbitrary. Whole books have been written about patterns, so it's impossible to cover them all. The ones we will see in this chapter are Strategy, Adapter, Decorator, Null Object, Iterator, and Composite. Several others will be covered in later chapters.

7.1 STRATEGY

The Strategy pattern is crucial, perhaps the most crucial pattern in modern object-oriented design. It's about creating pluggable, replaceable, reusable components. One example of this is the Template object described in the section on the single-responsibility principle in the previous chapter. If we pass the File and TemplateData objects into the constructor as suggested, we are getting close to a Strategy pattern.

For a more complete, yet still simplistic, example of the Strategy pattern, let's implement a basic example from earlier chapters using this pattern. This is a simplistic example, and the Strategy pattern is overkill in this case. But the example shows how the Strategy pattern is implemented and how it can be an alternative to implementation inheritance. We'll study the basic mechanics using "Hello world." The example is too simple to be meaningful in the real world, so in addition we'll discuss its usefulness in real situations.

The Strategy pattern will also recur in many contexts in later chapters.

7.1.1 "Hello world" using Strategy

Figure 7.1 shows the class diagram for the example shown in chapter 2. The parent class, HtmlDocument, implements the generic features represented by the start and end tags of the HTML document. The HelloWorld child class implements the specific features, represented by the actual content of the document. So to generate something other than a greeting, say an announcement, we can add another child class that generates the content of an announcement.

We can move the getContents() method to a Strategy object instead. Instead of using a subclass of HtmlDocument, we can use HtmlDocument configured with a Strategy object instead. In UML, this looks like figure 7.2.

This may look impressive; it's hard to tell from the UML diagram that it represents totally unnecessary complexity. We are just using it to make sure we understand the mechanical aspects of the pattern. HtmlContentStrategy might as well be

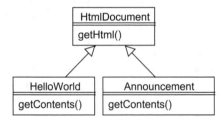

Figure 7.1
Class diagram of the simplistic HelloWorld example with related classes added

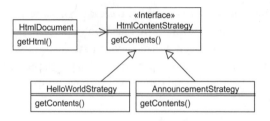

Figure 7.2
HelloWorld as a Strategy class

an abstract class, but I've defined it as an interface to make it clear that it doesn't need to contain any working code. This means that there is no implementation inheritance left in the design.

But what does it look like in code? The HtmlDocument class still generates the start and end of the document. But rather than get the content from a method that's implemented in a subclass, it gets it from the Strategy object.

```
class HtmlDocument {
    private $strategy;

    public function __construct($strategy) {
        $this->strategy = $strategy;
    }

    public function getHtml() {
        return "<html><body>".$this->strategy->getContents().
            "</body></html>";

    }
}
```

We want to be able to plug different Strategy objects into the HtmlDocument object. So the HtmlDocument object needs a consistent way to call the Strategy object. In other words, it needs a consistent interface, which is defined by an interface.

```
interface HtmlContentStrategy {
    public function __construct($name);
    public function getContents();
}
```

Now any HtmlDocument object will be able to use any Strategy object that implements this interface, since all it requires is the ability to call the get-Contents() method.

But wait a minute. What about the constructor? The interface defines that, too. The Strategy object for generating the "Hello world" message needs the world name as an argument to the constructor. Are we sure that other Strategy objects for generating HTML content will also need the same thing? I'm afraid not; in fact, I fear that they will need all sorts of other information to do their jobs.

What do we do about that? It's simple; we just eliminate the constructor from the interface. Since the HtmlDocument class doesn't instantiate the Strategy class, all objects that implement the interface can be used even if their constructors differ. So the interface just needs the `getContents()` method:

```
interface HtmlContentStrategy {
    public function getContents();
}
```

Now we can implement the "Hello world" feature as a Strategy class:

```
class HelloWorldStrategy implements HtmlContentStrategy {
    var $world;
    public function __construct($world ) {
        $this->world = $world ;
    }

    public function getContents() {
        return "Hello ".$this->world ."!";
    }
}
```

What this class does is trivial, but the pattern is extremely useful in more complex situations.

7.1.2 How Strategy is useful

Using Strategy in place of implementation inheritance is the way to create pluggable components and is useful in implementing the open-closed principle.

The most important reason for this is the fact that parent and child classes are highly coupled. They depend on each other in ways that are not necessarily obvious. An object that belongs to a class hierarchy can call a method from any class in the hierarchy (unless it is a private method) simply by using `$this`. And `$this` gives no clue as to which of the classes in the hierarchy the method belongs to.

Contrast this with the situation in which an object holds a reference to an object that is not part of an inheritance hierarchy. Let's say we have a User object that contains an Address object. In a method in the user object, we can call a method on `$this` or `$this->address`. In either case, it is clear which class the method belongs to. And unless we give the User object a reference to the Address object, the Address object is unable to call methods belonging to the User object (except by creating a new User object). So we have a one-way dependency; this makes it much more likely that we can reuse the Address class in another context. This means that the classes are much easier to disentangle than a parent and a child class that may use each other's methods freely.

This shows why there is high coupling, but this high coupling can also be convenient, since it's easy to use all those methods.

Strategy can be used in so many different situations that it is almost impossible to narrow its range of application. It can be applied to express almost any difference in behavior.

While Strategy is about pluggable behavior for a class, the next pattern—Adapter—is about changing the interface of an existing class to make it pluggable in a different context than its original one.

7.2   ADAPTER

The Adapter pattern is typically used to retrofit a class with an altered API. You may need a different API to make it compatible with another, existing class. Or perhaps the original API is too cumbersome and hard to use.

An Adapter is extra complexity, so if you can, it might be better to refactor the original class so it gets the API you want in the first place. But there might be good reasons why you can't or don't want to do that. Two of the reasons may be

- The class is already in use by many clients, so changing its interface will require changing all the clients.
- The class is part of some third-party software, so it's not practical to change it. You can, of course, change open-source software, but that means you're in trouble when the next version arrives.

In an ideal world, you might get to design everything for yourself and redesign it when necessary. Then you would rarely need Adapters, if ever. But in the real world, they become necessary because of constraints such as these.

In this section, we'll start with an extremely simple example, moving from there to an example showing how to adapt real template engines. Then we'll see an even more advanced example involving multiple classes. Finally, we'll discuss what to do if we need compatibility between several different interfaces so that a more generic interface is required.

7.2.1   Adapter for beginners

Sometimes all you need to do when creating an Adapter is change the names of methods. This is easy. If we have a template class with the method `assign()` and we want the name `set()` instead, we can use a simple Adapter that just delegates all the work to the template class.

Take our "simplest-possible template engine" example, the Template class from the previous chapter. It has the methods `set()` and `asHtml()`. What if we want to use the names Smarty uses instead: `assign()` and `fetch()`? The example in listing 7.1 shows how this can be done.

> **Listing 7.1   The Simplest-possible template adapter class**

```
class SimpleTemplateAdapter {
    private $template;

    public function __construct($template) {
        $this->template = $template;
    }
```

```
    public function assign($var,$value) {
        $this->template->set($var,$value);
    }

    public function fetch() {
        return $this->template->asHtml();
    }
}
```

To use this class, all we have to do is wrap the template object in the adapter by passing it in the constructor:

```
$template = new SimpleTemplateAdapter(new Template('test.php'));
```

`$template` now uses the Smarty method names, but it does not work quite like a Smarty object, since it's still defined as a template rather than a template engine. In the next section, we will see how to overcome this more challenging, conceptual difference.

7.2.2 Making one template engine look like another

For a more realistic example, let's use two template engines: Smarty and PHPTAL. Smarty is perhaps the most widely-known and popular template engine. PHPTAL is interesting and different. We'll discuss that further in chapter 13; for now, we're just looking at the possibilities of the Adapter pattern, and these two template engines are different enough to make it a challenge.

In particular, the two template engines are conceptually different in their design. PHPTAL uses a template object that is constructed with a specific template file. So you set the template first, add the variables you want inserted into the HTML output, and then execute it:

```
$template = new PHPTAL_Template('message.html');
$template->set('message','Hello world');
echo $template->execute();
```

A Smarty object is a different kind of animal: it's not a template; it's an instance of the template engine. After you've created the Smarty object, you can hand it any template file for processing.

The conceptual difference creates a difference in sequence. With PHPTAL, you specify the template file first and then you set the variables; with Smarty, it's the other way around:

```
$smarty = new Smarty;
$smarty->assign('message','Hello world');
$smarty->display('message.tpl');
```

Imagine that our site is currently based on Smarty, but we want to change it to PHP-TAL. In order to avoid having to rewrite all the PHP code that uses the templates, we want the templates to still appear to the PHP code as Smarty templates, so we can leave the code that uses them mostly unchanged. In other words, the Smarty interface is the one we want to keep using, even though the actual templates are PHPTAL templates. So the Adapter class will give the PHPTAL template engine a Smarty "skin." With one exception, the methods we'll write are the most basic ones needed to display a simple HTML page based on a template. If we need more methods, we can add them later.

We'll start by defining the PHPTAL template interface formally. As always in PHP, declaring the interface is not strictly needed, but it gives us a useful overview of what we're doing.

```
interface SmartyTemplateInterface {
    public function fetch($template);
    public function display($template);
    public function assign($name,$value);
    public function get_template_vars();
}
```

The Adapter reflects the conceptual differences between the two template engines. A Smarty object requires no constructor arguments, so we can skip the constructor in this class. The PHPTAL_Template object has to be constructed, but it demands the template file name in the constructor. Since the Smarty interface does not supply the file name until we generate the output using `fetch()` or `display()`, we have to wait until then before constructing the PHPTAL template object. Listing 7.2 shows the Adapter class.

Listing 7.2 Adapter to make PHPTAL templates conform to the Smarty interface

```
class SmartySkin implements SmartyTemplateInterface {
    private $vars = array();

    public function assign($name,$value) {
        $this->vars[$name] = $value;    ←——❶  Store variables before
    }                                          PHPTAL object exists

    public function fetch($template) {
        $phptal = new PHPTAL_Template(                    ❷  Create and
                str_replace('.tpl','.html',$template));      execute
        $phptal->setAll($this->vars);                        PHPTAL object
        return $phptal->execute();
    }

    public function get_template_vars($name=FALSE) {     ❸  Emulate
        if ($name) return $this->vars[$name];               Smarty's
        return $this->vars;                                 variable getter
    }

    public function display($template) {        ❹  PHPTAL has no
        echo $this->fetch($template);              display()
    }                                              method
}
```

❶ Since we don't create the PHPTAL object before it's time to generate the output, we have to store the variables in the meantime. This is done using the Smarty-compatible `assign()` method. We keep the variable in the `$vars` array belonging to the Adapter.

❷ It's only when the `fetch()` method is called that we have the template file name available. So now we can create the PHPTAL_Template object. Since the Smarty and the PHPTAL templates normally have different file extensions, we convert from one (`.tpl`) to the other (`.html`). Now we can copy the variables from the Adapter class to the template. PHPTAL has a convenient `setAll()` method to do this. Since we now have both the template filename and the variables set, we can generate the output by using PHPTAL's `execute()` method.

❸ `get_template_vars()` is Smarty's way of retrieving a variable that has been set in the Smarty object. We emulate its behavior by returning a specific variable if its name has been specified, or the whole array of variables if it hasn't.

❹ PHPTAL has no `display()` method, but it's trivial to implement by echoing the output from the `fetch()` method.

7.2.3 Adapters with multiple classes

Sometimes we have to do even more tricks to get an adapter to work. If the API we're emulating uses more than one class, we may have to emulate all of them. One example is the opposite process of the one we just did. If we want to give a Smarty template a PHPTAL skin, we run into a different kind of challenge: The PHPTAL template class has no way of retrieving the variables you've set in it. Instead, you have to get an object called a Context from the template object and get the variables from that object:

```
$context = $template->getContext();
$message = $context->get('message');
```

This might not be a problem in normal use of the template engine, but if we have used the Context object (testing is a likely use for it), we might want it in the adapter interface.

Let's see how we can do that. Here is the PHPTAL interface:

```
interface PhptalTemplateInterface {
    public function set($name,$value);
    public function execute();
    public function getContext();
}
```

Now for the Adapter itself. Listing 7.3 shows how the Adapter uses a Smarty object internally to do the actual work, while appearing from the outside as a PHPTAL template with limited functionality.

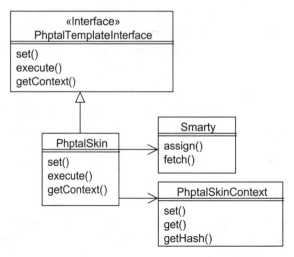

Figure 7.3   Adapting Smarty to make it look like PHPTAL

Figure 7.3 is a class diagram showing the structure of the design. The interface, the PhptalSkin class, and the PhptalContext class all belong to the adapter, but all the real work is done by the humble Smarty class.

In the real world, the Smarty class is not so humble. This example is simplified to utilize only a few basic methods of the PHPTAL interface and the Smarty object. We have shown only two methods of the around 40 methods of the Smarty object. In practice, we would be likely to implement more of them, although in most projects there is no good reason to implement more than we actually need.

Listing 7.3 shows how the PhptalSkin class is implemented.

Listing 7.3   Adapter to make Smarty templates conform to the PHPTAL interface

```
class PhptalSkin implements PhptalTemplateInterface {
    private $smarty;
    private $path;
    private $context;
    public function __construct($path) {
        $this->smarty = new Smarty;
        $this->path = str_replace('.html','.tpl',$path);
        $this->context = new PhptalSkinContext;
    }

    public function execute() {
        return $this->smarty->fetch($this->path);
    }

    public function set($name,$value) {
        $escaped = htmlentities($value,ENT_QUOTES,'UTF-8');
        $this->smarty->assign($name,$escaped);
        $this->context->set($name,$escaped);
    }
```

❶ Create Smarty and Context objects

❷ Execute with template name

❸ Set value in Smarty and Context

```
    public function getContext() {
        return $this->context;     ◁────    getContext() as
    }                                   ❹   with real
}                                           PHPTAL
```

❶ The Smarty object is the Smarty template engine, the object that's going to do the real work. The PHPTAL interface requires that we specify the template file when we construct the template object. Since the Smarty object does not store the name of the template file, we have to keep it in the Adapter. The file name conversion is the inverse of the file name conversion from the previous Adapter.

Since a PHPTAL template returns a PHPTAL_Context object, the adapter needs an object that does a similar job without being an actual PHPTAL_Context object. For this purpose, we use a PhptalSkinContext object. We'll take a look at the class in a moment. It is just a simple variable container, and for now, all we need to know about it is that we can store variables in it with a set() method.

❷ The execute() method calls Smarty's equivalent, the fetch() method. Since the fetch() method requires the template name (or more specifically a template resource), we give it the template name that was supplied to the constructor.

While we're at it, let's change the way the assign() method works to make it more secure. All output should be escaped to prevent cross-site scripting (XSS) attacks. With Smarty, this means you either have to escape the strings before adding them to the template or explicitly use Smarty's escaping features. The problem is that the escaping in this example is primitive and not applicable to anything beyond simple values. It would have to be made much more sophisticated to allow it to work in existing applications. The subject of template security will be discussed further in chapter 13.

❸ The set() method sets the corresponding variable in the Smarty object. It also sets the variable in the context object so that it can be retrieved in the PHPTAL fashion.

An alternative way to implement this would be to store the variables in the Adapter and to copy all of them into the Context or Smarty object when they're needed. The current solution duplicates the data, but there is no reason right now why that should cause problems, so there is probably little practical difference between the alternatives.

❹ We can use the getContext() method to return the PhptalSkinContext object, so that we can retrieve the variables in the same way as with a real PHPTAL_Context object.

Listing 7.4 shows the PhptalSkinContext class. This is just a thin wrapper around a PHP array.

```
class PhptalSkinContext {
    private $vars = array();

    public function set($name,$value) {
        $this->vars[$name] = $value;
    }

    public function get($name) {
        return $this->vars[$name];
    }

    public function getHash() {
        return $this->vars;
    }
}
```

The class has a subset of the interface of PHPTAL_Context class. `get()` retrieves a single variable; `getHash()` retrieves all of them.

7.2.4 Adapting to a generic interface

You may ask, why not use inheritance? Why not let the Adapter be a child class of Smarty or PHPTAL? In fact, the Gang of Four book indicates this as an option. The effect of letting the first of our Adapters inherit from the Smarty class will be to allow the use of any Smarty method that's not in the PHPTAL interface. The Adapter's interface then becomes a somewhat messy mixture of Smarty and PHPTAL methods. But if we're switching to Smarty anyway, that might be just as well. Developers could gradually switch to using the Smarty interface.

But there is one more consideration: in Uncle Bob's terminology, we've now taken the first bullet. We were cruising happily along, using PHPTAL templates for all our web pages, and suddenly someone hits us with the requirement to use Smarty instead. We know now that a certain kind of change can happen: switching template engines. And if it happens once, it could happen again. So what we probably want to do is to protect the system from further changes of the same type. The way to go in this case would be to move toward a generic template interface, which would not be identical to either the PHPTAL interface or the Smarty interface. The generic interface should be as easy as possible to adapt to a new template engine. In other words, it should be easy to write an Adapter that has the generic interface and delegates the real work to the new template engine.

So far, we have at least some indication of what's needed for a generic Template-Adapter interface. It will need to have an interface that re-creates the functionality of both the PHPTAL and the Smarty objects. We don't want to have to use fancy tricks such as the Context object. So the interface should have a method to get variables. It should also have a `display()` method. And the need to convert the template name is a tricky thing that needs to be smoothed over. If we assume that the template only needs a single template file name in some form, the generic interface might just require the file name without the extension and add the extension automatically.

Adapter is a pattern that works by wrapping an object in another. A Decorator also does that, but for a different purpose.

7.3 DECORATOR

Adapters are the tortillas of object-oriented programming. You wrap an object in an Adapter, and it looks completely different but tastes almost the same. Decorator is another kind of wrapper, but the intent is not to change the interface. Instead, a Decorator changes the way an object works—somewhat—but leaves its appearance relatively intact. So it's more like sprinkling salt on the dish: the result tastes slightly different, but looks similar.

But technically, what Adapters and Decorators do is mostly the same: you wrap the decorator around another object. A term that has been used to describe this principle is Handle-Body. There is a "Handle" object that wraps a "Body" object.

For an example, we'll use a so-called Resource Decorator for a database connection. Then we'll discuss how to make sure we can add multiple Decorators to an object.

7.3.1 Resource Decorator

For an example, let's try a Resource Decorator [Nock]. This is typically used to add extra behavior to a database connection. Let's say we're dissatisfied with the way PEAR DB handles errors. We want to use PHP 5 exceptions instead. One way to achieve that is to wrap the PEAR DB connection in a class that generates the exceptions. We'll start with a simple example using only one decorator (see listing 7.5).

> **Listing 7.5 Decorator that wraps a PEAR DB object and generates exceptions if errors occur**

```
class PearExceptionDecorator {
    private $connection;
    public function __construct($connection) {        Use PEAR DB  ❶
        $this->connection = $connection;                 connection
        if (DB::isError($this->connection)) {
            throw new Exception($this->connection->getMessage());
        }
    }

    public function query($sql) {                    query() method with  ❷
        $result = $this->connection->query($sql);       error handling
        if (DB::isError($result)) {
            throw new Exception($result->getMessage()."\n".$sql);
        }
        return $result;
    }
}
```

```
        public function nextID($name) {
            return $this->connection->nextID($name);
        }
    }
```

❸ One example of simple delegation

❶ The constructor accepts a PEAR DB object as an argument. This means that we can create our decorated connection as follows:

```
$connection = new PearExceptionDecorator(DB::Connect(
    'mysql://user:password@localhost/webdatabase'));
```

Passing the "Body" object in the constructor is typical of decorators, but in this simple case, it would work even if we instantiated the PEAR DB connection inside the constructor.

❷ The query() method calls the PEAR DB connection's query() method and throws an exception if there is an error (an SQL syntax error, for example).

❸ The nextID() method just delegates to the PEAR DB object. This method is really just one example of many methods that are available from the PEAR DB object that we don't need to change. To get the decorated object to work like the original object, we might want to implement a lot of these delegating methods.

In this case, there are at least two benefits to using a Decorator. One is that we can't simply change the PEAR package to add this feature to it. (Strictly speaking, we can change it, since it's open source, but then we have to maintain it afterward, and that's not worth the trouble.) The other is that our way of handling exceptions is more likely to change than the PEAR package. The PEAR package is relatively stable; it has to be, because it has lots of users. The Decorator might change because we need a different kind of error handling. Perhaps we want to use exceptions in a somewhat more sophisticated way, using a more specific exception class, for instance. Perhaps we want compatibility with PHP 4. We could have a similar decorator that would work in PHP 4, using some error handling or logging capability that is not exception based, and just swap the decorators depending on the PHP version.

7.3.2 Decorating and redecorating

The previous example is the simplest form of a decorator. The more advanced thing to do is to decorate and "redecorate." Since the decorated object works in a way that's similar to the original object, you can apply more than one Decorator to add different responsibilities. For example, if we had a Decorator to add logging to the connection, we could do something like this.

```
$connection = new PearLoggingDecorator(
    new PearExceptionDecorator(
    DB::Connect('mysql://user:password@localhost/webdatabase')));
```

But what if we have a lot of delegating methods—such as the next ID() method in the Decorator we've just seen? We don't want to duplicate all those in both Decorators. So we'll make a parent class to keep the delegating methods in (see listing 7.6).

Listing 7.6   Decorator parent class to make redecoration easier

```
abstract class PearDecorator {
    protected $connection;

    public function __construct($connection) {
        $this->connection =  $connection;
    }

    public function query($sql) {
        return $this->connection->query($sql);
    }

    public function nextID($name) {
        return $this->connection->nextID($name);
    }
}
```

As in the previous example, a practical version of the class is likely to contain many more delegating methods.

Any decorator for a PEAR DB object can now be derived from the abstract parent class. We need only override the methods we want to change. Figure 7.4 shows this simple inheritance hierarchy. The parent class is abstract, but its methods are not. Any method that is not implemented in a child Decorator will work like the method in the decorated object. The Logger class is just a helper for the logging Decorator.

Therefore, the PearExceptionDecorator no longer needs the next ID() method or any other method it doesn't add anything to. This is shown in listing 7.7.

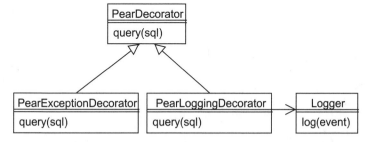

Figure 7.4   Using a parent class for Decorators to provide default method implementations and to make sure the Decorators are compatible

```php
class PearExceptionDecorator extends PearDecorator {
    public function __construct($connection) {
        $this->connection = $connection;
        if (DB::isError($this->connection)) {
            throw new Exception($this->connection->getMessage());
        }
    }

    public function query($sql) {
        $result = $this->connection->query($sql);
        if (DB::isError($result)) {
            throw new Exception($result->getMessage()."\n".$sql);
        }
        return $result;
    }

}
```

Now we can implement the logging Decorator using the same procedure. What we want to log will depend on the circumstances, but for the example, let's log every query. Perhaps we would want to do that while our application is in the testing stages. When it becomes stable, we can remove the Decorator. A more conventional alternative would be to disable logging; the advantage of the Decorator is that we can get rid of the logging code entirely so it doesn't clutter the application.

Listing 7.8 shows the logging Decorator.

```php
class PearLoggingDecorator extends PearDecorator {
    private $logger;
    public function __construct($connection) {
        $this->connection = $connection;
        $this->logger = Log::factory(
                'file', '/tmp/out.log', 'SQL');
    }

    public function query($sql) {
        $this->logger->notice('Query: '.$sql);
        $result = $this->connection->query($sql);
        return $result;
    }
}
```

We are using the PEAR Log package. In the constructor, we store a logger object in an instance variable. When we call the query() method on the decorated connection, it logs the SQL statement as a notice before executing the query.

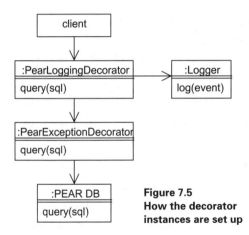

**Figure 7.5
How the decorator
instances are set up**

While figure 7.4 illustrates the relationships between the classes, the configuration of objects at runtime is something else. This is shown in the UML object diagram in figure 7.5. The colons (:PearLoggingDecorator) indicate that we are dealing with objects—instances of the named classes—rather than with the classes as such.

The PearLoggingDecorator uses the PearExceptionDecorator, which uses the PEAR DB object. The `query()` call is passed from the top to the bottom of this chain, and the results are passed back up.

NOTE   There is no deeper meaning to the words "top" and "bottom," "up" and "down" in this context. They just refer to the placement of the objects in the diagram. This placement is arbitrary.

The decorators are set up in an order that seems logical, but if we swapped the two decorators, it would still work, and we might not notice the difference.

From a pattern skeptic point of view, we may ask some critical questions when a Decorator is suggested. Is the decorator really needed? Do the component and the Decorator really need to be separate, or can they be merged into one class? You might want to keep them separate because the Decorator's behavior is not always needed, or to comply with the single-responsibility principle: if the decorator's behavior is likely to change for different reasons than the component's. Resource Decorators may be considered an example of this: the software that handles the database might change, but it's probably more stable than what you are adding to it.

Strategy is for changing and replacing behavior. Decorator is a way to add behavior. When we want to stop a behavior from happening, we can either write a plain old conditional statement or use a Null Object.

7.4   NULL OBJECT

"Don't turn on the dark light," my five-year-old son reproaches me when I turn out the lights in his room. The mental model revealed by this statement is an interesting and striking simplification of the physics involved. Instead of being opposites, he sees turning the light off and on as variations of the same process. There's a bright and a dark light, and you can turn either one on. In object-oriented lingo, both the bright light class and the dark light class have a `turnOn()` operation or method. Like the `dress()` method of the Boy and Girl classes in chapter 4, this is polymorphism, a case of different actions being represented as basically the same.

In this section, we'll see how Null Objects work, and then discover how to use them with the Strategy pattern.

7.4.1   Mixing dark and bright lights

A Null Object is the dark light of our object-oriented world. It looks like an ordinary object, but doesn't do anything real. Its *only* task is to look like an ordinary object so you don't have to write an `if` statement to distinguish between an object and a non-object. Consider the following:

```
$user = UserFinder::findWithName('Zaphod Beeblebrox');
$user->disable();
```

If the UserFinder returns a non-object such as NULL or FALSE, PHP will scold us:

```
Fatal error: Call to a member function disable() on a non-object
in user.php on line 2
```

To avoid this, we need to add a conditional statement:

```
$user = UserFinder::findWithName('Zaphod Beeblebrox');
if (is_object($user))
    $user->disable();
```

But if $user is a Null Object that has `disable()` method, there is no need for a conditional test. So if the UserFinder returns a Null Object instead of a non-object, the error won't happen.

A simple NullUser class could be implemented like this:

```
class NullUser implements User {
    public function disable() { }
    public function isNull() { return TRUE; }
}
```

The class is oversimplified, since it implements only one method that might be of real use in the corresponding user object: `disable()`. The idea is that the real user class, or classes, would also implement the interface called User. So, in practice, there would be many more methods.

7.4.2   Null Strategy objects

A slightly more advanced example might be a Null Strategy object. You have one object that's configured with another object that decides much of its behavior, but in some cases the object does not need that behavior at all.

An alternative to using the Logging decorator shown earlier might be to build logging into the connection class itself (assuming we have control over it). The connection class would then contain a logger object to do the logging. The pertinent parts of such a connection class might look something like this:

```
class Connection {
    public function __construct($url,$logger) {
        $this->url = $url;
        $this->logger = $logger;
        // More initialization
        // ...
    }

    public function query($sql) {
        $this->logger->log('Query: '.$sql);

        // Run the query
        // ...
    }
}
```

Since this class accepts a logger object as input when it's created, we can configure it with any logger object we please. And if we want to disable logging, we can pass it a null logger object:

```
$connection = new Connection(
    mysql://user:password@localhost/webdatabase,
    new NullLogger
);
```

A NullLogger class could be as simple as this:

```
class NullLogger implements Logger{
    public function log {}
}
```

Figure 7.6 shows the relationships between these classes. The interface may be represented formally using the `interface` keyword or an abstract class, or it may be implicit using duck typing as described in chapter 4.

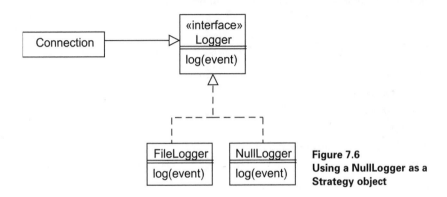

Figure 7.6
Using a NullLogger as a Strategy object

The PEAR Log package has a Null logger class called Logger_null that is somewhat more sophisticated than the one we just saw.

Although a Null Object might do something such as return another Null Object, frequently it's about doing nothing at all. The next pattern, Iterator, is about doing something several times.

7.5   ITERATOR

An *iterator* is an object whose job it is to iterate, usually returning elements one by one from some source. Iterators are popular. One reason may be that it's easy to understand what they do, in a certain limited way, that is. It is relatively easy to see how they work and how to implement one. But it's less obvious how and when they're useful compared to the alternatives, such as stuffing data into a plain PHP array and using a foreach loop to iterate.

In this section, we will see how iterators work, look at some good and bad reasons to use them, contrast them with plain arrays, and see how we can improve iterators further by using the Standard PHP Library (SPL).

7.5.1   How iterators work

An iterator is an object that allows you to get and process one element at a time. A while loop using an SPL (Standard PHP Library) iterator has this form:

```
while ($iterator->valid()) {
    $element = $iterator->current();
    // Process $element
    $iterator->next();
}
```

There are various interfaces for iterators, having different methods that do different things. However, there is some overlap. Above all, to be useful at all, every iterator needs some way of getting the next element and some way to signal when to stop. Table 7.1 compares the SPL iterator interface with the standard Java iterator interface and the interface used in the Gang of Four [Gang of Four] book.

Table 7.1   Comparing three different iterator interfaces

	Gang of Four iterator	Java iterator	PHP SPL iterator
Move to next element	Next()	next()	next()
Return the current element	CurrentItem()		current()
Check for end of iteration	IsDone()	hasNext()	valid()
Start over at beginning	First()		rewind()
Return key for current element			key()
Remove current element from collection		remove()	

7.5.2 Good reasons to use iterators

Three are three situations in which an iterator is undeniably useful in PHP:

- When you use a package or library that returns an iterator
- When there is no way to get all the elements of a collection in one call
- When you want to process a potentially vast number of elements

In the first case, you have no choice but to use the iterator you've been given. Problem 3 will happen, for example, when you return data from a database table. A database table can easily contain millions of elements and gigabytes of data, so the alternative—reading all of them into an array—may consume far too much memory. (On the other hand, if you know the table is small, reading it into an array is perfectly feasible.)

Another example would be reading the results from a search engine. In this case, problems 2 and 3 might both be present: you have no way of getting all the results from the search engine without asking repeatedly, and if you did have a way of getting all of them, it would far too much to handle in a simple array.

In addition to the undeniably good reasons to use iterators, there are other reasons that may be questioned, because there are alternatives to using iterators. The most important alternative is using plain arrays. In the previous situations, using plain arrays is not a practical alternative. In other situations, they may be more suitable than iterators.

7.5.3 Iterators versus plain arrays

The general argument in favor of iterators is that they

- Encapsulate iteration
- Provide a uniform interface to it

Encapsulation means that the code that uses an iterator does not have to know the details of the process of iteration. The client code can live happily ignoring those details, whether they involve reading from a database, walking a data structure recursively, or generating random data.

The *uniform interface* means that iterators are pluggable. You can replace an iterator with a different one, and as long as the single elements are the same, the client code will not know the difference.

Both of these are advantages of using iterators. On the other hand, both advantages can be had by using plain arrays instead.

Consider the following example. We'll assume we have a complex data structure such as a tree structure (this is an example that is sometimes used to explain iterators).

```
$structure = new VeryComplexDataStructure;
for($iterator = $structure->getIterator();
    $iterator->valid();
    $iterator->next()) {
    echo $iterator->current() . "\n";
}
```

The simpler way of doing it would be to return an array from the data structure instead of an iterator:

```
$structure = new VeryComplexDataStructure;
$array = $structure->getArray();
foreach ($array as $element) {
    echo $value . "\n";
}
```

It's simpler and more readable; furthermore, the code required to return the array will typically be significantly simpler and leaner than the iterator code, mostly because there is no need to keep track of position as we walk the data structure, collecting elements into an array. As the Gang of Four say, "External iterators can be difficult to implement over recursive aggregate structures like those in the Composite pattern, because a position in the structure may span many levels of nested aggregates." In other words, iterating internally in the structure is easier.

In addition, PHP arrays have another significant advantage over iterators: you can use the large range of powerful array functions available in PHP to sort, filter, search, and otherwise process the elements of the array.

On the other hand, when we create an array from a data structure, we need to make a pass through that structure. In other words, we need to iterate through all the elements. Even though that iteration process is typically simpler than what an iterator does, it takes time. And the `foreach` loop is a second round of iteration, which also takes time. If the iterator is intelligently done, it won't start iterating through the elements until you ask it to iterate. Also, when we extract the elements from the data structure into the array, the array will consume memory (unless the individual elements are references).

But these considerations are not likely to be important unless the number of elements is very large. The guideline, as always, is to avoid premature optimization (optimizing before you know you need to). And when you do need it, work on the things that contribute most to slow performance.

7.5.4 SPL iterators

The Standard PHP Library (SPL) is built into PHP 5. Its primary benefit—from a design point of view—is to allow us to use iterators in a `foreach` loop as if they were arrays. There are also a number of built-in iterator classes. For example, the built-in DirectoryIterator class lets us treat a directory as if it were an array of objects representing files. This code lists the files in the `/usr/local/lib/php` directory.

```
$iter = new DirectoryIterator('/usr/local/lib/php');
foreach($iter as $current) {
    echo $current->getFileName()."\n";
}
```

In chapter 19, we will see how to implement a decorator for a Mysqli result set to make it work as an SPL iterator.

7.5.5 How SPL helps us solve the iterator/array conflict

If you choose to use plain arrays to iterate, you might come across a case in which the volume of data increases to the point where you need to use an iterator instead. This might tempt you to use a complex iterator implementation over simple arrays when this is not really needed. With SPL, you have the choice of using plain arrays in most cases and changing them to iterators when and if that turns out to be necessary, since you can make your own iterator that will work with a foreach loop just like the ready-made iterator classes. In the VeryComplexDataStructure example, we can do something like this:

```
$structure = new VeryComplexDataStructure;
$iterator = $structure->getIterator();
foreach($iterator as $element) {
    echo $element . "\n";
}
```

As you can see, the foreach loop is exactly like the foreach loop that iterates over an array. The array has simply been replaced with an iterator. So if you start off by returning a plain array from the VeryComplexDataStructure, you can replace it with an iterator later without changing the foreach loop. There are two things to watch out for, though: you would need a variable name that's adequate for both the array and the iterator, and you have to avoid processing the array with array functions, since these functions won't work with the iterator.

The previous example has a hypothetical VeryComplexDataStructure class. The most common complex data structure in web programming is a tree structure. There is a pattern for tree structures as well; it's called Composite.

7.6 COMPOSITE

Composite is one of the more obvious and useful design patterns. A Composite is typically an object-oriented way of representing a tree structure such as a hierarchical menu or a threaded discussion forum with replies to replies.

Still, sometimes the usefulness of a composite structure is not so obvious. The Composite pattern allows us to have any number of levels in a hierarchy. But sometimes the number of levels is fixed at two or three. Do we still want to make it a Composite, or do we make it less abstract? The question might be whether the Composite simplifies the code or makes it more complex. We obviously don't want a Composite if a simple array is adequate. On the other hand, with three levels, a Composite is likely to be much more flexible than an array of arrays and simpler than an alternative object-oriented structure.

In this section, we'll work with a hierarchical menu example. First, we'll see how the tree structure can be represented as a Composite in UML diagrams. Then we'll implement the most essential feature of a Composite structure: the ability to add child nodes to any node that's not a leaf. (In this case, that means you can add submenus or menu options to any menu.) We'll also implement a so-called fluent interface to make the Composite easier to use in programming. We'll round off the implementation by using recursion to mark the path to a menu option. Finally, we'll discuss the fact that the implementation could be more efficient.

7.6.1 Implementing a menu as a Composite

Let's try an example: a menu for navigation on a web page such as the example in figure 7.4. Even if we have only one set of menu headings, there are still implicitly three levels of menus, since the structure as a whole is a menu. This makes it a strong candidate for a Composite structure.

The menu has only what little functionality is needed to illustrate the Composite. We want the structure itself and the ability to mark the current menu option and the path to it. If we've chosen Events and then Movies, both Events and Movies will be shown with a style that distinguishes them from the rest of the menu, as shown in figure 7.7.

First, let's sketch the objects for the first two submenus of this menu. Figure 7.8 shows how it can be represented. Each menu has a set of menu or menu option objects stored in instance variables, or more likely, in one instance variable which is an array of objects. To represent the fact that some of the menus and menu options are marked, we have a simple Boolean (TRUE/

Figure 7.7   A simple navigation menu

FALSE flag). In the HTML code, we will want to represent this as a CSS class, but we're keeping the HTML representation out of this for now to keep it simple. Furthermore, each menu or menu option has a string for the label. And there is a menu object to represent the menu as a whole. Its label will not be shown on the web page, but it's practical when we want to handle the menu.

A class diagram for the Composite class structure to represent menus and menu options is shown in figure 7.9 It is quite a bit more abstract, but should be easier to grasp based on the previous illustration. Figure 7.8 is a snapshot of a particular set of object instances at a particular time; figure 7.9 represents the class structure and the operations needed to generate the objects.

There are three different bits of functionality in this design:

- Each menu and each menu option has a *label*, the text that is displayed on the web page.
- The add() method of the Menu class is the one method that is absolutely required for generating a Composite tree structure.
- The rest of the methods and attributes are necessary to make it possible to mark the current menu and menu option.

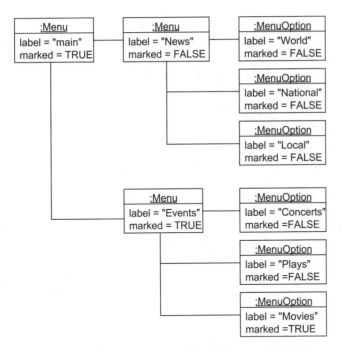

Figure 7.8 **An object structure for the first two submenus**

The two methods `hasMenuOptionWithId()` and `markPathToMenuOp-tion()` are abstract in the MenuComponent class. This implies that they must exist in the Menu and MenuOption classes, even though they are not shown in these classes in the diagram.

The leftmost connection from Menu to MenuComponent implies the fact—which is clear in figure 7.8 as well—that a Menu object can have any number of menu components (Menu or MenuOption objects).

Methods to get and set the attributes are not included in the illustration.

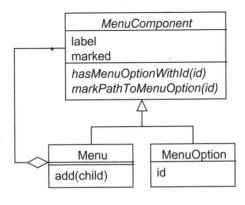

Figure 7.9
A Composite used to represent a menu with menu options in which the current menu option can be marked

7.6.2   The basics

Moving on to the code, we will start with the MenuComponent class. This class expresses what's similar between menus and menu options (listing 7.9). Both menus and menu options need a label and the ability to be marked as current.

> **Listing 7.9   Abstract class to express similarities between menus and menu options**

```
abstract class MenuComponent {
    protected $marked = FALSE;              Set and retrieve  ❶
    protected $label;                         marked state

    public function mark() { $this->marked = TRUE; }
    public function isMarked() { return $this->marked; }
                                                          Accessors
    public function getLabel() { return $this->label; }  ❷ for the
    public function setLabel($label) { $this->label = $label; }  label

    abstract public function hasMenuOptionWithId($id);
                                                         Marking
    abstract public function markPathToMenuOption($id);  ❸ operation
}
```

❶ mark() and isMarked() let us set and retrieve the state of being marked as current.

❷ We have simple accessors for the label. We will also set the label in the constructor, but we're leaving that part of it to the child classes.

❸ markPathToMenuOption() will be the method for marking the path; both the menu object and the menu option object have to implement it. hasMenuOption-WithId() exists to support the marking operation.

To implement the most basic Composite structure, all we need is an add() method to add a child to a node (a menu or menu option in this case).

```
class Menu extends MenuComponent {
    protected $marked = FALSE;
    protected $label;
    private $children = array();

    public function __construct($label) {
        $this->label = $label;
    }

    public function add($child) {
        $this->children[] = $child;
    }
}
```

`add()` does not know or care whether the object being added is a menu or a menu option. We can build an arbitrarily complex structure with this alone:

```
$menu = new Menu('News');
$submenu = new Menu('Events');
$menu->add($submenu);
$submenu = new Menu('Concerts');
$menu->add($submenu);
```

7.6.3 A fluent interface

This reuse of temporary variables is rather ugly. Fortunately, it's easy to achieve what's known as a *fluent interface*:

```
$menu->add(new Menu('Events'))->add(new Menu('Concerts'));
```

All we have to do is return the child after adding it:

```
public function add($child) {
    $this->children[] = $child;
    return $child;
}
```

Or even simpler:

```
public function add($child) {
    return $this->children[] = $child;
}
```

A mentioned, this is all we need to build arbitrarily complex structures. In fact, if the menu option is able to store a link URL, we already have something that could possibly be useful in a real application.

7.6.4 Recursive processing

But we haven't finished our study of the Composite pattern until we've tried using it for recursion. Our original requirement was to be able to mark the path to the currently selected menu option. To achieve that, we need to identify the menu option. Let's assume that the menu option has an ID, and that the HTTP request contains this ID. So we have the menu option ID and want to mark the path to the menu option with that ID. Unfortunately, the top node of our composite menu structure cannot tell us where the menu option with that ID is located.

We'll do what might be the Simplest Thing That Could Possibly Work: search for it. The first step is to give any node in the structure the ability to tell us whether it contains that particular menu option. The Menu object can do that by iterating over its children and asking all of them whether they have the menu option. If one of them does, it returns TRUE, if none of them do, it returns FALSE:

```
class Menu extends MenuComponent...
    public function hasMenuOptionWithId($id) {
        foreach ($this->children as $child) {
            if ($child->hasMenuOptionWithId($id)) return TRUE;
```

```
        }
        return FALSE;
    }
}
```

The recursion has to end somewhere. Therefore, we need the equivalent method in the MenuOption class to do something different. It simply checks whether its ID is the one we are looking for, and returns TRUE if it is:

```
class MenuOption extends MenuComponent {
    protected $marked = FALSE;
    protected $label;
    private $id;

    public function __construct($label,$id) {
        $this->label = $label;
        $this->id = $id;
    }
    public function hasMenuOptionWithId($id) {
        return $id == $this->id;
    }
}
```

Now we're ready to mark the path.

```
class Menu extends MenuComponent...
    public function markPathToMenuOption($id) {
        if (!$this->hasMenuOptionWithId($id)) return FALSE;
        $this->mark();
        foreach ($this->children as $child) {
            $child->markPathToMenuOption($id);
        }
    }
}
```

If this menu contains the menu option with the given ID, it marks itself and passes the task on to its children. Only the one child that contains the desired menu option will be marked.

The MenuOption class also has to implement the markPathToMenuOption() method. It's quite simple:

```
class MenuOption extends MenuComponent...
    public function markPathToMenuOption($id) {
        if ($this->hasMenuOptionWithId($id)) $this->mark();
    }
}
```

But our traversal algorithm is not the most efficient one. We're traversing parts of the tree repeatedly. Do we need to change that?

7.6.5   Is this inefficient?

We have deliberately sacrificed efficiency in favor of readability, since the data structure will never be very large. The implementation uses one method (hasMenuOptionWithId) to answer a question and another (markPathToMenuOption) to make a change. This is a good idea, which is why there is a refactoring to achieve this separation, called *Separate Query from Modifier*.

To make it slightly faster, we could have let the first method return the child that contains the menu option we're searching for. That would have enabled us to avoid the second round of recursion. But it would also have made the intent of the `has-MenuOptionWithId()` method more complex and therefore harder to understand. It would have been premature optimization.

And this premature optimization would have involved a premature, low-quality decision. If we did want to optimize the algorithm, approaching optimization as a task in itself, we should be looking at more alternatives. For example, we could do the search, have it return a path to the menu option as a sequence of array indexes, and then follow the path. Or we could do it with no recursion at all if we kept a list of all menu options indexed by ID and added references back to the parents in the composite structure. Starting with the menu option, we could traverse the path up to the root node, marking the nodes along the way.

One thing the Composite pattern does is to hide the difference between one and many. The Composite, containing many elements, can have the same methods as a single element. Frequently, the client need not know the difference. In chapter 17, we will see how this works in the context of input validation. A validator object may have a `validate()` method that works the same way whether it is a simple validator or a complex one that applies several different criteria.

The Composite View pattern (which is the main subject of chapter 14) is related, though not as closely as you might think.

7.7   SUMMARY

While design principles are approximate guidelines, design patterns are more like specific recipes or blueprints; they cannot be used mindlessly. To apply them, we need to understand where, how, and why they're useful. We need to look at context, consider alternatives, tweak the specifics, and use the object-oriented principles in our decision-making.

We have seen a small selection of design patterns. All of them are concerned with creating pluggable components. Strategy is the way to configure an object's behavior by adding a pluggable component. Adapter takes a component that is not pluggable and makes it pluggable. Decorator adds features without impairing pluggability. Null Object is a component that does nothing, but can be substituted for another to prevent a behavior from happening without interfering with the smooth running of the system. Iterator is a pluggable repetition engine that can even be a replacement for an array. Composite is a way to plug more than one component into a socket that's designed for just one.

In the next chapter, we will use date and time handling as a vehicle for making the context and the alternatives for design principles and patterns clearer.

CHAPTER 8

Design how-to: date and time handling

Applying object-oriented principles and patterns tends to be more art than science, more improvisation than ritual, more understanding than precise skill. At worst, it's like movie weddings. Real weddings are notoriously predictable and strictly organized. But in movie weddings, shock and awe is the rule: someone makes a blunder like saying "your awful wedded wife," the bride or the groom runs away, the wedding guests start fighting, or worse.

We want to avoid making software that acts like a runaway bride. Therefore, we want to learn to handle all the discrepancies and unexpected twists. It comes with experience; you have to try it out, look at examples in a real context, and think long and hard about them. How does everything relate? What are the alternatives? What are the consequences of these alternatives? To help us do this, we'll study a well-known domain that provides a more realistic context for some of the principles and patterns.

Exploring all the ins and outs of date and time handling is far too much material for a book chapter. But investigating some of the basics and finding out how to deal with them will shed some light on the design challenges involved and be helpful to us anytime we try to implement our own date and time objects, extend existing ones, or even just use an existing package without modification.

In this chapter, we will look at why we want to take an object-oriented approach to date and time handling. We'll discuss what abstractions and concepts need to be represented. Then we'll study a couple of important design challenges that arise in the process. Since date and time classes are prime candidates for reuse, we need to know how to deal with large-scale structure to understand how they can fit into an application. We also look at value objects; they are another object-oriented technique that is particularly useful in the date and time domain. Finally, we see the highlights of a possible implementation.

8.1 WHY OBJECT-ORIENTED DATE AND TIME HANDLING?

Date handling is difficult because calendars are fiendishly irregular. They were by no means designed with computing in mind.

FACT   Calendars are a mixture of ancient mathematics, religion and astronomy, not to mention politics. The heavens are irregular to start with, of course: The Earth completes an orbit around the Sun in approximately 365.24 times the amount of time it takes to revolve around its own axis. The ancients simplified this by pretending it was exactly 365 times. But then they made it difficult again by introducing weeks spanning across months and making the months unequal in length. The month of August supposedly has 31 days because the Roman senate decided that they couldn't give Emperor Augustus a month that was shorter than the one that was named for his predecessor Julius Caesar. (Wikipedia rudely spoils this excellent story by saying it is "almost certainly wrong," but that does not diminish the complexity of the subject.)

Fortunately, the built-in PHP data and time functions make things a lot easier for us. Many of the trickiest calculations are made easier. But it's also easy to underestimate the complexity of the task.

In this section, we'll look at just one example of how complex date and time handling can get. We'll also take a look at what we gain when we put an OO spin on date and time handling.

8.1.1 Easier, but not simpler

In procedural PHP applications, we typically work with a "Unix timestamp" that equals the number of seconds since January 1, 1970. Suppose you want to add a day to the timestamp. Since the timestamp is in seconds, it's tempting to try to add a day by adding the appropriate number of seconds:

```
$timestamp = mktime(23,30,0,3,24,2007);
echo strftime("%B %e",$timestamp)."\n";
$timestamp += 60*60*24;  // Add 24 hours
echo strftime("%B %e",$timestamp)."\n";
```

Unfortunately, this outputs the following:

```
March 24
March 26
```

We tried to add one day, but it seems we got two for the price of one. The reason is daylight saving time. The PHP date and time functions handle daylight saving time automatically. If daylight saving time begins on March 25, and you start in the hour before midnight on the previous day, you end up in the hour after midnight on March 26, because March 25 is only 23 hours long according to the clock.

This kind of difficulty indicates how procedural PHP code, although seemingly very logical, does not fully represent the logic inherent in date and time handling. This indicates a need to use objects to achieve greater flexibility and expressiveness. Let's explore what we can gain from an object-oriented approach.

8.1.2   OO advantages

In chapter 4, we went over a number of advantages of object orientation. Most of them apply to date and time handling.

Classes help us organize our program. The number of different calculations and manipulations is so large that having separate procedural functions for all of them would be confusing. Being able to sort out date and time functions from the rest by putting them in classes helps keep us from getting lost in the fog.

We can tell objects to do things. If you want to add something—say, a week—to a timestamp, trying to do it by calculating the number of seconds is often not sufficient, as the example in the previous section shows. At the very least, you need procedural functions for this kind of work.

In addition, we can hide different representations and give them a uniform interface. The best way to represent a point in time depends on the task at hand. If you represent time as a Unix timestamp, there are PHP functions that allow you to easily output it in the format you want. On the other hand, if you want to do calculations, it might be more appropriate to use separate numbers for the year, month, day of the month, hour, minute, and second. Or perhaps—if you're working with a number of days—you want to represent the date as the year and the day of the year? With objects, this format confusion can be hidden by letting the objects convert to whatever format is necessary.

We can bundle data. For example, the start time and end time of an interval can be stored and manipulated together as a unit.

We can reuse classes and objects. The complexity of date and time handling makes it hard to reuse procedural functions created for a specific application. It can be too hard to find the function you want, and if you do, perhaps it requires as input a date and time representation that is different from the one we have already.

Objects provide type safety. As mentioned in chapter 4, if we represent dates and times as objects, bugs will cause the code to fail faster and more obviously than if we represent them as numbers and strings that may be mistaken for something else.

We can give concepts a name. We can represent concepts such as date, time, duration, and interval with classes in a way that makes it clearer what the code is doing. Complex interactions become more meaningful and easier to understand.

But what concepts, specifically, and what names? This is the subject for the next section.

8.2 FINDING THE RIGHT ABSTRACTIONS

The concepts we use when programming date and time handling must be both more abstract and more precise than what we use in everyday life. We think we know exactly what a week is, but it's actually ambiguous. If the convention is that the week starts on Monday, a week could be a time span that starts at midnight on one Monday and ends at midnight the next Monday. But what about the time span that starts on Thursday at 11 a.m. and ends the next Thursday at the same time? Is that not a week as well?

Actually, these are at least two distinct meanings of the word *week*. If I say, "I will finish the project next week," I'm using the first of these two meanings: a week that starts on whatever day is "the first day of the week." If I say "I will finish the project in a week," or "a week from now," I'm probably using the other meaning: a week that starts right now. In everyday life, we juggle these meanings with no apparent problems. But computers are too stupid to do that, so we need a set of concepts that are precise enough for the computer, as intuitive as possible for us humans, and expressive enough to capture all the various things we want to tell the computer.

The most common date and time abstractions belong to two categories: representations of single times, and representations of time spans or intervals. In the rest of this section, we'll study these two categories in turn.

8.2.1 Single time representation: Time Point, Instant, DateAndTime

Martin Fowler has described an analysis pattern called Time Point [Fowler Time Point]. In his discussion of the pattern, he points out two different issues that make it more complex than it might seem: *precision* and *time zones*.

The typical time point representation in PHP is at a precision of one second. One of these might be represented as, for example, November 16 2006 3:05:45 p.m. But in business transactions, the time of day is sometimes irrelevant, and the only thing that matters is on which day an event (such as a payment) occurs. So what we need is a lower-precision object that only handles the date, November 16 2006. Figure 8.1 illustrates this ability of time points to have different precisions.

For that matter, a time point could be a year, a century, or (in principle) something even larger such as the Mesozoic era.

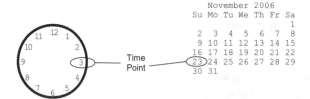

Figure 8.1
A point in time can be represented at different precisions, as a specific time of day or just the date.

Then there is higher-precision time, which might be necessary or convenient when short time spans matter or when several events can occur in the same second and need to be distinguished. Two obvious applications would be profiling an application or providing feedback to the user on how much time it took to process a request. In PHP, this is provided by the `microtime()` function.

In the open-source Java date and time package Joda Time, the standard implementation of a time point is the DateTime class. This class implements an interface called ReadableInstant. The only methods in the DateTime class are getters for time properties such as `getDayOfMonth()`.

To implement a date object with the time of day unspecified, how would we represent it? We could represent it as a time span from midnight to midnight. Or we could use just the time point at midnight at the start of the day. Joda has a separate class, DateMidnight, to express this. Or we can represent it as three numbers, specifying the year, month, and day of the month. The last option might be the most intuitive; for one thing, the implementation is clearly independent of time zones.

For the sake of simplifying the discussion in this chapter, we will limit our investigation as follows:

- No time zones. In practice, this means working with local time exclusively.

- Standard Gregorian calendar within whatever range the operating system will gracefully support. This means that we can use the built-in PHP date and time functions to do the actual calculations.

The alternative to using the built-in functions is to have some sort of pluggable engine to do the calculations. This is called an *engine* in PEAR Calendar, a *calendar* in the standard Java library, and a *chronology* in Joda Time. Joda Time has Chronology classes for interesting variations such as Coptic and Buddhist calendars.

As you can see, representing even a single time can be complex. Representing time spans adds yet another dimension of complexity. But knowing what concepts we are dealing with helps keep us out of trouble. We'll get specific about this in the next section.

8.2.2 Different kinds of time spans: Period, Duration, Date Range, Interval

Fowler also has another analysis pattern called Range, which simply means an object that defines a range of values by its end points. A special case of this is the Date Range, consisting of two Time Point objects.

This covers a lot of ground. You can represent days, weeks, months, or any time span as long as both the end points are defined. In Joda Time, a date range is called an *interval*.

Yet there is something missing; for instance, we may want to represent a "month" that has an unspecified start time, so that we can add a month to a given time point which is not known before the program runs. Something like this:

```
$monthlater = $now->add($month);
```

The $month in this expression is not a date range, since we're supposed to be able to add it to any time point. In other words, its start and end points are not fixed. So what object can represent this added time, the $month in this expression? One possibility is adding a number of seconds (or microseconds). This is known in Joda Time as a *duration*.

But since we're dealing with months, and months are irregular in duration, that won't work.

Another possibility is letting $month be a constant that defines the time unit. The Java Calendar class does this. Or even use a Month class that contains the information necessary to do the calculation.

But why have separate representations for the different time units when all we need is one class? We can do what Joda Time does. Joda Time has the concept of a *period*, which consists of a set of time fields; so for instance it can represent 6 years + 2 months + 15 days.

Using periods, $month in the previous example can be represented as a period with one month and zero years, weeks, days, hours, minutes, and seconds.

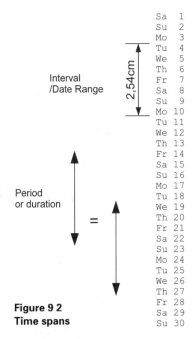

Figure 8.2 shows how an interval or date range has specific start and end points, while periods and durations are defined only by their size and can start anywhere.

The abundance of concepts in date and time handling creates a need for conversions between different representations. This in turn requires flexibility in how the objects are constructed. We will look at this next.

Figure 9 2
Time spans

8.3 ADVANCED OBJECT CONSTRUCTION

Constructing objects is an important subject in object-oriented design. In the simplest cases, plain constructors are all we need. But as we start creating more complex designs, constructors can become unmanageable. There are several distinct reasons why it's sometimes useful to have some more advanced construction tools in our toolbox:

- Construction can be complex just because of the complexity of the object being constructed.
- We might have different raw materials on hand depending on the situation. For example, as we will see shortly, date and time objects can be constructed from a Unix timestamp, a string, or other representations.
- We may want to configure an object differently depending on what we want it to do.
- We may want to encapsulate object creation so that we can change the creation process without affecting client code.

In this section, we'll see three different strategies to achieve this: creation methods, multiple constructors, and factory classes.

8.3.1 Using creation methods

A typical object construction challenge is to construct an object from several alternative representations. For instance, if we have a class representing a date and time, we might want to construct it from the Unix timestamp, an array of single values (year, month, day, hour, minute, second), a subset of this array (for example, year, month, and day; year, week number and day; year and day in year), a formatted human-readable date string, an object of the same type we're constructing, and so forth.

One way to do this is to have a single constructor method and use a `switch` statement or some other conditional construct to decide how to initialize the object. But this has a tendency to get messy. Another alternative is to use creation methods. This is pretty much a standard way of creating objects when something more than an ordinary constructor is required. Listing 8.1 shows how a class can use creation methods to construct a date and time object from different raw materials.

> **Listing 8.1 DateAndTime class using creation methods to allow different raw materials**

```
class DateAndTime {
    private $timestamp;
    public function __construct($timestamp=FALSE) {        ❶ Default to
        if (!$timestamp) $timestamp = time();                current date
        $this->timestamp = $timestamp;                       and time
    }
```

```
public function createFromDateAndTime(DateAndTime $datetime) {
    return new DateAndTime($datetime->getTimestamp());
}
public function createFromString($string) {
    return new DateAndTime(strtotime($string));
}
public function getTimestamp() {
    return $this->timestamp;
}
}
```

❸ Create DateAndTime object from string

❶ The constructor has a bit of conditional logic that initializes the object to the current date and time if no timestamp is specified.

The constructor should be complete, simple, and general enough to let any creation method work by calling it. Since any time point representation can somehow be converted into a timestamp, this one will do.

❷ The `createFromDateAndTime()` method takes a DateAndTime object and creates a new, identical DateAndTime object. Cloning the object would accomplish the same.

❸ The `createFromString()` method creates a DateAndTime object from a string representation such as "2 Mar 2005" or "2005-03-02 13:45:10". The built-in PHP function `strtotime()` takes care of converting the string into a timestamp.

Creation methods are a simple way to construct objects in varying ways. Another approach that is common in other languages is to use multiple constructors.

8.3.2   Multiple constructors

Let's work some more on the challenge of creating date and time objects from different raw materials. In Java, the plain vanilla way of solving this challenge is to use multiple constructors. It is possible in Java to define several different constructors with different signatures—in other words, using different sets of arguments. That makes it easy even without resorting to creation methods. You could create the DateAndTime object using new DateAndTime and some appropriate argument, and the correct constructor would be called automatically.

In PHP, we could achieve the same effect by using switch or other conditional statements, but the result tends to get messy and complex, especially if we want to check both the type and number of arguments. It's easy to end up with intricate logical expressions or nested conditional statements.

There is a trick to do something similar in PHP as in Java, but it has some drawbacks. Let's try it as an experiment so that we can assess the possibilities and limitations of our toolbox. We need a way to automatically call a given method based on the types of the method arguments. This is possible; the first thing we need is a way to generate a method signature based on the types of an array of arguments.

The class ClassUtil, shown in listing 8.2, does this basic job.

Listing 8.2   The ClassUtil class makes multiple constructors possible

```
class ClassUtil {
    public static function typeof($var) {                    ❶ Return type of
        if (is_object($var)) return get_class($var);            single variable
        if (is_array($var)) return 'array';
        if (is_numeric($var)) return 'number';
        return 'string';
    }

    public static function typelist($args) {                 ❷ Return types
        return array_map(array('self','typeof'),$args);         for an array
    }

    public static function callMethodForArgs(                ❸ Method to generate
        $object,$args,$name='construct')                        method name

                                        Construct the method name ❹
    {
        $method = $name.'_'.implode('_',self::typelist($args));
        if (!is_callable(array($object,$method)))

                                        Check that the method exists ❺

            throw new Exception(              Generate readable ❻
                sprintf(                        error message
                    "Class %s has no method '$name' that takes ".
                    "arguments (%s)",
                        get_class($object),
                        implode(',',self::typelist($args))
                    )
                );
        call_user_func_array(array($object,$method),$args);    Call the
                                                               generated
    }                                                       ❼ method
}
```

❶ The typeof() method returns a string representing the type of a single input variable: If it's an object, it returns the class name; if not, it returns either `'array'`, `'number'`, or `'string'`.

❷ The typelist() method takes an array of arguments and returns an array of type strings. What the array_map() function does in this example is equivalent to looping through the array and processing each element by calling self::typeof($variable). A comment for the extracted method would make it still clearer.

Although using `array_map()` instead of a loop saves keystrokes, that's not why we should use it. We should use it if it makes the method more readable. If you find an explicit loop more readable, it might be better to use that. But even if we're comfortable with it, the `array_map()` function is sufficiently cryptic to justify wrapping it in a method whose name summarizes its purpose.

❸ Now for the method that does the real work. `callMethodForArgs()` generates a method name based on the arguments to the method and then calls the method. By default, the method name will start with "construct." For example, if you call it with one argument that is a string and one that is an object belonging to a class called Template, it will perform the equivalent of this method call:

```
$object->construct_string_Template($string,$template);
```

❹ We generate the method name by gluing together the contents of the type list array, using underscore characters between each type string.

❺ Mistakes are likely when we call this method, so we need some error handling. If there is no method with the generated name, we should throw an exception to get an error message that is more informative than the one PHP will generate. We use `is_callable()` to check whether the method is available.

❻ For the exception message, we generate a representation of the type list using commas as separators to make it more readable.

❼ Finally, we use `call_user_func_array()` to call the method. We could have called the method more simply by using `$object->$method($args)`. That's less convenient, since the method gets all the arguments as a single argument—an array containing the actual arguments—instead of as a normal argument list.

Listing 8.3 shows a relatively simple example of how this can be used. It does the same job as listing 8.2, but instead of creation methods, we can now write any number of different constructor methods that will respond to different arguments.

Listing 8.3   DateAndTime class using the ClassUtil class to make multiple constructors possible

```php
class DateAndTime {
    private $timestamp;

    public function __construct() {
        $args = func_get_args();
        ClassUtil::callMethodForArgs($this,$args);
    }

    public function construct_() {
        $this->timestamp = time();
    }

    public function construct_DateAndTime($datetime) {
```

```
        $this->timestamp = $datetime->getTimestamp();
    }

    public function construct_number($timestamp) {
        $this->timestamp = $timestamp;
    }

    public function construct_string($string) {
        $this->timestamp = strtotime($string);
    }

    public function getTimestamp() {
        return $this->timestamp;
    }
}
```

All of these will now work:

```
$datetime = new DateAndTime();
$datetime = new DateAndTime(mktime(0,0,0,3,2,2005);
$datetime = new DateAndTime("2 Mar 2005");
$datetime = new DateAndTime("2005-03-02 13:45:10");
$datetime = new DateAndTime($datetime);
```

This is very elegant from the client's point of view. But there are a couple of problems. The most obvious one is that it takes processing time to do this. It may well be that we want to create lots of DateAndTime objects. Then that processing time could become significant.

The less obvious problem is that we're creating dependencies. As long as we're dealing with plain strings and numbers, that may not be significant; but as soon as we use the name of a specific class, we are hard-coding the name of the class into the method name. It's like a class type hint, only more restrictive. Consider a class type hint such as the following:

```
public function createFromDateAndTime(Instant $datetime) {}
```

If Instant is an interface, this will allow any object implementing the Instant interface (or, if Instant is a class, any descendant class). But the method construct_DateAndTime will *only* respond to DateAndTime objects; any parent classes or implemented interfaces are irrelevant.

For these reasons, this approach to constructors must be considered experimental. It might be useful in some circumstances, but it would be wise to use it with caution and to choose equivalent creation methods in most cases.

8.3.3   Using factory classes

Another way to handle object creation is to use factories. The basic principle is simple: if you have a class that contains a few creation methods, you can extract those methods, and presto, you have a factory class. In other words, a factory is responsible for creating objects that belong to other classes.

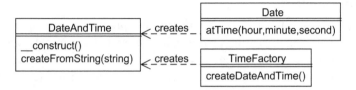

Figure 8.3 Different ways of creating an object: constructor, creation method, creation by related object, factory

Figure 8.3 shows some alternative ways of creating a DateAndTime object. There is a constructor and a creation method in the DateAndTime object itself. We also have a Date object that's able to create a DateAndTime object corresponding to a specific time on the date. Finally, there is a specialized TimeFactory whose sole responsibility is to create DateAndTime objects and other time-related objects.

Factories are a large and complex subject that we will be returning to. There are all sorts of design considerations, ways of using factories, and reasons why we would want to use them (and use them in specific ways). There are also design patterns that demonstrate some advanced ways of creating objects. It's common to consider Factory a pattern in and of itself. In contrast, the book *Design Patterns* [Gang of Four] has a pattern called Abstract Factory, but no plain Factory. For now, let's just note that we can make separate classes that specialize in creating objects. In particular, large and complex objects consisting of different pluggable components often require complex processes to construct them. Keeping complex construction logic in the class that's being created—or in another class that has other responsibilities—is possible, but not always a good idea. As Eric Evans points out in his book *Domain-Driven Design* [Evans], a car is completely separate from the machinery used to produce the car. Software objects are somewhat similar: the responsibility of creating an object is very different from the responsibilities of the object itself. So keeping them in separate classes is often an excellent idea.

Object creation is relevant to date and time handling because there are so many different kinds of objects. Another subject that comes up when dealing with time is how to handle name conflicts between classes. If every application has its own Date class, it's impossible to combine them without running into fatal errors. To avoid those conflicts, we want some understanding of the challenges of large-scale structure.

8.4 LARGE-SCALE STRUCTURE

Large-scale or high-level structure is important in complex applications. It's also difficult, and you need to learn to walk before you can fly. You need to understand classes before you can understand larger structures such as packages.

In this section, we'll find out what packages and namespaces are and check out what the lack of a namespace feature in PHP means to us. Then we'll look at some ways to deal with the name conflicts that can happen as a result of PHP's lack of namespace support.

8.4.1   The package concept

The word *package* has different meanings in different programming languages. A reasonable general meaning is the one used in UML, in which it's simply a grouping of classes and other elements. A package always has a namespace so that two classes in different packages can be named the same without confusion. Since (at this writing) there are officially no namespaces in PHP, we are forced to use workarounds to create a similar effect. But the general idea of a package is just as valid.

In Java, a package has additional characteristics such as a directory location, but these are not necessary to the package concept.

In his book, Robert C. Martin discusses a number of principles for package design [Uncle Bob]. An in-depth look at these is beyond the scope of this book. It's also difficult to summarize them in a simple way, but let's look at what the idea of a package means.

The most naïve way to think about packages is to think of them just as a way of grouping related classes. A slightly more sophisticated way is to consider packages a way of managing dependencies. Whenever a class uses another, that creates a dependency. We want to be able to think about dependencies, not just between classes, but between packages as well. We want these dependencies to be manageable. That will involve putting classes that depend heavily on each other in the same package. This can reduce the dependencies between packages, but there will have to be some, otherwise the packages will be separate programs or applications.

If we extract a class from another, it's typically a candidate to remain in the same package, but not always. Let's say we have a UserForm class. From this class we extract a parent class called Form. These two classes are in the same package, say UserView. But what if we have another package called NewsView that contains a news form class that needs to inherit from the UserForm class? Now we have the situation in figure 8.4.

Does this seem reasonable and logical? Hardly; the placement of the Form class in the UserView package looks completely arbitrary. It could just as well be in the NewsView package. The logical thing to do is to extract the Form class into another package outside the two view packages.

The package design principle at work here is called the common-reuse principle (CRP): *The classes in a package are reused together. If you reuse one of the classes in a package, you reuse them all.*

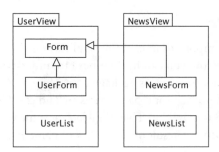

Figure 8.4
A class in the NewsView package uses a parent class in the UserView package. Is this a good idea?

The point is that in figure 8.4, the NewsView package depends on the UserView package, but the NewsView package does not need the UserForm class. So it has an unnecessary dependency on this class.

All of this is about language-independent design considerations. But what is a package in programming terms in PHP? How do we implement it? Since there is no package, module, or subsystem concept in PHP 5, there is no official answer to this. A package is simply a set of classes. Typically, a package is implemented as a directory containing several files. Each of the files can contain one or more classes. But it is also possible to put all classes for a package in a single file.

The technical implementation also needs to work around the biggest problem caused by the lack of package support in PHP. The problem is that of name conflicts between classes. The following section will focus on that.

8.4.2 Namespaces and packages

The subject of namespaces causes some confusion. One web document attempts to show how inferior PHP is to Perl by claiming that two functions named `read()` in PHP will clash since there are no namespaces to distinguish them.

This overlooks the most important part of the equation. Yes, in Perl, you can import a function into the current namespace so that you can use it without qualification. But if you're willing to use a qualified name such as `MyFile::read()`, or even object-oriented syntax, a class in PHP does the same job as a Perl package for this simple case. Even the syntax for calling a function with a qualified name is the same in PHP and Perl. And if you do have two identically named functions, using the qualified name lessens the risk of confusion. Perl 5 has no formal class concept, and that may obscure the similarity. In general, the meaning of keywords such as *package* differs between programming languages.

The real issue is how to work with structures that are larger than classes and how to avoid name conflicts between classes. The problem is not avoiding name conflicts between functions; it's avoiding name conflicts between classes. Therefore, the lack of a formal namespace abstraction on a scale larger than a class is a real deficiency in PHP. Fortunately, there are workarounds.

To get an idea of how a namespace system should work, Java's package concept is as good a comparison as any.

Java solves class name conflicts by allowing us to qualify the class name. For example, the two standard Java packages `java.sql` and `java.util` both contain a class called Date. If we import just one of these packages, there is no problem. We can create a Date object thus:

```
Date now = new Date();
```

But if we import both `java.util` and `java.sql`, the plot thickens. If we try `new Date()`, we get a compilation error. Fortunately, this is easily solved by using the qualified name.

```
java.util.Date now = new java.util.Date();
```

Other classes whose names are not in conflict can still be used without qualification.

In PHP, since there are officially no packages, things are not that simple. If two classes in two different packages have the same name, we get a fatal error as soon as we include both of them. And the only way around it appears to be replacing all occurrences of the name of one of the classes. This is a potential maintenance nightmare. The problem can be solved or at least alleviated, but that's by no means trivial.

8.4.3 PHP's lack of namespace support

Examining the problems associated with PHP's lack of namespace support, there is good news and bad new. The good news is that these problems are not noticeable at all—until you actually run into them. As long as you develop a single application and you're in control of naming all the classes, you can easily live with the fact that you have to name all of them differently.

(At this writing, it seems likely that namespace support will be added to PHP, but it is not yet clear when that will happen. That might make some of the practical advice in the next section less relevant.)

The bad news arrives only in some circumstances. If you want to reuse some code from one application in another application, or if you want to integrate two existing applications, you might be in trouble. If you're lucky, there will be no name conflicts. If not, a moderately large amount of work might be required to make the components work together.

Another troublesome situation occurs with versions. Having two versions of the same package available concurrently is impossible without renaming the classes in one of them.

Here is the scenario: you develop a date and time handling package for a statistics application called CornyStats. Then you reuse it in an e-commerce application, CornyStore. CornyStore needs additional date and time features that were not needed in the CornyStats. So you develop a new and improved version for the e-store application. Along the way, you realize there are some major problems with the API, so you change it a bit.

But now the next version of CornyStats is due soon, and it's clear that the new features developed for CornyStore are needed there, too. But since the API has changed, you can't simply switch versions; they're no longer compatible. You want to make the change gradually, but you can't, since when you try to include both the old and the new version, you get the dreaded error message:

```
Fatal error: Cannot redeclare class date in Date.php on line 3
```

There is an additional item of bad news: the way you can include files in PHP tends to cause confusion as to which classes are actually present and where they come from. Since file A can include file B, which includes file C, and so on, you can easily come across surprises when a class clashes with one you had no idea you had included.

8.4.4   Dealing with name conflicts

Now that we've identified name conflicts as the primary problem, the obvious question is what to do with it. How can we prevent name conflicts? How can we solve them when they do occur?

PEAR-type naming

Perhaps the most obvious way to avoid name conflicts is to adopt naming conventions from the start. This is what PEAR does. It works if you have control of all naming, but otherwise there is always the chance of running into an identical name invented by someone else. Do we want to name a class Calendar_Day? If we do, it will potentially clash with the PEAR class called Calendar_Day. Worse yet, you don't know what the PEAR developers might come up with next. Anything you do that uses a PEAR-like naming scheme, concatenating package and class names in the same way, risks clashing with a future PEAR package. If you have a well-factored design with many classes, the risk increases further.

URL-like naming

The only certain way to avoid all conceivable name clashes is to have a URL-like naming system that guarantees a unique name for everything. Java package naming conventions work like this: the Joda Time package is called `org.joda.time`. If we have a simple domain name like the publishers of this book, we could do this without too much pain:

```
class com_manning_DateAndTime implements com_manning_Instant {}
```

Or if the name of the package is original enough, it might be unlikely to conflict with an existing package. Joda is a good example of a name that's probably original enough to avoid name conflicts.

Burdening every single occurrence of a class name with this kind of information is cumbersome, but might be worth it in a complex application.

Doing the simplest thing

The next obvious alternative is to keep it simple until the need for complexity arises—that is, use whatever names come naturally at the time of coding. This will keep us happy until trouble rears its ugly head, and that might never happen.

When name conflicts do happen, there is not much to do except change the names of all the classes. This may be less formidable than it seems, though, even if we have a lot of classes to rename. At that point, a good PHP refactoring tool might have solved our problems, but none exist at the time of this writing.

On the other hand, if you have good test coverage, changing a few class names won't kill you. That is, unless the class names are widely used in client applications and libraries. In that case, the job of tracking down all occurrences of a class name might be difficult and risky.

Finding hidden occurrences of classes

One problem in solving name conflicts is the fact that PHP just gives you a fatal error message when you try to declare a class that has already been declared. That leaves us with no clue as to where the first declaration is; it may not be obvious.

There are a couple of simple tricks to find these classes. Let's say we are including a couple of class files as follows:

```
require_once 'Date.php';
require_once 'Template.php';
```

When we run this, we get the following error message:

```
Cannot redeclare class template in Template.php on line 2
```

Ugh. It's telling us about the second occurrence of the Template class, but that's the one we intended to include. We're looking for the first occurrence. Clearly Date.php either contains a Template class, or some file that is included from Date.php does.

The first and simplest trick is this:

```
class Template {}
require_once 'Date.php';
require_once 'Template.php';
```

Now the Template class is already defined when PHP finds the hidden occurrence of the class, and we get a message telling us where it's located.

If that's not enough, the two functions get_declared_classes() and get_included_files() can help us locate classes. For example:

```
require_once 'Date.php';
print_r(get_declared_classes());
print_r(get_included_files());
require_once 'Template.php';
```

This will print all files that have been included via Date.php and all classes that have been defined as a result of those includes. It will not print the files or classes that have been included or defined as a result of including Template.php.

Changing lots of class name occurrences

Even if the package is not widely used by clients, a name clash may affect lots of classes used in lots of places inside the package. Changing class names will involve some drudgery. On the other hand, by juggling a few regular expressions, we can automate 90 percent of the task or more. The class shown in listing 8.4 can take a chunk of code as input and replace one class name with another in a somewhat intelligent way.

The class has at least two distinct shortcomings: it will not rename class type hints nor multiple interfaces implemented by one class. The example is primarily intended as an illustration of how a simple and imperfect solution can be built using regular expressions, affectionately known as regexes.

Listing 8.4   Class for renaming classes using regular expressions

```
class ClassRenamer {
    private $oldName;
    private $newName;

    public function __construct($old,$new) {          ❶
        $this->oldName = $old;
        $this->newName = $new;
    }

    public function replaceKeywords($string) {
        $re =
            '/(interface|class|extends|implements|instanceof)\s+'.   ❷
            $this->oldName.'\b/';          ❸
        return preg_replace($re,'$1 '.$this->newName,$string);   ❹
    }

    public function replaceStaticCalls($string) {
        $re = '/\b'.$this->oldName.          ❺
            '\s*::\s*'.          ❻
            '(\$)?'.          ❼
            '(\w+)/';          ❽
        return preg_replace($re,$this->newName.'::$1$2',$string);   ❾
    }

    public function process($string) {          ❿
        return $this->replaceStaticCalls(
            $this->replaceKeywords($string)
        );
    }
}
```

❶ In the constructor, we configure the object with the old and the new class names.

❷ Our first regular expression takes care of the most important keywords that can precede a class name. It starts with either one of those keywords followed by one or more whitespace characters.

❸ This is followed by the class name, ending with a word boundary assertion (\b). Unless we include the word boundary assertion, we might get more replacements than we wanted. For instance, when trying to replace Date with YearMonthDay, we might inadvertently replace DateAndTime with YearMonthDayAndTime.

❹ The string matched by the regular expression is replaced with the keyword (represented by the back reference $1) followed by the new class name.

❺ After we've done the keywords, we start getting into places where the class name is not associated with a keyword. This is more difficult. The most common case is static method calls.

We'll build the regular expression using string concatenation to get the pieces on separate lines. (The other way to split the regex this way is to use the x modifier.) We start with the class name, starting at a word boundary.

❻ The next part of the regex is the double colon, with optional whitespace before and after. It's not customary to have spaces before or after the double colon. The Eclipse IDE does that, though, and PHP accepts it.

❼ Next is an optional dollar sign. This makes the regex match a static variable as well as a method or constant. If present, the dollar sign is captured by the parentheses and will be available as $1 in the replacement string.

❽ The end of the regex matches a string of "word" characters (letters, digits, and underscores). This is the name of a method, variable, or constant. The name is captured by the second set of parentheses and will be available as $2.

❾ The string matched by the regex is replaced by the new class name followed by a double colon, the dollar sign if present, and the method, variable, or constant name.

❿ To perform both transformations, we replace first the keyword-related occurrences of the class name and then the ones implying a static method call, variable, or constant.

Using factory classes

Using factory classes is the standard object-oriented procedure if we want to avoid mentioning the names of classes explicitly. That means we can use factories to alleviate potential name conflicts by reducing the number of occurrences of each class name.

Imagine that you are using several related classes. To instantiate them, you will normally use new in each and every case:

```
$start = new DateAndTime(time() - 3600);
$end = new DateAndTime;
$interval = new Interval($start,$end);
```

As you can see, every use of new involves mentioning a concrete class name. If we have a factory class instead with static creation methods, we can use just the factory class name instead:

```
$start = TimeFactory::createDateAndTime(time() - 3600);
$end = TimeFactory::createDateAndTime();
$interval = TimeFactory::createInterval($start,$end);
```

Figure 8.5 is a simple sequence diagram showing how a static call creates a DateAndTime object. The "metaclass" notation, while odd, officially expresses the fact that a static call to a class is a call to an instance of a metaclass. Craig Larman [Larman] helpfully suggests that "it may help to drink some beer before trying to understand this."

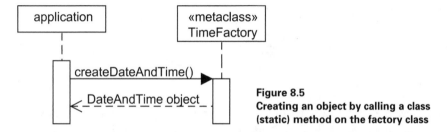

Figure 8.5
Creating an object by calling a class (static) method on the factory class

With static calls, there's only one class name—the names that were previously class names are now method names. But the code is slightly more verbose, and we might want to name the creation methods even more simply:

```
$start = TimeFactory::DateAndTime(time - 3600);
```

Still, the one class name occurs repeatedly. To change all those occurrences because the name is in conflict with another class might be a scary prospect.

There are a couple ways to deal with this. One is simple, but somewhat unsafe. We can define a child class of the factory class:

```
class MyTimeFactory extends Timefactory {}
```

If we use MyTimeFactory instead of TimeFactory and TimeFactory gets into a name conflict, we only need to change the TimeFactory name in one place. But if another class called MyTimeFactory appears, we're back to square one.

The way to avoid that is to create an instance of the factory class and use that to create the time objects as shown in figure 8.6.

A simple way make this available is to let the factory object be global.

```
$GLOBALS['TIME'] = new TimeFactory;
```

Then we can use that to create all the other objects:

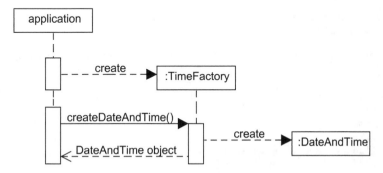

Figure 8.6   Creating an object by making a call to an instance of the factory class

```
public function checkInterval() {
    global $TIME;
    $start = $TIME->DateAndTime(time - 3600);
    $end = $TIME->DateAndTime();
    $interval = $TIME->Interval($start,$end);
    //...
}
```

Now the application has only one concrete class name that's associated with the date and time package, and the name occurs only once. This should prevent the worst-case scenario we discussed earlier, in which concrete class names are strewn across many applications and libraries.

Using eval

Inside the package itself, the factory strategy is not quite as effective. We might need to instantiate more classes, even ones that are not part of the public interface of the package.

Worse yet, factories won't let us get rid of all occurrences of the class names. Specifically, the class declarations themselves have to contain literal class and interface names:

```
class DateAndTime implements Instant {}
```

If we use the earlier strategy of ensuring that the classes have unique names, even this will not be a problem unless we want to use two parallel versions of the same package.

If we absolutely need to make the naming fully configurable, our last resort is the function that makes dreams—or is it nightmares?—come true: eval().

Using eval(), we can read the PHP classes as text from the file, replace the class names, and then execute the code with eval(), creating the renamed classes.

Let's say we have a file containing some classes and interfaces. All class and interface names are prefixed with a unique prefix, in this case com_example_. Here are a couple highlights just to show the principle:

```
abstract class com_example_Instant {}
class com_example_DateAndTime extends com_example_Instant {}
```

Instead of including this file in the standard way using require_once, we'll use a function to read and execute it:

```
function import_prefixed($file,$prefix) {
    $code = str_replace(
        'com_example_',
        $prefix,
        file_get_contents($file));
    eval ('?>'.$code.'<?php ');
}
```

This simple function reads the PHP code as text from the file, replaces the com_example prefix with any other prefix you specify, and executes the code.

Using this is now quite simple. We just import the file with our preferred prefix, and the re-prefixed class is ready to use:

```
import_prefixed('SimpleDateAndTime.php','com_manning_');
$datetime = new com_manning_DateAndTime;
```

Now we have some tricks at our disposal when faced with the prospect of class name conflicts. But there is yet another problem that surfaces when working with dates and times as objects: the fact that object references do not work as intuitively as they do with many other kinds of objects. The solution to this problem is called *value objects*.

8.5   USING VALUE OBJECTS

As described in chapter 2, objects in PHP 5 (but not PHP 4) are represented by references. You might think you are copying an object when you assign it to a variable, but you are actually only copying a reference to it. Then when you change one, the other one changes, too. This behavior can be confusing when you're working with dates.

In this section, we'll see exactly why this is a problem and how to use a mechanism called *value objects* to solve it.

8.5.1   How object references can make trouble

Say payment is due 10 days after delivery. You copy the delivery date and add 10 days to it. If you do that by adding 10 days to the timestamp inside the due date, you've also changed the delivery date, which probably isn't what you intended. The following is a recipe for confusion, if not disaster:

```
$deliveryDate = new DateAndTime;
$paymentDate = $deliveryDate;
$paymentDate->addDays(10);
```

If you thought that $paymentDate is now different from $deliveryDate, you're right in PHP 4, but wrong in PHP 5.

It's very simple: we need something that works the same way as plain values. Using ordinary numbers or strings to represent a date and time illustrates this:

```
$deliveryDate = time()
$paymentDate = $deliveryDate + 3600 * 24 * 10;
```

The previous problem—that both versions of the date change—doesn't occur in this case. We got $paymentDate by adding to $deliveryDate, but $delivery-Date didn't change. And no matter what we do to one of them, the other will remain the same. They are separate copies. With objects in PHP 5, it's different. The principle is shown in figure 8.7.

What we need is an API that lets us handle time points as if they were plain values. We want to do this:

```
$deliveryDate = new DateAndTime;
$paymentDate = $deliveryDate->addDays(10);
```

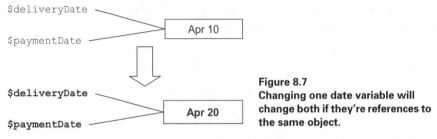

**Figure 8.7
Changing one date variable will
change both if they're references to
the same object.**

To make that possible, we want `$deliveryDate` to remain unchanged in that second line. The `$paymentDate` that is returned cannot be a reference to the original object; it must be a copy. The two objects must be identical but separate as shown in figure 8.8.

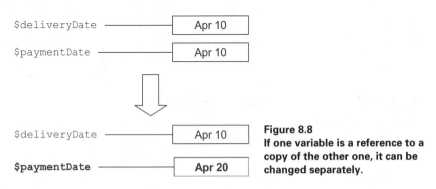

**Figure 8.8
If one variable is a reference to a
copy of the other one, it can be
changed separately.**

This kind of mechanism is known as a *value object* (sometimes named as a design pattern: *Value Object*). Value objects are objects whose identity is unimportant. Any copy of February 10, 2005, is interchangeable with any other copy. The date object is only defined by the value(s) inside it. A person, on the other hand, has an identity. If I copy a reference to a User object and change the email address, it's probably appropriate for the change to manifest itself in both places, since the two most likely represent the same user whose email address has changed.

Typical examples of value objects are dates, money amounts, and colors. All the time-related objects can be represented as value objects.

8.5.2 Implementing value objects

The problem we encountered earlier was the change in the delivery date. It was supposed to stay the same, but didn't. There is a way to make sure it stays constant: we can make it *immutable*—in other words, build it so that there is no way to change it. Making the internal representation private and only providing getter methods (no setters) is a good start:

```
class DateAndTime {
    private $timestamp;
    public function __construct($timestamp=FALSE) {
```

```
        if (!$timestamp) $timestamp = time();
        $this->timestamp = $timestamp;
    }

    public function getTimestamp() {
        return $this->timestamp;
    }
}
```

This class doesn't do much work. In fact, it might be hard to see the advantage of this over using "naked" timestamps.

It starts to make more sense when we add more methods. The simplest ones would be methods to get the components of a time point (such as the day of the week; these are called *properties* in Joda) and methods to compare time points.

But there might be a hidden benefit even with a class as simple as this one: If you come across a DateAndTime object somewhere in the code, you have the class as documentation of how it works.

8.5.3   Changing an immutable object

We've made the DateAndTime object immutable. On the other hand, we need to be able to manipulate it: we want to be able to add durations to it, subtract from it, and so on.

But it's not necessary to change the original object to achieve these changes; instead, we want to create a copy that is changed in the appropriate way. One way to achieve this is to clone the object.

```
class DateAndTime {
    public function addDuration($seconds)  {
        $clone = clone $this;
        $clone->timestamp += $seconds;
        return $clone;
    }
}
```

First we use the PHP 5 clone feature to get a copy of the object. Then we add the specified number of seconds to the cloned object. We can access the $timestamp variable in the clone directly, even if it's private, because $clone belongs to the DateAndTime class. That is, unless the addDuration() method is being called on an object belonging to a parent or child class of the DateAndTime class. In that case, $timestamp would have to be protected rather than private.

Cloning creates only a so-called *shallow copy*, meaning that objects inside the cloned object are not cloned, but that's not a problem in this case.

Another way to achieve the same thing, and slightly simpler in this case, is to create a fresh object:

```
class DateAndTime {
    public function addDuration($seconds)  {
        return new DateAndTime($this->timestamp + $seconds);
```

```
        }
    }
```

This is workable in most cases, since value objects are typically simple enough to allow easy construction of a new object.

The great advantage of using immutable objects is predictability. Calling a method on an immutable object is always "side-effect free." There is no risk of unexpected effects in other parts of the system.

On the other hand, it might be more efficient, performance-wise, to change a mutable object rather than create a new one. Joda Time gives you a choice of mutable and immutable time objects so that you can choose to use mutable ones if you want to make many changes.

8.6   IMPLEMENTING THE BASIC CLASSES

We now have the knowledge we need to implement the most important classes for date and time handling. We only have room for the highlights, so let's take a look at them.

We'll implement a DateAndTime class for single time points, Property and Field classes to represent parts of a single date and time, a Period class for a time span without a specific start and end, and an Interval class to represent the time between two specific time points.

8.6.1   DateAndTime

The date and time handling requirements of different applications differ widely. Often, one application needs one set of features, while the next one needs another, unrelated set of features. Some examples of the different capabilities required by different applications might be

- Do date and time arithmetic (add, subtract...).
- Compare dates and times.
- Get the weeks in a month and the days in a week (as for a calendar).
- Format and display dates and times.
- Find database rows within a time interval.

We might stuff all these features into one class, but it's hardly advisable. The single-responsibility principle (SRP) comes into play here. Better to keep most of it in separate classes that can change independently of the basic DateAndTime class.

In Joda Time, most of the methods of DateAndTime class are accessors for properties. There are also comparison methods such as `isAfter()` and `isAfter-Now()`, which are inherited from a class called AbstractInstant.

Since comparison methods are simple and not likely to change much, we might want to add them to the DateAndTime class. For example:

```
class DateAndTime {
    public function isAfter($instant) {
```

```
            return $this->timestamp > $instant->getTimestamp();
        }
    }
```

There are some alternative possibilities, including the following:

- Put the comparison methods in a parent class as in Joda time. There seems to be no particular reason to do that as long as we keep everything simple.
- Create a separate comparator class and use that explicitly in the client code when we want to compare two instants. That's cumbersome and likely to become tiring.
- Create a comparator class and let the DateAndTime class use that behind the scenes.

A separate comparator class would be useful if we needed to change the way we compare time points. That seems unlikely.

8.6.2   Properties and fields

Properties, as used in Joda Time, relieve the central DateAndTime class of the responsibility of knowing anything about days, weeks, days of the week, or similar complexities of date and time handling.

Let's try to emulate the Joda API. If we have a DateAndTime object, we should be able to get, set, add, or subtract a number of time units, such as day, by using a property. For example, to add six days to a time on August 9, 2006, we could do the following:

```
$format = "%a %e %b %Y %H:%M:%S";
$datetime = new DateAndTime(mktime(12,32,55,8,9,2006));
echo strftime($format,$datetime->getTimestamp)."\n";
$later = $datetime->dayOfMonth()->addToCopy(6);
echo strftime($format,$later->getTimestamp)."\n";
```

We want this to output the following:

```
Tue  9 Aug 2006 12:32:55
Mon 15 Aug 2006 12:32:55
```

But how will we do that? We'll have to look more closely at the code, since the property object is not explicit in the example. What actually happens is that we first get an object representing the day of month property:

```
$property = $datetime->dayOfMonth();
```

This property object is "any color we want, as long as it's black." We want to be able to do anything as long as it relates to days of the month: get the day of the month, set it, or add days.

But all of these are meaningless without the particular time point the property is related to. This means that the property has to know about the DateAndTime object it came from. Let's sketch a UML class diagram to express this (see figure 8.9).

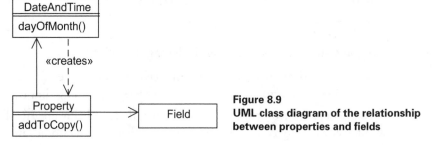

Figure 8.9
UML class diagram of the relationship between properties and fields

The `addToCopy()` method is just one of the methods we would want, but it's enough to illustrate the design.

The Property object uses the DateAndTime object, and it also has to know what *kind* of property it represents. Where is the information about what kind of property it represents? There are at least three alternatives:

- Child classes (DayOfMonthProperty, YearProperty, and so forth)
- Data values in the property object
- A separate object that knows nothing about a specific date and time, but does know whatever is specific to one property as opposed to another

Using data values to represent the difference between property types is the simplest solution, and it might be feasible for the properties that can be directly manipulated by `mktime()`, but otherwise it's likely to be too simple.

Joda Time uses a separate object called a *field*. This is the Strategy pattern.

That seems like a clean design with conceptually separate classes, so let's try it. The next question is: does the Property object do the calculations necessary to add the value to the copy, or does it delegate that work to the Field object?

Are the calculations complex enough to make us want to take them out of the Property object? Most calculations can be done simply with `mktime()`, and for `mktime()` the only difference between different fields is their position in the list of arguments. So the difference can be represented by a single integer value.

But the key information here is the fact that not all time fields are that simple. When we want to add a week, we have to do something quite different. Since the Field object is supposed to represent the difference between different property and field types, this specialized code has to go there.

Let's look at some code. To make this understandable, we need to start at the core: the fields. The abstract field class is just an interface definition:

```
abstract class TimeField {
    abstract' public function get(Instant $time);
    abstract public function setCopy(Instant $time, $value);
    abstract public function addToCopy(Instant $time, $value);
}
```

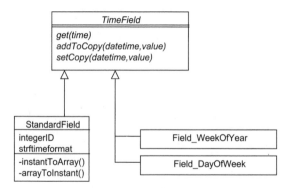

Figure 8.10   A single class to represent all fields that can be handled in a simple way with PHP functions; custom classes for more complex cases

Most of the fields can be handled in a uniform way by using the standard time functions built into PHP. These fields correspond to the numbers in an ISO date such as 2006-03-02 13:45:10. Figure 8.10 shows that we can use a single class to represent all of these fields while the others, such as those involving weeks, call for custom classes.

The StandardField class has the methods and attributes needed to convert the time representation so that it can be processed by the PHP functions.

Listing 8.5 is the standard field class.

Listing 8.5   Standard field class for all the fields that can be handled by the PHP time functions

```
class StandardField extends TimeField {
    private $integerID;
    private $strftimeFormat;

    public function __construct($integerID,$strftimeFormat) {
        $this->integerID = $integerID;
        $this->strftimeFormat = $strftimeFormat;         ❶
    }
    public function get(Instant $time) {
        return strftime(                                 ❷
            $this->strftimeFormat,
            $time->getTimestamp());
    }

    public function setCopy(Instant $time,$value) {
        $array = $this->instantToArray($time);           ❸
        $array[$this->integerID] = $value;
        return $this->arrayToInstant($array);
    }

    public function addToCopy(Instant $time,$value) {
        $array = $this->instantToArray($time);           ❹
        $array[$this->integerID] += $value;
        return $this->arrayToInstant($array);
    }
}
```

```
        private function instantToArray(Instant $instant) {
            return explode('-',
                strftime(
                    '%H-%M-%S-%m-%e-%Y',
                    $instant->getTimestamp())
                );
        }

        private function arrayToInstant($array) {
            return new DateAndTime(
                call_user_func_array('mktime',$array));
        }
    }
```

❶ `$integerID` and `$strftimeFormat` are the instance variables for the Field class. Each specific time unit has an integer ID, which represents its position in the list of arguments to `mktime()`. It also stores its `strftime()` format specification.

❷ The `get()` method uses the format specification stored in the class to generate a value for the field. So, for instance, a StandardField representing a month has `$strftimeFormat` set to `%m`.

❸ `setCopy()` indirectly uses `mktime()` to set the value of whatever Field the current class represents. It generates an array of values from the DateAndTime object. These correspond to the values `mktime()` accepts. Then it sets the appropriate value and converts the array back to a DateAndTime object.

❹ `addToCopy()` is almost identical to `set()`, but instead of setting the value, we want to be able to add an arbitrary number of the relevant unit.

There is obvious duplication between these two methods, but it's hardly worth eliminating. There are only two occurrences, they are close together, and using some sort of callback is relatively verbose in PHP.

`instantToArray()` and `arrayToInstant()` are primarily utility methods for the `get()`, `setCopy()`, and `addCopy()` methods, making it possible for them to work by setting or getting one of the array values.

❺ `instantToArray()` uses `strftime()` to generate a hyphen-separated list of time components (in the same sequence that PHP's `mktime()` accepts them), explodes the list into an array, and returns the array.

❻ `arrayToInstant()` accepts the time array, generates a timestamp using `mktime()`, and returns a new DateAndTime object based on the timestamp. As mentioned, `mktime()` will accept out-of-range values (too large or negative) and make sense of them. For example, if you ask for "the zeroth of January," it will give you December 31 of the previous year instead. So we can easily use it to add or subtract any number of time units, provided that the time unit is one that's part of the list of arguments to `mktime()`. We're using `call_user_func_array()` to make mktime() accept all the arguments as a single array. This is convenient, but the PHP manual tells us it's for calling user-defined functions, as its name indicates. It works with a built-in function, though.

But since it's not in the manual, this must be considered an undocumented feature. The possibility that this would be changed may seem remote, but it is safer to do it like this:

```php
return new DateAndTime(mktime(
    $array[0],
    $array[1],
    $array[2],
    $array[3],
    $array[4],
    $array[5]
));
```

Other field classes, particularly the ones involving weeks, will need specialized code to handle addition and setting. We'll use the week of the year field as an example:

```php
class Field_WeekOfYear extends TimeField {
    public function get(Instant $time){
        return strftime('%V',$time->getTimestamp());
    }

    public function addToCopy(Instant $time,$value){
        return $time->dayOfMonth()->addToCopy($value * 7);
    }
}
```

The addToCopy() method expresses the well-known fact that adding a week is the same thing as adding seven days.

The only responsibility of the Property class is to coordinate a DateAndTime value and a TimeField object. It delegates all the real work to the field object:

```php
class Property {
    private $datetime;
    private $field;

    public function __construct($datetime,$field) {
        $this->datetime = $datetime;
        $this->field = $field;
    }

    public function setCopy($value) {
        return $this->field->setCopy($this->datetime,$value);
    }

    public function addToCopy($value) {
        return $this->field->addToCopy($this->datetime,$value);
    }

    public function get() {
        return $this->field->get($this->datetime);
    }
}
```

Now all that's missing is a set of methods to allow the DateAndTime object to return the Property objects. The following is just a selection to show the principle:

```
class DateAndTime {
    public function hour {
        return new Property($this,new StandardField(0,'%H'));
    }

    public function dayOfMonth() {
        return new Property($this,new StandardField(4,'%e'));
    }

    public function weekOfYear() {
        return new Property($this,new Field_WeekOfYear);
    }
}
```

Additional methods are easy to add by looking up the codes in the PHP manual (`strftime()` and `mktime()`).

The sequence diagram in figure 8.11 shows the whole process. When we call the `hour()` method on the DateAndTime object, it creates and returns a Property object representing its `hour` property. Then we call `addToCopy(12)` to add 12 hours. The Property object knows what DateAndTime object we're dealing with, but not how to do the addition, so it needs the StandardField object to help to that. The Standard-Field object knows how to do the addition, but does not hold a reference to the Date-AndTime object, so the Property object has to pass this reference along.

The way we create the StandardField object is cryptic; it's not immediately obvious that the values 0 and %H represent the hour field. That is OK if this is the only place in the code we want to create field objects, but if that's not the case it's safer to move creation to a factory class so that these cryptic values are encapsulated in a single class. We also eliminate a tiny amount of duplication this way. We could create a separate factory class or use the abstract TimeField class:

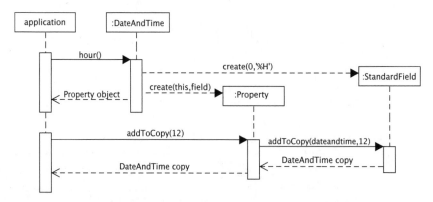

Figure 8.11 Sequence diagram showing the details of the interaction between DateAndTime, Property, and Field objects

CHAPTER 8   DESIGN HOW-TO: DATE AND TIME HANDLING

```
abstract class TimeField {
    public static function WeekOfYear() {
        return new Field_WeekOfYear; }

    public static function DayOfMonth() {
        return new StandardField(4,'%e'); }

    public static function Hour {
        return new StandardField(0,'%H');
    }
}
```

We now have a uniform interface for creating the field objects, one that hides the differences between the StandardField class and the others.

```
class DateAndTime {
    public function dayOfMonth() {
        return new Property($this,TimeField::dayOfMonth());
    }

    public function weekOfYear() {
        return new Property($this,TimeField::weekOfYear());
    }

    public function weekOfYear() {
        return new Property($this,TimeField::weekOfYear());
    }
}
```

This last change makes the code slightly more complex by adding an extra class. This is a double-edged sword: On the one hand, we have to go back and forth a lot between classes to follow the full sequence of operations. On the other hand, the uniform interface is a kind of conceptual simplicity that might make the code easier to understand.

8.6.3 Periods

A *period* in Joda Time is a time span that can start at any point in time and lasts for a specified number of years, months, weeks, days, hours, minutes, and seconds.

We want to be able to do things such as add a period to an Interval or DateAndTime. In the simple, abstract notation used in the Joda documentation, the principle can be described as follows:

```
instant  + period = instant
interval + period = interval
```

As usual, weeks are the jokers. All the other time units can be added simply with mktime(). And although it's not hard to do the calculation by first converting the weeks to days, it's even simpler and more uniform to do it by using fields.

There is one complication: a field is just an abstract concept that has no particular value, but we need to keep track of the fields and the field values together, since we're now cutting them off from the DateAndTime object. One logical way to do that would be to bundle them together in a wrapper class.

```
class FieldWithValue {
    private $field;
    private $value;

    public function __construct($field,$value) {
        $this->field = $field;
        $this->value = $value;
    }

    public function addToCopy($datetime) {
        return $this->field->addToCopy($datetime,$this->value);
    }

    public function getValue() {
        return $this->value;
    }
}
```

This might seem bureaucratic, but it's conceptually clean. Now the design is clear (see figure 8.12). A period consists of several FieldWithValue objects. Each of these can add themselves to the DateAndTime object. When all of them in turn have done so, the period has been added to the DateAndTime object.

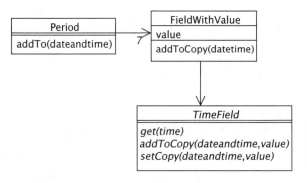

**Figure 8.12
Using a FieldWithValue class
to keep the calculation separate from the value**

The Field object and the FieldWithValue object are different in their behavior. A simpler alternative would be to just add a value variable to the field object itself, but that involves potential duplication and conflict. Since a property has both a field and an instant attached to it, the field value might conflict with the corresponding value in the instant object.

Now the Period class is very simple:

```
class Period {
    private $fields;
    public function __construct($years,$months,$weeks,$days,
                                $hours,$minutes,$seconds)
    {
        $this->fields = array(
            'years' => new FieldWithValue(
                TimeField::Year(),$years),
            'months' => new FieldWithValue(
                TimeField::Month(),$months),
```

```
        'weeks' => new FieldWithValue(
            TimeField::WeekOfYear(),$weeks),
        'days' => new FieldWithValue(
            TimeField::DayOfMonth(),$days),
        'hours' => new FieldWithValue(
            TimeField::Hour(),$hours),
        'minutes' => new FieldWithValue(
            TimeField::Minute(),$minutes),
        'seconds' => new FieldWithValue(
            TimeField::Second(),$seconds),
    );
}
public function addTo($datetime) {
    foreach ($this->fields as $fieldValue) {
        $datetime = $fieldValue->addToCopy($datetime);
    }
    return $datetime;
}
```

The calculation is not optimal, since we keep creating new objects in the loop, so if this is a library for heavy use, we will probably want a mutable DateAndTime object that will allow us to add values repeatedly. We might even have the DateAndTime object remember the values and only call mktime() when we're finished.

8.6.4   Intervals

The interval is Fowler's Date Range. It's basically just a start time and an end time:

```
class Interval {
    private $start;
    private $end;

    public function __construct($start,$end) {
        $this->start = $start;
        $this->end = $end;
    }

    public function getEnd() { return $this->end; }
    public function getStart() { return $this->start; }
}
```

In fact, this class could represent any kind of range, not just a date/time range. It could be a range of temperatures, pages, or lines in a file, for that matter.

Since we already have a way to add a period to an instant, we can easily add a period to an interval by adding it to the end time.

Other typical methods for an interval are comparisons such as contains(), overlaps(), and isAfter().

8.7 SUMMARY

Date and time handling is complex and tricky, but not for technological reasons. That makes it a good testing ground for object-oriented techniques and their ability to represent concepts and relationships.

Appropriate abstractions help make our code easier to understand and to maintain. Looking carefully at the way we represent time, there are several conceptually different ways to represent times and time spans.

Along the way, we bump into the problems of large-scale structure and packages, since date and time handling is a separate world apart from the rest of our application.

Most date and time abstractions are best represented as immutable value objects. This makes them more intuitive and predictable.

Actually implementing the classes is an interesting challenge that requires a lot of thinking beyond the basic understanding of abstractions. Our approach has been to simplify this challenge by using the built-in PHP date and time functions and to keep the central DateAndTime object simple while adding the main functionality in the surrounding classes.

We started this chapter by saying we wanted to handle discrepancies and unexpected twists. We have used a challenging example to see how such puzzles can be handled. But to really learn the process in practice, we need to experiment with it on a small scale at first. One of the most useful aids to making this work is test-driven development. Working test-first gives us another perspective on design. In the next chapter, we will start learning the art of unit testing by working through a simple example.

PART 2

Testing and refactoring

Object-oriented programming and design may seem theoretical and hard to follow. In part 2 of this book, we get to the techniques that will help make them clearer in practice. Unit testing and refactoring (improving the design of existing code) are ways to improve the quality of software, making it easier to maintain and allowing us to prevent bugs. This makes a programmer's job easier and saves time in dreary debugging. Just as important, test-driven development and refactoring are a unique learning process that let you discover the difference between good and poor application design on your own.

Testing and refactoring are related subjects, since refactoring depends on full test coverage. We will study unit testing to test an application piece by piece. We will use a test-first approach, applying it to an example that will evolve into a simple, but working web application. We will also see how to test this application from the outside using web tests. And we will take a tour of refactoring, looking both at well-known refactorings and some web-specific techniques.

CHAPTER 9

Test-driven development

I misplaced my cellphone once and could not find it anywhere. This happens to me sometimes, and I know exactly what to do about it: I pick up another phone and call the cellphone. Usually, this makes it easy.

But this particular late night, something spooky happened. Although I could hear it, I simply could not locate it. The sound appeared to be coming from somewhere inside a bookshelf, and although I had no idea why I would have left the phone there, I kept looking, listening, and groping for it.

But to no avail. I could still hear it, and I believed I had found the approximate location of the sound, but there was no way I could pinpoint its location. Another odd thing was the fact that I could hear only the vibrating alert, but not the regular ring-tone, even though I believed I had done nothing to silence it.

I had practically given up, when it dawned on me: *it's on the other side of the wall.* I went into the living room, and there it was. Now I could even hear it ringing. I had been looking for it in vain for at least half an hour, trying to narrow down the search as best I could. But what I really needed was to expand my perspective. Then it was easy to find.

To me, this story captures one of the most bothersome aspects of software bugs: all too frequently, they are on the other side of the wall. We believe we know approximately where the bug is located, and we search for it with mounting annoyance, even to the point of despair. Just as we are ready to give up, or perhaps after a good night's sleep, we realize it could be located in some place we had not searched.

It also summarizes perhaps the most important reason for the modern practices of unit testing and test-driven development (TDD). Since searching for bugs in the wrong place is a supreme waste of time and energy, any technique that helps you avoid those bug hunts in the first place will make you more productive.

The solution is having good test coverage and tests that are specific enough to tell us exactly where the problem is. That means having many tests, each of them exercising a small portion of the code. And the easiest way to get this kind of test coverage even in the early stages is to work test-first.

We will learn exactly how to do this. In this chapter, we'll work through a single, coherent example (a database transaction class), learning new techniques as we go along. We start by developing a basic, general requirements specification for the example. Then we implement the ability to retrieve data, using a step-by-step procedure for working test-first. Next, we'll add the ability to update and insert data, learning how to clean up tests and make them more readable. Finally, we'll make the class able to use real database transactions, tackling the difficult problem of testing that concurrent transactions are properly handled. But first, let's take a look at the background.

9.1 BUILDING QUALITY INTO THE PROCESS

Beginning with Fredrick Taylor's "scientific management," twentieth-century manufacturing depended on mass production to control quality. Note the word "control" here. The objective was not high quality, but a minimum standard of consistency. A production line is about efficiency and reducing waste. It's about quantity at low cost. If you had the money, you would buy the hand-made version.

This system reached its pinnacle in 1945. Who cared if a Russian or American tank was inferior to its German counterpart if you could have four times as many? As Stalin said, "Quantity has a quality all of its own." This wasn't about wealth creation or craftsmanship; this was a battle of attrition.

The chain of command owed much to the military, too. To a production manager, workers were naturally lazy and would avoid work if they could. Because workmanship would have to be checked-up on, quality assurance was given to a separate department. This was a self-fulfilling prophecy. Stripped of the power to improve quality, there wasn't any. Managers instructed workers, after all; not the other way around. With feedback from the line workers ignored—the very workers that could improve the manufacturing process—there was only stasis.

By 1980, the U.S. was no longer the only industrial superpower, and was in a manufacturing recession. By contrast, Japanese goods, cars especially, were considered more reliable and were often cheaper, too. An NBC television program called *If Japan Can... Why Can't We?* captured the feeling of defeat. Overnight, an unknown William Edwards Deming became famous.

In 1950, Deming had conducted a lecture tour of Japan, explaining process control to executives, for members of JUSE (Japanese Union of Scientists and Engineers). The tour was about controlling manufacturing with statistics. This had also been developed in the second world war, but had fallen into disuse. With his new Japanese colleagues, Deming created a system called *Total Quality Management (*TQM*)*. The central tenet of TQM was building quality into the process.

In TQM, this is achieved locally. A quality problem was still a management problem, but management won't know everything. For this reason, workers are empowered to make design changes themselves. Locally, design improvements can happen at a much faster rate. Targets are different, too. The drive to quality means that a low defect rate is given priority over raw production figures. If a problem is found late in the process, it involves more people and takes longer to fix. This means that quality control has to be local, too, ensuring rapid feedback. Each person in the manufacturing cell is his own QA department. High quality keeps the process local, while keeping the process local improves quality.

9.1.1 Requirements for the example

The idea of building quality into the process is the foundation of local unit testing and test-driven development. Quality control in software is about squashing bugs, and that starts with testing. We are going to be aggressive about this. Every function point will be tested the moment it is written. How do we achieve this? We'll write the test before we write the code. So where do we start? We want to write the tests first, but we can't write a test without some idea of what we want to develop. Normally we would be driven by a need in the application, but this is a book example. We'll be a little artificial. We'll write something that is a basic building block of many PHP applications, the database. We want to connect to MySQL like so:

```
$transaction = new MysqlTransaction( ... );
$transaction->execute(
        'insert into authors (name) values ("Dagfinn")');
$transaction->execute(
        'insert into authors (name) values ("Marcus")');
$transaction->execute(
        'insert into authors (name) values ("Chris")');
$transaction->commit();
```

How would we test this?

We could do the usual: write a few lines of *ad hoc* code, run it, and then have a look in the database to see if anything happened. It won't work, so we fix it and run it again. We do this for a few more features until we have seen every feature work at least once, although not all at the same time, and then tick off the task as done. Any bugs that show up will be caught by the QA department. Or the beta testers.

There is a lot wrong with this approach. Besides the lack of a complete test run at the end, we don't feel that the work is complete. Likely another developer will encounter this class and find mistakes in it, or have to extend it. She will have to create her own tests all over again, probably different from ours. Her tests might not cover some of our features, inevitably breaking some of our code. She might have a different opinion on what the class should do, leading to a confused design, unless she rewrites from scratch. Relying on QA or beta testing cycles to fix things is also expensive. This is just hacking.

We'll do things differently. Every test we write will be in the form of a script. This means that any time we have any doubt in the code, we can run our test again. This alone will save some time. The test will be checked into our version control alongside the code. The test is precious. When we add another test, we'll add it to the same script. Thus, the script will accumulate tests. Any time we have doubt in the code, we can run all of them.

9.1.2   Reporting test results

We also need some reasonably tidy way of reporting test results so they will make sense even when run in a large test suite. In our code snippet, we inserted three rows, so our test script could echo them back:

```
Dagfinn
Marcus
Chris
```

That means something to us right now, but it will look like a random jumble when we have 15 different tests all echoing various data with no indication of what they mean. Instead we want something like this:

```
Test of inserting three rows - passed.
```

Even another developer can see our intent now, and if it fails he can examine the test code to figure out what we really wanted to happen. When he edits the code, any time he thinks he broke something, he can run the tests. He can even use the tests to explore the code. As he adds tests, we can see what he intended, too. Communication is a big benefit of having test-covered code, but that's getting ahead of ourselves. We still haven't written a test.

9.2   DATABASE SELECT

How do we start? We know we want to test the transaction class and its ability to query the database. That's relatively complex, and we want to make the process easier by going one step at a time. Therefore, our first goal is just to get some kind of test up and running. Something like a "Hello world" of testing; the minimum test code that will tell us that the basic infrastructure actually works.

9.2.1   A rudimentary test

We start by creating our new class in a folder called `classes`, and within that folder we will have another called `tests`, where we will place our first test script. The `classes/tests` folder needs to be viewable by the web browser, which means making it available to the web server on your machine. (Alternatively, you can run the tests from a command line, but here we'll be using the web browser.)

The first test script is called transaction_test.php. Here it is:

```php
<?php
?>
```

A joke? I admit it's not much of a test script. Nevertheless, we fire it up in the browser and make sure we see a blank page. Isn't that what you would have really done? Strange seeing this in print, isn't it? Testing as we go is not really that new. We actually do it all of the time, and know it's a good thing.

If we start coding the tests from scratch, we could end up with a lot of duplicated code. We can write something like this:

```
print "Running email test\n";
//...
if ($email == 'me@myself.com') {
    print "OK\n"
} else {
    print "Not OK\n";
}
```

After a few repetitions of this `if-else` statement, we realize we need a function to handle it. But that's not all we will need. In a large test suite, we want more sophisticated reporting. At the least, we want a summary at the end telling us whether all the tests were OK. If not, we want to know how many tests failed.

We need consistent reporting with summaries and a way of organizing tests into test suites. Clearly, it would be nice if we could avoid programming all that stuff ourselves. Fortunately, there are test tools that will save us time in writing the testing mechanics. In the Java world, the standard unit testing tool is called JUnit. PHP has several JUnit-like tools available, of which the most popular are PHPUnit2 within PEAR (http://pear.php.net/package/PHPUnit2/) and SimpleTest (http://simpletest.org/, http://simpletest.org/wiki). We will be using SimpleTest. This is pure bias on our part, as one of the authors of this book (Marcus Baker) is also the lead developer for this project. Appendix A has a summary and comparison of these PHP test tools.

SimpleTest can be downloaded from Sourceforge (http://sf.net/projects/simpletest/) as a tarball, a PEAR install, or an Eclipse plug-in. For simplicity, we'll use the tarball, and we'll unpack it into our `tests` folder. It's ready to run straight away. Here is a minimal, do-nothing test script:

```php
<?php
require_once('simpletest/unit_tester.php');
require_once('simpletest/reporter.php');
```

❶ Require the SimpleTest files

```
class TestOfMysqlTransaction extends UnitTestCase {
}
$test = new TestOfMysqlTransaction();
$test->run(new HtmlReporter());
?>
```

❷ Extend the test case class

❸ Instantiate and run

❶ Breaking this down line by line, first we `require` two sections of the library. unit_tester.php is nearly always loaded and has the UnitTestCase base class. reporter.php has the standard means of displaying test results, and has the class Html-Reporter, which we use a few lines later.

❷ To create tests in SimpleTest (or PHPUnit, for that matter) we subclass the base test case. Here our test case is called TestOfMysqlTransaction, but you could give it any name.

❸ Finally, we instantiate our test case and run it. Soon our test case will contain a bunch of tests that will send any passes and failures to the reporter. Reporters can be customized for a project in elaborate ways, but we will use a basic built-in version for the browser called HtmlReporter. For command-line testing, use TextReporter instead.

Viewing this in the browser, we should see the result in figure 9.1.

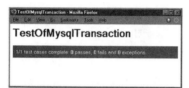

Figure 9.1
Running the TestOfMysqlTransaction test case with no tests defined yet

The big green bar means that there were no failures. Of course, there were no tests either. We'll move on to a test that assumes real functionality: a database select.

9.2.2 The first real test

Remember that we're trying to work test-first. Therefore, the next thing we want to do is add a test for a database select feature while disregarding the fact that the code doesn't exist yet. We pretend the feature is already implemented and write the test code as if we're using it. We will eventually want something along the lines of figure 9.2, allowing us to run a SELECT, get a result set, and then get rows from the result set. The diagram doesn't cover all the details of the interface, though.

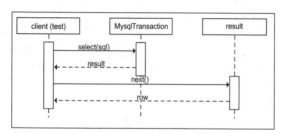

Figure 9.2 We want to create a MysqlTransaction class that is capable of SQL SELECT.

The test plays the part of a typical piece of client code. By writing the test first, we get to play with the interface of our class a little before we commit to it. In effect, we get to try it out first in the test.

We already have an empty test class called TestOfMysqlTransaction. Each individual test will be implemented as a method in the test class. Here is our first real test:

```php
require_once('../transaction.php');

class TestOfMysqlTransaction extends UnitTestCase {
    function testCanReadSimpleSelect() {           ❶
        $transaction = new MysqlTransaction();
        $result = $transaction->select('select 1 as one');     ❷
        $row = $result->next();
        $this->assertEqual($row['one'], 1);         ❸
    }
}
```

❶ SimpleTest does some magic here. When the test case executes, it searches itself for all methods that start with "test" and runs them. If the method starts with any other name, it will be skipped. We'll make use of this later, but for now just remember to put "test" at the beginning of each method you want to run.

❷ Now we start pretending that the feature has been implemented as outlined in figure 9.2. "Select" sounds like a good name for an SQL select method. We pretend that the transaction class has a select() method that is able to run an SQL SELECT. We also pretend that the results of the select() call will come back as an iterator (see section 7.5). Each call to next() on the iterator will give us a row as a PHP array(). Here we only expect to fetch one row, so the usual iterator loop is absent.

❸ The assertEqual() method is a SimpleTest assertion, one of quite a few available. If the two parameters do not match up, a failure message will be dispatched to the test reporter and we will get a big red bar.

Figure 9.3 is a simplified class diagram of the test setup. The MysqlTransaction and MysqlResult classes are in gray because they don't exist yet. They are implied by the code in the test method. The UnitTestCase class is part of the SimpleTest framework. Only one method of this class is shown, although it has many others.

When we run this test case, we don't get to see the red bar. Instead the results are quite spectacular, as in figure 9.4.

We haven't yet created the file classes/transaction.php, causing a crash. This is because we are writing the tests before we write the code, any code, even creating the file. Why? Because we want the least amount of code that we can get away with. It's easy to make assumptions about what you will need and miss a much simpler solution.

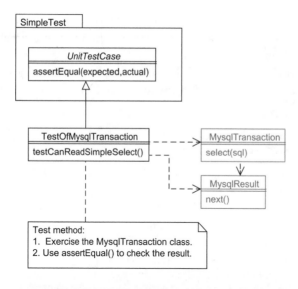

Figure 9.3 Our first real test, the infrastructure needed to make it work, and the classes implied by the test

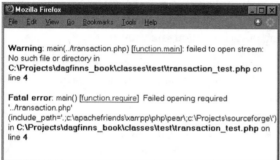

Figure 9.4 Now the test causes a fatal error, since we have a test, but the code to be tested does not exist yet.

9.2.3   Make it pass

The test result tells us what we need to do next. It's telling us that it's unable to open the file transaction.php. This is not surprising, since the file does not exist. We have to create the file.

If we create an empty transaction.php file and run the test again, it will tell us that the MysqlTransaction class does not exist. If we create the class, we get another fatal error telling us that we are trying to run a nonexistent method.

This process leads us to the following code, the minimum needed to avoid a fatal PHP error:

```php
<?php
class MysqlTransaction {
    function select() {
        return new MysqlResult();
    }
}
```

```
class MysqlResult {
    function next() {
    }
}
?>
```

It isn't fully functional, but does prevent a PHP crash. The output is in figure 9.5.

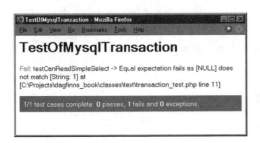

Figure 9.5
The test case no longer crashes,
but the test fails since the code is
not fully functional yet.

It takes only a single failure to get that big red bar. That's the way it works. This might seem brutal, but there are no partially passing test suites, in the same way as there is no such thing as partially correct code. The only way to get the green bar back is with 100 percent passing tests.

We can achieve a green bar simply by returning the correct row:

```
class MysqlResult {
    function next() {
        return array('one' => '1');
    }
}
```

And sure enough, we get the green bar (see figure 9.6).

Notice the small steps: write a line, look at the tests, write a line, check whether it's green. Did we just cheat by simply hard-coding the desired result? Well, yes we did. This is what Kent Beck, the inventor of TDD, calls the FakeIt pattern. We will find it's easier to work with code when we have a green bar. For this reason, we get to the green bar any way we can, even if it's a simplistic, stupid, fake implementation. Once green, we can refactor the code to the solution we really want.

In a way, the code is actually correct despite our hack. It works; it just doesn't meet any real user requirements. Any other developer looking at the tests might be a bit disappointed when she sees our current implementation, but it's pretty obvious that we

Figure 9.6
We've made the test pass by
hard-coding the output of the
desired result.

have done a temporary hack. If we were run over by a bus, she could carry on from this point without confusion. All code is a work in progress, and in a way this is no different.

9.2.4 Make it work

Since we weren't run over by a bus and we're still alive, it's still our job to write some more code. We want to go from the fake implementation to code that actually does something useful. Instead of just returning a hard-coded value that satisfies the test, we want to get the real value that's stored in the database and return it. But before we can get anything from the database, we need to connect to it, so let's start with this:

```
class MysqlTransaction {
    function select($sql) {
        $connection = mysql_connect(
                'localhost', 'me', 'secret', 'test', true);
        return new MysqlResult();
    }
}
```

Not much of a change, just adding the connect call and doing nothing with it. The choice of call is quite interesting here. Assuming that we want to be backward compatible with version 4.0 of MySQL and don't currently have PDO installed, we use the older PHP function `mysql_connect()` rather than the newer Mysqli or PDO interfaces. Note that this doesn't affect the tests. If you want to write your Mysql-Transaction class using PDO, it won't substantially affect this chapter.

When we run the tests, we get the result in figure 9.7.

We haven't set up the access to MySQL, and so PHP generates a warning about our failure to connect. SimpleTest reports this as an exception, because it cannot be tied to any failed assertion.

Note that we only added one line before we ran the test suite. Running the tests is easy, just a single mouse click, so why not run them often? That way we get feedback the instant a line of code fails. Saving up a whole slew of errors before running the tests will take longer to sort out. With a small investment of a mouse click every few lines, we maintain a steady rhythm.

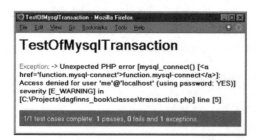

Figure 9.7
This time we're unable to get the MySQL connection, and the test case tells us what's wrong.

CHAPTER 9 TEST-DRIVEN DEVELOPMENT

Once the user name, password, and database have been set up, we are back to green. We'll skip a few steps here and go straight to the resulting code (see listing 7.1). Normally this would take a couple of test cycles to sort out.

Listing 9.1 The MysqlTransaction class fully implemented

```php
class MysqlTransaction {
    private $connection;

    function __construct($host, $user, $password, $db) {
        $this->connection = mysql_connect(
                $host, $user, $password, $db, true);
    }

    function select($sql) {
        $result = @mysql_query($sql, $this->connection);
        return new MysqlResult($result);
    }
}

class MysqlResult {
    private $result;

    function __construct($result) {
        $this->result = $result;
    }

    function next() {
        return mysql_fetch_assoc($this->result);
    }
}
```

Depending on the settings in your php.ini, you will receive various warnings about MySQL queries. We are going to trap all errors with exceptions, so we'll suppress the legacy PHP errors with the "@" operator. The test has also been modified slightly, so that the connection now takes the connection parameters from the test case:

```php
class TestOfMysqlTransaction extends UnitTestCase {
    function testCanReadSimpleSelect() {
        $transaction = new MysqlTransaction(
                'localhost', 'me', 'secret', 'test');
        $result = $transaction->select('select 1 as one');
        $row = $result->next();
        $this->assertEqual($row['one'], '1');
    }
}
```

Job done. We have implemented our first feature. In doing so, we have left a trail of tests (OK, just one) which specify the program so far. We have also gone in small steps, and so written only enough code to get the test to pass. 100 percent test coverage and lean code. That's a nice benefit of this style of coding. We are building quality in.

Right now we are green, as shown in figure 9.8.

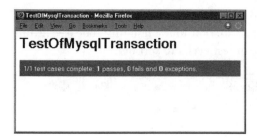

Figure 9.8
Finally, when the feature has been fully implemented, the test passes.

At last our Transaction class is up and running, and we have implemented the `select()` feature. From now on, things get faster. We need to implement the ability to write to the database as well. But first, we want to do some error checking.

9.2.5   Test until you are confident

The rules of this game are, write a test and watch it fail, get it green, modify (refactor) the code while green. This cycle is often abbreviated "red, green, refactor." We only add features once we have a failing test. We are only allowed to add a test once all the other tests are passing. If you try to add features with other code not working, you just dig yourself into a mess. If you ever catch yourself doing that, stop, roll back, and recode in smaller steps. It will be quicker than floundering.

We are green, so let's add a test for some error checking:

```
class TestOfMysqlTransaction extends UnitTestCase {

    function testShouldThrowExceptionOnBadSelectSyntax() {
        $transaction = new MysqlTransaction(
                'localhost', 'me', 'secret', 'test');

        $this->expectException();
        $transaction->select('not valid SQL');
    }
}
```

❶ Long, intention-revealing method name

❷ We had better get an exception

❶ That's a long method name, isn't it? We prefer long test method names that exactly explain what the test does. This makes the test more readable, makes the test output more readable when things go wrong, and also helps to keep us focused. With a woolier name such as `testErrorChecking()`, we might be tempted to test many more things. With a precise goal, we know when we are finished and ready to move on to the next feature. A test has to tell a story.

❷ This time there is a funny sort of assertion. `expectException()` tells SimpleTest to expect an exception to be thrown before the end of the test. If it isn't, SimpleTest registers a failure. We must get an exception to get to green.

Getting the test to pass is pretty easy, and involves changing only the `select()` method of our transaction class:

```
class MysqlTransaction {

    function select($sql) {
        $result = @mysql_query($sql, $this->connection);
        if ($error = mysql_error($this->connection)) {
            throw new Exception($error);
        }
        return new MysqlResult($result);
    }
}
```

Normally we would add more error checking here. In fact, we would keep adding tests until we had covered every type of error we could think of. At that point, we are confident in our code and can move on. For brevity, we are going to skip connection errors and so on, and move on to the `execute()` method. We have a lot of ground to cover.

9.3   DATABASE INSERT AND UPDATE

We are now the proud owners of a read-only database transaction class. It can do SQL SELECT, but no INSERT or UPDATE. We need some way to get data into the database as well; typing it manually on the MySQL command line gets tedious. Insert and update is actually simpler than select, since we

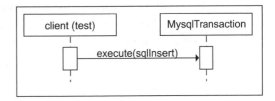

Figure 9.9   Inserting or updating data involves just one call from the client to the MysqlTransaction class.

need not worry about how to process the result. Figure 9.9 shows how simple it is.

We'll add an `execute()` method to our MysqlTransaction class. The `execute()` method is like the `select()` method, but returns no result. It's used for inserting or updating data. Because we have been moving forward successfully, we'll also move in larger steps. That's one of the joys of test-driven development; you can adjust the speed as you go. Clear run of green? Speed up. Keep getting failures? Slow down and take smaller steps. The idea is steady, confident progress. In the first subsection, we'll take a first shot at writing a test and then clean it up by separating the database setup code from the test itself. In the second subsection, we'll implement the `execute()` method, committing a small sin by cutting and pasting from the `select()` method. Then we'll atone for our sin by eliminating the duplication we just caused.

9.3.1   Making the tests more readable

We want to write data to the database. Since we already have a way to read data, we can test the ability to write data by reading it back and checking that we get the same value back. Here is a test that writes a row and reads it back again. It's a more aggressive test, but it's not well written:

```
class TestOfMysqlTransaction extends UnitTestCase {

    function testCanWriteRowAndReadItBack() {
        $transaction = new MysqlTransaction(                    Create the  ❶
                'localhost', 'me', 'secret', 'test');              table
        $transaction->execute('create table numbers (integer n)');  ◄
        $transaction->execute('insert into numbers (n) values (1)');
        $result = $transaction->select('select * from numbers');
        $row = $result->next();                    Insert and retrieve data  ❷
        $this->assertEqual($row['n'], '1');
        $transaction->execute('drop table numbers');  ❸  Drop the table
    }
}
```

❶❸ We need a test table in the database so that we insert and retrieve data without affecting anything else. Before the main test code, we create and drop the table.

❷ We use the transaction class to insert a value into the database and retrieve it. Then we assert that the value retrieved is the equal to the one we inserted.

What we see here is that the setup code (creating and dropping the table) and the test code are hopelessly intermingled. As a result, this test doesn't tell a story. It's difficult to read. We'll rewrite the test case to make things clearer. First the schema handling:

```
class TestOfMysqlTransaction extends UnitTestCase {

    private function createSchema() {
        $transaction = new MysqlTransaction(
                'localhost', 'me', 'secret', 'test');
        $transaction->execute('drop table if exists numbers');
        $transaction->execute(
            'create table numbers (n integer) type=InnoDB');
    }

    private function dropSchema() {
        $transaction = new MysqlTransaction(
                'localhost', 'me', 'secret', 'test');
        $transaction->execute('drop table if exists numbers');
    }
}
```

We've pulled the schema handling code out into separate methods. These methods won't be run automatically by the testing tool, because they are private and don't start with the string 'test'. This is handy for adding helper methods to the test case, useful for common test code.

Note that you will need a transactional version of MySQL for the following to work. That type=InnoDB statement at the end of the table creation tells MySQL to use a transactional table type. MySQL's default table type is non-transactional, which could lead to a surprise. You might need to install MySQL-max rather than the standard MySQL distribution for this feature to be present, depending on which version you are using.

CHAPTER 9   TEST-DRIVEN DEVELOPMENT

Extracting this code makes the main test flow a little easier. We have a setup section, the code snippet, the assertion, and finally we tear down the schema:

```
class TestOfMysqlTransaction extends UnitTestCase {

    function testCanWriteRowAndReadItBack() {
        $this->createSchema();
        $transaction = new MysqlTransaction(
                'localhost', 'me', 'secret', 'test');
        $transaction->execute('insert into numbers (n) values (1)');
        $result = $transaction->select('select * from numbers');
        $row = $result->next();
        $this->assertEqual($row['n'], '1');
        $this->dropSchema();
    }
}
```

Later on, we will find a way to clean this code up even more.

Why so much effort getting the tests to read well? After all, we only get paid for production code, not test code. It's because we are not just writing test code. It's about having an executable specification that other developers can read. As the tests become an executable design document, they gradually replace the paper artifacts. It becomes less about testing the code, and more about designing the code as you go. We'd put a lot of effort into our design documents to make them readable, so now that the tests are specifying the design, we'll expend the same effort on the tests. The other developers will thank us.

9.3.2 Red, green, refactor

Right now, the test will crash. Our next goal is not to get the test to pass, but to get it to fail in a well-defined, informative way by giving us a red bar. To get the test from crash to red, we have to add the `execute()` method to `MysqlTransaction`.

Then we're ready to go for green. Here is the MysqlTransaction code I added to get to green, running the tests at each step. In the first step, we had never selected a database after logging on. This is easily fixed by selecting a database in the constructor and checking for errors:

```
class MysqlTransaction {

    function __construct($host, $user, $password, $db) {
        $this->connection = mysql_connect(
                $host, $user, $password, $db, true);
        mysql_select_db($db, $this->connection);
        if ($error = mysql_error($this->connection)) {
            throw new Exception($error);
        }
    }
    //...
}
```

Then we have to actually write the execute() method. Most of the code is already in the select() method. As we want to get to green as quickly as possible, we'll cut and paste the code we need from the select() method to the execute() method.

```
class MysqlTransaction {

    function execute($sql) {
        mysql_query($sql, $this->connection);
        if ($error = mysql_error($this->connection)) {
            throw new Exception($error);
        }
    }
}
```

OK, the cut and paste got us to green, but we have a lot of duplicated code now. Once green, though, it's much easier to refactor the code. We just go in small steps and run the tests each time. If we tried to do this on red, trying to get a perfect solution in one go, likely we would get into a tangle. Refactoring is easier with passing tests.

First we'll create a new method:

```
class MysqlTransaction {

    private function throwOnMysqlError() {
        if ($error = mysql_error($this->connection)) {
            throw new Exception($error);
        }
    }
}
```

We run the tests. Next we make select() use the new method:

```
class MysqlTransaction {

    function select($sql) {
        $result = mysql_query($sql, $this->connection);
        $this->throwOnMysqlError();
        return new MysqlResult($result);
    }
    //...
}
```

We run the tests again (still green) and then factor the error check out of the constructor and the execute() method (not shown). Once we are happy that the code cannot be improved, we are ready to add another test.

That's a strange order to do things. Normally we design, then code, then test, then debug. Here we test, then code, then design once the first draft of the code is written. This takes faith that we will be able to shuffle the code about once it is already written. This faith is actually well placed. Did you notice we no longer have a debug step?

You would have thought that making changes would now involve changing tests as well as code. Sometimes it does, but that's a small price to pay. The biggest barrier to change is usually fear: fear that something will break, and that the damage will not show up until later. This results in the code becoming rather rigid as it grows more complicated. Sadly, this fear often blocks attempts to remove complexity, so this is a bad situation to be in. Having good test coverage removes the fear and allows changes to happen more often. The code is much easier to refactor with tests around it. Paradoxically, unit tests make the code more fluid. It's a bit like tightrope walking. You go faster with a safety net.

It can be difficult to get used to writing code before putting in a lot of design work. Personally, I have always found this aspect hardest to deal with, feeling that I should have a clear vision before I start. This is that production-line mentality creeping in again. The trouble is that when you try the clear-vision approach on complicated problems, it turns out that the clear visions aren't really that clear. Sometimes they are even completely wrong. Nowadays I have a rule of thumb: "No design survives the first line of code." I still do some early design, but I just make it a rough sketch. Less to throw away after we have started coding.

We've implemented all the basic features of the class, except the actual database transactions. It's time to get that done as well.

9.4   REAL DATABASE TRANSACTIONS

All this talk about design might leave you thinking that TDD is *not* about testing, and there is a grain of truth to this. It *is* about testing as well, and to prove it we still have a knotty problem to sort out. Our class is called MysqlTransaction and yet we haven't tested any transactional behavior.

In this section, we'll first find out how to test transactions. Then we'll add the actual Mysql transactional behavior to our code. Based on our experience from the example, we'll discuss whether testing really removes the need for debugging, and what else we need to do to ensure that we've done all we can to produce code of high quality.

9.4.1   Testing transactions

We'll add a `commit()` method to the tests and have the rule that nothing is committed to the database until this method is called. This means that some of our test code won't yet make sense. In particular, when we build and drop the schema, we have to commit these steps, too. For example, here is a fixed `createSchema()` method in the tests:

```
class TestOfMysqlTransaction extends UnitTestCase {

    function createSchema() {
        $transaction = new MysqlTransaction(
                'localhost', 'me', 'secret', 'test');
        $transaction->execute(
            'create table numbers (n integer) type=InnoDB');
        $transaction->commit();
    }
}
```

Of course, we add an empty method to the code to get the tests back to green. Now that our tests match the desired interface, we can move on.

Testing transactions is tricky, to say the least. For the transaction test, we'll set up a sample row of data, and then we'll start two transactions. The first will modify the data, hopefully successfully. Then the second transaction will attempt to modify the data before the first one has been committed. We should get an exception when the second update query is executed.

We shall see that this is a tough test to get right. Still, this extra effort is easier than finding out later that your website has some mysteriously inconsistent data. Here is the helper method to set up the data:

```
class TestOfMysqlTransaction extends UnitTestCase {

    function setUpRow() {
        $this->createSchema();
        $transaction = new MysqlTransaction(
                'localhost', 'me', 'secret', 'test');
        $transaction->execute('insert into numbers (n) values (1)');
        $transaction->commit();
    }

}
```

That was easy. Here is the test:

```
class TestOfMysqlTransaction extends UnitTestCase {

    function testRowConflictBlowsOutTransaction() {
        $this->setUpRow();                    ❶  Insert
        $one = new MysqlTransaction(              test rows
                'localhost', 'me', 'secret', 'test');
        $one->execute('update numbers set n = 2 where n = 1');
        $two = new MysqlTransaction(
                'localhost', 'me', 'secret', 'test');
        try {
            $two->execute('update numbers set n = 3 where n = 1');
            $this->fail('Should have thrown');
        } catch (Exception $e) { }
        $this->dropSchema();                  Second
    }                                         transaction ❸

}
```

❶ Create transaction, no commit ❷ Second transaction ❸

❶ We start by running the helper method that inserts the row that the transactions will compete for.

❷ Then we create and run the first transaction without committing it.

❸ The second transaction is similar and should throw an exception as soon as we try to execute it. The test for the exception is similar to the one we used earlier in this chapter.

We're only testing the failure behavior here. There is no need for any commits in the test, since we're not supposed to get to commit anyway. Note that we haven't used expectException() here, because we want to ensure that dropSchema() is run. The `fail()` method just issues a failure if we get to it. Of course, we should have thrown by then. If we do, our test reaches the end without failures.

Now that we have a failing test, let's code.

9.4.2 Implementing transactions

In order to get real transactional behavior, we need to open the transaction and commit it. We want to open it implicitly when the MysqlTransaction object is created, and commit it only when `commit()` is called explicitly. We start by opening a transaction in the constructor:

```
class MysqlTransaction {

    function __construct($host, $user, $password, $db) {
        $this->connection = mysql_connect(
                $host, $user, $password, $db, true);
        mysql_select_db($db, $this->connection);
        $this->throwOnMysqlError();
        $this->begin();
    }
    //...
}
```

Opening the transaction is fairly technical. Here is the version for MySQL:

```
class MysqlTransaction {

    private function begin() {
        $this->execute(
                'set transaction isolation level serializable');
        $this->execute('begin');
    }
    //...
}
```

The isolation level is chosen for maximum MySQL consistency. In other words, it's the safest and slowest isolation level. By contrast, the `commit()` method is pretty generic:

```
class MysqlTransaction {

    function commit() {
        $this->execute('commit');
        mysql_close($this->connection);
        unset($this->connection);
    }
}
```

Once the transaction is committed, we don't want to send any more statements. Closing the connection will ensure any further queries throw exceptions.

If you run this test, you will likely get a web server timeout. On my default installation, the web server page timeout is set to 30 seconds, but the MySQL deadlock timeout is set at 50 seconds. This causes the page to timeout first. If you increase the page timeouts in your web server and your php.ini file, you will see the test pass after 50 seconds. This is too long. Unit testing works because of the fast feedback. We like to run the tests after each code edit. We cannot afford to wait 50 seconds for one test, as that would kill a lot of the benefit.

For a web environment database server, the deadlock wait is actually too long anyway. In your my.ini (Windows) or my.cnf (Unix), you can change the timeout with

```
innodb_lock_wait_timeout=1
```

This causes the test to take just 1 second. Even that extra second is not ideal, but we could live with this. We won't have permission to change this setting in a production environment, so we will tend to move all of the slow tests into their own test group. They are run less often, usually when rolling out to a server, or overnight on a special test machine. You might want to do this for your development box as well, just to keep the tests fast. When classes depend on the outside world like this, you often have to make some testing compromises. In the next chapter, we'll look at ways to ease such problems.

9.4.3   The end of debugging?

Our code is starting to look quite well-tested now, and hopefully we have managed to head off a lot of future disasters. Is unit testing the end of debugging? Sadly, no.

If you are developing the usual hacky way, your manual tests will catch about 25 percent of the bugs in your program (see *Facts and Fallacies of Software Engineering* by Robert Glass). By *manual tests,* we mean print statements and run-throughs with a debugger. The remaining bugs will either be from failure to think of enough tests (35 percent), or combinatorial effects of different features (around 40 percent). How does TDD make a dent on these figures?

By testing in very small units, we reduce combinatorial effects of features. In addition, the code we write is naturally easy to test, as that was one of the running constraints in its production. This also helps to make features independent during time. As we combine our units of code, we will also write integration tests specifically aimed at testing combinations of actions. These are much easier when we know that the underlying parts are working perfectly in isolation.

Simply forgetting a test happens less often when you have the attitude that "we have finished when we cannot think of any more tests." By having an explicit point in the process, this thought allows us to explore new testing ideas. Again, we would expect a small reduction in missing tests due to this pause.

If optimistically we reduce both these bug counts by a factor of two, we have a conundrum. Teams adopting TDD often report dramatic drops in defect rates, much more than a factor of two. What's happening?

In contrast to testing, code inspection can reduce defect rates by a factor of ten. Code is easier to inspect if it's minimal and the intent is clear. As TDD pushes us away from grand up-front designs, to a series of lean additions, it naturally leads to cleaner code. If this is the case, part of the effect of unit testing may be the incidental boost it gives to code inspection. Test-protected code is much easier for multiple developers to work on and play with. As each one improves the code, he finds new tests and fixes that help to clean it up. The code keeps getting better as you add developers, rather than backsliding.

This is the benefit of building quality in. By reducing confusion, you reduce development time, too. To contradict Stalin: "Quality has a quantity all of its own."

9.4.4   Testing is a tool, not a substitute

It's up to us to write correct code. Because code inspection is still part of the process, writing code that feels right is still important. That's why we have refactoring as the last stage. The code is not finished just because the tests pass; it's finished when the tests pass and everyone is happy with the code. Right now, I am not happy with the way our transaction class doesn't clean up after itself in the face of exceptions. I want a destructor:

```
class MysqlTransaction {

    function __destruct() {
        if (isset($this->connection)) {
            @mysql_query('rollback', $this->connection);
            @mysql_close($this->connection);
        }
    }
}
```

I've used the raw `mysql_query()` function here. If we used our own `execute()` method, failure would result in another exception. Throwing exceptions in a destructory is bad form.

9.5   SUMMARY

In the next chapter, we will build further on our knowledge of unit testing, learning how to set up test suites properly. We will also use mock objects and other fake software entities to make it easier to test units in isolation.

Are you happy with the code you see? Can you think of any more tests? Do you feel in charge of the quality of the code that you write?

And William Edwards Deming? Building quality into the system had its own rewards for the twentieth-century Japanese economy. With less money being spent on finding defects, especially finding them late, industry was actually able to cut costs while raising quality. Buyers of Japanese products benefited not just from a lower price, but more reliability and better design. TQM would turn Japan into an industrial power. In 1950, though, shocked at Japan's post-war poverty, Deming waived his fee.

C H A P T E R   1 0

Advanced testing techniques

Once, as I was zapping TV channels, I happened upon an unfamiliar soap opera. A man was saying to a woman, "We're *real people*; we have *real feelings*." If I had been following the program from the start, I would probably have been mildly amused by this. But coming in suddenly, it struck me how extraordinary a statement this was, a fictional character bombastically proclaiming himself real.

Working with software, we're used to juggling the real and the unreal. In computing, it's a matter of taste whether you consider anything real or not, other than hardware and moving electrons. Ultimately, it's mostly fake. The kind of fiction in which dreams and reality mingle in complex ways (like *The Matrix*) seems like a natural thing to us.

But the idea that some software objects are "fakes," in contrast to normal objects, is important in testing. Most fake objects are referred to as *mock objects*. Their fakeness does not imply that ordinary objects are as real as chairs or giraffes. Instead, the fakeness of mock objects is determined by the fact that they work only in the context of testing and not in an ordinary program.

For an interesting example of fakeness from the presumably real world of physical technology, consider incubators, the kind that help premature infants survive. From our unit-testing point of view, an incubator is a complete fake implementation of a womb. It maintains a similar stable environment, using a high-precision thermostat, feeding tubes, and monitoring equipment. It might be less than perfect from both an emotional and a medical point of view, and yet it has some definite practical advantages. Above all, it's isolated. It has few dependencies on its environment beyond a supply of electrical current. In my (perhaps totally misguided) imagination, given slightly more automation than is common in hospitals, a baby could survive for weeks or even months in an incubator even if no other human beings were around.

A womb, on the other hand, although itself a highly predictable environment, depends on a complex and unpredictable biological system known as a human being. (A woman, to be precise; I'm using the term *human* being to emphasize the fact that gender is irrelevant to this discussion.)

In addition to their inherent complexity, human beings have their own dependencies on environmental factors. To state the obvious, they need food, water, housing, clothes, and even have complex psychological needs. The existence of dependencies, and dependencies on dependencies, means that you need real people (even the kind that have real feelings) to staff the maternity ward.

These issues, dependencies and predictability, are crucial in software testing. When a single component has a failure, we don't want other tests to fail, even if those other parts use the failing component. Most importantly, we want the tests to be controlled and not subject to random failure. We want our code to run in a tightly controlled environment like an incubator or a padded cell.

The need for this increases with rising complexity. Testing a single class as you code it is usually straightforward. Continually testing an entire code base day in and day out, perhaps with multiple developers and multiple skills, means solving a few additional problems.

We have to be able to run every test in the application, for a start. This allows us to regularly monitor the health of our code base. We would normally run every test before each check-in of code.

In this chapter, we will be building the internal workings of a contact manager that implements persistence using the MysqlTransaction class from the previous chapter. Working test-first as usual, we will first implement the Contact class and its persistence feature. Then we'll design and implement a feature that lets us send an email to a contact. To test that, we'll be using mock objects. Finally, we'll use a program called fakemail to test the sending of the email for real.

10.1 *A CONTACT MANAGER WITH PERSISTENCE*

Our examples are now going to get more realistic. We are going to build a simple customer relationship manager. This will be a tool to keep track of clients, initiate contact with web site visitors, and manage personal email conversations. It will eventually be capable of sending and storing every kind of message and contact detail we will ever need. All that is in the future, though. Right now, we are just getting started.

Since we need to add another group of tests, we start this section by finding out how to run multiple test cases effectively. Then we write a test case for contact persistence. Working from the test case, we implement simple Contact and ContactFinder classes. We clean our test case up by implementing `setUp()` and `tearDown()` methods to eliminate duplication. At that point, surprisingly, our implementation is still incomplete, so we finish up by integrating a mail library. If you thought you needed to start at the bottom, coding around a mail library, then you are in for a pleasant surprise.

10.1.1 Running multiple test cases

A contact manager must be able keep track of an email address in a database and send a message to it. So this is the aspect that we'll tackle first. Of course we start with a test case:

```php
<?php
class TestOfContact extends UnitTestCase {
}
?>
```

We place this snippet into a classes/test/contact_test.php file. We already have a test file called transaction_test.php in the same directory. It's a good idea to run all the tests together until the full test suite becomes so large that it's no longer practical. We want to be able to run all these tests at once, even though they are in multiple files.

You might be thinking that we have skipped all of the SimpleTest scaffolding at this point. What happened to including SimpleTest, and all that stuff about running with a reporter that we have in the transaction test script? In fact, it is rarely needed. Instead, we will place the test scaffold code into its own file called classes/test/all_tests.php. Here it is:

```php
<?php
require_once('simpletest/unit_tester.php');          ❶ Require the
require_once('simpletest/reporter.php');                SimpleTest files

class AllTests extends TestSuite {                    ❷ Create a
    function __construct() {                             test suite
        parent::__construct('All tests');
        $this->addTestFile('transaction_test.php');   ❸ Add the test
        $this->addTestFile('contact_test.php');          from the files
    }
}
$test = new AllTests();                               ❹ Run the full
$test->run(new HtmlReporter());                         test suite
?>
```

❶ This includes the SimpleTest toolkit as before.

❷ Next we create a test suite. The 'All tests' string is the title that will be displayed in the browser.

❸ Then the magic happens. In the constructor, we add the test using `addTest-File()`. Now each test file will be included with a PHP `require()`. SimpleTest will scan the global class list before and after the include, and then any new test classes are added to the test suite. For this to work, the test file must not have been included before. A test file can have any number of test classes and other code, and any number of test files can be included in a group. In case you were wondering, suites can nest if a group definition is itself loaded with `addTestFile()`. The resulting test structure, test cases and groups within groups, is an example of the Composite pattern that we introduced in section 7.6.

❹ All that's left is to run the `AllTests` group.

The all_tests.php file will get executed when we want to run the tests. Right now, that doesn't work, because our transaction_test.php file from the last chapter messes things up. Our TestOfMysqlTransactionTest gets run twice. This is because it is still set to run as a standalone script. To make further progress, we must go back and strip away the runner code from our first test:

```php
<?php
require_once('../transaction.php');

class TestOfMysqlTransaction extends UnitTestCase {

}
$test = new TestOfMysqlTransaction();
$test->run(new HtmlReporter());
?>
```

When we run all_tests.php, we still get a failure, but this is just SimpleTest warning us that we haven't entered any test methods yet.

With the runner code in its own file, adding more tests just means including the files under test, and then declaring test classes. Adding a test case is a single line of code and adding a test is a single line of code. We don't like duplicating test code any more than we like duplicating production code. You can have as many test cases in a file as you like, and as many tests in a test case as you like.

That's enough about how SimpleTest works; let's return to our contact manager application.

10.1.2 Testing the contact's persistence

Our contact manager won't do us much good if the contacts have to be re-entered every time we run it. The contacts have to persist across sessions. That means we have to be able to save a contact to the database and retrieve it again. Where do we start? We write a test, of course:

```php
<?php
require_once('../contact.php');

class TestOfContactPersistence extends UnitTestCase {

    function testContactCanBeFoundAgain() {
        $contact = new Contact('Me', 'me@me.com');
        $transaction = new MysqlTransaction(
                'localhost', 'me', 'secret', 'test');
        $contact->save($transaction);

        $finder = new ContactFinder();
        $contact = $finder->findByName($transaction, 'Me');
        $this->assertEqual($contact->getEmail(), 'me@me.com');
    }
}
?>
```

The first part of the test saves a new contact to the database. Right now, we assume a Contact object is just a name, an email address, and a save() method. After saving it, we immediately try to retrieve a copy. For finding contacts, we'll not surprisingly use a ContactFinder class. We'll take a guess for now, and assume that we will need to find a contact by name. This isn't unreasonable, but this is not the usual thinking when designing an application. In real life, there would be a requirement driving the code, and we would only add the methods that we definitely need. A complete application would be too much to absorb for an example, so our design is proceeding bottom-up. In the coming chapters, we'll complete our survey of test driving code, and demonstrate how an application can be built top-down.

The approach is now similar to our transaction_test.php in the previous chapter. We let the test define the interface, and then write enough code to avoid a PHP crash. Here is the minimum code in classes/contact.php that gives us a red bar instead of a crash:

```php
<?php
class Contact {

    function getEmail() {
    }

    function save($transaction) {
    }
}

class ContactFinder {
    function findByName($transaction, $name) {
        return new Contact();
    }
}
?>
```

To get the test to pass, we use the FakeIt pattern again, or "cheating" if you prefer. Since the test says that the `getEmail()` method should return me@me.com, all we need to do is hard-code this particular email address:

```
class Contact {

    function getEmail() {
        return 'me@me.com';
    }
    //...
}
```

Since the code now has the ability to return this email address only, it's not general enough. It should be able to return any email address we want. Looking back at the test, what is the Contact object doing? Ignoring the fact that it's being saved to and then re-created from the database, its own work is accepting the contact's name and email address as arguments to the constructor and returning the email address when we ask for it. The test also implies that it has some way of returning its name, but the details are up to the implementation. Notice how deftly the test defines the interface. It only requires what is absolutely needed.

10.1.3 The Contact and ContactFinder classes

At this point, it might occur to us that the test we've written is actually pretty elaborate in its workings. We have the choice of writing another, very simple, test case specifically for the Contact class. Alternatively, we can assume that it's not necessary, since our existing test case seems to be exercising all of the Contact object's very simple features. It comes down to what you consider a "unit" in unit testing. To me, Contact and ContactFinder are so closely tied that it makes more sense to test them together.

Let's just implement the Contact class and see what happens:

```
class Contact {
    private $name;
    private $email;

    function __construct($name, $email) {
        $this->name = $name;
        $this->email = $email;
    }

    function getEmail() {
        return $this->email;
    }
    //...
}
```

Now the test fails. We have a red bar, and the simple reason is that the ContactFinder is still rudimentary. We are dumping a fully formed Contact object into a black hole and re-creating a new, empty one without the correct email address. To get back to green quickly, we can do another FakeIt. The last time, we hard-coded the return value from the Contact object. Now we hard-code the return value from the Contact-Finder:

```
class ContactFinder {
    function findByName($transaction, $name) {
        return new Contact($name, 'me@me.com');
    }
}
```

This works and we are green. If it hadn't worked, our best bet would have been to take a step back and actually implement a separate test (or tests) for the Contact object to make sure the email getter was working. As mentioned in the previous chapter, you can adjust your speed. And you know you need to adjust it if you lose track and become unsure of what's happened and where to go. If you take a step and lose your footing, go back and then take a smaller step forward. As it is, though, the step we have taken is small enough and pushes our design along nicely.

Another small step is to let the ContactFinder read the data for the contact object from the database:

```
class ContactFinder {
    function findByName($transaction, $name) {
        $result = $transaction->select(
                "select * from contacts where name='$name'");
        return new Contact($name, 'me@me.com');
    }
}
```

We're still returning the hard-coded Contact object; that practically guarantees that the assertEqual() in our test will still pass. However, we do get an exception from our MysqlTransaction, which says "Table 'test.contacts' doesn't exist." This leads us to the thorny issue of where to create the schema. Although this chapter is a discussion about thorny issues and testing techniques, it's not about how to organize an application into packages. We'll take the simplest approach: using an SQL script to create the table that the exception is screaming about. To avoid mixing SQL scripts with our PHP code, we create a top-level directory called database and place the following scripts in it. The first is database/create_schema.sql:

```
create table contacts(
    name varchar(255),
    email varchar(255)
) type=InnoDB;
```

Then there is the corresponding database/drop_schema.sql:

```
drop table if exists contacts;
```

We need to add these scripts to our test case. We will call them through our well-tested MysqlTransaction class:

```
class TestOfContactPersistence extends UnitTestCase {
    function createSchema() {
        $transaction = new MysqlTransaction(
                'localhost', 'me', 'secret', 'test');
        $transaction->execute(file_get_contents(
                '../../database/create_schema.sql'));
        $transaction->commit();
    }
    function dropSchema() {
        $transaction = new MysqlTransaction(
                'localhost', 'me', 'secret', 'test');
        $transaction->execute(file_get_contents(
                '../../database/drop_schema.sql'));
        $transaction->commit();
    }
}
```

At this point, we could call these methods at the beginning and end of our test, as we did in the TestOfMysqlTransaction class in the previous chapter. In that class, we wanted to use these methods in only a few tests, and we wanted them used differently each time. In our new situation, we will want to create and drop the schema for every test. That means adding calls to createSchema() and dropSchema() for every method. That's a lot of repetitive clutter.

10.1.4   setUp() and tearDown()

Again, the original JUnit authors have thought of this situation, and both SimpleTest and PHPUnit have copied the solution. SimpleTest test cases come with a setUp() method that is run before every test and a tearDown() that is run after every test. By default, these methods do nothing, but we can override them with our own code:

```
class TestOfContactPersistence extends UnitTestCase {
    function setUp() {
        $this->dropSchema();
        $this->createSchema();
    }

    function tearDown() {
        $this->dropSchema();
    }
    //...
}
```

Note that we call dropSchema() in the setUp() method as well as the tear-Down(). This doesn't cause us any harm and ensures we start with an up-to-date schema when we change things between tests. By repeating the action in the tear-down, we make sure that we leave no trace of our test. If we do leave a trace, this could inadvertently affect a developer's environment or another test case.

Are you shocked that we would drop the whole database and re-create it for every test, possibly hundreds of times? It turns out that this doesn't significantly slow the tests down. What's nice is it absolutely guarantees that the database starts in a clean state each time. The alternative is to create the schema once, then delete just our test data. This is possible, but carries a risk, since we might easily forget to delete some of it. When a test leaves test data in the database, the next test might perform differently, causing a different test result than we would get when running the test completely on its own. This problem is known as *test interference*.

If it takes us a year to develop our customer relations software, then there will be many changes of schema and many changes of individual tests. If any of these lead to test interference, we could waste hours trying to track down a bug that doesn't exist. Worse, we could have incorrect code when one test falsely relies on data entered by another. That's a lot of wasted effort, just to save a fraction of a second on our test runs. We also miss out on the confidence and cleaner tests we get from a complete drop. It pays to be brutal with our test setup.

10.1.5 The final version

Back to our ContactFinder class. When we last looked, it was still basically a fake. We got the result object from the database, but then we threw it away and returned a hard-coded Contact object created to match the test. We'll complete it by getting the database row from the result object and creating the Contact object from the row:

```
class ContactFinder {
    function findByName($transaction, $name) {
        $result = $transaction->select(
                "select * from contacts where name='$name'");
        $row = $result->next();
        return new Contact($row['name'], $row['email']);
    }
}
```

This is supposed to be the finished version of the ContactFinder, but we can't be sure yet, since the test fails because of an incomplete Contact class. The row is not being written to the database, since the Contact object's save() method is an empty stub. Filling it out, we end up with this:

```
class Contact {

    function save($transaction) {
        $transaction->execute(
                "insert into contacts (name, email) " .
                "values ('" . $this->name . "', '" .
                $this->email . "')");
    }
}
```

We don't want duplicate rows in our database, but at the same time, the name field is unlikely to be unique. We could use the email field as a database key, but this doesn't completely solve the problem. Suppose we make contact with someone, but have an incorrect email address. When we find out her real email address, we naturally want to overwrite our current entry. The trouble is, writing out a new Contact will still leave the old version unless we explicitly delete the incorrect one. Worse, what if two people are sharing the same email address? Or someone uses multiple email addresses? What about merging two similar databases? Keeping historical records? Human identity is a complex problem.

The problem is so complex that we will skip it and return to the subject of data class design in chapter 21. Whatever scheme we come up with, we should be able to write tests for our current test case. Here, we'll tackle another problem instead—actually sending a mail.

10.2 *SENDING AN EMAIL TO A CONTACT*

We want to be able to use the contact manager to send an email to a contact. To this end, we'll put a `send()` method in the Contact class. It will accept the message text as an argument and send the text to the email address stored in the Contact object.

Just the tiniest bit of up-front design is appropriate here. We need to know what classes will be involved and the basics of how they will interact. We may change our minds about both of those things when we write the tests and implement the classes, but it helps to have a mini-plan.

We will start this section with that design. To test it without sending actual emails, we turn to mock objects, first using a manually coded mock class, and then using SimpleTest's mock objects. This enables us to implement the email feature in the Contact class without having implemented the underlying Mailer class. This means that we're implementing top-down, and mock objects make that possible. Finally, we discuss the limitations of mock objects and the need for integration testing.

10.2.1 Designing the Mailer class and its test environment

There is an appropriately named `mail()` function built into PHP. At first sight, the simplest thing that could possibly work is to use that. If we spray `mail()` calls all over our code, though, we will find ourselves sending emails on every test. Instead we use a separate Mailer class for this work. As we will see shortly, a Mailer class will be a requirement for building our padded cell or incubator. So let's have a look at the basic class design to get a rough idea of what we're aiming for (see figure 10.1). The Contact object will be able to send the message by using the Mailer, which is introduced as an argument to the Contact's `send()` method.

Trying to test this brings on tougher challenges than before, since the end result is an email, and emails end up outside our cozy class environment. The obvious way to test whether an email has been sent by the Contact object is to set up the test to mail

Figure 10.1
Class design for Contact class using a Mailer

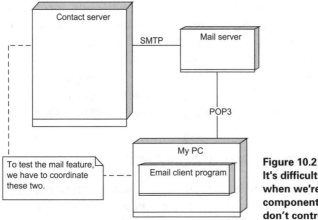

Figure 10.2
It's difficult to automate testing when we're dealing with many components, some of which we don't control.

it to yourself. Then you run the test, wait a few seconds, and then check your incoming mail. This obviously won't work if another developer is running our tests. It breaks our model of automating tests. How can we test email on a single click?

One way is to set up a special test mail server in such a way that we can read the mail queue. This is clumsy and slow, and we like to avoid slow tests when we can. It's also a lot of work to set up such a server. How about a mail server on the development box itself? Again this is a lot of work, and we still have to read the mail queue. Figure 10.2 shows how complex our test might be.

10.2.2 Manually coding a mock object

Hang on for a second; are we tackling this problem the right way?

We only want to assert that the Contact object attempted to send an email. We are not testing the Mailer class; we are testing our Contact class. What happens if there is a bug in our Mailer class? When we run our test of the Contact class, we will get failures that are not our fault. Besides wasting a lot of our time, it shows we are testing more than we need to. Let's not test the mailer at all if we can.

As the request leaves our application code, it enters the test environment. The quicker we intercept the message, the fewer related classes we need to test. Suppose we test it straight away. Suppose the only application code in our tests is the class we actually want to test. That means intercepting the message as soon as it leaves Contact. There is a neat trick which actually accomplishes this.

We'll add the following to our contact_test.php file:

```php
class MockMailer {
    public $sent = false;

    function send() {
        $this->sent = true;
    }
}

class TestOfContactMail extends UnitTestCase {
```

```
    function testMailWasSent() {
        $mailer = new MockMailer();
        $contact = new Contact('Me', 'me@me.com');
        $contact->send('Hello', $mailer);
        $this->assertTrue($mailer->sent);
    }
}
```

The MockMailer is a stand-in for our real Mailer object. It's a complete fake, totally unable to deliver a real email, and a figment of our test code. It does have a primitive ability to remember what has been done to it, though. This is the distinguishing feature of mock objects: they are able to *sense* what the code we are testing is doing. We feed it to our class under test, Contact, which is blissfully unaware of our deception. By controlling calls made by our application object, as well as the calls we make on it, we place our class in its own padded cell.

Now instead of the complexity of figure 10.2, we are using the much simpler structure in figure 10.1, with the Mailer replaced by a lookalike, or rather, a workalike.

But our mock object is still rather primitive, since it can only sense the fact that the send() method has been called and nothing more. We need something a bit more powerful for a satisfactory test.

10.2.3   A more sophisticated mock object

The preceding test asserts only that we called the send() method on the Mailer. Really, we would like to check the contents of the mail and the address it was sent to. We could add an if clause to our hand-coded mock just for this test and that would work fine. Suppose, though, we add another test. We would need to have another if clause, or some way to program in the expected parameters. Suddenly that's a lot of mock code, and pretty repetitive, too.

SimpleTest can automate a lot of this work for you. First, we have to include the mock objects toolkit in our all_tests.php file:

```
<?php
require_once('simpletest/unit_tester.php');
require_once('simpletest/mock_objects.php');
require_once('simpletest/reporter.php');
//...
?>
```

Once this is done, we can rewrite our test more concisely:

```
Mock::generate('Mailer');        ❶ Generate the mock class

class TestOfContactMail extends UnitTestCase {

    function testMailWasSent() {
        $mailer = new MockMailer();
        $mailer->expectOnce('send', array(                    ❷ Set expectations
                'me@me.com', "Hi Me,\n\nHello"));                 and run test
        $contact = new Contact('Me', 'me@me.com');
        $contact->send('Hello', $mailer);
```

```
        }
}
```

❶ The `Mock::generate()` call is where most of the work is done. This code generates a whole new class. The default name for this class is the `generate()` parameter with the word "Mock" in front. This generated class has no real code in common with the original, but has the same method signatures and interfaces. We can then instantiate our MockMailer objects as often as we want in our tests.

❷ The mock object is a programmable clone, and has a lifetime of one test. Here we tell it that `send()` will be called just once. If this does not happen, an error is sent to the test suite. The expectation also contains a parameter list that, when not matched exactly, will also result in failure. Note that we no longer need the unit test assertion, as the mock object will talk to the test suite directly. The result is a precise, yet very lean test. Mock objects add considerable firepower to your unit testing armory.

Unfortunately, the test currently fails. It's a fatal error with "Class 'MockMailer' not found."

10.2.4   Top-down testing

The test fails because we haven't written the Mailer class yet, and since SimpleTest uses the real class to generate the corresponding mock class, the mock version is not generated. Do we now have to implement the Mailer anyway, just to get the mock version?

Fortunately, we don't. We only need to sketch out the Mailer class. We don't have to write any Mailer code, only the basic interface. In a file mailer_.php we can write:

```php
<?php
class Mailer {
    function send($address, $message) {
    }
}
?>
```

Once this file is included by contact.php, our crash is replaced by a failing test, as shown in figure 10.3.

Our MockMailer now correctly reports that `send()` was not called by Contact, when it should have been. The test code is so ruthless, it almost tells us the code to type into our Contact class:

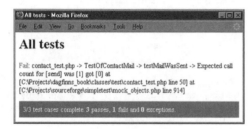

**Figure 10.3
The test fails because the
mock object's expectation
was not fulfilled.**

CHAPTER 10   ADVANCED TESTING TECHNIQUES

```
class Contact {
    function send($message, $mailer) {
        $mailer->send($this->getEmail(),
                "Hi {$this->name},\n\n$message");
    }
}
```

With the mock satisfied, we are green.

We have a passing test, but we don't yet have a functioning Mailer class. With conventional unit testing, you have to build all of the small pieces first. This isn't considered a problem if you assume that the design is done by the time the testing phase has come around, but we no longer assume that. Instead, we expect design and testing to be a continuous process. Normal unit testing thus forces us to design bottom up, because the lower-level objects must be functioning before the higher-level ones can be tested. Mock objects break that dependency, and so allow us to design top-down. again.

With our current example, Contact has forced Mailer into having one method signature, send(), but this is only the story so far. Other parts of the code may force other methods to be added later. No immediate implementation is needed in any case, and the specification for our new class is free to evolve.

The test decoupling shows in other ways. While we are coding the Mailer, suppose we break it. This would ordinarily cause multiple test failures all over the test suite, including our Contact tests. With most of the dependent tests using mocks, only the Mailer tests fail. The test suite tells you precisely what code has been broken, without spurious reports on other classes.

Figure 10.4 shows how the Contact class is decoupled from the Mailer during the mock test. The mailer interface is not explicitly represented in the code. The fact that they have the same methods is not because we've programmed them using interface inheritance; it's because one is generated from the other. The resulting relationship between them is similar, though.

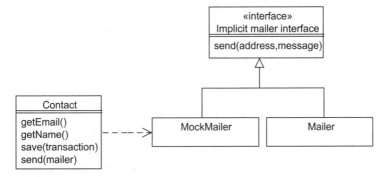

Figure 10.4   The mock Mailer has the same interface as the real one, but if the real Mailer fails or changes its implementation, the test of the Contact object will still work.

10.2.5 Mock limitations

There is an obvious problem with mocks. The mock objects will catch changes of interface, and type hints are carried over into the mock versions, but more subtle mismatches can creep through. We could assume a method behaves a certain way in a test, but the behavior might be different in real life. As a result, we could program our mock differently from the code it is meant to simulate. For example, we could have got the parameters the wrong way around on the Mailer's `send()` method, but our tests would still pass if both tests and code make the same assumption. Or perhaps the mailer needs the email address in a different format, such as "`<Me>` `me@me.com`." For this reason, we often add an integration test or two without mocks. This is to make sure all of the pieces are wired up correctly.

You might be thinking, "If we have to create an integration test anyway, why bother mocking in the first place?" Good question, but imagine a larger number of tests. Integration tests are hard work; tests with mock objects are not. If we write most of our tests with mocks, and confirm the wiring together with just a few integration tests, we win. In practice, we win big.

The other obvious problem is that we cannot use mock objects to test the Mailer class itself. The whole point of this class is to talk to the outside world. If we draw our application as a space holding a web of interconnected classes, the Mailer would appear on the outer edge, as shown in figure 10.5.

The Transaction and Mailer classes can be thought of as gateways to the outside world. Our Contact class is purely internal. The gateways make excellent pieces to mock when testing the internals. The internal unit tests run at the full speed of the microprocessor and nothing can go wrong. Testing the gateways needs special consideration, as the tests are likely to be fiddly, like our timing problem in the Transaction tests.

As the Mailer is definitely a gateway, this throws us back into our original quandary—how to test email without setting up a complete mail environment.

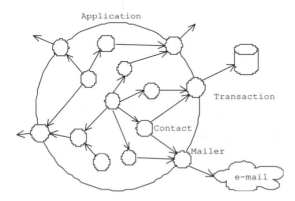

Figure 10.5
The application as a web of interconnected classes that talks to the outside world through gateways

CHAPTER 10   ADVANCED TESTING TECHNIQUES

10.3 A FAKE MAIL SERVER

When someone says they stubbed something, they are usually referring to their toe. When programmers *stub* something, they mean that they created a fake version just for testing. We want to stub the mail server. Like most Internet protocols, mail is just shoveling text through network sockets. Writing a simulator for such resources is a job, but not a complex one. Creating a fake Internet server is usually a few days' work at most.

This might sound like a lot of work just to test one mail class, but it actually isn't. If you are going to be working on an application for a year, spending three days automating such testing will repay itself many times over. We won't just use the stub for the little class test we are about to write, we will reuse it every time we test the whole application. We'll look at application testing in chapter 12.

In this section, we'll see how to install fakemail, devise a test with it, and implement the Mailer class accordingly. Then we'll discuss how the implementation is actually an Adapter on a Zend framework class.

10.3.1 Installing fakemail

So how do we create a fake mail server? As it happens, one of the authors was faced with exactly this task while working on a recent project. The resulting spin-off was the *fakemail* project on Sourceforge (http://sf.net/projects/fakemail/). Rather than write our own stub, we'll use this one.

Installing fakemail is fairly straightforward, and you can choose from Perl or Python versions. The Perl version needs the CPAN module `Net::Server::Mail::SMTP` (see http://cpan.perl.org/) and the Cygwin version of Perl (http://www.cygwin.com/) if you are using Windows. The Sourceforge tarball unpacks into a fakemail folder, inside which is the file fakemail. To make sure that everything is working, we'll fire up fakemail next.

To start the server, we run the script:

```
perl fakemail --host=localhost --port=25 --path=.
```

The host should match your machine's host name, and the port is the one you want to listen to for initial connections. The Simple Mail Transport Protocol (SMTP) listens on port 25 by default, so for a quick and dirty test, we'll use that port. On Unix systems, you will not have access to ports below 1024 unless you are the superuser. The `path` parameter tells fakemail where to store the incoming mails.

If you've started fakemail in a terminal, it will output:

```
Starting fakemail
Listening on port 25
```

The server is now waiting for incoming mail. Next, we fire up a mail client and create a new account. This account will use our local machine as the mail server. The

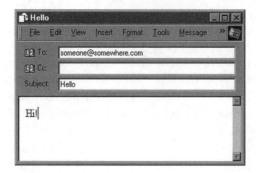

Figure 10.6
Example of configuring a
mail client to use fakemail

exact configuration obviously differs depending on the mail client, but figure 10.6 is an example.

We now send a mail as we normally would, as shown in figure 10.7. We then find that fakemail has captured it into a file called someone@somewhere.com.1. If we were to send another mail to the same address, it would be saved as someone@somewhere.com.2. We stop fakemail by hitting Ctrl-C in the terminal. The captured mail should look something like this:

```
Message-ID: <001301c640b9$6f5a63c0$0401a8c0@home>
From: Marcus <marcus@localhost>
To: <someone@somewhere.com>
Subject: Hello
Date: Mon, 6 Mar 2006 01:00:59 -0000
Content-Type: text/plain; charset="iso-8859-1"
Content-Transfer-Encoding: 7bit

Hi!
```

Note that fakemail captures both the headers and the mail body. It's a very simple script.

Now that we've seen the how the fake mail server works, we want to use it to test our Mailer class—or rather, to develop the Mailer test-first. So our first goal is to write a workable test of the Mailer's main feature: sending mail.

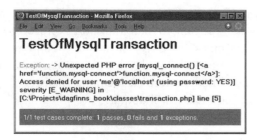

Figure 10.7
Sending a test mail
to fakemail

CHAPTER 10 ADVANCED TESTING TECHNIQUES

10.3.2   A mail test

Now that fakemail, our test tool for the occasion, is installed, we can put it to use. Our test class will be called TestOfMailer. To be able to use fakemail, the test class must start fakemail before running the actual tests and stop it afterward. The most convenient way to do that is to start it in the setUp() method and stop it in the tearDown() method. That way, it will start and stop for every single test.

```
require_once('../mailer.php');

class TestOfMailer extends UnitTestCase {
    private $pid;

    function setUp() {                              ❶ Start
        $command = 'perl fakemail/fakemail ' .         fakemail
                '--host=localhost --port=10025 ' .
                '--path=temp --background';
        $this->pid = `$command`;
    }

    function tearDown() {                           ❷ Stop
        $command = 'kill ' . $this->pid;               fakemail
        `$command`;
    }
}
```

❶ We define the fakemail start command and use the PHP backtick operator to run it. The parameters are similar to our fakemail installation check, but with a few important differences. Because a production server will already have a mail server, we cannot use port 25 in our tests. Instead the setUp() method uses port 10025. This means that our eventual Mailer class will have to be able to change its port to match. The path to save the captured mails is set to temp, and this folder will have to be created in the classes/test folder. It will also need to be writable by the web server. This sort of tedious setup is often necessary for gateway classes. Finally, the background flag tells fakemail to start as a background task in a detached subshell. If this were not done, our testing process would jam, waiting for fakemail to stop. As we need our current process to send the very mail that would clear the jam, we would be deadlocked. We need a second process. When fakemail runs as a background process, the process ID is printed to the screen. We capture this process ID, so that we can kill it again in the tearDown() method.

❷ The tearDown() method, again using the backtick operator, kills the process using the process ID we stored in the $pid instance variables.

Now that we control the environment, we actually test something:

```
class TestOfMailer extends UnitTestCase {

    function testMailIsSent() {
        $mailer = new Mailer('localhost', 10025);
        $mailer->send('me@me.com', 'Hello');
```

```
            $this->assertMailText('me@me.com', 'Hello');
        }
    }
```

This might seem cryptic. We were supposed to be using fakemail, but there is no trace of it in this test. Where is it? It's hidden inside the `assertMailText()` call. It's no good scurrying off to the SimpleTest manual to look up `assertMailText()`, because it isn't there. One of the advantages of having classes as the test cases is that we can supplement them with custom assertions when we think we will use them often. Here we are going to create a new mail assertion just to make the test easier to read. The tests are our documentation, after all.

Here is the new assertion:

```
class TestOfMailer extends UnitTestCase {

    function assertMailText($address, $expected) {
        if (! file_exists("../../temp/$address.1")) {    ❶ Fail if
            $this->fail("No mail for $address");             no file
            return;
        }
        $content = file_get_contents("../../temp/$address.1");
        $this->assertNotIdentical(                        ❷ Pass if
                strstr($content, $expected),                contents
                false,                                      are OK
                "Cannot find $expected in $address");
    }
}
```

❶ If no file has been saved, we immediately fail and finish the test.

❷ If fakemail has saved the incoming mail, we do a simple `strstr()` call to see if the text is present. The `assertNotIdentical()` is the opposite of `assertIdentical()` in SimpleTest. So what's `assertIdentical()`? It compares not just the value, like `assertEqual()`, but also the type. As the PHP `strstr()` function returns false on no match, we test for exactly that value. We also make sure that the assertion outputs a meaningful message to anyone faced with our failing test.

All this file saving is going to lead to a lot of debris, and that in turn could lead to test interference. We make sure the temporary files are cleaned up by going back to the `setUp()` and `tearDown()` calls:

```
class TestOfMailer extends UnitTestCase {

    function setUp() {
        $command = 'perl fakemail/fakemail ' .
                '--host=localhost --port=10025 ' .
                '--path=temp --background';
        $this->pid = `$command`;
        @unlink('../../temp/me@me.com.1');
    }

    function tearDown() {
```

```
        $command = 'kill ' . $this->pid;
        `$command`;
        @unlink('../../temp/me@me.com.1');
    }
    //...
}
```

The test is done; now to the code. Of course, we are not going to implement an entire mail client to pass this test. Instead we'll use a library.

At the time of writing, the first cut of the Zend framework has just been released and, conveniently for us, it contains a mail component. We'll import the library into a folder called Zend in the top-level directory. The Zend mailer is made up of a container for the email information, called Zend_Mail, and a gateway of its own, called Zend_Mail_Transport. Because we want to be able to change the server port programmatically, we'll choose the more flexible Zend_Mail_Transport_Smtp version of the transport.

The resulting Mailer class that just passes the test is:

```php
<?php
set_include_path(get_include_path() . PATH_SEPARATOR .
        dirname(__FILE__) . '/../Zend/library');
require_once('Zend/Mail.php');
require_once('Zend/Mail/Transport/Smtp.php');

class Mailer {
    private $transport;

    function __construct($host, $port) {
      $this->transport =
              new Zend_Mail_Transport_Smtp($host, $port);     }

    function send($address, $message) {
        $mail = new Zend_Mail();
        $mail->setFrom('me@localhost', 'Me');
        $mail->addTo($address);
        $mail->setBodyText($message);
        @$mail->send($this->transport);
    }
}
?>
```

The version of the Zend framework I was using, version 0.10, throws warnings within the mail components. For this reason, the PHP error suppressor is used on $mail->send() until this bug is fixed.

The first test is green, but we are still a long way short of completing our Mailer class. We'll need some way to set the "from" address and the subject of the mail. We'll also need some error handling, probably with exceptions. As that's not really the point of this chapter, this is left as an "exercise for the reader." The main achievement is the closing of the feedback loop. From this point on, it's red, green, refactor. If we break the Mailer, we will know about it.

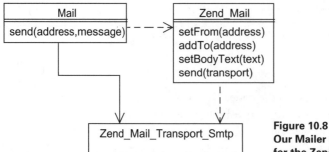

Figure 10.8
Our Mailer class is an Adapter for the Zend_Mail class.

10.3.3 Gateways as adapters

The Mailer acts as a simple wrapper to change the interface of the Zend_Mail class and hides the transport class. This is the Adapter pattern from chapter 7; figure 10.8 shows how it works in this case.

You are probably wondering why we bothered with our own Mailer class, when all it does is use the Zend framework to do its work. Why not just use the Zend classes in our application? Has testing led us down the wrong path?

We could have mocked the Zend_Mail class and used that as the gateway instead, if we knew we were going to go down that road. The thing is, we didn't need to know that. By controlling the gateway, we could defer or modify our work on sending email without affecting progress on the rest of the application. Not only that, but we are free to choose our own interface, one that is clearest to us and fits our own coding standards. We are also insulated from changes in the Zend framework.

This change of dependency, from the gateway affecting us to us dictating the gateway, is known as *dependency inversion*. We described it at great length at the end of chapter 6. It's an important technique in decoupling application components, and yet it arose naturally as a result of our testing techniques. If you need to swap out components to mock them, naturally you are going to be able to swap out components to change them as well. Testing could easily have hamstrung us as classes depended on other classes to work. Testing with mock objects and simple gateways has actually encouraged a decoupled design.

10.4 SUMMARY

Testing an entire application is not just about the mechanics of running a lot of test files; an application contains huge numbers of dependencies. As we start to wear the three hats of tester, coder, and designer, we have to manage these dependencies in our tests as well as our code. Sometimes, such as with gateways to the outside world, testing these can be quite a bit of work.

Designing tests naturally gets us into designing interfaces. Designing tests with mocks and stubs allows us to concentrate on one task at a time, and to control everything else. With conflicting problems isolated, we can more thoroughly test each component. We can also work on each component in any order we wish, ideally with top-down design. Perhaps in test-driven development, we should call it "mock-down design"?

As we've said before, full test coverage is the prerequisite for refactoring, and refactoring is the subject of the next chapter. Tests act as a safety net while we shuffle code around. Enabling code to be modified after it is written enables us to change the design. Some of the things we will learn include separating HTML markup from PHP code, improving readability, eliminating duplication, and making procedural code object-oriented. All of these are design improvements added to existing code. We are ready to examine the third stage in our process of test, then code, then design.

Refactoring web applications

You can't know a town, neighborhood, or landscape well until you've been around it. You need to explore it to the point where most places are familiar to you. That means roaming most of the roads and streets. Just traversing it a couple of times is not enough.

You learn more if you're on foot or on a bicycle. Traveling by car, even if you're driving, you might forget where the slopes or even hills are located. When you're foot-powered, you're likely to remember the exact ups and downs.

A software design is a landscape of possibilities. If you take the time to explore them, you're likely to learn something new every time.

In the real world, there is limited time for this. But refactoring opens up an opportunity. The obvious benefits of refactoring are improving the design and preventing it from deteriorating as a result of changes. The less obvious benefit is to allow us to explore and see the effect of different design approaches.

Refactoring is a large and fertile subject, and showing full examples takes up a lot of space in a book. If you want to refactor code that is already object-oriented, there is plenty of literature on how to do it, and even though PHP is not well-represented, the examples are usually relevant to PHP.

But this does not reflect the real world of PHP web programming. Most books and articles about refactoring use pure object-oriented program code as a starting point for refactoring. Real-world PHP web applications are not pure program code (HTML markup is involved), and frequently the PHP code is not object-oriented. This chapter focuses particularly on the challenges posed by such typical PHP applications. Refactoring web applications is a large subject; an entire book could easily be written about it. We will concentrate on a few challenges that are particularly important in PHP:

- Separating HTML markup and program code
- Dealing with changes that are different in PHP than in the languages that are typically used in refactoring books
- Inherently difficult refactorings, especially those involving conditionals

Based on this, we will start by discussing the place of refactoring in the development process. Then we'll cover the classic aims of refactoring—improving readability and eliminating duplication—and see a couple of basic examples of how they can be achieved. That should get us in the mood to discuss the more difficult challenges: separating HTML and PHP code and simplifying conditional expressions. Finally, we'll take a look at some tricks for getting from procedural to object-oriented.

11.1   REFACTORING IN THE REAL WORLD

To remind you of what was said in chapter 1, *refactoring* means improving the design of existing code. The behavior of the code does not change; we're not fixing bugs or adding new features. This helps keep the program flexible, readable, and maintainable, so that the next time we fix a bug or add a feature, it is easier to see what needs to be done and easier to make the change.

Refactoring makes it easier to find bugs. When it becomes easier to see what the code is doing, it's also easier to see how what it does differs from what it should do. Changes are easier because refactoring typically leads to simpler code, and when it's easier to understand the code, it's easier to make changes. Changing messy code is like moving things around when they're stacked in a random pile rather than sorted neatly on shelves.

Refactoring, like unit testing and many other good things in life, is simple. In fact, it's deceptively simple and easy to do. It's a set of small, unambiguous steps that tend to lead to unforeseen, sometimes magical, results.

In this section, we'll discuss refactoring and its place in different real-world situations. We'll look at the difference between refactoring as a regular practice to keep code clean and refactoring as a way of saving code that has never been kept clean before. Then we'll discuss the question of when it might be better to reimplement rather to refactor.

11.1.1 Early and late refactoring

There are two different scenarios for refactoring. One is refactoring as a regular practice, integral to software development. This is what the gurus of agile development recommend. Even the best experts are unable to keep a design clean at all times without refactoring. Requirements change, and even if we could keep them constant as defined in some document, there would still be new and unexpected requirements that would shift the balance so that changing to a somewhat different design is desirable.

The other scenario is refactoring *legacy code*; code that has not been refactored along the way and might therefore be far from ideal design-wise.

This is more difficult in many ways. This chapter will focus heavily on this kind of challenge, since most PHP developers will meet it, and since it's a way to learn better alternatives to practices—such as mixing program code and HTML markup—that are common in PHP applications but not very useful in the long run.

Refactoring depends on good test coverage. If there are no tests to alert us when we introduce a bug, we risk spending too much time searching for bugs after a refactoring session.

There is an expression "You can't get there from here":

> *YouCantgetThereFromHere is a kind of a problem that I once saw Bugs Bunny have in a cartoon. He kept driving around in circles and coming back to the same hamburger stand and asking directions. Eventually the hamburger stand guy said "Well gee, come to think of it you can't get there from here."* (http://c2.com/cgi/wiki?YouCantGetThereFromHere)

Strictly speaking, in programming there is no such thing as not being able to get there from here. If you can get there at all, you can get there by throwing your existing code into the bit bucket and reimplementing whatever you need.

But refactoring is based on the assumption that there is usually an easier way to get there from here by changing the code incrementally.

But in refactoring and redesign, especially of legacy code, the straight line from here to there invariably goes through a swamp. In refactoring, we go in baby steps around the swamp. We take whatever detours are necessary to keep from getting wet—that is, to keep the tests running correctly except for short periods—typically, a few minutes at most.

I've learned more about good program design from refactoring than from anything else. In second place comes reading well-designed code. All the theory, including design patterns, comes after that.

Although refactoring legacy code is possible, how far can we stretch our ability to do it? When is it better to reimplement?

11.1.2 Refactoring versus reimplementation

What do we do if a bunch of spaghetti code is dumped in our lap? There are two basic strategies for dealing with it: one is to refactor incrementally, the other is to bail out and build something similar from scratch.

There is no sure way to know when it's better to throw the old code out. Simple logic tells us that there must be such cases. There are times when the code is so bloated and unreadable—when large amounts of code do very little and the work just to understand what it does is a major undertaking—that it seems obviously better to start afresh.

At the other extreme, reimplementation is sometimes just an expression of the "not invented here" principle. Someone wants to start from scratch because he believes he's so much smarter than those who developed the existing system. So he starts building something new with little effort to avoid the mistakes that were made during the previous implementation.

When developers reimplement a program that was developed by someone else, there is no guarantee that the new program will be better than the old one. It could be worse. There are a few reasons why it's likely to be better, though:

- There is normally an expectation that it will be better, and that at least motivates the developers to try.

- Even though some programmers are not good at learning from past experience, and especially that of others, some understanding is usually transferred from the old crowd to the new.

- The existing program makes it easier to discover the requirements for the new one.

- Finally, sometimes technological progress intervenes and makes it easier to do things right the second time.

Whatever the situation, nontechnical considerations play an important part. If you're making an open-source application in your spare time, you're free to reimplement, but in the commercial world, tight schedules tend to make full reimplementations impossible. It might be painfully slow to add new functionality to the existing application, but customers and managers are typically not willing to wait half a year or more for a completely new program if they could have that urgent new feature in two weeks instead. If we say it's good for them in the long run, why should they trust us? Unless, that is, the old application is somehow in crisis and they know something drastic has to be done.

By refactoring incrementally, we can avoid the trap of having to spend so much time on code improvement that we break our schedules. The principle is that whenever we need to change something, we do any necessary refactorings first. With chaotic code, that can sometimes be difficult, but it usually helps. Changing duplicated code the same way in several places is a slow and error-prone process.

Another possibility is to reimplement only parts of the application. That can also help us get some improvement on a tight schedule.

The advantage of refactoring instead of reimplementation, besides the fact that it makes it easier to keep schedules, is that it nearly always goes from worse to better. If done competently and without excess ambition, it will make the program more manageable and more maintainable and make it easier to add new features.

Now that we've done some thinking about the place of refactoring in development, it's time to see how it's done. We'll start with the classic aims of refactoring and see a few simple examples of how they can be achieved.

11.2 REFACTORING BASICS: READABILITY AND DUPLICATION

Refactoring is both difficult and surprisingly easy. It's easy in simple cases and on a small scale because the procedures and the aims are simple and relatively easy to understand. And although it can be a heavy challenge to perform large refactorings to change the entire architecture of an application, the fact that refactoring can be practiced on a small scale first helps a lot to prepare us for that kind of undertaking.

The most basic goals of refactoring are to improve readability and eliminate code duplication. Frequently, refactoring leads to obvious improvements in these two areas. In this section, we'll take these goals in turn and study them in the context of realistic examples.

11.2.1 Improving readability

Improving the readability of PHP code is important and usually easy—up to a point. We can usually start with the simple improvements. When we've exhausted those, the harder ones are easier to do because of the improvements we've already made.

All refactoring aims at making code easier to read and understand, but the main tool to improve readability is one of the simplest refactorings: *Extract Method*. Probably all programmers have done it at some point. Even if you've never written a line of object-oriented code, you've probably extracted a function from procedural code, and that's the same thing in principle.

Extracting functions or methods to enhance readability is simple in theory. If we have a few lines of code whose intention can be described in a few words, we make it a separate method or function. What is challenging sometimes is the fact that enclosing code in a function or method makes all the variables local to that function or method. Long stretches of procedural code tend to have lots of temporary variables that might or might not be used before or after the chunk we want to extract. To make it work, we may have to pass one or more variables as arguments and return one or more variables. The idea is to do it if it enhances readability and to ignore temporarily other problems we're not currently working on; the result doesn't have to be perfect or "right," just better.

Let's look at an example that may seem overly simplistic, but actually demonstrates the principle quite well. If you have some experience with PHP and MySQL, you're likely to find this simple script fairly easy to read:

```
$mysqli = new mysqli('localhost','app','secret','news');
$result = $mysqli->query('SELECT * FROM News');
while ($array = $result->fetch_assoc()) {
    echo $array['headline']."\n";
}
```

But remember that the ease with which you read it is a result of experience. Someone who hasn't used the MySQL functions would find it harder. Or if the code used some less-known library, an XML database, perhaps, it would be less obvious. So let's pretend we want this to be easier to read for someone who is not so familiar with MySQL. Adding comments would help:

```
// Connect to news database
$mysqli = new mysqli('localhost','app','secret','news');

// Get news articles from database
$result = $mysqli->query('SELECT * FROM News');

// Show headlines
while ($array = $result->fetch_assoc()) {
    echo $array['headline']."\n";
}
```

Now we've used about three times as many lines, but it's probably slightly easier to read even for someone with the relevant background.

Comments are helpful, but as mentioned before, if the same information is in the form of function and class names, it's harder to forget to change it when you move parts of it around.

The next step is simply to extract each of these sections into a separate function:

```
function createMysqlConnection() {
    return new mysqli('localhost','app','secret','news');
}

function getNewsArticlesFromDatabase($mysqli) {
    return $mysqli->query('SELECT * FROM News');
}

function showHeadlines($result) {
    while ($array = $result->fetch_assoc()) {
        echo $array['headline']."\n";
    }
}
```

We've just taken the comments and transformed them mechanically into function names. Now the main code can be written like this:

```
$mysqli = createMysqlConnection();
$result = getNewsArticlesFromDatabase($mysqli);
showHeadlines($result);
```

This may seem mildly absurd; and admittedly, extracting so many functions from such a short stretch of code is an extreme example. In most cases, each function or method will be longer than these. The most interesting part of this experiment is just reading and comparing the examples.

Also, you might not want the function names quite as verbose as these. But it is possible, and with a program editor or IDE that has some kind of automatic completion feature, it's not likely to cost much typing.

Another issue that crops up at this stage is object orientation. Although we've used the object-oriented mysqli extension, the code around it is not object-oriented. But there are two reasons why what we've done so far is pointing us in the direction of objects:

- We have to pass arguments from one line to the next to maintain context. The code would be even more readable if we didn't have to do this.

- The functions are small. If we split all the code into chunks this small, we are likely to end up with so many functions that we can never remember all of them, and we're likely to get into name conflicts. Keeping the functions in a class helps us avoid that.

Generally, anything that improves readability tends to be worth doing. Some improvements may seem trivial, but those are usually easy to make.

11.2.2 Eliminating duplication

As mentioned earlier, duplication is one of worst diseases of software. It encourages bugs and security holes, since making parallel changes in several near-identical code segments is almost certain to fail sooner or later. Either we will forget to change one of the copies, or the change will not work in all of them, as shown in figure 11.1.

Duplication comes in varying degrees of awfulness, from one or two lines of code that are somewhat or almost identical, to the web application that's been copied several times in its entirety and modified differently each time.

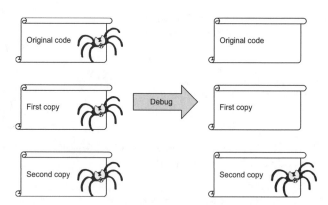

Figure 11.1 Trying to fix a bug that exists in three copies

Some say you should refactor as soon as you have two similar chunks of code. Some say you should wince at the second occurrence and refactor when you get to the third. Some even wait for the fourth.

But it seems clear that the decision has to be based on more than the number of occurrences. The volume of duplicated code seems to be of obvious importance. Here is an example of a tiny volume of duplication:

```
echo strftime("%a %e %b %Y %H:%M:%S",$time1);
echo strftime("%a %e %b %Y %H:%M:%S",$time2);
```

Do we want to make a separate function or method for this? Create a constant or variable for the `strftime()` format string? It could possibly make the code more readable, but it hardly seems necessary for the sake of eliminating duplication. And adding one more occurrence would hardly tip the scales in favor of refactoring.

But if there are 500 lines of duplicated code, the usefulness of eliminating the duplication seems obvious.

As the example stands, it would be quite a feat to change one of them without noticing the other. But if the two lines in the previous example were further apart, there would be a chance that we might change just one of them. That might cause an undesirable inconsistency in the user interface. Clearly the distance between the occurrences also has some relevance. To sum up, the need to eliminate duplication depends on at least these three factors:

- The number of occurrences
- The volume of duplicated code
- The distance between occurrences

Table 11.1 lists some of the classic refactorings that are most useful for eliminating duplication.

Extracting functions or methods to eliminate duplication is the same thing in principle as doing it to improve readability, only better, since we usually get an improvement in readability as a bonus.

Listing 11.1 is another slightly altered excerpt from a real web application. Each `print` statement was originally a single line; I've broken the lines, making it slightly more readable. Still, it's the kind of thing that can seem overwhelming and tempt us to hack whatever changes we need.

Table 11.1   Some refactorings for eliminating duplication

Location of duplication	Refactoring
Inside conditional	Consolidate Duplicate Conditional Fragments
In procedural code	Extract Function
Inside a class	Extract Method
In different classes	Extract Superclass, Extract Class

Listing 11.1 Duplication inside URLs

```
<td align="right" valign="top" colspan="2">
<?php
 if ($lang=="no") {
   if ($monitor==="") {
       print "    
       <a href=\"$PHP_SELF?show=search\" target=\"_self\"
       class=\"headlink\">Rediger</a>\n";
       print "    
       <a href=\"$PHP_SELF?show=search&action=new\"
       target=\"_self\" class=\"headlink\">Ny</a>\n";
   }
 } else {
   if ($monitor=="") {
       print "    
       <a href=\"$PHP_SELF?show=search\" target=\"_self\"
       class=\"headlink\">Edit</a>\n";
       print "    
       <a href=\"$PHP_SELF?show=search&action=new\"
       target=\"_self\" class=\"headlink\">New</a>\n";
   }
 }
?>
</td>
```

At least this example uses some CSS styling. Still, it could be simplified further by using CSS:

- The ` ` characters can and should be replaced with CSS margin and/or padding, since that is their real purpose.

- Repeating the class attribute seems unnecessary. If every link in the table is styled in the same way and the table cell that's being generated is inside a table with `id="search"`, the styling for the links can be specified as in this example:

```
table#search a { color: green; margin-left: 4em; }
```

But the CSS issues are nit-picking compared to the real duplication problem. That problem is fairly obvious from the example: the `if` and `else` branches of the outer conditional statement differ only in the texts displayed. The first set is in Norwegian; the second in English.

Strictly speaking, this calls for a *Consolidate Duplicate Conditional Fragments* refactoring or *Extract Method*. That would require us to move the duplicated code outside the `if-else` statement or replace the text strings with method calls. But because of the complexity of the statement, the simplicity of the strings, and the fact that we expect to end up with a template eventually, we'll replace the text strings with variables instead. For example,

```
$strings =
    $lang == 'no'
    ? array('edit' => 'Rediger', 'new' => 'Ny')
    : array('edit' => 'Edit', 'new' => 'New');
if ($monitor==="") {
    print "<a href=\"$PHP_SELF?show=search\" target=\"_self\"
    class=\"headlink\">".$strings['edit']."</a>\n";
    print "<a href=\"$PHP_SELF?show=search&action=new\"
    target=\"_self\" class=\"headlink\">".$strings['new']."</a>\n";
}
```

This is an unsophisticated approach to internationalization. I'm not suggesting it's the "correct" one. At the very least, the strings need to be moved into separate files. It's not supposed to be perfect, just better. We're trying out what it's like to refactor by small steps, solving problems one by one.

There is still some duplication. We may want to generate the URLs separately and keep them as variables in a template, eventually.

We have started on the difficult task of improving code that contains both HTML markup and PHP program code. In most cases, this requires separating the two as cleanly as possible. Let's see how we can do that.

11.3 *SEPARATING MARKUP FROM PROGRAM CODE*

The subject of separating HTML markup from PHP program code has been mentioned before, and we will return to it, particularly in chapter 13. Figure 11.2 illustrates the basic idea, seen from the point of view of refactoring. Many PHP applications mix PHP and HTML sections rather freely. Since this gets messy except in very simple cases, we want to pull the two apart, keeping them (mostly) in separate files: HTML in template files and PHP code in scripts or classes.

There are two distinct approaches to separating markup and program code. From a traditional refactoring point of view, the more obvious one is to place the entire HTML output under test and start making the division in small steps. But this can be

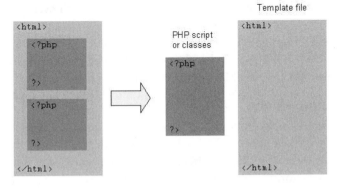

Figure 11.2   Separating HTML and PHP

difficult and cumbersome, especially with large amounts of HTML. It's too easy to do something that makes the test fail—by accidentally replacing a space character with a newline, for instance. The difference might not be important to the end result (line breaks are mostly irrelevant in HTML), and still we have to spend time fiddling with it to keep the tests passing. We get bogged down in layout details when what we really want to do is to make the transfer of data into the template work.

The other approach is to start by creating the template from the output, identify the variables needed, and then put the test harness on the variables instead of the final HTML output. This is usually more straightforward.

In this section, we'll start by discussing the rationale behind the separation. We'll take a quick look at the role of CSS, and then we'll see two examples that illustrate the two different approaches mentioned.

11.3.1 Why the separation is useful

I was rather surprised to find that one PHP book actually recommends outputting all HTML code from PHP echo or print statements.

There is a sort of flexibility to this approach: once you have everything in PHP code, it's easy to add conditional logic, move some of it into functions, and do all sorts of other manipulations.

The problem is that this kind of practice fragments the markup in a way that makes it almost impossible to see and modify the layout in the context of the web page as a whole.

For instance, if we want to have a professional web designer improve the layout, we might be utterly lost. We might not think we will ever need to do that, but unless the application is our personal open-source project and we have 100 percent control over it, we really can't be sure. In a commercial setting, it's risky. Even if no web designers are ever involved, we might get a request like this one: "We need this application with a different layout. Can you make it look like our new customer's web site?" Suddenly we have to use this sample page, whatever its HTML qualities, for the layout. If the existing HTML is in a template or a long HTML section, we can copy the HTML from the sample and add dynamic content to it. If it's scattered all over the PHP code, we're in trouble.

Another, related difficulty is optimizing the HTML code itself. Making systematic changes to make the HTML more readable and less bloated (see the next section) is next to impossible unless the HTML is fairly concentrated in a few places.

11.3.2 Using CSS appropriately

Although this is not a book about CSS, it is worth mentioning the benefits of using CSS appropriately. Proper use of CSS makes the HTML code more readable and reduces its volume. Indirectly, this can affect the PHP code as well, and it is one of the considerations in refactoring web applications.

In spite of an increasing number of broadband users, the size of the HTML file sent across the network to the user is one of the factors that determine response time. And response time can be a key factor affecting whether the user chooses to stay at your site or go somewhere else.

This is one reason for using CSS markup sensibly. Unnecessary tags and attributes slow down browsing. And simpler, more readable HTML is easier to maintain. Here is a slightly altered excerpt from an open-source PHP application downloaded in 2005:

```
echo "<tr bgcolor=00ffff>";
echo "  <td bgcolor=dddddd align=middle>";
echo "    <font size=2 color=ff4499 face=sans-serif>$i</font>";
echo "  </td>";
echo "</tr>";
```

The majority of the markup in this example is deprecated according to the HTML 4.01 specification, which was published in 1999. It seems it was still popular six years later. In a minimal survey of five open-source PHP applications I downloaded in 2007, all of them used the deprecated `bgcolor` attribute, but there weren't many occurrences in each application.

But the practical disadvantages are more important than the lack of conformance to W3C recommendations. The unnecessary markup obfuscates the PHP code it's embedded in, consumes bandwidth, and is much less flexible than its CSS equivalent. With CSS and using an HTML section instead of the echo statements, it can be reduced to this:

```
<tr>
  <td>
    <?php echo $i ?>
  </td>
</tr>
```

And here is the CSS code for good measure:

```
table tr { background-color:#00ffff; }
table td { background-color:#dddddd; font-size: 0.8em;
           color: #ff4499; font-family: sans-serif;
           text-align: center; }
```

Of course, this has to be sent across the network, too, but normally only once, since the browser caches the CSS code if it's in a separate style sheet.

11.3.3 Cleaning up a function that generates a link

For our first example, we will try the first approach to separating markup and code. We will place the HTML output under test and change the PHP code slowly and incrementally so that the code is always working and the tests never fail. This is manageable in this case since there is not much HTML.

The example is loosely based on a part of a real application. All the problems are real ones from that application. But the example is much simpler and cleaner than the original, which had several additional global and local variables and used these to build the URL.

```php
function print_link($search,$form,$link_text,$blank_target) {
    if( !($search || $form))
        echo "<a href=\"index.php\"";
    else {
        if(!$search) {
            echo "<a href=\"form.php\"";
        }
        else {
            echo "<a href=\"index.php?action=search\"";
        }
    }

    if($blank_target)
        echo " target=\"_blank\">";
    else
        echo ">";

    echo "$link_text</a>\n";
}
```

Full test coverage is absolutely necessary, or at some point we might discover that we made a mistake at an earlier stage, and it will be hard to recover.

Here are the requirements for the test class. It has to exercise all three branches in the first conditional statement and both branches of the second one. The first conditional is controlled by the two arguments $search and $form; the second one is controlled by the argument $blank_target. The tests will have to set the two global variables in three different combinations and use output buffering to catch the output. Listing 11.2 shows the test case.

Listing 11.2   Test case for link function

```php
class LinkTest extends UnitTestCase {
    function getEchoed($search,$form,$blank_target=FALSE) {   ❶ Test some
        ob_start();                                               arguments
        print_link($search,$form,'hello',$blank_target);          to catch
        $html = ob_get_contents();                                output
        ob_end_clean();            Run with output
        return $html;              buffering ❷
    }

    function testFirstIf() {                          ❸ Test-first
        $html = $this->getEchoed(FALSE,FALSE);           branch
        $this->assertEqual(
            '<a href="index.php">hello</a>'."\n",
            $html);
    }
```

```
function testSecondIf() {
    $html = $this->getEchoed(FALSE.TRUE);
    $this->assertEqual(
    '<a href="form.php">hello</a>'."\n",
    $html);
}
function testElse() {
    $html = $this->getEchoed(TRUE,FALSE);
    $this->assertEqual(
        '<a href="index.php?action=search">hello</a>'."\n",
        $html);
}
function testBlankTarget() {
    $html = $this->getEchoed(FALSE,FALSE,TRUE);
    $this->assertEqual(
        '<a href="index.php" target="_blank">hello</a>'."\n",
        $html);
}
}
```

Test other ❹
cases

❶ In order to test the different paths, we need to feed different combinations of arguments to the function and catch the output so we can check it. getEchoed() does this job.

❷ We start output buffering so we can catch the output. Then we run the function, using "hello" for the one argument that's constant for all the tests. Finally, we end output buffering and return the results.

❸ To test the first if branch (the one in the outer conditional), we feed FALSE in the two first arguments to the function and test the output.

❹ The rest of the tests are just variations using different arguments.

When the tests are in place, we can start refactoring. The nested conditionals look like an awkward implementation of if...elseif...else. So let's change that:

```
if( !($search || $form))
    echo "<a href=\"index.php\"";
elseif(!$search) {
    echo "<a href=\"form.php\"";
}
else {
    echo "<a href=\"index.php?action=search\"";
}
```

The <a href is duplicated in all the conditional branches. Duplicated markup is always a hindrance when we want to concentrate all the markup in one place. So we'll use the refactoring called *Consolidate Duplicate Conditional Fragments* to put it in one place. Figure 11.3 is a somewhat abstract flowchart to illustrate this refactoring.

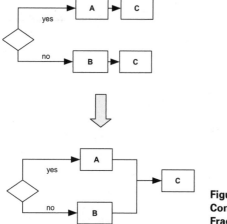

Figure 11.3
Consolidate Duplicate Conditional
Fragments refactoring

In our example, this means extracting the string `<a href="` and echoing it before the `if` statement:

```
echo "<a href=\"";
if( !($search || $form))
    echo "index.php\"";
elseif(!$search) {
    echo "form.php\"";
}
else {
    echo "index.php?action=search\"";
}
```

From a mechanical point of view, we could have moved `$page.php`, too. But strategically, it might be better to keep the URL itself apart from the HTML tag it's in.

Then there is the other conditional near the end of the function. Here, we find another small dose of duplication:

```
if($blank_target)
    echo " target=\"_blank\">";
else
    echo ">";
```

Since that `>` character is output in both cases, we can remove the `else`. We might as well change the outer quotes to single quotes while we're at it, so we don't need to escape the ones inside:

```
if($blank_target)
    echo ' target="_blank"';
echo ">";
```

Now for a somewhat larger and more important step. We want to extract the code that generates just the URL. The URL is not part of the HTML markup and cannot be styled, so all the processing that goes into generating the URL itself can safely be done in a PHP function. This part of the code always executes only one `echo` statement, so instead of printing, we can just return the result:

```
function get_url($search,$form) {
    if( !($search || $form)) {
        return "index.php";
    }
    elseif(!$search) {
        return "form.php";
    }
    else {
        return "index.php?action=search";
    }
}
```

The if-elseif-else structure is no longer necessary. Also, we can reverse the sense of the conditions, move them around, and end up with this:

```
function get_url($search,$form) {
    if ($search) return "index.php?action=search";
    if ($form) return "form.php";
    return "index.php";
}
```

Now the main function is looking more readable:

```
function print_link($search,$form,$link_text,$blank_target) {
    echo '<a href="';
    echo get_url_($search,$form);
    echo '"';
    if($blank_target)
        echo ' target="_blank"';
    echo '>';
    echo "$link_text</a>\n";
}
```

We are now close to being able to separate out all the markup by concentrating it at the end of the function. The `if` test for the target attribute is the only remaining PHP logic. We could probably move everything but the attribute value outside the `if` statement, so if `$blank_target` is false, we get an empty target attribute instead of no attribute. But instead, we'll keep the code working in exactly the same way, generating `$target_attr` variable that is either empty or contains the attribute with the `_blank` value. A convenient way to do this is to use the ternary operator:

```
$target_attr = $blank_target ? ' target="_blank"' : '';
```

If `$blank_target` is TRUE, `$target_attr` becomes `target="_blank"`. Otherwise `$target_attr` will be an empty string. Now we can write the next version of the `print_link()` function as follows:

```
function print_link($search,$form,$txt_link,$blank_target){
    $target_attr = $blank_target ? ' target="_blank"' : '';
    $url = get_url($search,$form);
```

```
        print '<a href="';
        print $url.'"';;
        print $target_attr;
        print '>';
        print "$txt_link</a>\n";
}
```

It is now becoming clear how we can use this in an HTML section or template. If we have a function to generate the URL and one to generate the target attribute then we're ready to go, because the only remaining variable, the link text ($txt_link), need not be processed by a function at all.

```
function get_target_attr($blank_target) {
    return $blank_target ? ' target="_blank"' : '';
}

function print_link($search,$form,$txt_link,$blank_target){
    $target_attr = get_target_attr($blank_target);
    $url = get_url($search,$form);
    ?>
    <a href="<?php echo $url>"<?php echo $target_attr?>>
    <?php echo $txt_link?></a>
    <?php
}
```

Now assuming we have a template file and are using the (cleaned-up) print_link() function in it, we can achieve an even better separation of PHP and HTML by using the component functions instead of print_link().

```
<a href="<?php echo get_url()?>"<?php echo get_target_attr()?>>
<?php echo $txt_link?></a>
```

We will deal with the template issue in the next section as well, as we discover how it may be applied in a context—the SimpleTest test reporter—if we want to output different formats, not just HTML

11.3.4   Introducing templates in SimpleTest

A true story this time: At one point, I wanted a different layout for the SimpleTest error report. This was entirely possible by making my own test reporter class. But as I considered the task, I saw the way SimpleTest's HtmlReporter class was outputting HTML markup in print statements, and I realized that I would prefer to be able to specify the layout by using a template.

There were relatively good reasons why the HtmlReporter had been done with print statements. It was designed to output the parts of the test report as soon as they became available. So the report header would be output immediately through a method called paintHeader(). As the tests finished, if there were failures, each of them were reported along the way. Finally, the statistics for all the tests were output using paintFooter().

Using templates in this design would have involved a number of small templates, and that would not necessarily be practical.

On the other hand, there is a different way to do it: store all the test results and output them at the end. But that means losing the ability to show the results immediately as they arrive.

So it comes down to requirements: The existing SimpleTest way of doing it was fine given the requirement for immediate output, but that was not what I was looking for. Most of my tests run quickly, so I can live with waiting until the end to hear about failures. Others don't, but that's not important for our purposes. We're just experimenting to see how this can be refactored.

Making SimpleTest template-compatible involved two challenges. One was to make the test reporter class store the results and only report them at the end. That could be done by letting most of the "paint" methods remember the results in instance variables, and letting `paintFooter()` take care of the output. This is slightly inelegant, but only because of the way the methods are named. Had they been named as in JUnit (`endTest()` instead of `paintFooter()`, for example), it would have seemed perfectly valid.

The other challenge was to establish the template itself. First, what is a template? Something that can be fed to a major template engine such as Smarty? Possibly, but to keep our experiment simple, we'll use an ordinary PHP file as our template. If we want to introduce a template engine, we can do that later.

We'll use the simplest test reporter—the TextReporter class—as our starting point. The resulting template should be easy to convert into an HTML template.

To make the template, we first need some output. Since a failing test contains more information, we'll start with that. Let's have two failures so that we can test looping in the template. There is no reason to make the messages more complex than necessary, so some simple assertions will suffice:

```
class SomeTest extends UnitTestCase {
    function testSomething() {
        $this->assertEqual(1,2);
        $this->assertEqual(2,3);
    }
}
```

On running this test, the text-based reporter outputs the following:

```
SomeTest
1) Equal expectation fails because
   [Integer: 1] differs from [Integer: 2] by 1 at line [8]
        in testSomething
2) Equal expectation fails because
   [Integer: 2] differs from [Integer: 3] by 1 at line [9]
        in testSomething
FAILURES!!!
Test cases run: 1/1, Passes: 0, Failures: 2, Exceptions: 0
```

This is all we need to create the template file. We take this output, stick it in a file, and call it something original like template.php.

What we are doing here is actually a form of Kent Beck's FakeIt pattern [Beck]. It's analogous to what we did in chapter 9 to make the TestOfMysqlTransaction pass. We make the code work by hard-coding the data that will make the tests pass; then we can start inserting real data. As a first step toward real data, we create a PHP section at the beginning, set the desired data as variables, and use the variables in the HTML section at the end of the template file. After we make our test reporter class generate the variables, we can remove this PHP section. The "template" is shown in listing 11.3.

Listing 11.3 PHP "template" file created from the test output

```php
<?php
$testname = 'SomeTest';
$run = 1;        //Number of cases actually run
$cases = 1;      //Total number of cases
$passes = 0;
$failures = 2;
$exceptions = 0;
$count = 0;      //Start counting tests at 0
$ok = FALSE;
$failreports = array(
    array(
    'message'=>"Equal expectation fails because [Integer: 1]".
        "differs from [Integer: 2] by 1 at line [8]",
    'breadcrumb'=>'testSomething'
    ),
    array(
    'message'=>"Equal expectation fails because [Integer: 2]".
        "differs from [Integer: 3] by 1 at line [9]",
    'breadcrumb'=>'testSomething'
    ),
);
?>
<?=$testname ?>
<?php foreach ($failreports as $failure): ?>

<?=++$count ?>) <?=$failure['message'] ?>

        <?=$failure['breadcrumb'] ?>
<?php endforeach; ?>

<?php if ($ok): ?>
OK
<?php else: ?>
FAILURES!!!
<?php endif; ?>
Test cases run: <?=$run ?>/<?=$cases ?>, Passes: <?=$passes ?>,
Failures: <?=$failures ?>, Exceptions: <?=$exceptions ?>
```

The template consists mostly of variables; in addition it has the essential logic for generating the output:

- A foreach loop to show the test failures
- A $count variable to keep track of how many failures we've displayed
- An if-else conditional to display a different message depending on whether some tests failed

The first half of the file just sets the variables; the second half is the actual template that outputs the results. The second half is what would normally be an HTML section, although in this case, there is no actual HTML markup. Instead, it contains lots of small PHP sections that mostly just display a single variable. This might seem excessive and not very readable as it stands, but the point is layout flexibility. The layout elements can be treated like layout elements instead of code; if you add spaces, they will show up in the command-line output without the need to use print or echo. More importantly, by adding HTML markup, this template can easily be converted into an HTML-based template for browser viewing.

Our next goal is to generate the required variables from the class. Since we are not in control of the SimpleTest code, we need to make a copy of TextReporter and call it TemplateBasedReporter. Following the test-first principle, the next thing we need is a test of the ability of the class to generate the variables. For the sake of the test, it's just as well to have a separate method called templateVars() that returns the variables for the template. To get the correct assertions for the test, we just copy and mechanically transform the assignments in the template. This test case is shown in listing 11.4.

Listing 11.4 Testing that our reporter class can generate the variables we want

```
function testOutputVars() {
    $reporter = new TemplateBasedReporter;      ❶ Create reporter
    ob_start();
    $test = new SomeTest();                      ❷ Run test with output buffering
    $test->run($reporter);
    ob_end_clean();
    extract($reporter->templateVars());          ❸ Extract variables
    $this->assertEqual('SomeTest',$testname);    ❹ Test the variables
    $this->assertEqual(1,$run);
    $this->assertEqual(1,$cases);
    $this->assertEqual(0,$passes);
    $this->assertEqual(2,$failures);
    $this->assertEqual(0,$exceptions);
    $this->assertEqual(FALSE,$ok);
}
```

❶ Create reporter
❷ Run test with output buffering
❸ Extract variables
❹ Test the variables

```
$this->assertEqual(array(
    array(
        'message'=>"Equal expectation fails because ".
            "[Integer: 1] differs from [Integer: 2] ".
            "by 1 at line [8]",
        'breadcrumb'=>'testSomething'
    ),
    array(
        'message'=>"Equal expectation fails because ".
            "[Integer: 2] differs from [Integer: 3] ".
            "by 1 at line [9]",
        'breadcrumb'=>'testSomething'
    ),
),$failreports);
}
```

Failure data in complex arrays ⑤

❶ We start by creating an instance of our test reporter class.

❷ We're only interested in testing the method that will return the template variables. The old test output is still active, but we don't need any output for this test, so we turn on output buffering to keep it from bothering us. Then we run the test. We could have used a mock object in place of the real test, but since the test is so simple, we just run it.

❸ We want to get the variables in a form that is easily digested by our template. Since it is a plain PHP include file, we extract the variables from the array returned by the templateVars() method.

❹ We test all the simple variables with asserts that have been mapped from the assignments in the template.

❺ For the failure data, we need complex arrays. Since we started with the template, we know that the form of this data is reasonable for use in the template.

The next step is another FakeIt. We create the templateVars() method and just hard-code the variables we need to return.

The test will pass, and then we can replace the variables one by one with real ones generated during the test run. This is where much of the real work happens, but we won't go into all the details involving the intricacies of the test reporter class.

Eventually, we end up with a templateVars() method that returns real data exclusively. Note the use of compact() here to match the extract() in the test method. In effect, we are transferring all those variables via the return statement by packing them into an array and then unpacking them again.

```
class TemplateBasedReporter {
    function templateVars() {
        $testname = $this->test_name;
        $run = $this->getTestCaseProgress();
        $cases = $this->getTestCaseCount();
```

```
        $passes = $this->getPassCount();
        $failures = $this->getFailCount();
        $exceptions = $this->getExceptionCount();
        $ok = ($this->getFailCount() + $this->getExceptionCount() == 0);
        $failreports = $this->failreports;
        return compact("testname","run","cases","passes","failures",
            "exceptions","count","ok","failreports");
    }
}
```

Now we've implemented most of what we need. We have made sure the template does its job (testing by visual inspection); we have made sure the test reporter class is capable of returning the variables the template needs. What's lacking is to connect the dots. As mentioned, the `paintFooter()` method can do all the output work. Now all it needs is to get the template variables and include the template file.

```
class TemplateBasedReporter
    function paintFooter() {
        extract($this->templateVars());
        include('template.php');
    }
}
```

Finally, we can remove the PHP code at the beginning of the template file, and the template will display the variables it has been fed by the reporter class instead.

Total intermingling of PHP code and HTML markup is probably the number-one refactoring issue in legacy PHP applications. The second most important issue is overly complex and nested conditional expressions and loops.

11.4 SIMPLIFYING CONDITIONAL EXPRESSIONS

Conditionals tend to be particularly hard to read and refactor. In PHP applications, it's not uncommon to see five or more levels of nested conditionals and loops. It's almost impossible to do anything about it without some way to identify small steps for the refactoring.

Testing is another thorny issue. Complete test coverage of a complex conditional statement requires that all paths through the statement are covered. Writing a separate test for each path is advisable. But this is easier said than done. Trying to get by with incomplete test coverage is possible, but entails the risk of introducing bugs that are found at some inconvenient later time. Writing complete unit tests is not that hard if you know exactly what the conditional statement is supposed to do, but frequently this is not the case. There might be special cases you have ignored, and you risk writing tests that turn out to be pointless eventually.

If you know exactly what part of the web interface the conditional statement affects, it may be possible to get by with web tests only (see the next chapter). If the web interface is not going to change, these tests will stay useful.

We'll discuss these testing problems some more in the section on refactoring from procedural to object-oriented. There is no magic bullet that will make it easy, but at least we can learn the tricks and try them out, as in the examples to follow.

11.4.1 A simple example

Listing 11.5 is another example from a real application, but with all variable names changed. What's happening here? It seems clear that the code is intended to help interpret the HTTP request. (In fact, it seems to be doing something similar to register_globals, which is highly discouraged. It's included here only to show the mechanics of refactoring.) But the deep nesting makes it harder to see what's going on. In general, both conditionals and loops can be handled by extracting functions or methods externally or internally:

Externally: extract the whole conditional statement or the whole loop.

Internally: extract one branch—or each branch—of the conditional or the contents of the loop.

We'll consider some possible refactorings of listing 11.5 without going into detail on how to do it.

Listing 11.5 Nested if and for statements

```
for ($i=0; $i<count($vars); $i += 1) {          ❶ Use foreach
    $var = $vars[$i];                              instead      ❸  Use
    if (!isset($$var)) {           ❷ Replace with function       Reverse
        if (empty($_POST[$var])) {                               Conditional
            if (empty($_GET[$var]) && empty($query[$var])) {
                $$var = '';
            } elseif (!empty($_GET[$var])) {
                $$var = $_GET[$var];
            } else {                        Extract as  ❹
                $$var = $query[$var];         function
            }
        } else {
            $$var = $_POST[$var];
        }
    }
}
```

---

❶ These two first lines define the loop itself. They could be replaced with the simpler

```
foreach($vars as $var) {
```

❷ This if statement could be extracted as a separate function. It represents the entire content of the loop, since the first two lines just define the loop. The obstacle is the fact that there are two non-global variables that are being used inside the if block: $var (which is actually the name of the variable $$var) and the $query array.

The simple way to handle that is just to pass the variables into the function. Then the first line can be changed to a `return` statement instead of an `if`. That gets rid of one level of nesting:

```
function getVariable($var,$query) {
    if (!isset($$var)) return;
```

Alternatively, without the function, we could still get rid of the nesting by using `continue` to skip the rest of the loop iteration:

```
    if (!isset($$var)) continue;
```

❸ When we have an `if-else` conditional with a relatively long `if` and a short `else`, one possible refactoring is *Reverse Conditional*. By reversing the sense of the test (`empty` becomes `!empty`), it becomes easier to see the logic:

```
if (!empty($_POST[$var])) {
    $$var = $_POST[$var];
} else {
    if (empty($_GET[$var]) && empty($query[$var])) { }
}
```

Aha! When an `else` block starts with an `if`, that's an `elseif`. That means we can get rid of another level of nesting.

Another possible refactoring here is *Decompose Conditional*, which involves extracting the test and the branches of the conditional statement as separate methods. The `if` part is the hottest candidate for extraction, since it's the most complex. In the next section, we will see a fuller example of *Decompose Conditional*.

❹ If the remaining `if-elseif-else` statement is inside a function, we can return values instead of collecting the result in a variable. We could end up with something like this:

```
if (!empty($_POST[$var]) return $_POST[$var];
if (!empty($_GET[$var]) return $_GET[$var];
if (!empty($query[$var]) return $query[$var];
return '';
```

By now it's starting to become obvious what the code is actually doing. It looks right, but since we haven't actually done the refactoring with full test coverage, there is no guarantee it would not break something in the other parts of the application.

11.4.2   A longer example: authentication code

Let's look at a longish example: a form for submitting news articles. The form requires the user to log in before accessing it. In a real application, there would typically be a news list page as well, which would contain links to the form for the purpose of editing news articles and submitting new ones. So the example is slightly unnatural in that we would normally not be led directly to the form after logging in; on the other hand, it's entirely normal that the form is login-protected so that if we happened to type the form URL into the browser without having logged in first, we would in fact be asked to log in. The reason for this example is that a form illustrates more web programming principles than a list page would.

The news entry form

The example assumes that `register_globals` is turned on. That's the directive that lets us use session variables, GET and POST variables, and others as if they were simple global variables with simple names. As the PHP manual reminds us repeatedly, `register_globals` shouldn't be turned on. It should be avoided like the plague for security reasons. But there is always the chance that you might come across it, years after it was officially denounced.

There is another reason to avoid it as well: it's critical to avoid confusion and chaos. For reasons of clarity, a session variable and a request variable should never have identical names, and with `register_globals` turned off, they never will.

This point—why unmarked globals are confusing—is one of the things listing 11.6 demonstrates.

Even the refactored version is far from perfect and should not necessarily be emulated. The process of refactoring is what we're trying to learn here. The example has problems that we will not be focusing specifically on. Some of these are security issues:

- As mentioned, `register_globals` is dangerous.
- The login mechanism itself is rather primitive.
- The database code is not secured against SQL injection attacks.
- There is no validation or error-checking of user input.

Listing 11.6   Login-protected news entry form

```
session_start();                                    ❶ Use $_SESSION
session_register('current_user');                      instead
mysql_connect('localhost','dbuser','secret');
mysql_select_db('ourapp');                          ❷ Logging in or
if ($username || $current_user)                         logged in
    if ($username) {                                              ❸ Check
        $sql = "SELECT id,username,password FROM Users ".            password
            "WHERE password = '".md5($password)."' ".
            "AND username = '".$username."'";
        $r = mysql_query($sql);
        $current_user = mysql_fetch_assoc($r);
    }
    if ($current_user) {          ❹ Start application
        if ($headline) {              code
            if ($id) {                              ❺ Updating an
                $sql = "UPDATE News SET ".             existing article
                "headline = '".$headline."',".
                "text = '".$text."' ".
                "WHERE id = ".$id;
```

```
    } else {                                    ⑥ Creating new
        $sql = "INSERT INTO News ".                article
            "(headline,text) ".
            "VALUES ('".$headline."','"
            .$text."') ";
    }                                 ⑦ Execute
    mysql_query($sql);    ◄─────         SQL
    header("Location: http://localhost/newslist.php");   ⑧ Redirect
    exit;                                                   to news
} else {                                                    list page
    if ($id) {                                          ⑨ Retrieve
        $sql = 'SELECT text, headline '.                   an
            'FROM News WHERE id = '.$id;                    existing
        $r = mysql_query($sql);                            article
        list($text,$headline) = mysql_fetch_row($r);
    }
    echo '<html>';
    echo '<body>';                              The news ⑩
    echo '<h1>Submit news</h1>';                  form
    echo '<form method="POST">';
    echo '<input type="hidden" name="id"';
    echo 'value="'.$id.'">';
    echo 'Headline:';
    echo '<input type="text" name="headline" ';
    echo 'value="'.$headline.'"><br>';
    echo 'text:';
    echo '<textarea name="text" cols="50" rows="20">';
    echo ''.$text.'</textarea><br>';
    echo '<input type="submit" value="Submit news">';
    echo '</form>';
    echo '</body>';
    echo '</html>';
    }
}
} else {
    echo '<html>';
    echo '<body>';                              The login ⑪
    echo '<h1>Log in</h1>';                        form
    echo '<form method="POST">';
    echo 'User name: <input type="text" name="username">';
    echo '<br>';
    echo 'Password : <input type="password" name="password">';
    echo '<br>';
    echo '<input type="submit" value="Log in">';
    echo '</form>';
    echo '</body>';
    echo '</html>';
} ?>
```

❶ When register_globals is turned on, session_register() lets us use
$current_user instead of $_SESSION['current_user']. In general, this is
a bad practice; we're doing it here to illustrate it and to show how to avoid it.

② `$username` is an HTTP variable; `$current_user` is a session variable. There is nothing to indicate that fact. This way of doing it is convenient (less typing), but makes it harder to guess what the variables are doing. If instead we were to use `$_SESSION['current_user']` and `$_POST['username']`, it would effectively document where each variable was coming from.

The purpose of these variables here is to tell us where we stand with regard to login. If `$username` is set, it means the user just submitted the login form. If `$current_user` is set, it means the user is already logged in. The reason there is one conditional branch for both of these cases is that they are the alternatives that don't require showing the login form.

③ If the user has submitted the login form, we check whether the user exists in the database and has the password the user entered. The passwords are stored in the database table encrypted using the PHP `md5()` function. They can't be decrypted, but we can check whether a string matches the password by encrypting the string.

④ This is where the application code (as opposed to the authentication and login code) starts. `$current_user` is a session variable. If it's set, we know that the user is already logged in, no authentication is needed, and we can display the form.

⑤ If the HTTP request contains a news article ID, we assume that the user is editing an existing article and build an `UPDATE` statement based on that.

⑥ If not, we assume the user wants to create a new news article and build an `INSERT` statement.

⑦ Then we execute the `UPDATE` or `INSERT` statement.

⑧ After the database has been successfully updated, we redirect to the news list page. (No, there's no validation and no error checking. That's because we want to avoid dealing with too many kinds of complexity in one example.)

⑨ If there is a news article ID present when we are ready to show the news form, we assume that it came from an edit link and get the article from the database.

⑩ The news form has all the HTML code inside echo statements. This is another bad practice that is used in this example just for the sake of illustration.

⑪ Finally, the login form, which is displayed if the user is not already logged in or trying to log in.

Isolating login and authentication

How do we start to refactor a beast like this? There are several places we could start. The simplest thing to begin with would be to change some of the long sections of echoed HTML markup into HTML sections. On the other hand, the greatest complexity and difficulty is in the conditionals.

How can we make it clearer which parts of this example do what? The outer conditionals are involved in login and authentication. The part that properly belongs to this particular web page is all inside the conditional branch following `if ($current_user)`. So a way to separate the page-specific code from login and authentication is to extract everything inside this branch into a separate function. Or we could place it in a file and `include` it. The problem with using `include` for the application content is that it's exactly the wrong way around. The URL would belong to the login page, and since login will be used for most or all pages, all pages get the same URL. It is possible, and common, to do it that way, and we will get to that later. But we don't want that to be our only option. So for now it's better to have URL belong to the news form page, and let that page `include` the login and authentication code.

To do that, it will be helpful to make the login and authentication code more manageable. In listing 11.7, the conditional statements related to login and authentication have been isolated so they're easier to see.

Listing 11.7 Authentication-related conditional logic from the previous example

```
if ($username || $current_user) {
    if ($username) {
        // Check for the username and password in the database
    }
    if ($current_user) {
        // Do the news form with all its ifs and elses
    }
} else {
    // Show the login form
}
```

There is a standard refactoring we can apply to get started. It's called *Decompose Conditional*. The principle is to take the content of branches, and the tests as well, if necessary, into separate methods or functions. Figure 11.4 shows how this works in principle. The flowchart at left represents the conditional statement.

Let's try it. We'll make a function out of every single branch in the authentication logic and test to get a feel for how that works (see listing 11.8).

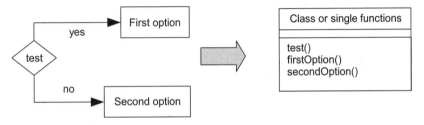

Figure 11.4 Decompose Conditional refactoring

```
if (loggedIn() or loginSubmitted()) {
    if (loginSubmitted()) {
        authenticate();
    }
    if (loggedIn()) {
        showPage();
    }
} else {
    showLoginForm();
}
```

Like the previous example, this is just the structure of the conditionals all by themselves. But while listing 11.7 was not a real, working example, this one is. Isolating the conditional statements makes it easier to understand exactly how they work. It also enables us to play with the structure of the conditionals without moving large blocks of code around.

Some of the functions will be pretty trivial. `loggedIn()`, for instance:

```
function loggedIn() { return $_SESSION['current_user']
                                ? TRUE : FALSE; }
```

We can choose to be satisfied with the structure of these conditionals, or we can try to make them even more readable. As they are, they look odd, since the inner tests duplicate the outer test. The outer test might seem unnecessary, and would be except for the fact that the result of `authenticate()` affects the following `if` test.

One possibility is the solution in listing 11.9, which may be cleaner and less confusing even though it's somewhat longer. (You may agree or disagree; my primary mission here is to show how to do this kind of refactoring.) Notice that the first conditional statement has the same sequence as the actual events when logging in: display the login form, submit the login form, and show the application page.

```
if (firstRequest()) {
    showLoginForm();
} elseif (loginSubmitted()) {
    tryAuthenticate();
} else {
    showPage();
}

function firstRequest() {
    return !loggedIn() && !loginSubmitted();
}

function tryAuthenticate() {
    authenticate();
    if (loggedIn()) {
```

```
        showPage();
    } else {
        showLoginForm();
    }
}
```

Now we can move all the authentication-related code (listing 11.9 and the two functions `authenticate()` and `showLoginForm()`) into a separate file, so that we can use login and authentication on any web page. The only inconvenience is that the actual application code has to be wrapped in a function called `showPage()`:

```
function showPage() {
    // Actual contents of the web page,
    // possibly including calls to templates
}
```

Fortunately, that's easy to fix. All of these tests and branches eventually end up running `showLoginForm()` or `showPage()`. We'll change these two just a little. If we add a dummy `showPage()` function, `showPage()` becomes the equivalent of running whatever code comes after all the functions:

```
function showPage() {
    // Do nothing, wait for the rest of the script to execute
}
```

Another alternative—which will work in some circumstances—is to actively include the application page:

```
function showPage() {
    include($_SERVER['ORIG_PATH_TRANSLATED']);
}
```

This is an odd thing to do, since this is now an include file that includes the file that included it. It works, but only under the following conditions:

- We use `include_once` or `require_once` (rather than `include` or `require`) in the first file.
- There are no functions and classes in the first file.

If there are functions and classes in the first file, we get a "Cannot redeclare" error.

We also have to add an `exit()` at the end of the `showLoginForm()` function to keep the application page from showing up after the login form. Then we can dispense with the enclosing `showPage()` function in the web pages.

11.4.3 Handling conditional HTML

One of the hardest things to refactor is a PHP page that has lots of conditional logic with echoed HTML code inside. The classic way to simplify complex conditionals is what we just did, the refactoring known as Decompose Conditional: we extract each test and each conditional branch into its own function or method. This works even when there is HTML markup inside the branches, provided that the HTML is in relatively long continuous stretches, at best an entire web page.

But if the HTML markup inside the conditional branches is in small chunks, different strategies are required. Sometimes we can extract duplicated markup as we saw in the section on cleaning up a function that generates a link.

However, sometimes it's necessary to output different HTML depending on some condition. A typical example is when users have different authorization. For example, administrators may have an extra button available that ordinary users are not allowed to see.

All serious template engines have some way to output HTML conditionally. In plain PHP, it would be like this example:

```php
<?php if (is_webmaster()): ?>
  <div class="ActionLinks">
    <a href="newsform.php" class="CommandLink">
      Add news
    </a>
  </div>
<?php endif; ?>
```

The important thing to remember is that we want the template to be as HTML-like as possible, even if it's technically a plain PHP file.

Conditional expressions can be present—and can be refactored—in both procedural and object-oriented code, but they're generally easier to deal with if the surrounding code is already object-oriented. In the next section, we'll summarize some problems and see some techniques that are useful to transform procedural code to object-oriented.

11.5 REFACTORING FROM PROCEDURAL TO OBJECT-ORIENTED

In principle, we can refactor procedural code just as we can do with object-oriented code. But in practice, effective refactoring depends on having unit tests in place. And unit testing requires well-defined units that depend as little as possible on other units. Long stretches of script code don't meet this criterion. And even functions might have troublesome dependencies on other functions. When an object depends on another object, it can often be replaced with a mock object. And even when it can't (for example, because it creates the object it depends on internally), it's relatively simple to change it so it can be replaced. This is what Michael Feathers calls an *Object Seam* [Feathers].

It's different when we work with functions, because functions are harder to replace.

In this section, we'll first discuss how to get procedural code under test, and then we'll see some techniques that are useful when we want to make it object-oriented.

11.5.1 Getting procedural code under test

In a certain ideal sense, the best way to make procedural code testable is to make it object-oriented first. Or rather, it would be if we weren't likely to break it on the way from procedural to OO. We really need some way to make it testable without such radical surgery. We want to be able to make procedural code testable without having to make it object-oriented first. There are three ways to do this without changing the code.

Use web tests to test the end-user interface. These help, and are useful anyway as acceptance tests. But for enabling refactoring, web tests won't quite replace unit tests. One reason is because they don't pinpoint the location of a problem the way unit tests do. And when we want to make just one small change somewhere, we might need a lot of web tests to ensure that it's working properly.

- Test a PHP file by running it with output buffering.
- Test single functions. This may be the place to start if there are already functions, but unfortunately, there are scripts that have no functions. Searching for "function" in all the files of a PHP application sometimes turns up just JavaScript functions.
- Testing an existing function is often straightforward, but there are some potential problems. The function may depend on global variables, it may depend on other functions, and it may depend on built-in functions that don't necessarily act predictably.

A dependency on global variables is relatively easy to handle in a mechanical sense. We can always get rid of them by making them arguments to the function instead. Sometimes you see this kind of thing:

```php
function print_link()
{
    global $search;
    global $form;
}
```

This can usually be replaced with the following:

```php
function print_link($search,$form)
{
//...
    return ($search,$form);
}
```

We also have to call it like this:

```php
list($search,$form) = print_link($search,$form);
```

Whether we actually need to go to such lengths—having them as arguments *and* return values—depends on where they occur.

When we test the function, we may also have to understand what the global variables actually mean. That's not always trivial.

Functions that are called inside a function that's under test narrow our options in testing. Objects can be replaced with mock objects. Not so with functions. But we can sometimes replace a function with a call to a global object. Or by including a different function library, containing a set of functions that have the same names but work differently, we can replace the functions with something that's guaranteed to have the same behavior every time.

This works with user-defined functions, but not with built-in functions, since there is no way to eliminate the existing definitions. (Except by compiling a separate PHP executable for testing and disabling the feature that the built-in function belongs to. I've never tried this, but it could conceivably be useful in some situations.)

To work around that, we have to replace the function names. For a simple substitution such as a prefix, that should be safe enough.

11.5.2   Doing the refactorings

There are many ways to write procedural code and many refactorings that might be useful. A complete guide is beyond the horizon at present. But I can try to give some advice and some hints that might help.

Trying to refactor the messiest code may be a tedious, exacting, time-consuming task, and it's hard to know when it's worth it and when it's better to reimplement. As mentioned, there are times when large amounts of code do very little; in that case, reimplementing is almost certainly much more efficient. On the other hand, when you only need to make a small change in a large PHP file, throwing everything out may be much too demanding, in the short run at least.

Turn off register_globals

As you may know, `register_globals` is highly discouraged for security reasons. Avoiding it also helps refactoring.

PHP has several distinct categories of global variables. The most important ones are the superglobal request arrays (`$_GET`, `$_POST` and `$_REQUEST`), session variables (`$_SESSION`), and plain globals. The plain globals are the ones whose scope are the current file and any files that include the current file or are included in it.

If `register_globals` is turned off, you are forced to find all request and session variables in one of the arrays or in some object or variable derived from these. This means that it's usually easy to find out which category a variable belongs to. But if `register_globals` is turned on, you have less information, since these variables appear with plain names without any clear category identification.

Knowing which category variables belong to can be important when refactoring. If you try to extract some code into a function or method, all the global variables become local. More likely than not, the code stops working, and there's no obvious way to find the guilty variables except through meticulous debugging. On the other hand, if all request or session variables are referred to as elements of the superglobal arrays, these at least won't cause this type of problem. Also, knowing which variables are request variables makes it easier to see how the HTTP requests work and to refactor the code that interprets the HTTP requests (this belongs to the Controller in the Model-View-Controller pattern; see chapters 15 and 16).

If you have an application that depends on `register_globals`, changing the usage of these variables and using the arrays instead of the plain variables will make later refactorings easier.

In other words, handling globals lays the groundwork for cleaning up the application. So it's an important first step if it's needed, but it's also difficult. Looking for `session_register()` can help locate session variables, and URLs and forms should contain most GET and POST variables. Unless, that is, the variable names are somehow constructed by the PHP code.

Encapsulate script includes

One of the worst problems in PHP web applications is includes that run PHP code in the form of a script.

In PHP, it's possible to use an include file that only contains PHP code that is not in the form of functions and classes and just executes the code at the point where it's included. Typically, the include file uses global variables that are set in the including file.

This resembles a function call, but it's less explicit and harder to reuse. In a function, you typically pass in some values as arguments and return one or more values. The include file, in contrast, uses global variables in place of these explicit input and output values. That makes it hard to use it anywhere else or even to move the include statement because the global variables might not be set or might be set incorrectly.

Figure 11.5 gives some idea of the difficulty. The global variable `$items` is set in the main script file, changed in the include file, and then used again in the main file, but there is no simple way to keep track of its changes. Even doing a full search through the main file could be misleading, since you will miss the place where `$items` is set to 0.

The way to deal with this is to wrap the entire contents of the file in a function. Unless you have a specific reason to keep the include in place, you may also want to

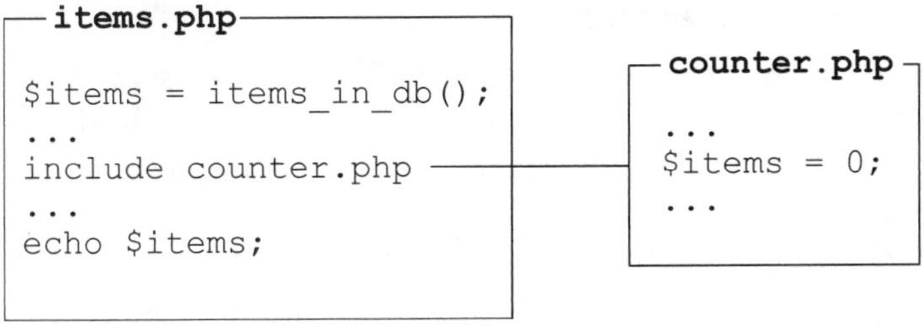

```
┌─items.php──────────────┐
│                        │          ┌─counter.php─┐
│  $items = items_in_db();│          │             │
│  ...                   │          │  ...        │
│  include counter.php ──┼──────────┼─ $items = 0;│
│  ...                   │          │  ...        │
│  echo $items;          │          │             │
│                        │          └─────────────┘
└────────────────────────┘
```

Figure 11.5 Changes to global variables can be hard to identify when they occur in an include file.

move it to the beginning of the file and call the function in the place where the include used to be.

This is difficult if there are lots of variables that have the function of communicating between the including file and the included file. If it's too hard to find these variables, it might be a better idea to extract functions from the include file first to get more control of the variables.

Extract small, testable functions or classes

When refactoring legacy code, we typically refactor only what we need in order to make functional changes. If the change we need can be localized, we can extract that part of the code into a function. The difficulty is in knowing which variables are temporary variables within the stretch of code we're extracting, and which occur before or after. Unless they are global variables that are used in other files as well, we can find them by searching in an editor. The ones that occur before can be passed as arguments to the function; the ones that occur later can be returned from the function. Since this kind of refactoring often requires us to return several variables, it's useful to return them from the function as an array:

```
function get_parts($string) {
    return array($start,$middle,$end);
}
```

Then we can recover the variables returned from the function by using `list()`:

```
list($start,$middle,$end) = get_search();
```

When refactoring script code, object orientation is not the first priority. To refactor gradually, it's often just as well to start by extracting functions and adding them to classes as the need arises. If we extract several functions, we may start seeing that the same variables keep recurring in the argument lists of these functions. That kind of variable is a prime candidate for becoming an instance variable in a class.

Alternatively, if we have some idea of the design we're moving toward, we may know what kind of class we need. In that case, it might be better to start with a class in the first place.

Concentrate SQL statements

SQL statements often contain heavy duplication of column lists and the like. Moving SQL statements to data access classes makes it easier to see the duplication.

We will look at object-oriented data storage in depth in part 3 of this book.

Replace HTML echo sections with HTML sections

As mentioned before, it may be better to start by creating templates from scratch using the HTML output of the application and just eliminating all parts of the code that echo HTML markup. But that might be too much work in the short term.

But if we're not creating a complete template, it helps to at least replace the sections that echo HTML markup with HTML sections.

We will look at a less-than-obvious example. There are more obvious examples that simply echo long stretches of static HTML code. This example is fairly short and contains PHP control logic.

```php
$sql = 'SELECT id, text, headline FROM News';
$result = mysql_query($sql);
while ($a = mysql_fetch_assoc($result)) {
    echo "<a href=\"newsform.php?id=".$a['id']."&command=edit\">";
    echo "<h2>".$a['headline']."</h2>";
    echo "</a>";
    echo $a['text'];
}
```

This is PHP code with some HTML markup inside it. By switching the roles, embedding some PHP code inside the HTML section instead, we get this:

```php
$sql = 'SELECT id, text, headline FROM News';
?>
<?php while ($a = mysql_fetch_assoc($result)): ?>
  <a href="newsform.php?id=<?php echo $a['id'] ?>&command=edit">
    <h2><?php echo $a['headline'] ?></h2>
  </a>
  <?php echo $a['text'] ?>
<?php endwhile; ?>
```

This may not seem like much of an improvement, but it has some definite advantages. It takes the focus off the relatively trivial PHP code, which is not likely to change much, and puts the focus on the HTML code, which is likely to change for visual reasons. In this way, we achieve the following things:

- It's easier to see the structure of the HTML output; we can easily indent it.

- It's much easier to change the HTML output, especially for a web designer.

- It's easier to change into a template later.

11.6 SUMMARY

More than any other practice, refactoring is the key to ensuring that software can be maintained in the long run. By improving readability and eliminating duplication, we keep the code supple and make it easier to modify and add to it.

Refactoring is also a phenomenal learning experience. Comparing different solutions to similar problems sharpens our ability to distinguish poor design from good design and mediocre design from excellent design.

There is plenty of material available on refactoring relatively clean object-oriented code. The kind of code that is more common in PHP applications is harder to refactor. Sometimes it's also hard to be sure it's worth it. But frequently, reimplementation is not even an option.

But refactoring is possible. We can transform complex, nested conditional statements and loops into simpler, more manageable functions and methods. We can get legacy code under test gradually. And we can perform small, relatively safe refactorings that slowly but surely improve the quality of our code.

In the next chapter, we will return to the subject of testing. We will learn how to test the final product: the web interface itself. In the process, we will see how web testing can drive development and how to configure web tests to run on different computers. We will also take a hard look at the advantages and disadvantages of this approach to testing and gain an understanding of how it fits into development process.

C H A P T E R   1 2

Taking control with web tests

Programming is an intellectual *Jackass* stunt. We take risks, underestimating the difficulty of a programming task, and often the consequences are unexpected and catastrophic failure. When we implement some code, the possibility that it might fail seems so remote that we don't even consider it. But in the real world, it's subject to Murphy's Law and fails anyway.

But although we know that from repeated experience, we still do it. We keep setting ourselves on fire no matter how many times we get burned.

Admittedly, this is a somewhat sensationalized account. Fortunately, the burns are rarely serious. And it is possible to learn to be more careful; in fact, most do. But Murphy's Law is a natural mode of thinking only to paranoid or pessimistic people. Although some claim it's a real phenomenon with natural causes, it seems to run counter to level-headed logic and reason.

I am fascinated (perhaps morbidly) by how Murphy's Law works in real, physical, technological disasters. Sinking ships and nuclear accidents give me a sense of *déjà vu*. The way a trivial, ridiculous error can have vast, catastrophic consequences reminds me of some software projects. Some software companies are as unsinkable as the Titanic and sink just as dramatically.

Nuclear power is interesting as an example of a technology in which extreme safety requirements have inspired extreme safeguards.[1] One of the most obvious of these is the containment building. Even though the reactor is supposed to be built so that release of radioactive substances will not happen, there is a steel or concrete shell around it in case a leak happens anyway.

To keep our application as safe from bugs as possible, we need a containment building or a safety net: integration and acceptance tests to ensure that the units work properly together and that the application as a whole is performing as intended. In the context of web programming, these tests are typically web tests. Even though unit tests are supposed to cover every behavior and prevent all possible bugs, in practice they don't. And, especially when we use mock objects, there are sometimes leaks between the tests, causing integration bugs. Web tests will catch most—hopefully the vast majority—of these remaining defects.

There is more to web testing, though. In addition to catching and preventing bugs, it allows us to use test-driven design at the top level of our application. In this chapter, we'll see how to start with the user interface and build the application top-down from there.

We'll start by revisiting the contact manager and setting up web tests for it. We'll add the tests and the missing persistence pieces needed to get the contact form to work. Then we'll go back to the top level of the application and make sure our tests are complete. Finally, we'll get a general overview of how to handle a complete legacy application.

12.1   REVISITING THE CONTACT MANAGER

Back to our contact manager example from chapter 10. We've been building it wrong.

We would never design a web application by starting with a low-level transaction class. In the beginning, we don't know if we need a transaction class. We could try to get around this by trying to design the application first. If we could actually manage this, we would know what we needed and could write a low-level object first. Of course, it's nearly impossible to fully design the application up front. That's not the main problem, though. We deny options to the business.

At the early stages of building a web site, building infrastructure is just not the highest priority. Far more important is getting the overall design in front of our clients as quickly as we can, to get feedback on the general direction. Any code that doesn't press ahead with the top-level design is likely to be wasted when the client sees the first version and changes his mind. Clients will change their minds. These decisions are how the business progresses. Denying them the opportunity to change things early will

---

[1] I am, of course, not implying any judgment about the controversial issue of how successful (or not) these safeguards are.

slow down the development of the business. Starting at the top of the code doesn't just make good programming sense, it makes good business sense.

For a PHP developer, the top-level code pushes out HTML, but the test-driven approaches we have looked at so far deal with testing classes, not web pages. In this chapter, we get to see the coding step we should have carried out first. We'll write some web tests.

A word of warning: web testing is very much about taking control of messy situations. This is a down-and-dirty chapter, with quite a bit of code, hacking, and temporary tricks to get things working. Sorry, but that's just the way early prototypes are in real life. At the end of such a process, we can hope to leave behind a fledgling, breathing project. One that will be forever improving.

In this section, we'll start by seeing an HTML mock-up of the basic web pages. Then we'll set up web testing that defines the behavior we want, even though that behavior hasn't been implemented yet. We'll satisfy those tests by doing as little as possible, simulating real interaction but using no real data. Finally, we'll find out how to configure the web tests so that they can be run on different machines.

12.1.1 The mock-up

The first step of any project is requirements-gathering and communication with our client, usually called the project owner or project visionary. It's unlikely at this early stage that the vision will be understood by the project owner, never mind us. To help clear the mists, the first code we write will probably be just a static page mock-up, or maybe just a paper mock-up of the design. It's transitioning from a mock-up to working code where the first testing phase kicks in.

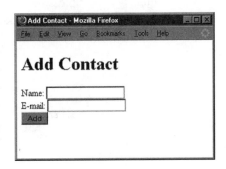

Figure 12.1 A mock-up page for adding a new contact

We'll assume that the client has seen a visual mock-up of our interface, and is happy for us to proceed. Figure 12.1 is our mocked up page for adding a new contact.

I won't embarrass myself by displaying my graphic design skills, so this is a bare-bones prototype. Here is the code:

```html
<html>
    <head><title>Add Contact</title></head>
    <body>
        <form method="post">
            <h1>Add Contact</h1>
            <label>Name: <input type="text" name="name" /></label>
            <br />
            <label>E-mail: <input type="text" name="email" /></label>
            <br />
            <input type="submit" name="add" value="Add" />
```

```
        </form>
    </body>
</html>
```

Our user story is simple. When we enter a new contact, we should see that person displayed in the contacts listing. The contacts listing page, also the default home page, will show all the contacts we have. Later on, the real contact manager application would have too many contacts for that to scale. If we have several thousand contacts, we won't be able to comfortably view them all on a single page. When that happens, we'll change it to something else, probably by adding paging, alphabetical navigation, or a search facility. We are confident enough in our refactoring skills that we will tackle these problems as we get to them. Right now, we want to get working code in front of the project visionary as quickly as possible, so we want the simplest home page.

Figure 12.2 Mocked-up home page for our project

We've produced a mock-up of that, too (see figure 12.2). Right now, everything is static:

```
<html>
    <head>
        <title>Show Contacts</title>
        <style>
            td, th {border: 1px inset gray}
            table {border: 1px outset black}
        </style>
    </head>
    <body>
        <h1>Show Contacts</h1>
        <table>
            <tr><th>Name</th><th>E-mail</th></tr>
            <tr>
                <td>Me</td>
                <td>me@me.com</td>
            </tr>
        </table>
        <a href="add.php"></a>Add contact</a>
    </body>
</html>
```

Our first problem is to get the form submission under the control of a test.

12.1.2 Setting up web testing

We won't even consider testing this form manually. If manually testing a class is hard enough, testing forms with a browser is excruciating. Modern browsers have a habit of caching pages and auto-filling form fields, which can be confusing when testing.

Not only that, but most web site testing involves cookies, sessions, and authentication. Having to manually reset that lot between each test run can soak up hours of our time. Mistakes would be a certainty.

There are a huge number of tools available for web testing, both commercial and free. A fairly complete list is maintained at http://www.softwareqatest.com/qatweb1. html. It's well worth scanning through this list, as it's easy to end up reinventing the wheel. For this chapter, we'll take the easy option and make use of the web tester built into SimpleTest. This tool lacks support for JavaScript, so for really complex dynamic sites, you may want to look at Selenium (http://www.openqa.org/selenium/).

For security reasons, we don't want our test cases visible from the web server. We'll place our two HTML pages into site/add.php for the form and site/index.php for the landing page, as we want the contact list to be the default view. We'll start our web testing in a folder called acceptance. The choice of name will become clear shortly. We write the test runner script into acceptance/all_tests.php:

```php
<?php
require_once('simpletest/web_tester.php');
require_once('simpletest/reporter.php');

class AllAcceptanceTests extends TestSuite {
    function __construct() {
        parent::__construct('All acceptance tests');
        $this->addTestFile('adding_contact_test.php');
    }
}
$test = new AllAcceptanceTests();
$test->run(new HtmlReporter());
?>
```

The format is the same as the runner for our unit tests. The only difference is the inclusion of the SimpleTest web_tester.php file instead of unit_tester.php. We've already added our first test script to the suite, even though we haven't written it yet. Here is enough of the acceptance/adding_contact_test.php file to get a green bar:

```php
<?php
class TestOfAddingContacts extends WebTestCase {
    function testNewContactShouldBeVisible() {
    }
}
?>
```

Of course, getting a green bar is easy when you are not actually testing anything, so let's add some test code. The WebTestCase acts pretty much like the UnitTestCase from the previous chapters, except it contains a native PHP web browser. You write the tests as scripts, as if you were walking around the site with a real browser. Here is the test. We go to the home page, click on "Add contact," fill in the form, click submit, and then check that we can see our new contact:

```
class TestOfAddingContacts extends WebTestCase {          ❶ Get the
    function testNewContactShouldBeVisible() {               home page
        $this->get('http://greedy/dagfinn/site/index.php');  ⤶
        $this->click('Add contact');                      ❷ Fill in the
        $this->setField('Name:', 'Me');                      form
        $this->setField('E-mail:', 'me@me.com');
        $this->click('Add');                              ❸ Submit and
        $this->assertText('Me');                             check the
        $this->assertText('me@me.com');                      result
    }
}
```

❶ The test starts with a simple GET request to the home page. The WebTestCase does some limited parsing of the current page, enough to recognize links and form elements. This means that once we get to the home page, we can navigate the site as we would normally.

❷ We use the click() method to effectively click on the link and take us to the add.php page. The click() method looks for visible links or buttons or, failing that, image alt text. The setField() method just fills in form elements and uses the label text by default. You can use setFieldByName() or setFieldById() if the HTML doesn't have label tags.

❸ Once done, we can click() again to submit the form. As we see, coding the test is easy. It's the surrounding resources that give us the most work. Navigating the site is not our only intention; we want to check content. The assertText() methods look for visible text, and issue a failure to the test suite if no match is found. Right now the test fails, because our form submits to itself, not to the index.php script.

12.1.3   Satisfying the test with fake web page interaction

At this stage of development, submitting to ourselves is a good stepping stone. It's convenient at this point that form handling can be dealt with from within the same script, rather than having the form creation in one file and the handling code in another. It also prevents the form handling code from getting mixed in with other functionality or with other form handlers. If we submitted directly to our index.php page, we would mix showing the contacts with adding contacts. As every other form would probably want to return to this page, it would have to have a form handler for each one. It would bloat fast.

We have another advantage if we combine this approach with redirecting to index.php after handling the form. Not redirecting could cause browser problems. If the page is bookmarked after adding a new user, every time the bookmark is looked up, the form would be resubmitted. Therefore, we will let our first test version work as shown in the sequence diagram in figure 12.3.

When the user submits the form (which is, strictly speaking, not identical to add.php, since it's actually the HTML output from add.php), it generates a POST request to add.php. Since form submissions go by default to the URL of the script that

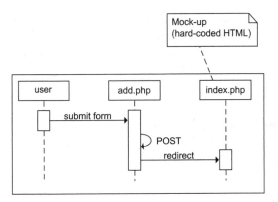

Figure 12.3
Mostly fake web application
that passes the first test

generated the form, this is already implemented. The index.php mock-up is also already implemented. The only thing missing is the redirect from add.php to index.php:

```php
<?php
if (@$_POST['add']) {
    header('Location: index.php');
}
?><html>
    <head><title>Add Contact</title></head>
    ...
</html>
```

Our first bit of code and our tests now pass. Sadly, the only reason our tests pass is because we have hard-coded the correct result. It's not the only thing that's hard-coded. The test will only pass on my home machine, because we hard-coded the starting URL. To make this test run on any development box, we need a way to read the correct start URL for each box. This gets us into configuration.

12.1.4   Write once, test everywhere

It's not just the web server configuration we must have control of, but every other resource that could change for testing. It's something of a luxury to be able to develop and roll out to a bank of identical machines, with virtual machines or chroot installations. Usually machines have differences. This includes such things as the database connections, mail servers, and web services. Because we are now making HTTP requests, we cannot modify the actual code to add mocks. This makes some kind of automatic selection within the application itself necessary, and the usual way to do that is with a configuration file.

If you repetitively hand code a separate configuration file for every server, the chance of error is high. Nor can you check a hand-coded file into your version control system without affecting the configuration of other machines. Otherwise, this would force you to make a copy of a template configuration and hand-tune it for your machine every time you checked out the code. It's nice if the configuration choice is automatic.

There are several ways a single configuration can adapt to the machine it's on. It could read an environment variable, the host name, the current user, or the current path, for example. We'll go for the simplest solution, reading the host name. Here is a possible configuration file:

```
[www.actual-live-site.com]
home = http://www.actual-live-site.com/
...
[greedy]          My home Windows box has a host
                  name of "greedy," but why?
home = http://greedy/dagfinn/site/index.php
db_host = localhost
db = test
db_username = me
db_password = secret
mail_host = localhost
mail_port = 10025
```

We can call this file configuration.php and place it in our project root directory. Now each developer can add her own host to the file and check in her version of the configuration. If a developer changes or adds configuration keys, she can update the other machines at the same time as her own. If there is a problem on a developer's box, she can look at how other machines are configured to help diagnose the problem.

In our classes folder, we can create the following class in configuration.php:

```php
<?php
class Configuration {
    private $all;
    private $host;

    function __construct() {
        $this->all = parse_ini_file(
                dirname(__FILE__) . '/../configuration',
                true);
        $this->host = trim(`hostname`);
    }

    function getHome() {
        return $this->all[$this->host]['home'];
    }

    //...
}
?>
```

I've only listed the getHome() accessor here, but it's easy to add others as needed. I've also skipped the all-important unit tests that go with this class.

Our modified test file now looks like this:

```php
<?php
require_once(dirname(__FILE__) . '/../classes/configuration.php');

class TestOfAddingContacts extends WebTestCase {
    protected $configuration;
```

```
    function __construct() {
        parent::__construct();
        $this->configuration = new Configuration();
    }

    function testNewContactShouldBeVisible() {
        $this->get($this->configuration->getHome());
        $this->click('Add contact');
        ...
    }
}
?>
```

❶ Create Configuration instance in constructor

❷ Configured rather than hard-coded value

❶❷ To avoid repeated file reads, we've created the Configuration instance just once in the test constructor. This trick does not work in PHPUnit unit tests, because the test case is instantiated anew for each test method. (Besides, there is no web tester in PHPUnit unless you install Selenium.) PHPUnit is more like JUnit in this regard. SimpleTest creates the test case just once upon the first test. This is more natural, but you have to be wary about possible interference from test to test. Here we are using it to our advantage. Instead of a hard-coded URL, we can use the configured value.

At the end of the previous section, we observed that we had hard-coded both the result web page (index.php) and the installation-dependent configuration data. With the configuration file in place, you can now add your own web server URL to the site/index.php script.

Having dealt with the configuration data, we can start replacing the fake web page with something that actually works. Our tests are green, and we will be keeping them green.

12.2 GETTING A WORKING FORM

To change the fake web interface into a real one, we need to add persistence code that saves the Contact object and retrieves it again. We're aiming for an interaction like the one in figure 12.4. The diagram has been simplified by grouping all the persistence classes under the single heading *Data Source*.

The interaction from figure 12.4 remains, and persistence functionality has been added. add.php saves the Contact object to the database; index.php retrieves all the Contact objects and lists them. For the sake of the test, we want to list just the single one we've saved.

In this section, first we'll implement what we think we need to save the form data. When we do, we'll discover that there is no database, and so we will set it up. Finally, we'll do another trick to make the test pass: stubbing out the ContactFinder class.

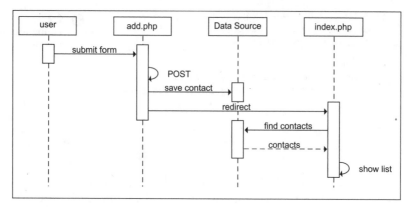

Figure 12.4 Mostly real web application that fleshes out the "add contact" feature defined by the first test

12.2.1 Trying to save the contact to the database

The first challenge is to get a Contact object written to the database. Let's modify our add.php script to achieve this.

```php
<?php
require_once(dirname(__FILE__) . '/../classes/configuration.php');
require_once(dirname(__FILE__) . '/../classes/transaction.php');
require_once(dirname(__FILE__) . '/../classes/contact.php');

if (@$_POST['add']) {
    if (@$_POST['name'] && @$_POST['email']) {
        $configuration = new Configuration();
        $transaction = new MysqlTransaction(
                $configuration->getDbHost(),
                $configuration->getDbUsername(),
                $configuration->getDbPassword(),
                $configuration->getDb());
        $contact = new Contact($_POST['name'], $_POST['email']);
        $contact->save($transaction);
        $transaction->commit();
    }
    header('Location: index.php');
}
?><html>
    ...
</html>
```

① Our trusty configuration

② We only process the "add" action on this page

③ These methods will have to be added to Configuration

④ Create the Contact instance in memory

⑤ Send the data to the database

① First we must include all the code we are going to use. Perversely, we've already written it in the previous chapters.

② Then we can pull all the strands of our previous code together. We are using the Configuration object to get the database connection parameters and the MysqlTransaction and Contact classes together to write the Contact object to the database.

Figure 12.5
A confusing test failure, but at least we know something is wrong

❸ Anything machine specific now goes through our configuration class so that we can switch to test versions when needed.

❹❺ We create and commit our new contact.

This code is a little too complex to live in a top-level script, and doesn't even catch any exceptions that could be thrown. That's typical at this stage. Right now we are just trying to get everything hooked up. Once we have some tests passing from end to end, we'll think about refactoring and error handling.

The tests don't pass. Instead we get the rather confusing failure in figure 12.5.

SimpleTest echoes the first hundred or so characters of the web page when it fails. If the error message appears at the top, as it does here, then you get to see a truncated version of it. Web testing can often be a poor diagnostic tool, but makes an excellent safety net. We'll return to this point later. In practice, it means you often end up walking the site with the real browser to find out what went wrong, or using the SimpleTest debugging methods to see the output: showText(), showSource(), show-Headers(), or showRequest().

12.2.2 Setting up the database

If you navigate our miniature web site, or add a showSource() just after the click(), you'll see that we couldn't save any data. The database schema does not exist. This is the same problem we had when testing the Contact class. By analogy with those tests, we'll create and drop the schema on every test run. This makes sure that we have a clean slate for every test. Here are the setUp() and tearDown() methods:

```
class TestOfAddingContacts extends WebTestCase {

    function setUp() {
        $this->dropSchema();
        $this->createSchema();
    }
```

```
    function tearDown() {
        $this->dropSchema();
    }
    //...
}
```

Now that we have a separate Configuration class, we can write much-improved versions of these compared to our TestOfContactPersistence class from chapter 10:

```
class TestOfAddingContacts extends WebTestCase {
    function createSchema() {
        $this->sqlScript('create_schema.sql');
    }

    function dropSchema() {
        $this->sqlScript('drop_schema.sql');
    }

    function sqlScript($script) {
        $transaction = new MysqlTransaction(
                $this->configuration->getDbHost(),
                $this->configuration->getDbUsername(),
                $this->configuration->getDbPassword(),
                $this->configuration->getDb());
        $transaction->execute(file_get_contents(
                "../database/$script"));
        $transaction->commit();
    }
}
```

In real life, we would go back and change the other tests from chapter 10, using the Configuration class. Right now, we'll press on, maintaining our focus on getting our web application from fake to real.

The tests are green again, so we can keep refactoring. The index.php page needs to read our data:

```
<?php
require_once(dirname(__FILE__) . '/../classes/configuration.php');
require_once(dirname(__FILE__) . '/../classes/transaction.php');
require_once(dirname(__FILE__) . '/../classes/contact.php');

$configuration = new Configuration();
$transaction = new MysqlTransaction(
        $configuration->getDbHost(),
        $configuration->getDbUsername(),
        $configuration->getDbPassword(),
        $configuration->getDb());
$finder = new ContactFinder();
$contacts = $finder->findAll($transaction);
?><html>
    ...
</html>
```

This is where our example gets a bit more realistic. Until now, we have been using code that was written in previous chapters. If we were designing top-down, we would have to create these components as we went along. Time has been going backward, because of the order in which we have been explaining things. At this point we hit a method that we haven't written yet, called findAll(). How do we deal with this?

12.2.3 Stubbing out the finder

What we don't do is leave the test script crashing. Failing is OK, but crashing isn't. That will log-jam everyone else on the team unless they are willing to delete our new code. As developers are a polite bunch, they will likely leave the script as it is and work around it. This is called *code ownership* and is not something you want.

If you are using modern version control such as CVS, Subversion, or Perforce, you will know that monumental effort goes into preventing developer code locks, that is, sections of the code being worked on by one developer that prevents other developers from working on the same section of code. These modern version control systems allow all developers to work simultaneously on whatever part of the system they desire. We are about to ride roughshod over that infrastructure. By leaving the tests broken while we work on another piece of code, we've effectively locked it anyway. No one can figure out what we were trying to achieve. We've taken ownership of it.

To get around the code ownership problem, we are going to stub out the finder until we've finished working on the web scripts. Here is the rest of our index.php script that leaves us with a failing test:

```php
<?php
//...
?><html>
    ...
    <body>
        <h1>Show Contacts</h1>
        <table>
            <tr><th>Name</th><th>E-mail</th></tr>
            <?php
                while ($contact = $contacts->next()) {
                    print "<tr>\n";
                    print "<td>{$contact->getName()}</td>\n";
                    print "<td>{$contact->getEmail()}</td>\n";
                    print "</tr>\n";
                }
            ?>
        </table>
        <a href="add.php">Add contact</a>
    </body>
</html>
```

Now the advantages of top-down design start to shine through. The top-level code is dictating the interface to the lower-level code. Stubbing this in our contact.php file is easy. We must add the findAll() method to ContactFinder:

```
class ContactFinder {

    function findAll($transaction) {
        return new ContactResultSet();
    }
}
```

We don't test for this yet, as we are just trying to get our main test case working. The ContactResultSet is a simple iterator. Later it will wrap a MySQL result, but for now we'll make it obvious it's just a fake:

```
class ContactResultSet {
    private $contacts;

    function __construct() {
        $this->contacts = array(new Contact('Me', 'me@me.com'));
    }

    function next() {
        return array_shift($this->contacts);
    }
}
```

By making the fakery blatantly obvious, other developers know they are free to fill out this code. If we don't think it's obvious enough, then we add a code comment saying "Stubbed for adding_contact_test.php." Usually I find that the test suite is guidance enough.

The only remaining detail is the extra accessor needed for the Contact class:

```
class Contact {

    function getName() {
        return $this->name;
    }
}
```

If we were to strictly stub this, we would just return the string "Me." Here the code is sufficiently simple that we write the finished code straight in. Testing is a tool, not an orthodox religion. We tune the degree of testing, turning it down when we are confident in our code, turning it up the second we get an unexpected failure.

Our contact-adding test is finally green and is testing real scripts. There is still some stubbed code, and the scripts are frankly rubbish, but we are up and running. We now have two paths we can follow. We can refactor our top-level code, or we could implement the stubbed ContactFinder method. It's more effective to get the top-level code working first. So if being unfinished does not bug you too much, we now go on to refactor the entire web application.

12.3   QUALITY ASSURANCE

The contact manager is almost finished; we've left a gaping hole with the stubbed-out ContactFinder class, but instead of the relatively easy task of implementing the finder, we want to tie up the loose ends at the top level of the application.

One of those loose ends is unit testing the top-level scripts. The other one is considering the relationship between our tests and user requirements.

12.3.1   Making the contact manager unit-testable

There is a lot of repetition in the top-level application scripts. With the test case as a safety net, let's gather the code into a class. The add.php code is the easiest. All we have to do is save a new Contact and redirect if successful. The top-level code should really look like this:

```php
<?php
require_once('../classes/add_contact_controller.php');

$controller = new AddContactController($_POST);
if ($controller->added()) {
    header('Location: index.php');
}
?><html>
    ...
/html>
```

This makes the top-level navigation clearer, and puts a lot of the resource management into the AddContactController class. As a pattern, it's called the Page Controller. It's a known design, but here we are allowing it to emerge as a result of our refactoring process. We will see it again in a different variation when we have a closer look at the controller patterns in chapter 17.

Once all the controllers are in classes, commonality can be factored out. Here is the complete class after it has been copied into the classes/add_contact_controller.php file:

```php
class AddContactController {
    private $added = false;

    function __construct($request) {
        if (@$request['add']) {
            if (@$request['name'] && @$request['email']) {
                try {
                    $this->saveContact($request['name'],
                                        $request['email']);
                } catch (Exception $e) {
                }
                $this->added = true;
            }
        }
    }

    private function saveContact($name, $email) {
        $configuration = new Configuration();
```

```
        $transaction = new MysqlTransaction(
                $configuration->getDbHost(),
                $configuration->getDbUsername(),
                $configuration->getDbPassword(),
                $configuration->getDb());
        $contact = new Contact($name, $email);
        $contact->save($transaction);
        $transaction->commit();
    }

    function added() {
        return $this->added;
    }
}
```

The sequence diagram in figure 12.6 shows how the process of saving the contact works.

Moving the code into its own class, and then its own file, are two trivial steps that can be done under the control of our web test. Once we add more validation and other more-complex behavior into the mix, using web tests becomes clumsy. Then it's best to write unit tests for our controllers.

Partly this is because web tests are slow. Even when testing through the local-host interface, a large test case can take several seconds to run. The sheer complexity of some pages can make them take longer than that. I've seen full site tests that take 20 minutes or more to run. This was why we placed the web tests into a separate test runner script early on; we wanted to keep the unit tests separate and fast. By moving as much controller code as possible out of the top-level scripts and into unit tests, we get back our fast feedback cycle.

The bigger problem with web testing is that when something fails, it can be difficult to isolate. Suppose a database query produces an error deep in the code. At the web page level, all we would get would be some bland message such as "server error,

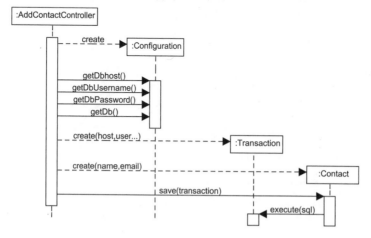

Figure 12.6   What the AddContactController does to save the contact to the database

please retry." Hardly much help when we are debugging. Unit tests test individual components and classes. When that component fails, the unit test makes it clear where the problem is. Only that unit test will fail, as long as the other tests use a mocked database. By contrast, a database failure could break every single web test. Hardly much help tracking down the problem. Web tests make a great safety net, but make a poor diagnostic tool.

12.3.2 From use case to acceptance test

Web tests do have one big advantage: they are very readable. This makes it easy to translate a specification into a series of tests. Tests of the functional specification are usually dictated by the client to confirm completion of a project, so they are called *acceptance tests*.

Acceptance tests are usually derived from a written specification, or if we are lucky, we have the customer sitting next to us while we write them. Let's say they tell us something like this:

Adding a new contact:

We can add a new contact from a home page link. Right now a contact is just a name and an email address. We need to be able to edit an existing contact by clicking on the name on the front page listing.

When we enter the new person, error handling should be as follows:

1. An invalid email address should let us try again, saying "invalid address" or something.

2. A missing name shouldn't matter; it should get entered anyway.

3. A database failure should just display a message.

The new contact should be shown at the top of the home page listing.

This is called a *use case*. It includes not just the "happy path" when everything goes well, but also the failure stories. It also includes explicit descriptions of the final state after the action is carried out. You can tell from the language that this specification was written with a developer present, and probably with a visual mock-up too. Once in this form, it translates straight into web tests:

```
class TestOfAddingContacts extends WebTestCase {

    function testNewContactShouldBeVisible() { }
}
```

We already have this one. Let's deal with clicking on the name to edit the email address and with the response to the invalid email address, as shown in listing 12.1.

Listing 12.1   A test class based on our use case

```
class TestOfAddingContacts extends WebTestCase {
    function addContact($name, $email) {                              ❶
        $this->get($this->configuration->getHome());
        $this->click('Add contact');
        $this->setField('Name:', $name);
        $this->setField('E-mail:', $email);
        $this->click('Add');
    }

    function testNewContactShouldBeVisible() {                        ❷
        $this->addContact('Me', 'me@me.com');
        $this->assertText('Me');
        $this->assertText('me@me.com');
    }

    function testCanClickOnNameToEditContact() {                      ❸
        $this->addContact('Me', 'me@me.com');
        $this->click('Me');
        $this->setField('E-mail:', 'me@elsewhere.com');
        $this->click('Add');
        $this->assertText('me@elsewhere.com');
        $this->assertNoText('me@me.com');
    }

    function testInvalidEmailAddressShowsInvalidMessage() {          ❹
        $this->addContact('Me', 'invalid_email');
        $this->assertText('Invalid address');
        $this->assertTitle('Add Contact');
    }
}
```

❶ We refactor our tests just as we would refactor our regular code, and move the repeated code into its own method, addContact(). We don't usually remove duplication with quite the same zeal as we would in production code, though. The name of the game for tests is not flexibility, but readability. We will accept some duplication if it makes the story clearer. Try it with your client. Can you talk them through the test case? If not, move any technical code into its own methods, but leave the sequence of steps as they imagine it, even if you repeat some code in several tests.

❷ After addContact(), the "Me" contact should be available in the web interface. Here, we just test that the contact's name and email address is visible.

❸ The use case description says "We need to be able to edit an existing contact by clicking on the name on the front page listing." This test simulates clicking on the contact name, changing the email field, and clicking Add to submit the form. Then it checks that the new email address is present and that the old one is not.

❹ The test for error handling is partial, because this is not likely to be the final version. We use `assertTitle()` to confirm that we are still on the page with the form, and haven't been redirected. As the result of usability testing, it may be that the incorrect field is simply highlighted in red. Perhaps a different message will be used. What happens next is a different approach to what happens in unit tests. With unit tests, the programmer would simply edit the test and code together to get a working solution. With acceptance tests, a programmer would never change the test without going back to the project owner. Acceptance tests are an agreement between developers and their clients.

They are also a communication mechanism. Our use case will generate half a dozen tests in all, and this should be enough for the developers to implement the application. They give developers a clear goal, and help to prevent feature creep by being emphatic. They fail if there is still work to do; they pass if there isn't (except refactoring of course).

What happens next depends on development process. If you are in the Extreme Programming camp (XP), the tests will have been written when the "user story," a cut-down use case, was brought into the current project iteration. If the project has a distinct requirements-gathering phase, all of the specification can be converted to tests early on. Whichever technique is used, until the application code is written, the tests will fail. We either manage this, comment out the failing tests, or stub them into passing.

In our example, we stubbed the lower-level code while we worked on the acceptance test so that other developers could carry on working on the same code. This is not the only approach. We could also have used the branching mechanism in our version control to isolate any damage we were causing. A nice advantage of all of those failing acceptance tests is that they show project progress as they turn from red to green. If we comment them out, or spoof them with stub code, the project manager might believe that progress is more rapid than it really is.

Suppose we don't rigidly enforce the rule of tests being green for the acceptance test suite? If your tools support it, or you have two web test suites, you can trade in a simpler development environment for better feedback on how the project is going. Is this the better approach? We don't know.

We won't implement any of the previous tests. We are explaining things backward again. We would use the techniques in this chapter to get them passing, and then refactor controllers, requests, and other resources as in chapter 11. Then we would unit test these components, mocking out resources as in chapter 10. Finally, we would test these resources in detail, as we did in chapter 9.

Until now, we've been working on an example developed from scratch. An ideal world, but how can we introduce testing into an existing web application that doesn't follow any of our recommended rules or guidelines, one whose only claim to fame is that it works well enough, often enough, to be useful?

12.4 THE HORROR OF LEGACY CODE

Does your current code base induce dread? Is it a neglected ruin of a building where one false move can bring the roof falling in? When you take one bug out, do you put two more in? Does it lack tests, so that even when you think you've fixed something, you're not sure? If so, you've got legacy code.

You've also got a catch-22. To get this mess under control, you want to refactor. To refactor safely, you want to have unit tests. Unfortunately, you cannot get unit tests in place because of all the dependencies. That is, the code of a single class often doesn't run without bringing in all of the code it's entangled with. To get rid of the dependencies, you need to refactor...

A big problem with unit tests is code that doesn't have them. The win comes when you have pretty-complete test coverage. You can make any change to the application you want, secure in the knowledge that the test suite will catch any breakage. As soon as you have code without test coverage, you have to start checking that part manually. Adding unit tests to legacy code is also no fun at all. When you are just learning test-driven development, the last thing you want to be doing is all testing and no development.

Let's invent the nightmare scenario. We join a project to find a code base that is edited directly on the live server and has grown organically over a few years. It's a mixture of coding styles, both procedural and OO. It has an occasional database backup, but no other copy, least of all one in version control. It also uses lots of external resources, such as web services. How to cope? Here is a battle-tested, step by step guide:

1 Duplicate the live environment on a dedicated "hack box."

2 Round up every piece of legacy code.

3 Test manually and fix the hack box application.

4 Set up databases.

5 Fix permissions.

6 Write web tests.

7 Check everything into version control.

8 Replace hard-coded paths to make the code work on other machines.

9 Automate the checkout.

10 Deploy to the live server.

11 Automate deployment.

Figure 12.7 summarizes the components used in the process. There is a "hack box" for cleaning up a copy of the application. Then there is a development machine, possibly one of many, to be used when the application is configurable enough to install from version control. And there is, of course, a live server, the production environment.

Now let's take a closer look at each step. Although the following is not down to the level of specific commands, it should serve as a rough guide.

Step 1: Duplicate the live environment

The first step is to set aside a machine dedicated to duplicating the live environment. You need to be able to commit all the crimes on this machine that have been committed on the live server, including strange email and network configuration. Don't use your day-to-day computer for this unless you are brave. Ideally, this development machine will have exactly the same operating system and libraries as the live box. In practice, this can be nearly impossible, so we have to adapt as we go. Get as close as you can. We're calling this machine "hack box," because it will be full of hacks. We can think of it as an operating table.

Step 2: Round up legacy code

Step 2 is to round up every piece of legacy code there is. If there is a web service call to another machine under our control, make a copy of that code as well. You want every scrap of legacy code duplicated on your development box, placed in exactly the same directories. This includes Unix cron jobs and other configuration scripts. We copy all of this code, in identical directories, onto the hack box. Our application is ready for surgery.

Step 3: Test manually

Now point your web browser at the home page on your machine. The result will be spectacular, probably with an error message or 20. The first problem will likely be hard-coded links, especially images. You need to edit the hosts file of this machine to make the host name identical to the live server host name. At this point, you will be glad you set up a separate development machine for this exercise, as the networking will now be screwy. Try to catch every external request unless it uses a web service from another site. If necessary, use a packet sniffer, such as ethereal (http://www. ethereal.com/), to make sure the application is self contained. You will have to edit the web server configuration to make sure all the paths and access files are correct. Yet more hacks to our hack box.

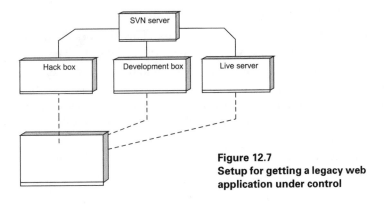

Figure 12.7
Setup for getting a legacy web application under control

Each time you click on a page, you will likely get some kind of configuration error. Each time, fix the problem, make a note of it, and move on. You will probably have to install some libraries, too. Once you start to hit database errors, you have finished step 3. Your hosts file will be a mess.

Step 4: Set up databases

Now for the databases. Take the last backup of the data along with a schema dump. Set up the identical configuration on the hack box and import the schema and data. By now the web site should look approximately right. You may have to take over `.htaccess` or other web server authentication files, too.

Step 5: Fix permissions

The remaining issue will be permissions. As you identify each of these, transfer them into a script that you can run in one go. Step 5 is done when the application is fully running in this new environment. Getting through these first five steps will typically take a week. It's a very difficult task to divide up among several people, so it typically involves one person (the unsung hero) working on it until done. From now on, life gets easier.

Step 6: Write web tests

The next step is writing the web tests. The application is treated as a black box throughout. If something is saved using a form, the web test logs into the administration interface to check that it is there. We don't read a database directly if we can avoid it. The objective is to cover the code, not exhaustively test every variation. It is enough to know that a web form saves information, for example, not that it validates every field. The good news is that this task can be split among many developers, and a few hundred tests can cover even quite-large applications.

This is the step that really unlocks the problem. From now on, any developer can inspect the hack box and the test suite to find out how the code should work.

Step 7: Check everything into version control

Step 7 is to check everything into version control. This includes the database schema and our permissions script. Next we back up all the code in the hack box and delete it. Now check out the code from version control and use a script to move it to the correct directory, if needed. The directory permissions will be broken, but the handy script we wrote earlier should take care of that. Get the tests back to green. Now any changes we make on this hack machine will be reflected in the version control when we check the code in.

We are connected to our version control. Think of this as life support.

Step 8: Replace hard-coded paths

We need to be able to get working copies of the code in front of the other developers. This means being able to check the code out to any machine, and into any directory.

Still on the hack box, write a configuration class similar to the one we used earlier. Add entries for host names, database connections, and fixed file system paths. Step 8 is to painstakingly replace every hard-coded path, host, and password with dynamically configured versions. At least we are now refactoring with some tests. Now the focus moves to our normal development boxes. Check out the code to your favorite machine, and fill out the new configuration options. Of course, the tests will fail. To get them passing, keep making changes to the hack box. Add more configuration if needed. The tests stay green on the hack box, and the results are checked. Each time we check out the code on our development box and retest. As the configuration changes take place on the hack box, more and more of the tests on the other development boxes should go green. When they all go green, the application has taken its first real breath.

Step 9: Automate the checkout

Automating the checkout is step nine. A script should build the database schema, change web server configurations, fix any permissions, or make any other sundry changes to get the code working. Step 9 is done when we can, on any development box, check out the code, run a few scripts, and get green tests. The work gradually shifts away from the hack box as we make the code base more portable. From this point on, any developer can work on the code. We are nearly there. Our patient is conscious, but unable to leave the hospital.

Step 10: Deploy to the live server

The final phase is the live server itself. We want to be able to deploy from the version control, straight to the server. In theory, our original hack box should provide the blueprint, but we won't be able to run the tests live without affecting data. Step ten is to add a testing version of the database to both the hack box and the live server. This shadow testing database should start empty of data. This will affect the web tests for sure, so you will need to fix these. The idea is that you can roll out to the live server, without affecting the current live deployment. This confirms that the application really will work with the modules that are on the live box.

After step 10, you can safely run the tests on the live server as long as you first switch configuration. How you switch configuration is up to you. As the legacy version will be hard-coded right now, we can just place the testing configuration under the live hosts entry in the configuration file. In the future, if we want to run a testing and live version on the same box, we will have get clever. That's later.

Of course, this manual step of switching configuration is extremely dangerous. We want to remove it before we do a serious roll-out.

Step 11: Automate deployment

Step 11 involves writing the automated deployment script. It's the final step. This should export the code from the version control, run the tests in the test database, and, if successful, switch to the live configuration. Our work is complete when we do our first rollout to the live server. The connection between a particular server and the code is gone. We have portable code. We can code and test on our own workstation, deploy to a staging server, and finally to a live server. The worst is over. We can even decommission our hack box.

We still don't have unit tests covering the code. The web tests will tell us only *if* we have broken something, not *where*, but unit tests can now be added incrementally. As we work on different sections of our now living and breathing code, we can leave a trail of better tests and better design. This is a virtuous circle of refactoring and greater test coverage. If we are in a hurry, we could even risk adding a feature or two. Our patient has taken its first steps. The health of our project should slowly recover.

12.5 SUMMARY

Web tests are easy to write and allow us to use test-driven design starting with the web interface itself. Use cases can be converted to web tests in an almost mechanical way. We start out satisfying the tests with a fake, hard-coded application consisting mostly of static HTML and flesh it out to make it do real work. One challenge is making the application and test suite configurable enough to work in different environments. Although web tests are easy, they are a blunt diagnostic. This makes them most useful when unit tests cannot be applied, or where unit tests are inappropriate. These include knotty HTTP issues, acceptance tests, and as a safety net or containment building. They are especially effective in the early stages of development. Even legacy code can be retrofitted with tests by starting with the web tests and moving on to add unit tests later.

The real value of unit testing, mocking, refactoring, and testing is the change it brings about in managing web projects. At this point, we are not merely a lone coder, but a software developer. We can adapt our process to business risk. We can share our work with others. We can turn code into a strategic asset and manage that asset.

In the next chapter, we will start exploring the specifics of web presentation. The key challenge is to separate HTML markup from PHP code. To meet this challenge, we will learn how to keep the HTML markup in template files by using template engines such as Smarty, PHPTAL, and XSLT. We will also look into additional techniques for keeping program logic out of templates and discover how to make templates secure. Our graphic designers will thank us.

PART 3

Building the web interface

The web interface itself is the challenge that is unique to web programming. Most complete programs have a user interface, but other types of user interfaces—such as command-line interfaces and rich-client graphical user interfaces—involve other kinds of issues and different species of complexity.

One unique issue is the separation of HTML markup and program code. Another is the handling of the HTTP request. Among PHP developers, the standard solution to the first problem is web templates, and the object-oriented solution to the second one is the Model-View-Controller (MVC) pattern. In this part of the book, we will put both of these under close scrutiny. We will also look at ways to construct complex web pages out of independent components and how to handle input validation and forms.

CHAPTER 13

Using templates to manage web presentation

Web presentation, in its simplest form, is a plain HTML document. PHP helps us insert dynamic content into the HTML document simply. But as the program code grows more complex, the combination poses new challenges. Increasingly, program code and HTML markup appear as Siamese twins: They're together all the time, but they might be better off spending some time apart. They might prefer to meet and work together when it's actually needed instead of being inseparably attached to each other. Adding to this is the fact that even though they're joined together, they have very different personalities. When we try to apply modern programming principles, we find that only the PHP code responds properly to it. HTML markup needs to be cared for in completely different ways. Doing this is much easier if we try to separate them.

So to be able to use the object-oriented tools and concepts presented in earlier chapters, we need to separate the two as cleanly as possible. Fortunately, object orientation also helps us achieve this goal. The way most PHP template engines work is by supplying one or more classes to encapsulate the process of adding dynamic content into an HTML page. Another example of how object-oriented techniques can work is the View Helper pattern that we will discuss later in this chapter.

In this chapter, we start by discussing the reasons why we want to separate presentation from the rest of the application and how templates can help us do that. Then we study some template engines and compare how they work. We also take a close look at XSLT, which may be used as a template engine. Then we go through some further techniques for keeping program logic out of templates. Finally, we'll see how to make sure templates don't compromise security.

13.1 SEPARATING PRESENTATION AND DOMAIN LOGIC

The need to separate presentation from business logic—also known as domain logic—is a fundamental principle of software design. It is relevant not just for web applications, but in all software that interacts with people. The separation is given somewhat-different names in different architectural models, but the basic principle is similar. In the Model-View-Controller architecture (we'll have a closer look at it in chapter 15), it's known as the *Model-View separation*; in the typical layered architecture, there may be a Presentation layer and a Domain layer.

In this section, we'll summarize some of the most-common rationales for divorcing presentation from business logic, then we'll take a closer look at the role of templates and the benefits they can bring.

13.1.1 To separate or not to separate...

You may have seen the reasons for this separation before, but let's summarize them.

- *Separation of concerns.* The user interface typically requires different rules, different techniques, and different ways of thinking than the business concepts. It also has a tendency to change more often, so it's a good idea to be able to make changes in the UI without affecting the non-UI parts of the program.

- *Pluggable user interface.* Sometimes, the same basic functionality is needed by different types of user interface. You can download a file from the Web by using a command-line utility or a graphical web browser. If you're programming both the utility and the browser, it makes sense for them to use the same code to do the real work of downloading.

- *Division of labor.* Often different people are assigned to the user interface and the domain logic. In the case of web applications, layout and styling of web pages is often done by web designers who are not programmers.

- *Easier testing.* User interfaces are difficult to test by automated test suites, so it makes sense to be able to test the underlying features separately. The user interface may be user-friendly, but the domain logic is typically more program-friendly and predictable.

In spite of all this, there are those who advocate mixing presentation information—in the form of HTML markup—into PHP code. As mentioned in chapter 11, I was surprised to find that one relatively recent PHP book actually recommends outputting all HTML code from PHP `echo` or `print` statements. Perhaps I shouldn't have been surprised. The conclusion from looking at a number of open-source web applications is that it *is* common practice.

It's flexible in some ways, but it fragments the markup, making web design difficult. And it's a one-way street: you burn the bridges behind you, and when the day of reckoning comes, you find yourself unable to go back.

13.1.2 Why templates?

In PHP, the standard answer to the perennial question of how to separate presentation from domain logic is to use a template engine. The template engine concept will be familiar to PHP programmers, but may be confusing to those who are used to different terminology that is prevalent in some other languages, particularly C++ and Java. (C++ templates and the Template Method design pattern [Gang of Four] both refer to template concepts that are distinct from the one discussed here.)

A template in our context is a web template—a page written in a language that consists mostly of HTML markup, but also has a way of expressing how dynamically generated content is to be included. A template engine is a software library that allows us to generate HTML code from the templates and specify the dynamic content to be included.

This is the basic idea behind PHP itself, JSP, and ASP. That means there is something mildly paradoxical about the idea of a template engine for PHP, since all template engines do the thing that PHP is perfectly capable of on its own: they generate HTML pages with embedded dynamic content.

So why use templates? To help achieve the separation of concerns and the division of labor made possible by keeping program code and HTML markup separate.

In addition, templates support security by making it harder for template designers to sneak in unwanted program code. And some template languages are XML formats that make it possible for other programs—beside the template engine—to handle the template.

For some reason, discussions of templates tend to turn into heated arguments. Some say that template engines are superfluous, since PHP is already basically a template language. And since most template engines don't enforce a separation between presentation and business logic anyway, self-discipline is required to keep them apart. Why not use the same self-discipline to create PHP files that are separated cleanly into HTML sections and script sections?

This is a valid point. Still, the empirical evidence seems to indicate that templates do succeed, to some extent at least, in *encouraging* the separation. They wouldn't be so popular if they were simply an unnecessary waste of processing cycles.

Encourage the separation

The main rationale behind templates is separating presentation and business logic. But, as Terrence Parr points out (http://www.cs.usfca.edu/~parrt/papers/mvc.templates.pdf), most template engines only *encourage* this separation rather than *enforce* it. Template engines tend to accumulate features that make them more and more like a complete programming language. That makes business logic creep into templates, and the distinction between presentation and domain goes out the window. To a lesser or greater extent, anyway.

It's a pragmatic issue. The separation is important; do whatever is necessary to make sure it's there. What's necessary depends on your context, your environment, and the people in it. Templates help; templates with restricted functionality help even more. Later in this chapter, we'll see ways to solve some of the problems that tend to tempt you to put lots of program logic in templates.

Promote division of labor

One of the reasons for keeping HTML markup in templates is enabling web designers and others, typically non-programmers, to change the layout of a web application.

Even if—typically on a small project—programmers are doing the design job, it's not safe to mix presentation and program code. As mentioned in chapter 11, you never know when you might need the help of a professional web designer or when an existing application might need to be adapted to a completely different layout. This kind of thing is almost impossible without separating PHP code from HTML markup.

Another, related difficulty is optimizing the HTML code itself. The size of the HTML file sent across the network to the user can be the key determining factor for response time, and response time can be the key factor to determine whether the user chooses to stay at your site or go somewhere else. So using CSS styling sensibly can be important. If you have the typical markup using nested tables and perhaps even <font> tags, you are outputting more HTML code than you need to. Changing this can reduce the size and increase the readability of the HTML code. But this is extremely difficult unless the HTML is fairly well-separated and concentrated in a few places.

Provide easier parsing than plain PHP

Some, but not all, template engines implement the template features using XML/XHTML syntax—as tags, attributes, or comments. Among other things, this allows us to pre- and post-process templates by using SimpleXML and the XML DOM.

Templates also have another advantage over plain PHP files: you can defer output. Template engines let you generate the output at one point in the program and output it later. You can do this with plain PHP, but you have to use the output buffering functions, which is more cumbersome.

Increase security

PHP files can't be left in the hands of people you don't trust. If web designers are given PHP files in order to develop the layout, they potentially have the power to delete files, send sensitive information from the server by email, alter database data, and so on.

Template engines help avoid this problem by limiting template designers' ability to perform unsafe operations. Although PHP template engines tend to have a way to execute PHP code, there is usually a way of preventing this. And if there isn't, you could always search for a PHP keyword in the templates. That should be much easier than inspecting PHP files manually, trying to figure out if any of the PHP code is insecure.

You might think this is a non-issue—that web designers have no interest in doing mischief—but that's not always the case. There have in fact been attacks from bloggers who have been given access to templates that were capable of executing code.

Now that we know why we want to use some sort of template engine approach, even if it might be a simple one, we are ready to ask the next question: which template engine is best for our needs? There are no final answers, but at least we can start to explore the issue.

13.2   WHICH TEMPLATE ENGINE?

There are many different template engines for PHP. My real-world experience with these different engines and approaches is insufficient to tell you what the best choice in all circumstances is.

It's crucially dependent on the situation, including the following considerations:

- Who is handling HTML layout and design? Is it done by a web designer, or are you doing it yourself?

- How critical is performance? While some web sites may potentially receive millions of hits per day, many more are specialized or restricted in ways that guarantee relatively light traffic.

- What tools are being used to edit the web pages? Is it done in raw HTML code, with a WYSIWYG editor, or with a combination of the two?

Sometimes the rational choice will be determined by technical problems, even bugs, that surface in a particular context. These are issues that may be decisive, but are practically impossible to address in a book because they may be solved by the time the book is published.

But even though I can offer no authoritative advice, we can study some of the most popular approaches and mention some of their more obvious pros and cons.

I admit that the selection of sample template engines is subjective: First, we want to try using plain PHP as a template language so that we can use it as a yardstick; the others must have some additional advantages, or they are useless. Then we'll look at Smarty because it's popular, PHPTAL because it's my personal favorite, and XSLT because it's very different from the others and has additional interesting features.

Throughout this section and the one on XSLT, we'll use an example list of user accounts to show various template techniques. Listing 13.1 is the user list in its first, non-template, version.

Listing 13.1   The user list in its original version

```php
<?php
require_once 'UserFinder.php';

$finder = new UserFinder;                        ❶
$users = $finder->findAll();

?>
<html>
  <head>
    <title>User administration</title>
  </head>
  <body>
    <div id="content">
      <h1>User administration</h1>
    <table id="AdminList" cellspacing="0">
    <tr>
      <th>Login name</th>
      <th>First Name</th>
      <th>Last name</th>
      <th>Email address</th>
      <th>Role</th>
      <th></th>
    </tr>
    <?php foreach ($users as $u) : ?>       ❷
      <tr>
        <td><?php echo htmlentities($u->getUserName()) ?></td>   ❸
        <td><?php echo htmlentities($u->getFirstName()) ?></td>
        <td><?php echo htmlentities($u->getLastName()) ?></td>
        <td><?php echo htmlentities($u->getEmail()) ?></td>
        <td><?php echo htmlentities($u->getRole()) ?></td   >
        <td><a href="userform.php?id=<?php
             echo htmlentities($u->getID()) ?>"
              class="CommandLink">Edit</a>
      </tr>
    <?php endforeach; ?>
    </table>
    </div>
  </body>
</html>
```

❶ We'll deal with the details of object-oriented database access in part 4 of this book. For now, we're just assuming we have the classes available. We have a UserFinder class that takes care of all the details of finding and getting users from the database. The findAll() method returns an array of User objects.

❷ To generate the table, we use a PHP `foreach` with the so-called alternative syntax for control structures. `if`, `while`, `for`, `foreach`, and `switch` can all be used in this way.

❸ The variables of each object are retrieved with accessors. To ensure against XSS attacks, we escape all of the strings using `htmlentities()`.

Now that we know what we want to do, we can start implementing it using template engines. First out is a minimal approach using plain PHP as a template language.

13.2.1 Plain PHP

You can use ordinary PHP files as templates. That means that you can write a PHP file that's as close as possible to pure HTML. Restrict the PHP sections to simple variable output and a minimum of control structures. Any longer PHP sections can be placed in another file.

Depending on your point of view, this might seem either harebrained, too obvious, or both. On the one hand, template engines are tailor-made for template handling, whereas PHP is a full programming language. On the other hand, what the template engines do is suspiciously similar to what PHP does in the simplest cases: they take a file that's mostly HTML and replace some special markup with dynamic content.

The primary objective of template engines is to facilitate separation of presentation from application logic and content. You can achieve that separation by simply keeping them separate, but it requires discipline. A first step in that direction could be to keep nearly all the PHP code in the beginning in a single PHP section followed by an HTML section, instead of interspersing PHP processing sections in the HTML code. But we can make the separation even clearer by keeping them in separate files. Listing 13.2 shows what the PHP script file looks like after the HTML code has been moved into a separate file called userlist_template.

> **Listing 13.2   The user list PHP code after extracting the HTML section**

```php
<?php
require_once 'UserFinder.php';
require_once 'HTTPPlus.php';

$finder = new UserFinder;
$users = $finder->findAll();

include 'userlist_template.php';
?>
```

This is clearly not rocket science, but it's worth considering. Template engines have some advantages beyond just basic separation of presentation and program logic. On the other hand, none of them are likely to be faster than plain PHP.

And as we've seen in chapter 6, it is possible—in fact, not very difficult—to develop this approach into a class with an API resembling most template engines, using template objects in PHP. The two basic tricks are encapsulating the `include` statement inside a method so you can control which variables will be set, and using output buffering to store the result of processing the template instead of just letting it output the result immediately.

Judging by some of the discussions I've seen lately, the "PHP as template" camp might be the biggest group among PHP programmers. But specialized template engines have their devoted followers as well. One of the biggest is Smarty, so let's see how it compares to plain PHP.

13.2.2 Custom syntax: Smarty

As you may know, Smarty is one of the most popular PHP template engines. There are several other template engines that are based on a similar principle: the template appears as an object in the PHP code, and you can set values from PHP that can be displayed using the template.

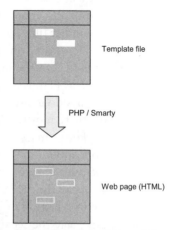

You might say that the template is a web page with "holes" that are filled by a PHP script. Figure 13.1 illustrates this simple principle, which is common to Smarty and many other template engines.

The template file itself has special markup that marks the "holes" into which you can insert dynamic content. This markup is not XML or HTML; it's a custom syntax that distinguishes Smarty's syntax from HTML or XML tags.

Figure 13.1   Smarty template viewed in a web browser

Listing 13.3, a Smarty template for the user list, illustrates how this works.

Listing 13.3   Smarty template for user list

```html
<html>
  <head>
    <title>User administration</title>
  </head>
  <body>
    <div id="content">
      <h1>User administration</h1>
      <table id="AdminList" cellspacing="0">
      <tr>
        <th>Login name</th>
        <th>First Name</th>
        <th>Last name</th>
        <th>Email address</th>
        <th>Role</th>
        <th></th>
```

```
    </tr>
    {section name=u loop=$users}
      <tr>
      <td>{$users[u]->getUsername()|escape:"htmlall"}</td>
      <td>{$users[u]->getFirstname()|escape:"htmlall"}</td>
      <td>{$users[u]->getLastname()|escape:"htmlall"}</td>
      <td>{$users[u]->getEmail()|escape:"htmlall"}</td>
      <td>{$users[u]->getRole()|escape:"htmlall"}</td>
      <td><a href="userform.php?id={$users[u]->getID()}">Edit</a>
      </tr>
    {/section}
    </table>
    </div>
  </body>
</html>
```

As you can see, this example is very similar to the original PHP file. The PHP foreach statement has been replaced with a Smarty section with a loop.

Also, we are using Smarty's mechanism to escape output. Even this is not quite ideal. For optimal security, we should specify character encoding as well:

```
{$users[u]->getLastname()|escape:"htmlall":"UTF-8"}
```

Using Smarty from PHP

The PHP file that uses the Smarty template (see listing 13.4) is another variation on the beginning PHP section of the original userlist.php file.

Listing 13.4   userlist.php, Smarty version

```
<?php
require_once 'UserFinder.php';
require_once 'HTTPPlus.php';
define('SMARTY_DIR','/usr/local/lib/php/Smarty/');
require(SMARTY_DIR.'Smarty.class.php');

$finder = new UserFinder;
$users = $finder->findAll();

$smarty = new Smarty;
$smarty->assign('users',$users);
$smarty->display('userlist.tpl');
?>
```

In addition to what we did before, we create a Smarty object, set Smarty's users variable to the array of user objects we got from the UserFinder, and ask the Smarty object to display it.

Hiding the Smarty markup

Let's pretend to be web designers for a moment. We want to be able to edit the template in a WYSIWYG HTML editor. The problem is that it will not look good unless the editor is capable of handling the braces that Smarty uses. It will look the same as in a web browser. Figure 13.2 shows how the template looks in a web browser.

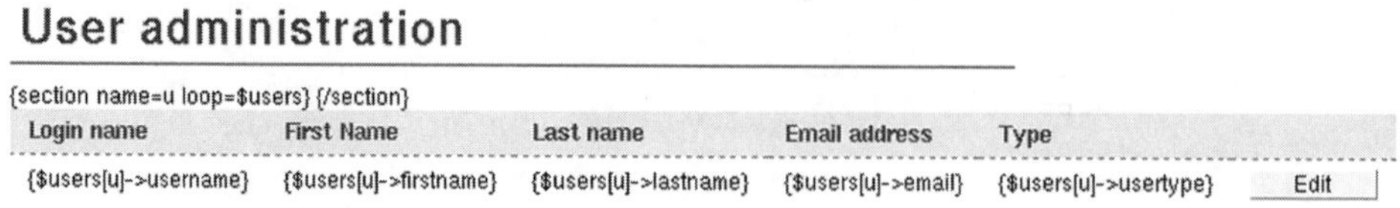

User administration

{section name=u loop=$users} {/section}

Login name	First Name	Last name	Email address	Type	
{$users[u]->username}	{$users[u]->firstname}	{$users[u]->lastname}	{$users[u]->email}	{$users[u]->usertype}	Edit

Figure 13.2 Smarty template viewed in a web browser

This is not terribly designer-friendly. But we can change it, since Smarty gives us some choice about how the template should look when viewed in WYSIWYG. Smarty lets us change the delimiters. So we can make the Smarty markup invisible in WYSIWYG view by enclosing them in HTML comments. We change the left and right delimiters, adding HTML comment characters so that the Smarty expressions look like this one:

```
<!--{$users[u]->username}-->
```

That changes WYSIWYG view as shown in figure 13.3.

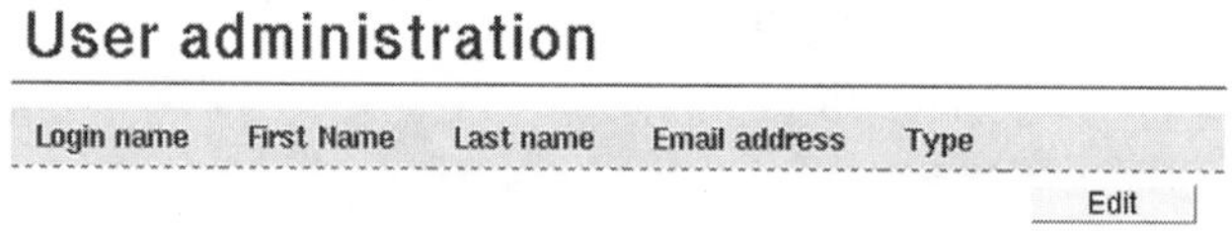

User administration

Login name	First Name	Last name	Email address	Type	
					Edit

Figure 13.3 Smarty template after changing Smarty's delimiters

Whether this is actually better is a matter of what you—and the web designers you might work with—prefer. Figure 13.2 has none of those weird and excessively long Smarty tags. On the other hand, you have absolutely nothing to tell you where the PHP-generated content will appear. That is not necessarily an advantage.

We've looked at Smarty, which is fairly typical of template engines. Our next candidate for admiration, PHPTAL, is less typical because it is based on a different principle.

13.2.3 Attribute language: PHPTAL

PHPTAL is a template engine that is based on yet another principle, radically different from what we've seen so far. *TAL* stands for *Template Attribute Language*. It is based on using XML attributes instead of specialized tags. So, for instance, where a Smarty template would have

```
<td>{$username}</td>
```

the PHPTAL equivalent would be

```
<td tal:content="username">Dummy user name</td>
```

PHPTAL is supremely friendly from a web designer's point of view. WYSIWYG HTML editing tools generally ignore unknown attributes, and PHPTAL lets you insert dummy content that will make the template look like the real web page when viewed in a WYSIWYG HTML editor—or in a web browser for that matter. Figure 13.4 shows what a PHPTAL template for the user list looks like when opened as a file in a web browser.

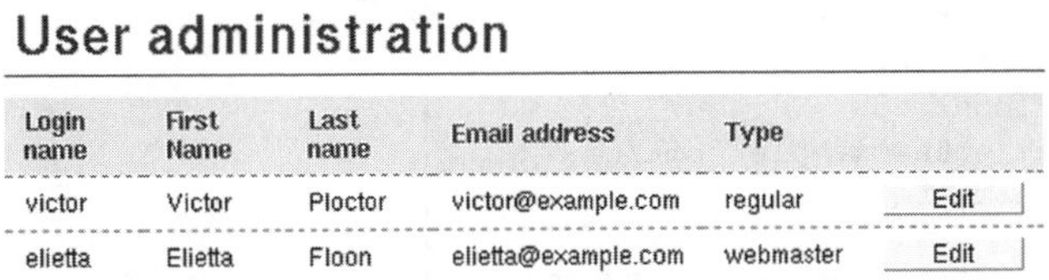

User administration

Login name	First Name	Last name	Email address	Type	
victor	Victor	Ploctor	victor@example.com	regular	Edit
elietta	Elietta	Floon	elietta@example.com	webmaster	Edit

Figure 13.4   PHPTAL template viewed in web browser

This is possible because of PHPTAL's ability to insert example content that disappears when the real application is run. Let's look at the PHPTAL template (see listing 13.5).

Listing 13.5   PHPTAL template for user list

```
<!DOCTYPE html PUBLIC "-//W3C//DTD XHTML 1.0 Transitional//EN"     ❶
    "http://www.w3.org/TR/xhtml1/DTD/xhtml1-transitional.dtd">
<html xmlns="http://www.w3.org/1999/xhtml">     ❷
  <head>
    <title>
      User administration
    </title>
  </head>
  <body>
    <div id="content">
      <h1>
        User administration
      </h1>
      <table id="AdminList" cellspacing="0">
        <tr>
          <th>Login name</th>
          <th>First Name</th>
          <th>Last name</th>
          <th>Email address</th>
          <th>Role</th>
          <th>
          </th>
        </tr>
        <tr tal:repeat="user users">          ❸
```

```
        <td tal:content="user/getUsername">victor</td>          4
        <td tal:content="user/getFirstname">Victor</td>
        <td tal:content="user/getLastname">Ploctor</td>
        <td tal:content="user/getEmail">victor@example.com</td>
        <td tal:content="user/getRole">regular</td>
        <td>
          <a href="userform.php?id=$user/getID"      5
             class="CommandLink">Edit</a>
        </td>
      </tr>
      <tr tal:replace="">                                        6
        <td>elietta</td>
        <td>Elietta</td>
        <td>Floon</td>
        <td>elietta@example.com</td>
        <td>webmaster</td>
        <td>
          <a href="userform.php?id=42"
             class="CommandLink">Edit</a>
        </td>
      </tr>
    </table>
  </div>
 </body>
</html>
```

1 The DOCTYPE declaration was generated by HTML Tidy. It expresses the fact that this is an XHTML document. PHPTAL will be just as happy if we replace it with a plain XML declaration such as `<? xml version="1.0">`. In fact, PHPTAL seems to accept the file without the declaration, but it's better to have a file that can be checked by an XML parser.

2 The `xmlns` attribute, generated by Tidy, declares the XHTML namespace to be the default namespace for this document. That means that all tags and attributes without an explicit namespace should be interpreted as belonging to the XHTML namespace.

3 The `tal:repeat` attribute is technically an XML attribute belonging to the TAL namespace. The namespace is a way of making sure an attribute is distinct from all other attributes. This makes it possible for us to use another `repeat` attribute from another namespace if we should happen to need it.

    What `tal:repeat` does in PHPTAL may be obvious: it iterates over the array of user objects in exactly the same way that `foreach` in PHP or Smarty does. The difference is that because `tal:repeat` is an attribute, we don't need to place a separate tag for it. Nor do we need an end tag; the `</tr>` tag is the end tag for `tal:repeat`.

4 `tal:content` replaces everything between the tags with the content taken from our user object. So the user name and other data inside the tags is only dummy or example content that makes the template easier to understand and to view in a WYSI-WYG editor.

No escaping is required, since PHPTAL does this by default.

❺ Most of the dynamic content in PHPTAL templates is represented as TAL attributes. To add content to an attribute, it's more intuitive to use a different syntax, which is what you can see here. To insert the user ID into the `href` attribute, we represent it as `$user/getID`. Again, the template is as close to the plain HTML representation as possible.

❻ Because of the `tal:replace` attribute, this entire table row is thrown out—replaced with an empty string—when the template is processed. The first table row in the template—the one that contains `tal:repeat`—generates all the table rows in the output. The dummy row is only there for the sake of the template: it makes the template resemble the web page that's generated when the application is run. We can add any number of such dummy rows if we want. They will all disappear when the template is processed.

The difference between `tal:replace` and `tal:content` is the following: `tal:content` removes the material between the HTML tags and replaces it with dynamic content. `tal:replace` removes what's between the tags *and* the tags themselves.

When we want to write the PHP code to process the template, we find that PHP-TAL is similar to Smarty and other template engines (see listing 13.6).

Listing 13.6   Processing the PHPTAL template

```php
<?php
require_once 'HTML/Template/PHPTAL.php';
require_once 'UserFinder.php';

$finder = new UserFinder;
$users = $finder->findAll();

$template = new PHPTAL('userlist.tal');
$template->set("users",$users);
echo $template->execute();
```

The difference between this and the Smarty example is slight. The methods are named differently and PHPTAL has no method for displaying the output directly, so we just echo the results of template processing.

One of the advantages of PHPTAL is that the templates are XML and can be processed using other XML-based tools. This is even more applicable to the next item on our agenda: XSLT.

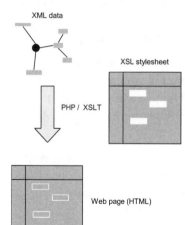

XML data

XSL stylesheet

PHP / XSLT

Web page (HTML)

Figure 13.5 XSLT works by transforming an XML data file using an XSL stylesheet.

13.3 TRANSFORMATION: XSLT

XSLT stylesheets are another popular way of expressing the HTML tag content of a web page. XSLT, the XML stylesheet language, is a way of transforming XML documents into HTML documents or into other XML documents. So if we want to use XSLT as templates in a PHP application, we first generate XML code, transform that using XSLT, and output it to the browser. Figure 13.5 shows how XSLT works when generating web pages. The stylesheet can be similar to the templates we've seen before, but is officially a recipe for the transformation of the XML file into HTML.

XSLT is very different from the other template systems. It's a powerful, non-procedural programming language. You can do all sorts of advanced things with it. But it's not necessarily the answer to all your template prayers. Its main advantage is its status as a cross-platform standard. Martin Fowler says:

> *You can use XSLT to transform XML created from J2EE or .NET, which can help in putting a common HTML view on data from different sources.*

Another way of putting it would be that a lot of different programming languages and environments, including PHP, have tools available for parsing and generating XML. Therefore, XML can be used to communicate between these languages and environments, and XSLT is a natural tool to use when you already have data in XML format.

Fowler also thinks that XSLT makes it "easier to keep the transform focused only on rendering HTML, thus avoiding having too much logic in the view." My experience is exactly the opposite: XSLT offers such interesting opportunities for implementing view logic that the temptation may be hard to resist.

13.3.1 "XMLizing" a web page

When you want to produce an XSLT stylesheet from an existing PHP file or from a sample HTML file, the first thing to do is to create something that's valid XML. One way to do this is the following:

- Replace the PHP processing instructions (`<?php ... ?>`) with something that an XML parser will take to be a plain string. For example, you can replace `<?` with `[` and `?>` with `]`.
- Run HTML Tidy to generate valid XML (XHTML).

HTML Tidy is a utility program that helps clean up HTML and convert it into XHTML. It's available at http://tidy.sourceforge.net. There is also a PHP Tidy extension. But for our current purposes, the command-line utility is fine. A typical way to run it would be as follows:

```
tidy -indent -asxml -wrap 150 userlist.xhtml
```

`-indent` produces indented output. `-asxml` specifies that the output should be XML. `-wrap 150` makes Tidy wrap lines at 150 characters rather than the default 68. With very complex web pages, this may be helpful, since they will sometimes be so deeply indented that there is little room left on the line.

Tidy sometimes only gives warnings. At other times, it reports fatal errors that require you to change the file manually. For instance, browsers are usually willing to render a web page even if table markup is incorrectly and inconsistently placed. Tidy (not to mention XML parsers) is not so forgiving.

After using Tidy, you can test the result using an XML parser such as the command line utility called `xmllint`. It's part of `libxml2`, the Gnome XML toolkit. The XML support in PHP 5 is based on `libxml2`. It's included in several Linux distributions and is also available for Windows.

13.3.2 Setting up XSLT

When setting up a PHP application based on XSLT, we can start by making the transformation work independently of PHP. To do that, we need

- An XML test file that is a representative sample of the XML the PHP application will generate
- The XSLT stylesheet
- A command-line XSLT tool

The command-line XSLT tool for `libxml2` is called `xsltproc`. You can run it as follows:

```
$ xsltproc userlist.xsl userlist.xml
```

You can generate the XML test file or write it manually. It's typically a very simple representation of the data from the database. Listing 13.7 shows how the user list may be represented.

Listing 13.7   XML file for testing XSLT template processing

```xml
<?xml version="1.0" ?>
<userlist>
  <user>
    <username>victor</username>
    <firstname>Victor</firstname>
    <lastname>Ploctor</lastname>
    <email>victor@example.com</email>
    <role>regular</role>
    <id>1</id>
  </user>
  <!-- More users on the same format -->1
</userlist>
```

13.3.3   The XSLT stylesheet

If you're not used to XSLT, the real challenge is in the XSLT stylesheet itself. The stylesheet shown in listing 13.8 tries to approximate ordinary HTML as much as possible. That means that using HTML-like constructs is more important than idiomatic XSLT. The reason for this is the same as with all the other templates: we want a web designer to find it easy to use.

Listing 13.8   XSLT stylesheet for the user list

```xml
<xsl:stylesheet version="1.0"
  xmlns:xsl="http://www.w3.org/1999/XSL/Transform">  ❶
  <xsl:output method="html">  ❷
  <xsl:template match="/">  ❸
    <html xmlns="http://www.w3.org/1999/xhtml">  ❹
      <head>
        <title>
          User administration
        </title>
      </head>
      <body>
        <div id="content">
          <h1>
            User administration
          </h1>
          <table id="AdminList" cellspacing="0">
            <tr>
              <th>Login name</th>
              <th>First Name</th>
              <th>Last name</th>
              <th>Email address</th>
              <th>Role</th>
```

```
        <th>
        </th>
      </tr>
      <xsl:for-each select="/userlist/user">        ❺
        <tr>
          <td><xsl:value-of select="username"/></td>
          <td><xsl:value-of select="firstname"/></td>        ❻
          <td><xsl:value-of select="lastname"/></td>
          <td><xsl:value-of select="email"/></td>
          <td><xsl:value-of select="role"/></td>
          <td>
            <a class="CommandLink"
              href="{concat('userform.php?id=',id)}">        ❼
              Edit
            </a>
          </td>
        </tr>
      </xsl:for-each>
    </table>
  </div>
  </body>
  </html>
  </xsl:template>
</xsl:stylesheet>
```

❶ Yes, you have to insert all this stuff just to get a valid XSL stylesheet. XSL is verbose.

❷ The output method is html, as we want to generate HTML code.

❸ xsl:template is where the real XSLT processing starts. The match expression is an XPath expression capable of matching a node or a set of nodes in the input XML document. The template is processed whenever XSLT encounters a node that matches. In this case, the template matches the root node. Since processing starts at the root node, XSLT will start on this template immediately. And since there are no other templates, processing this one is all it will do.

❹ All namespaces have to be declared. This goes for the html namespace as well.

❺ The xsl:for-each selects all the user elements and tells XSLT to process each one.
   From an XSLT-purist point of view, this is sinful: using xslt:for-each in this context is not idiomatic in XSLT. XSLT is a non-procedural programming language, and for-each is a procedural mode of expression, foreign to XSLT. The typical way to do it in XSLT would be to use a separate template for the repeating section. The reason for using for-each is not to make it cozy and familiar for PHP programmers. Instead, the intention is to make a single template that will resemble an HTML page.

❻ `xsl:value-of` is the XSLT equivalent of `echo` or `print` in PHP. Again, the `select` expression is an XPath expression. The expression is interpreted relative to the current node, so while XSLT is processing one of the user nodes, it outputs the content of, say, the `username` element in that user node.

❼ The expression that defines the link URL may be an ugly brute, but it's more HTML-like than some alternatives. The outer braces mean that what's inside is an XPath expression instead of a string. The `concat()` function is simple string concatenation. In this case, it concatenates the literal string `userform.php?id=` with the result of the XPath expression `id`, which happens to be the user ID.

13.3.4   Running XSLT from PHP

Although the functions needed to run XSLT from PHP are documented in the PHP manual, we'll see them in context using the user list again for a complete example. First we generate the XML code and then we transform it (see listing 13.9).

Listing 13.9   Generating the user list with XSLT

```php
$finder = new UserFinder;
$users = $finder->findAll();
ob_start();        ❶
?>
<?php echo '<?xml version="1.0" ?>'."\n"; ?>      ❷
<userlist>
  <?php foreach ($users as $u) : ?>
    <user>
    <username>
      <?php echo htmlentities($u->getUserName()) ?>
    </username>
    <firstname>
      <?php echo htmlentities($u->getFirstName()) ?>
    </firstname>
    <lastname>
      <?php echo htmlentities($u->getLastName()) ?>
    </lastname>
    <email><?php echo htmlentities($u->getEmail()) ?></email>
    <role><?php echo htmlentities($u->getRole()) ?></role>
    <id><?php echo htmlentities($u->getID()) ?></id>
    </user>
  <?php endforeach; ?>
</userlist>

<?php
$xml = ob_get_contents();        ❸
ob_end_clean();
print processXslt($xml,'userlist.xsl');        ❹

function processXslt($xml,$xslfile) {
    $dom = new DomDocument;        ❺
    $dom->loadXML($xml);
```

```
$xsldom = new domDocument();          6
$xsldom->load($xslfile);
$proc = new xsltprocessor;                    7
$proc->importStylesheet($xsldom);
return $proc->transformToXml($dom);
}
```

❶ Output buffering is an extremely versatile feature of PHP. Here we're using it to avoid having to put quotes around all the XML code. Instead, we can have an XML section, similar to the usual HTML sections. Instead of being output, it's kept until we ask for it.

❷ The XML section is basically a simplified version of an HTML section in a PHP file. All presentation-related elements have been stripped away, and all that's left is a data structure.

Again, we are escaping all the data. This is to be processed through XSLT, and XSLT will usually ignore HTML tags, so the risk of cross-site scripting attacks is less. It's more likely that suspicious content could generate a fatal syntax error, and using `htmlentities()` helps prevent that.

❸ We get the buffered XML code and turn off output buffering.

❹ The XSLT processing is packaged into a function that takes XML text and the name of the stylesheet file as arguments.

❺ Create a DOM based on the XML document in `$xml`.

❻ Create another DOM based on the stylesheet. We read this from a file instead of a string, since we have the XML code as a string and the XSLT stylesheet in a file. That's natural since the stylesheet is relatively constant, while the XML code contains database data that may change at any time.

❼ Instantiate an XSLT processor. Tell the XSLT processor to use the stylesheet represented by our second DOM. Then transform the XML using the XSL stylesheet.

We've seen how to use template engines based on various principles. Using templates goes a long way toward achieving separation between HTML and PHP code. But there is still the risk that we will start undermining the separation by adding too much programming logic to the template itself, either by using the template engine's built-in programming capabilities (XSLT has a lot of that), or by sneaking in significant amounts of PHP code (Smarty and PHTAL both have that option). In the next section, we'll study some tricks that will help us resist that temptation in particularly difficult cases.

13.4 *KEEPING LOGIC OUT OF TEMPLATES*

Most web application pages have a relatively simple structure, such as a form or a simple list. A loop and perhaps a few simple conditionals will suffice as logic for the presentation. That's no big problem in a template, since this minimal logic doesn't obscure the HTML layout of the page much.

But there are a few challenges that are harder to manage without putting more logic into the templates. Presentation logic is a gray area between domain logic and pure layout and design: logic that only determines how the data is presented on the web page but is still program logic.

These are the cases in which presentation logic gets more complex. An example that is often cited is alternating colors for table rows. There is no way (currently) to do this with HTML or CSS only. (It should be possible with the `nth-child()` pseudo-class in CSS 3, but browser support for this is practically nonexistent at this writing. It's also possible with the JavaScript DOM.)

Unless the template engine has a special feature that will help us with it, we need something like an `if` test embedded in a loop. That makes the logic in the template more complex and harder to read and manage.

Template designers can live with looping and simple conditionals. But when you start to get nested loops and complex conditionals, they find it at best annoying because it gets in the way of their work. At worst, it's confusing to designers and opens the door to the dreaded tangle of HTML markup and program code.

In this section, we'll first deal with a general pattern (View Helper) for handling logic that is part of the Presentation layer but is too complex to fit comfortably in a template. Then we'll look at a series of real-life situations that challenge our ability to keep program logic out of templates and suggest a solution to each of these situations.

13.4.1 View Helper

A common strategy for dealing with this is to put presentation logic in PHP classes outside the template (see figure 13.6). We can keep them in separate classes that only handle the View and do not touch the Domain layer. These classes should not generate any HTML code, but they can generate presentation-related information such as the depth of an item in a hierarchical display or CSS classes to allow alternating row colors in a table.

This is often considered a form of the View Helper design pattern. View Helper is a somewhat vague concept. But in this context, it has a specific responsibility: to

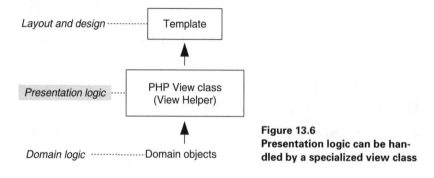

Figure 13.6
Presentation logic can be handled by a specialized view class

convert or translate the information in domain and data objects into a form that can be used in a template.

This approach makes it possible to use a very simple template language. In fact, you could probably make your own with little effort. Simple variable substitution, conditionals, and loops should be sufficient.

13.4.2 Alternating row colors

Alternating colors in the rows of a table is a popular way to make it easier to distinguish the rows in the browser. You might think this needs to be implemented with programming logic in the template because a designer might need to change it. The colors might change, or the designer might decide not to have alternating colors after all.

Some template engines have facilities that make this easier. For example, Smarty has a function called cycle that lets you alternate automatically between a set of values. The alternative, which will work with any template engine, is to do the alternation logic in PHP before passing the values to the template.

We definitely want to avoid having explicit color names or codes in the PHP program code. We don't want to have to change a PHP file for the sake of a styling change. The way to do it is to generate a table with alternating CSS classes for the rows. Then the colors can be defined in CSS, and the only thing that's left for PHP is the abstract alternation logic. The HTML code would look like this example:

```
<table>
<tr class="row1"><td>Banana</td></tr>
<tr class="row2"><td>Apple</td></tr>
<tr class="row1"><td>Orange</td></tr>
<tr class="row2"><td>Pineapple</td></tr>
</table>
```

And the template would have

```
<tr class="{$fruit.rowcss}"><td>{$fruit.name}</td></tr>
```

Now all we need is the PHP code to establish the $fruit.rowcss variables. Assuming that the fruit is in a plain array of associative arrays, we could pre-process it as follows:

```
foreach (array_keys($fruits) as $rownumber) {
    $fruits[$rownumber]['rowcss'] = 'row'.($rownumber % 2 + 1);
}
```

The template designer defines the colors for the CSS classes row1 and row2 and is happy. Making them all the same color can be done by letting the two CSS classes be identical. That is duplication, but not of a very harmful kind.

13.4.3 Handling date and time formats

Date and time formats are another challenge when we try to separate the programmer's job from the web designer's. The choice of format is purely a presentation issue;

there is no reason why it should depend on technical considerations. But, as with alternating colors, it has no native syntax in HTML and/or CSS. So ideally, we should provide the web designer with a way to specify the format inside the template. (There is an exception to this: if we know there is only one date format we ever want to use, we can just generate it in the PHP code.)

One way to do this is to use a modifier. Smarty has a built-in variable modifier called date_format that allows a designer to specify a date format using strftime() syntax:

{$smarty.now|date_format:"%H:%M:%S"}

But it would be less cryptic and probably more practical if the date format had a name. A web site will probably be using only a few different date formats that are used repeatedly on different web pages. So having two or three named date formats would make them easier to remember and make it possible to change a date format globally. For example, we might have a standard date and time format, one format for just the time, and a short format for cramped spaces on the page.

If the template engine has the ability to define custom modifiers, you could use that to define named date formats. But a solution which is more general—more independent of which template engine you're using—is to give the template a PHP object which has a method to generate the appropriate date format. For some reason, objects that represent date and time have not been common in PHP, but they're useful for this kind of task. Listing 13.10 shows a simplified class resembling the examples in chapter 8.

Listing 13.10   A simplified date and time class

```
class DateAndTime {
    private $timestamp;

    function __construct($timestamp=FALSE) {
        $this->timestamp = $timestamp ? $timestamp : time();   ❶
    }

    function isoformat() {
        return strftime("%Y-%m-%d %H:%M:%S",$this->timestamp);
    }                                                           ❷

    function rfcformat() {
        return strftime("%a %e %b %Y %H:%M:%S",$this->timestamp);
    }
}
```

❶ The DateAndTime object is constructed from a specified timestamp. If no timestamp is specified, the object represents the current time when it was created.

❷ The isoformat() and rfcformat() methods return the formatted date and time as a string.

So we could use the object like this:

```
$now = new DateAndTime;
echo $now->isoformat()."\n";
```

This is interesting, but the real practical value starts to appear when we use the Date-AndTime object to replace other ways of representing the date and time. Listing 13.11 shows a class representing a DiscussionMessage object that contains the knowledge of when it was created.

Listing 13.11 A DiscussionMessage class that uses the DateAndTime class

```
class DiscussionMessage {
    private $subject;
    private $text;
    private $created;

    function __construct($subject,$text,DateAndTime $created) {   ❶
        $this->subject = $subject;
        $this->text = $text;
        $this->created = $created;
    }

    function isotime() { return $this->created->isoformat(); }   ❷
    function rfctime() { return $this->created->rfcformat(); }

    function getSubject() { return $this->subject; }
    function getText() { return $this->text; }
    function getCreated() { return $this->created; }
}
```

❶ To make sure we construct the object correctly, let's use a type hint to require that the $created argument is already a DateAndTime object. Using a type hint is particularly appropriate in this case. It's easy to make a mistake and use an integer timestamp, and the mistake won't become apparent during construction.

❷ The isotime() and rfctime() methods just call the corresponding methods in the DateAndTime objects. They are not strictly needed if we have a convenient way to call a method on the DateAndTime object itself. Since we're using it in a template, that depends on the template engine.

The DiscussionMessage class can be used like this in PHP 5 code:

```
$message = new DiscussionMessage(
        'Re: Templates',
        'I love templates, too!',
        new DateAndTime
        );
echo $message->getCreated()->isoformat()."\n";
```

Since a template engine won't necessarily let us do the equivalent of that last line, it's convenient to be able to do this instead:

```
echo $message->isotime()."\n";
```

Now, if we happen to have a Smarty object lying around, we can assign the message object to the Smarty object and display the results using a template:

```
$smarty->assign('message',$message);
echo $template->fetch($mode.'.tpl');
```

The template can use the `isotime()` or `rfctime()` methods to display the date:

```
<div id="content">
  <h1>
    {$message->getSubject()}
  </h1>
  <p class="ArticleText">
    {$message->getText()}
  </p>
  <p class="ArticleInfo">
    {$message->isotime()}
  </p>
</div>
```

So far, we've populated the DiscussionMessage object by hard-coding its values. In practice, of course, we would typically be getting these from a database. We'll see how that's done in part 4 of this book.

13.4.4   Generating hierarchical displays

Threaded discussion forums—such as the one in figure 13.7—are good examples of hierarchical data to display on a web page.

An object-oriented tree structure is useful for processing this type of data. But how can we insert it into a template? The problem is that we don't know how many levels of replies we need to handle. So even a very complex (and not very readable) set of nested loops is inadequate for the task.

Subject	Posted by
Info on train robberies	Victor Ploctor
Re: Info on train robberies	Elietta Floon
Historical (Was:Re: Info on train robberies)	Administrator
Re: Info on train robberies	Administrator
When will rains run on time?	Victor Ploctor
Re: When will rains run on time?	Administrator

Figure 13.7   A threaded discussion view

Recursion is the normal way to process tree structures. So one possibility is to give the template engine the ability to do recursion. This will still not be very readable, nor will it be easy to test. Another way to do it is to simplify the data structure by first transforming it into a simple two-dimensional array or an array of objects. To show the threaded list using HTML, we need to insert it into rows and columns anyway. Figure 13.8 depicts this process. A tree, identical in structure to the one implied by figure 13.7, is transformed into an array.

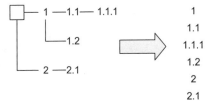

Figure 13.8 Transforming a tree structure into an array that is easier to display

By using a separate View-oriented class to do this, we can maintain the separation between presentation and domain logic while keeping the template from containing much more than the usual presentation logic. The class in listing 13.12 does the job of generating this plainer data structure. The most crucial part of the job is done by the getList() method, which operates on a discussion node, getting a sequential list of descendant nodes by recursion. getList() is what is known as a foreign method. It does something the node object might have done itself. The reason we don't let the node object do it is because we want to keep the presentation logic out of the discussion node.

Listing 13.12 shows the DiscussionView class. The list it generates is an array of arrays; so it's not an object-oriented structure at all, but it's a structure that's simple to use in a template. (You can use a simplified object-oriented structure instead if your template engine supports this.)

> **Listing 13.12   The DiscussionView class transforms a hierarchical threaded discussion into a linear data structure**

```
class DiscussionView {
    private $discussionID;

    function __construct($discussionID) {        ❶
        $this->discussionID = $discussionID;
    }

    function getDiscussionData() {
        $mapper = new DiscussionMapper;          ❷
        $discussion = $mapper->find($this->discussionID);   ❸
        $list = $this->getList($discussion);     ❹
        array_shift($list);      ❺
        return $list;
    }

    function getList($node,$depth=-1) {          ❻
        ++$depth;       ❼
        $array = $this->asArray($node);     ❽
        $array['depth'] = $depth;      ❾
```

```
            $result[] = $array;
            foreach ($node->getChildren() as $child) {
                $result = array_merge(
                        $result,
                        $this->getList($child,$depth));
            }
            return $result;
        }

    function asArray($node) {
        return array(
                'id'      => $node->getID(),
                'subject' => $node->getSubject(),
                'text'    => $node->getText(),
                'author'  => $node->getAuthor()
                );
    }

    function execute() {
        $template = new Template('discussion.html');
        $template->set('messages',$this->getDiscussionData());
        return $template->execute();
    }
}
```

(10)

(11)

❶ The DiscussionView class takes a discussion ID as input and does all the work of getting the data from the database and putting it into a form that is easy to display in a template. It might be tidier to give it the data instead, so that the View object doesn't depend on the database-related code.

❷ To get the data from the database, we use a Data Mapper called DiscussionMapper. Although we haven't introduced Data Mappers yet, to understand this example, you just need to know that it's a class that can be used for getting data from the database.

❸ The mapper's find() method takes the discussion ID and retrieves the discussion from the database. The discussion is an object-oriented tree structure composed of discussion nodes.

❹ Now we call the method that converts the Composite structure into a simple list in the form of an array.

❺ We remove the first element of the list. It's the root node representing the entire discussion, and we don't want that to show up on the web page. We just want the individual threads, which are the children of the root node.

❻ The getList() method returns the contents of the discussion as an array in the order the posts will be listed on the web page. This is where the recursion happens.

❼ We have a $depth variable to keep track of the current level in the hierarchy. When the method is called initially (on the root node), $depth is set to -1 and then incremented. So the root node's depth is 0. Then, when we call the method on the children of the root node, we pass $depth on and it gets incremented to 1. And so it keeps increasing as we move recursively to deeper levels.

An inelegant but relatively flexible way to use this is to generate separate CSS classes for each level (level1, level2, and so on). Assuming a limited number of levels, they can be separately styled in this manner:

```
table#AdminList tr.level2 td.threaded { padding-left: 2em; }
table#AdminList tr.level3 td.threaded { padding-left: 4em; }
table#AdminList tr.level4 td.threaded { padding-left: 6em; }
table#AdminList tr.level5 td.threaded { padding-left: 8em; }
```

❽ $array is an associative array representing a single node. The asArray() method converts the node from an object, potentially with children, to a plain associative array.

❾ $result is the list that will contain this node and all its descendants. We build the list starting with the current node.

❿ Each child generates a list of nodes, and we append the list to the result list.

⓫ Since a plain array is relatively easy to use with any template engine, generating an array from an object, as we're doing here, may be reasonable. However, if we can, it might be better to use the object directly or via a decorator. An object-oriented data structure is more flexible and easier to modify.

13.4.5   Preventing updates from the template

If we represent our data as objects, it's convenient to be able to pass the object to the template and use methods inside the template to display the data inside it. But what if this allows a template designer to modify the object and perhaps even store it in the database? Now we have the same kind of security problem as with template languages that allow PHP code, although perhaps to a lesser degree. In principle, a template should not be allowed to change anything. It should only have access to read-only data, or to its own copies that are not used anywhere else.

This is a case where the PHP 5 object model may be a hindrance rather than a help. In PHP 4, objects were copied by default, so a template would always get its own copies of the objects. So even if a template designer were to modify the object, it would not affect anything outside the processing of the template.

We can solve that problem by explicitly cloning the objects. This can be built into a template engine by decorating it or extending it with a subclass. (I would normally prefer a decorator to reduce the dependency on the template engine API, but we're using inheritance here to illustrate the possibility.)

```
class Template extends PHPTAL {
    public function set($name,$data) {
        if (is_object($data)) $data = clone $data;
        parent::set($name,$data);
    }
}
```

But there is another, potentially worse problem: The object may have methods that affect the outside world. In particular, it might have methods to insert, update, or delete itself in the database. A clone would have the same power to do that as the original object.

There are several ways we might handle this problem. We might

- Use Data Mappers. Data Mappers are specialized objects that handle database interaction. So a User object would not be able to insert itself into the database. Instead, we would have to use a UserMapper. And there would be no way to get hold of the UserMapper from the template unless it was PHP-enabled.

- Use a template engine-specific way to restrict access to methods. Smarty allows you to specify a list of allowed methods in Smarty's `register_object()` method.

- Decorate the object or copy it to a specialized View object containing the same data but having fewer capabilities.

Security considerations have been mentioned along the way in this chapter, but in the next section, we'll summarize and complete them.

13.5 TEMPLATES AND SECURITY

The most important issue is the danger of cross-site scripting (XSS) attacks. (For an introduction to this and other security-related concepts, see appendix B.) To prevent this, we need to escape all output. The template engines described in this chapter are very different in how they escape output. Preferably, we want the template engine to escape output by default. In other words, output escaping should be the easiest option for the programmer and/or designer. Template engines support this to different degrees and in different ways. In this section, we'll take a closer look at how it works in PHPTAL, Smarty, and XSLT.

13.5.1 PHPTAL

PHPTAL escapes all output variables by default. This is excellent for security. But using the `structure` keyword disables escaping for a variable:

```
<p tal:content="structure introduction">dummy intro</p>
```

Obviously, we should be careful when using `structure`. If the variable contains data that may come from the user, there is a risk. In addition, you should make sure output is escaped with the correct character encoding. The encoding should match the encoding set in the HTTP header. PHPTAL's default is UTF-8, which is often a good choice. However, if you do need to use a different encoding, you can set it with the constant PHPTAL_DEFAULT_ENCODING:

```
define('PHPTAL_DEFAULT_ENCODING', 'ISO-8859-1');
$tpl = new PHPTAL('abc.html');
```

Although this is probably less relevant, it's also possible to set the encoding for a single template:

```
$tpl->setEncoding('ISO-8859-2');
```

13.5.2 Smarty

Smarty has no default output escaping. To escape an output variable properly, you have to add the escape variable modifier manually:

```
{$introduction|escape:"htmlall":"UTF-8"}
```

This clutters the templates, and you're likely to forget to do it. Or rather, you're likely to use it only when you know the variable is unsafe. But it's more secure to escape all output.

This can be achieved by using the `$default_modifiers` variable:

```
$template->default_modifiers = array('escape:"htmlall:UTF-8"');
```

For the exceptional case, when we need to output a variable unescaped, we can use the nodefaults modifier in the template to get rid of the default modifiers:

```
{$safe_html|smarty:nodefaults}
```

Smarty also has a feature to prevent template designers from using PHP code and to restrict include capabilities. This can be turned on as follows:

```
$smarty->security = true;
```

13.5.3 XSLT

In general, XSLT will not output any tags that are not explicit in the stylesheet. This means that with most stylesheets, there is no way for tags such as `<script>` to be output as part of the dynamic content.

There is one exception: `xsl:copy-of` makes a deep copy of the current node in the input XML file, including child nodes.

As mentioned in the comments to listing 13.9, escaping variables from PHP may be necessary mainly to avoid XML syntax errors. The file to be transformed has to be valid XML or the XML parser will complain. If it contains arbitrary text, there is a high risk that the text will contain some characters that will make it invalid.

13.6 SUMMARY

One of the central dogmas of modern web programming is the need to separate HTML markup from program code. Although many believe this can be done effectively with plain PHP, others find it more appropriate to use a template engine. All the template engines meet roughly the same challenges, but they do so in syntactically different ways. Some, such as Smarty, use a custom syntax exclusively. XSLT, although not strictly a template engine, is a specialized programming language that transforms an XML file containing the data to be displayed, adding markup to it. PHPTAL uses XML attributes to specify dynamic content.

A powerful template engine typically has the ability to execute PHP code or other potentially advanced constructs. This makes it all too easy to slip back into an excessively strong mixture of markup and program code. Fortunately, there are additional techniques for handling the challenges—such as alternating row colors and date and time formatting—that tend to lead you into that particular swamp.

Templates pose particular challenges to security. To guard against attacks, we need to make sure we escape all output. This is always possible, though easier with some template engines than with others.

Web presentation becomes even more demanding when the web page is composed of many interacting components. In the next chapter, we will look into what is often called the Composite View pattern. We will see how to gain layout and content flexibility both for the whole web page and its parts and how to integrate existing applications into a Composite View.

C H A P T E R   1 4

Constructing complex web pages

A complex web page is like a zoo. There may be all sorts of different creatures, all with different habits and requiring different care, cleaning, and feeding. Some of them are in cages (typically the stuff that surrounds the main content, such as banners, ads, menus, and various kinds of sidebars); some of them range freely on the main expanse of the page.

Keeping all these coordinated is one of the great challenges of web programming.

In addition, different species play together. A menu may need to communicate with a news list as well as with itself. Making this work properly is actually a challenge that goes beyond the scope of this chapter, since that challenge involves user interaction. Here, we will focus mostly on the display or View part of the job.

In this chapter, we'll first introduce and discuss the Composite View pattern. Then we'll show how to implement a simple, straightforward composite template using Smarty or PHPTAL. Finally, we'll see how to solve a few more advanced challenges.

14.1   COMBINING TEMPLATES (COMPOSITE VIEW)

Modern web pages are not just complex; they tend to grow increasingly complex. But we have some tools to help us.

Assembling a page is not really difficult with PHP include files. You just use one include file for each part of the page, and one file that includes all of them. Most templates have include capabilities as well. There is no magic or rocket science involved. But careful thinking is needed to develop a structured approach that gets you the necessary flexibility and avoids inelegant hacks even when solving problems such as separate print-friendly views of a page. That's what we'll develop in this chapter.

14.1.1 Composite View: one or several design patterns?

The book *Core J2EE Patterns* (and its companion online pattern catalog) [Alur et al.] has Composite View listed as a design pattern and demonstrates several different strategies for implementing it. The Composite View itself is the idea of assembling a web page from pluggable, reusable components. The solutions to this problem are presented as different strategies that are actually completely different solutions to the same problem. This may be confusing if you're used to design patterns that give a reasonably specific solution to a problem.

That need not trouble us too much, though. The challenge is to achieve the kinds of flexibility we need for developing complex layouts. In PHP, this is typically achieved by using the built-in features of PHP or template engines.

14.1.2 Composite data and composite templates

The Composite View is one of the harder challenges in web programming. One key idea that is not widely recognized is this: assembling the template from components and assembling the data that goes into it (parts of the Model in Model-View-Controller terms) are two separate challenges. You can have a monolithic class that does the whole job of creating the data for the template even if the template itself is assembled from several pieces. And you can have a complex composite or collection of PHP components that assemble and insert the data into a template, even if the template is a single sheet of HTML with slots for dynamic information.

The following sections will focus mostly on creating the composite template. We'll first see how to do it in a typical, straightforward case.

14.2 IMPLEMENTING A STRAIGHTFORWARD COMPOSITE VIEW

To design a strategy for assembling web pages, we need to know the requirements. How much and what flexibility do we need? The solution featured in the J2EE book [Alur et al.] is based on the idea of pluggable components and pluggable layout, and uses custom tags to achieve it.

In this section, we'll first define more specifically what we need to do. Then we'll see how it can be implemented with two template engines; first Smarty, then PHPTAL. We'll also look at an additional, PHPTAL-specific way of doing it.

14.2.1 What we need to achieve

To get an idea of what it takes to implement a Composite View, let's do a simple example in plain PHP, starting with the simplest-possible implementation. Figure 14.1 shows the kind of layout we want.

We have four different components here: the banner, the menu, the main text, and the sidebar containing the news list. To implement this in "naive" PHP, we use plain include statements:

```
<html>
<head><!--The usual stuff goes here--></head>
<body>
<?php include 'banner.php' ?>
<?php include 'menu.php' ?>
<?php include 'welcome.php' ?>
<?php include 'news.php' ?>
</body>
</html>
```

So now we've assembled the page from a number of components. But they're not yet pluggable. We can fix that by replacing one or more of the file names with variables:

```
<?php include 'banner.php' ?>
<?php include 'menu.php' ?>
<?php include "$content.php" ?>
<?php include "$sidebar.php" ?>
```

Pretty basic, but we want basic. (As it stands, it's insecure if the variables can contain data supplied by the user. We are assuming here, and in the following examples, that they cannot.) We don't want a sophisticated solution if we can get by with a simpler one. The point is that this satisfies the first requirement of a Composite View.

The other concern addressed by the Composite View pattern is pluggable layout. We should be able to replace the overall layout of the page with a different one. Again staying within plain, blunt PHP, all we need to do is make a separate file out of the preceding code and include that from our main script:

**Figure 14.1
Composite View-type page
layout with several different
components**

```php
<?php
// Find out which $layout to use
// ...
include "$layout.php";
```

Wait a minute, you might say. There's no layout at all in the layout file! No HTML tags. Yes—and no. The only layout that's present is the presence and sequence of the components. We will assume that the rest is in CSS. Each of the included files will be an HTML <div> element with contents such as this:

```html
<div id="banner">
  <img src="hazycrazy2.png" width="519"/>
</div>
```

Each of these <div>s, and individual elements within them, can be styled, positioned, even hidden, using CSS. In fact, since CSS can be used for positioning and hiding, you might even question whether there is a need for the layout file at all. With CSS, you can position <div>s accurately and (somewhat) freely regardless of their sequence in the HTML markup. And you can hide them using display:none. But the

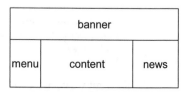

Figure 14.2 Names for the components of the page from figure 14.1

hidden elements will still be present in the web page that is downloaded to the browser. So they will still consume bandwidth, potentially making response times longer for the user.

Figure 14.2 shows how we've named the parts of the page.

14.2.2 Using Smarty

In our Composite View implementation, we want something that satisfies the requirements and leverages the tools we have available to make the solution as simple, easy, and maintainable as possible. We can use Smarty to do something similar to what we did with plain PHP in the previous section:

```
<body>
  {include file="banner.tpl"}
  {include file="menu.tpl"}
  {include file="$content"}
  {include file="$sidebar"}
</body>
```

As before, we have the pluggable components sidebar and content, whose names have to be assigned to the template. The pluggable layout is the main template itself:

```
$template->assign('content','welcome.tpl');
$template->assign('sidebar','news.tpl');
echo $template->fetch($current.'.tpl'); ❶
```

❶ Using `$current` this way is not as dangerous as using it in a PHP include. Still, if the variable can be altered by a user, there is a potential for retrieving a file from anywhere in the file system.

There is one more thing we might like to do. We need to handle the title of the HTML document as well. Frequently, the main content area has a heading, for example:

```
<div id="content">
  <h1>Event calendar</h1>
...
```

Typically, the heading should be the same as the document title or at least coordinated with it as figure 14.3 shows.

We could set the title in the PHP code and output the same variable in two places. But the title is ideally within the template designer's jurisdiction. The other simple alternative would be to use two template files. But there would be a risk that one would be updated and not the other. Having them both in one file would be better.

What we can do is use Smarty's `capture` feature to define a template section as a variable that can be used somewhere else. We would define the `title` and `content` sections in the same file as follows:

```
{capture name=title}
<title>Welcome to Hazycrazy.com</title>
{/capture}

{capture name=content}
<div id="content">
  <h1>Welcome to Hazycrazy.com</h1>
  ...
  ...
</div>
{/capture}
```

Now in our layout template, we can include the file and then use the variables:

```
{include file="$content"}
<html>
<head>
```

Figure 14.3 We want the same text for the title and the main heading, even though they are in separate parts of the page.

```
{$smarty.capture.title}
<link rel="STYLESHEET" href="hazycrazy.css"
  media="screen" type="text/css" />
</head>
  <body>
    {include file="banner.tpl"}
    {include file="$sidebar}
    {$smarty.capture.content}
    {include file="menu.tpl"}
  </body>
</html>
```

Of course, along with the title, you could include other markup that goes inside the header, such as a `<meta>` tag containing a page description or specialized CSS stylesheets or JavaScript.

14.2.3   Using PHPTAL

We can do the same thing in PHPTAL using PHPTAL's macro feature. Instead of captures, we define macros that can be used elsewhere:

```
<?xml version="1.0"?>
<html>
  <title metal:define-macro="title">Welcome to Hazycrazy.com
    </title>
  <div id="content" metal:define-macro="content">
    <h1>Welcome to Hazycrazy.com</h1>
  </div>
</html>
```

The `<html>` tags aren't actually used for markup; they won't ever appear on the web page, since they're not part of the macros. The reason they are there is because the PHP-TAL template must be a valid XML document. That means it needs a root element.

In PHPTAL, we also need to use macros in place of the plain includes. This is a good thing, since we can choose to have several macros per file, or just one.

Using one file for the pluggable content and one for the other macros, our main template file looks like this:

```
<html>
<head>
  <link rel="STYLESHEET" href="hazycrazy.css"
    media="screen" type="text/css" />
  <span metal:use-macro="{$content}.html/title"/>
</head>
  <body>
    <span metal:use-macro="macros.html/banner"/>
    <span metal:use-macro="macros.html/menu"/>
    <span metal:use-macro="${content}.html/content"/>
    <span metal:use-macro="macros.html/{$sidebar}"/>
  </body>
</html>
```

Unlike many attributes used in PHPTAL (such as `tal:content`), `metal:use-macro` accepts a string by default, not a variable. So to access the file name in the `content` variable, we have to use `${content}`.

14.2.4 Using page macros with PHPTAL

The PHPTAL solution shown in the previous example is the one that follows the same strategy we used for Smarty. This strategy is useful since it's generally applicable to most, if not all, template engines. In addition, PHPTAL allows us to be even more flexible by using what is known as a page macro. The web page as a whole can be defined as a macro, making it possible to handle the parts and the whole in one uniform fashion.

Listing 14.1 is a page macro example. Note first that this is *not* a template; it's a macro that defines what's common between many pages. If we forget that it's a macro and try to use it as a template, we get no output.

The general idea is that the page macro contains all of these elements:

- Static parts of the page such as the menu.
- "Slots" that can be filled by the template that uses the macro.
- Default content for the slots if the macro doesn't fill them.

Listing 14.1   DateAndTime class using creation methods to allow different raw materials

```
<html metal:define-macro="page">
  <head>
    <link rel="STYLESHEET"
      href="../css/hazycrazy.css" media="screen
    <title metal:define-slot="title">          ❶ The title is
      Hazycrazy.com default title                  a slot
    </title>
  </head>
  <body>
    <div id="banner">
      <img src="../img/hazycrazy2.png" width="519" />    ❷ Constant or
    </div>                                                   default
    <div id="menu">                                         content
      <a href="life.php">Life</a>
      <a href="pets.php">Pets</a>
      <a href="computers.php">Computers</a>
      <a href="social.php">Socializing</a>
    </div>
    <div id="content" metal:define-slot="content" />   ◄
    <div id="sidebar">                         No default    ❸
      <h1>News</h1>                             content
      <span tal:replace="news">
    </div>
  </body>
</html>
```

❶ The title is defined as a slot and has default content.

❷ The banner and the menu are both constant content. If this were to change—for example, if we were creating a new web page that needed a different menu—we could easily change either into a slot by adding a `metal:define-slot` attribute. This would not affect existing templates using the page macro, since the static content becomes default content that is displayed unchanged unless its slot is filled.

❸ The `content` slot has no default content. It will show up empty unless the template fills it.

To fill the slots, all we need to do is use the `metal:fill-slot` attribute.

```
<html metal:use-macro="macros.html/page">

  <title metal:fill-slot="title">Welcome to Hazycrazy.com</title>

  <div id="content" metal:fill-slot="content">
    <h1>Welcome to Hazycrazy.com</h1>
    <p>
      We love you...
    </p>
    <h2>We know everything</h2>
    <p>
      At HazyCrazy.com...
    </p>
  </div>
</html>
```

This template expresses only what's specific to the Welcome page. Both the title and the main content are specified.

A page macro is an exceptionally easy way to create pluggable layouts for a full web page. Although many general layout changes can be done in CSS, pluggable page layouts are the ultimate secret weapon when we need a sudden complete change of scenery, such as a print-friendly layout.

14.3 COMPOSITE VIEW EXAMPLES

Many web sites have layouts that are similar to the one we developed in the previous section. But in practice, there are usually additional challenges requiring us to do something extra in addition to the plain layout. Elements need to be added, static elements need to become dynamic, the application needs to communicate with other applications, and so on.

Let's exercise the Composite View pattern some more. In this section, we'll take what we've learned about combining templates and apply it to some specific challenges. As a first example, we'll tackle the problem of print-friendly versions of pages. Then we'll dip briefly into a large and complex subject: integrating existing applications into a Composite View. Finally, we'll take a look at Martin Fowler's Two-Step View pattern.

14.3.1 Making print-friendly versions of pages

Complex layouts are not well-suited for printing. That's why many sites have the ability to display "printable," "print-friendly," or "printer-friendly" versions of pages, particularly articles and others that have a great deal of text.

The simplest way to get a print-friendly layout is to do it with CSS only. If you have separate stylesheets for media="print" and media="screen", the print-friendly layout will automatically be applied when printing, with no need for an extra link to the print-friendly version.

Here, we'll take the slightly more powerful and complex route of controlling part of the layout from PHP by using a different template for printing. Creating a print-friendly layout will be a test to make sure our layout flexibility really works. What we need to do is to create another layout page that is more appropriate for a printout. Figure 14.4 shows how such a layout might look in a browser. The menu is not needed for a printout, so we remove that altogether. And sidebars often cause problems with printing, so we'll just move the news list on the right side so it's right at the beginning of the page.

Creating the layout itself is a simple matter of making a new layout template with the menu include removed, and making separate CSS stylesheets to control the positioning of the remaining elements. The print-friendly Smarty template looks like this:

Figure 14.4   Print-friendly page layout. We have removed the menu and moved the news from the right-hand side of the page to the beginning.

```
{include file="$content"}
<html xmlns="http://www.w3.org/1999/xhtml">
<head>
{$smarty.capture.title}
<link rel="STYLESHEET" href="hazycrazy.css"
  media="screen" type="text/css" />
<link rel="STYLESHEET" href="print.css"
  media="screen" type="text/css" />
</head>
  <body>
    {include file="banner.tpl"}
    {include file="$sidebar"}
    {$smarty.capture.content}
  </body>
</html>
```

Apart from the absence of menu.tpl, the only difference here is in the stylesheets. We have one stylesheet (hazycrazy.css) that contains all styling information that's used by both the standard and print-friendly layouts. In addition, we have one stylesheet for each layout containing just the styling information specific to that layout. In the previous example, that's print.css.

Let us look at the parts of the CSS stylesheets that control positioning, leaving out all fonts and colors. To generate the standard layout shown in figure 14.4, we use the following styles for positioning:

```
div#banner { position:absolute; top:0px; left:0px }
div#content { margin-left: 80px; margin-top: 60px;
  margin-right:170px;}
div#sidebar { position:absolute; top:0px; right:0px;
  padding: 10px; padding-top:0px; margin-left:10px;width:150px; }
div#menu { width: 80px; position: absolute;
  top: 60px; left: 0px; }
```

Simply summarized, this places the banner, menu, and sidebar in absolute positions relative to the whole page. The main text has margins that keep it from overlapping the other components.

The positioning does *not* depend on the sequence of the <div>s. So we can move the elements around as we please by just using CSS.

Not surprisingly, the print-friendly positioning is much simpler:

```
div#content { margin-left: 5px; margin-top: 0px;}
div#banner { position:absolute;top:0;left:0px }
div#sidebar { margin-top:60px; }
```

This positions the banner absolutely and lets the "sidebar" (although it's no longer a sidebar) and main text flow after it. Unlike the stylesheet for the standard layout, the print-friendly stylesheet does depend on the sequence of the <div>s. <div id="sidebar"> must be placed before <div id="content"> in the HTML code.

Now we can have a print-friendly version of each page by simply replacing the template. A more advanced challenge is merging several screen pages from an article into a single print-friendly page, as many sites do. To do that, we could still use the same templates and stylesheets, but we would have to put different content into the content template.

14.3.2   Integrating existing applications into a Composite View

Programming is simpler if you control all the code yourself. But sometimes, you may need to put something into the application that wasn't designed to be there. Maybe it's a legacy application; maybe it's an open-source or commercial product you want to use rather than do it yourself. An event calendar, perhaps, or a discussion forum. You would like to just plug it into the content area of the page, surrounded by the usual menus, navigation, sidebars, and other components.

Our rather modest goal is to just have the other application show up in the right place. To do that we run the other application first by using `include` and capture the output with the output buffering functions:

```
ob_start();
include('someboard.php');
$board = ob_get_contents();
ob_end_clean();
```

Then we give the template the entire HTML output as a variable, and set the template for the content component to one that's specialized for integrating other applications:

```
$template = new Template('standard.html','.');
$template->set('content','board_include.html');
$template->set('someboard',$board);
```

The pluggable template for the bulletin board application has a slot for inserting the finished HTML content and nothing else:

```
<?xml version="1.0"?>
<html>

<title metal:define-macro="title">Welcome to Hazycrazy.com</title>

<div id="main" metal:define-macro="main_content">
<span tal:replace="structure someboard"/>
</div>

</html>
```

`structure` is the PHPTAL keyword we need when we insert content that's already finished HTML, since PHPTAL escapes HTML markup characters as entities by default. Of course, this means that security depends on the included application's ability to escape output properly.

Some applications will actually work right off the bat when plugged in this way. For that to happen, all the URLs in the application must be links to a single PHP file. If the application doesn't work, you need to do more work. At least you've gotten started.

14.3.3 Multi-appearance sites and Fowler's Two Step View

Nearly all web sites have a consistent look and feel. If all of this look and feel is coded in the individual templates, it's hard to change it. And it's even harder to make several different consistent appearances for the same site. For instance, if you're selling an e-commerce application that online stores can have on their web sites, your customers will want the appearance to be consistent but distinctive to their particular site and to reflect their company profile. If you have to change every single template to do that, it could take a long time.

In his book on enterprise patterns [P of EAA], Martin Fowler presents an ingenious pattern for solving these problems. It's called the *Two Step View* and it involves generating an intermediate representation that contains the data the user will see on the screen (rather than the data in the database), but no formatting information.

But is Two Step View really necessary? You can achieve just about any desired change in a site's appearance by using CSS. In his examples, Fowler shows us how to use this to achieve alternating table row colors. But alternating colors can easily be done with CSS styling, as shown in the previous chapter. And so can many other, more advanced things, such as positioning.

> **NOTE** For a stunning demonstration of the power of CSS to create different appearances for the same web page, visit the CSS Zen Garden (http://www.csszengarden.com).

Fowler's examples illustrate how badly undervalued and underused CSS is. He uses the `bgcolor` attribute on the `<tr>` element for the alternating table row colors. But the `bgcolor` attribute is listed as deprecated in the HTML 4.0 specification from 1997; Fowler's book was published in 2003.

On the other hand, it's understandable that developers use deprecated features. Browsers are slow to adopt new recommendations, anyway. But in this case, using CSS stylesheets instead would have solved the problem Fowler is trying to solve in a simpler and more satisfying way.

Still, there might be situations where your need for layout flexibility is so extreme that you really need Two Step View. Perhaps you want dates formatted differently depending on which look and feel has been chosen. Even that could be done with CSS by outputting both formats in the HTML code and setting `display:none` for the date format(s) you don't want the user to see. So for a simple example:

```
<html>
<head>
<style>
.rfcdate { display: inline; }
.isodate { display: none; }
</style>
</head>
<body>
The current date is
<span class="isodate">2004-04-29</span>
```

```
<span class="rfcdate">Thu Apr 29 2004</span>
and the time is 10:30 PM.
</body>
</html>
```

This simple HTML file shows up in the browser as follows:

```
The current date is Thu Apr 29 2004 and the time is 10:30 PM.
```

So you can do that, but at some point, you may find that it's gone too far, that there are too many dates on the page and too many supported date formats. The Two Step View might be an alternative in such a case. Just realize that the Two Step View pattern is complex and you should have a good reason to use it.

In the previous example, to strip away unnecessary HTML, you could post-process the output to remove all date formats except the one you want. That would be one small step in the direction of a Two Step View.

14.4   SUMMARY

Modern web pages typically require us to combine different, independent elements on a single page. Menus, banners, logos, ads, images, and text content need to be merged in a way that is sufficiently flexible to allow parts to be changed independently.

There are several ways to implement a so-called Composite View so that the elements and the layout become separately pluggable. Fortunately, PHP itself and the template engines have capabilities that support inclusion of independent layout elements.

Nearly all layout variations can be achieved using just CSS styling, but if extreme flexibility is required, the design pattern known as Two Step View can be applied.

Although web presentation can be quite complex, two-way user interaction is inherently even more demanding. In the following chapter, we will start studying how to create a design that will ease this, too. This involves getting a handle on the Model-View-Controller architecture, understanding how it works, and how a basic implementation of it can be achieved.

User interaction

One-way communication is entertaining at best, rude and authoritarian at worst. So far we've looked at presentation as if there were little or no opportunity for the user to talk back to the application. This is obviously not enough for most web applications.

In some applications, though, talking back may not be necessary. You might just want to get the latest stock quotes from a database and display them in a list. That's relatively easy to do; eliminating interaction simplifies our job as programmers greatly.

When we do need interaction, there are challenges that are specific to creating that interaction, and it's a different kind of challenge with web interfaces than with other kinds of user interfaces.

I am not referring to interaction design in the sense of user interface design to improve usability. That is an important subject which is relatively independent of programming. There are books about it. What I intend to discuss here is not how to communicate effectively with the user, but how to make the user interface communicate effectively with the rest of the application. Many web applications are designed in a way that makes it hard for a programmer to know how to write the code that responds to a user's request or command. When we write that code, it's easy to get confused about what the user's intention is and where we are relative to the application as a whole. How do you know what intention the HTTP request expresses if it's just a

338

bunch of variables? What form or link generated the request? Do we need to know that? Is the PHP file we're looking at an independent web page or an include file?

As always, one of our main concerns is to keep our code readable. So let's start by having a look at how web applications become unreadable. They do, very easily, and it's by no means unique to PHP. Several factors conspire to make it easy to hack some code that's ugly, hard to follow, and almost impossible to change without causing bugs. One is the tendency to mingle HTML and program code too freely. Another is the fact that HTTP was designed for hypertext publishing, not programming.

If you have any experience at all in web programming, you've almost certainly seen web application code that leaves you with few or no clues as to what it does. Does it matter? Absolutely. Unless you understand how it works, you can't change it safely and effectively. The application will act like a house that's being changed at random (parts of it collapsing without notice) or like a rebellious teenager that has no interest in taking orders.

One page from a PHP application I downloaded uses the variable $t extensively. But what does it stand for? Time, trouble, truth? I had to search through the rest of the files to discover that the intended meaning was "type." Type of what? Searching a bit more, it seems to actually be some sort of user interface configuration parameter, but I'm still not sure what it does. And where does $t get its value from? Is it a global variable that's set inside some function call or include file? Is it a GET or POST variable? Is it a session variable? When register_globals is turned on (and it still happens, even after strong recommendations to the contrary), this can be especially hard to figure out.

Another difficult question could be: when and in what sequence is the code executed? Frequently, it's controlled by a series of if tests using different variables whose credentials are as dubious as those of $t. Some of these variables may be configuration parameters, some may be user input, others may be data from the database that has been stored in session variables.

And how do you know what place the page you're looking at has in the application as a whole? Sometimes it's hard to know which page the current page is called from and what's the logical next step.

So what do you do when you meet one of these disheveled web applications? Maybe you wrote it yourself a few months ago, but you've forgotten most of the details. Or maybe someone else generously bequeathed it to you. Do you keep hacking, do you clean it up, do you reimplement it, or what? If you want to clean it up, where do you start?

The buzzword that tends to be applied to try to solve these problems is Model-View-Controller (MVC). MVC is generally a good idea for web applications, but there is a lot of confusion surrounding it. In this chapter, we'll inspect it, deconstruct it, and try to find out when and how to apply it. We'll start by trying to understand what MVC is all about, follow up by formulating a pattern that captures the essence of what is normally left unsaid about it, and start to look at how a simple, "naive" web application can be improved by thinking in MVC terms.

15.1 THE MODEL-VIEW-CONTROLLER ARCHITECTURE

In chapter 13, we saw how to separate the presentation part of the application from the domain logic.

The Model-View-Controller (MVC) architecture is based on this separation. In MVC terms, it's the distinction between Model and View. But there is also a second separation: between View and Controller. In MVC, the Model component is the functional core of the program, or a piece of that functional core; the View is used to present information to the user. In addition, MVC has a component known as a Controller, which handles user input. This can become important in complex web applications because of the need to process the HTTP request.

Figure 15.1 shows the outline of how web MVC works. The arrows can be read in the UML sense: *uses.* (Someone may want to kill me for this interpretation of MVC, since there tends to be violent disagreement on the particulars, but I'll take the risk.) What is clear is the fact that the Model does not use the Controller or the View. It need not and should not know about them.

Table 15.1 summarizes what the components of the MVC architecture do.

The Web was originally designed as a collection of static HTML pages with hyperlinks. The principle is that the user requests a specific page—either by entering its URL in the browser or by clicking a link—and gets only that page. Adding dynamic content by using PHP (or other means) does not change that.

But the situation changes drastically when you have PHP code that makes decisions, not just about which data to fill the page with, but about which page is to be displayed. In simple hypertext, the user is always in control of page navigation. But complex web applications need to take some of that control away from the user. One example is validation or error checking: the application needs to display different web pages depending on whether the operation was successful or something went wrong.

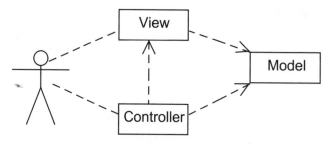

Figure 15.1   The Model-View-Controller architecture for the Web

Table 15.1   The components of a Model-View-Controller architecture

Program component	Purpose
Model	The part of the program that represents the data and the "domain logic," "business logic," or "core functionality." In other words, everything except the user interface.
View	The part of the program that displays results to the user. In a typical PHP application, this usually means one or more HTML sections.
Controller	The controller controls user input. In a web application, this is the part of application that deals with the HTTP request.

In this section, we'll work toward an understanding of MVC, what it means and what its variations are. We'll start by discussing the general meaning of MVC and its areas of application. We'll untangle the various concepts involved—including *command* or *action*. Finally, we'll look at the difference between MVC for web applications and rich-client interfaces.

15.1.1   Clearing the MVC fog

MVC—when applied to web applications—seems to confuse everyone, including the gurus. Even when the gurus claim to understand it, it's clear that they don't agree among themselves. The terminology varies; they draw the line between the components in different ways, and the details and explanations differ.

Some of the reasons for the MVC confusion are

- The terminology is inconsistent and confusing for both the patterns themselves and the basic terms such as "action."
- The difference between MVC as applied to traditional rich-client GUIs and web interfaces tends to be blurred.
- The MVC-based web presentation design patterns (including Front Controller and Page Controller) are an attempt to do something advanced without making the basics clear first. The patterns miss some of the most essential and basic pieces of the puzzle. Most of these pieces have to do with the way commands are coded in the HTTP request.

The existing descriptions of Front Controller and Page Controller are good enough that if you read the explanations and following the examples, you are likely to end up with a pretty good result. But they are not sufficient to allow you to understand existing MVC implementations that don't follow the patterns exactly, to participate in the many discussions on MVC, or to implement MVC successfully in another language such as PHP. So let's put MVC under the microscope and familiarize ourselves more with it.

MVC is approximate

Some dislike MVC because it seems to be a straitjacket. Some try to put the straitjacket on and implement the application while wearing it. That's usually not a good idea. MVC as straitjacket implies a misunderstanding of MVC and of design patterns in general. Martin Fowler says that "every time I use a pattern I tweak it a little here and there." Fowler is right, and this applies more than anything to the Model-View-Controller pattern because it is so broad in its scope. Trying to get all the details to fit the pattern is not productive.

It's more useful to think of MVC as a sorting principle. Any application that separates the Model, View, and Controller parts of the code uses MVC. M, V, and C don't even have to be in different classes or functions, but each of them needs to be lumped together rather than being freely interspersed and scattered around the application. This is the most important feature of MVC. People discuss how many Controllers there should be per View or which parts are allowed to communicate with each other at what time. These are all secondary issues compared to the basic separations. The most important separation is between Model and View. The next most important one is between View and Controller.

Some like to call MVC a "paradigm" rather than a design pattern, emphasizing the fact that you have freedom in how to apply it. The book *Pattern-Oriented Software Architecture* [POSA] lists it as an *architectural pattern* (as opposed to design pattern). Another architectural pattern in the book is "Layers," which is perhaps even more general and paradigm-like than MVC.

Think of it as a guideline rather than a blueprint. MVC is not an exam; it's a learning process. It's a means of achieving success, not a success criterion. The question to ask to evaluate a design is not "Does this design conform to MVC?" Instead we need to ask the same questions we should always ask: Is the code readable and understandable, and does it avoid duplication? Does it work? Is it reliable? Have we avoided unnecessary complexity? Does it have appropriate flexibility?

MVC is about user interaction

The MVC architecture will not help you make pizza, take better photographs, or quit smoking. Nor is it of any use for communicating with databases, calculating dates, or searching the Web. It's not the solution to everything. It deals with something broad but well-defined: handling user input and output. Whether you think of MVC as a general architecture for the entire application or for part of it is not important. The key is using it to solve the problem it's supposed to solve.

15.1.2 Defining the basic concepts

A major source of MVC fog is imprecise language. In many cases, terms are used by different people to mean different things, different terms are used to mean the same thing, or the same term is used in two or more distinct meanings without any explicit recognition of the ambiguity.

A good example of this is Martin Fowler's description of the Page Controller design pattern [P of EAA]. In order to understand what a Page Controller is, we first need to know what a page is. Fowler does not make this easy for us. He says:

The basic idea behind a Page Controller *is to have one module on the web server act as the controller for each page on the web site. In practice, it doesn't work out to exactly one module per page, since you may hit a link sometimes and get a different page depending on dynamic information. More strictly, the controllers tie in to each action, which may be clicking on a button.*

Let's try to guess what this means. It's called a Page Controller, but the currency it's trading in is not really pages; it's actions. And actions, the way he describes them, are user interface events. The way Fowler is using the term here, it is an action taken by the user rather than an action taken by the application in response to the user.

So in one paragraph, Fowler manages to blur the distinction between three concepts: page, action, and event. He may not be more confused than the rest of us, but he's not crystal clear, either.

It is difficult, but let's try to define some of the terms in a more precise way. The most problematic of them all may be *page*. A page is a clear and unambiguous term on a static HTML site, but in a web application, it gets blurred. Page is a user-oriented term which is well-known to anyone who browses the Web. So the concept of a page should probably correspond with the user's experience of what a page is. But if you have two separate screen shots from a browser, how do you know whether they represent the same page or separate pages? How much and what kind of difference is required? When potentially everything can be generated dynamically, that question is hard to answer unambiguously.

Table 15.2 shows definitions for some important terms.

Table 15.2 Some basic terms defined

Term	Definition
Event	A user interface event—in other words, an action performed by the user in the browser. In a web application that uses no JavaScript, this means a mouse click on a link or submit button or the keyboard equivalents of these clicks. If JavaScript is used, it may be any event recognized by JavaScript. For instance, a <select> menu can be programmed to submit a form.
Command	A message that expresses the intention behind an action performed by the user in the browser.
View	In web MVC, a relatively fixed set of HTML markup with slots for dynamic content. This is frequently implemented as a template.

In a simple static hypertext—plain HTML—web site, there is a one-to-one relationship between event, command, page, and view. All events are hyperlink clicks. The event always expresses the user's intention to view a specific page. Figure 15.2 shows this very simple relationship.

Figure 15.2 Good old-fashioned hypertext is based on a simple one-to-one relationship between the user's actions and the application's response

But once we introduce forms into the application, this situation changes, because the user's intention is no longer always to view a certain page.

For example, when I post a message to an online forum, my intention is to post the message, to make it available to the other participants. What appears after that—the forum, the thread, or my message for further editing—is secondary. I may have preferences about what I wish to see, but those preferences are definitely less important to me than my wish to post the message. Primarily, I want the application to process my data, not to show me anything. Figure 15.3 shows a typical case. You submit a form. The application checks whether your input is valid. If it is, the application shows whatever is the natural continuation of the dialog. If not, it re-displays the form so that you can correct the input.

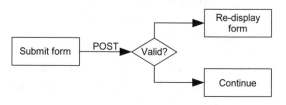

Figure 15.3 Web applications make decisions so that the relationship between user action and the "page" that's shown becomes ambiguous

This distinction—between a user request for processing and a user request for viewing a page—is conceptually the same as the distinction between an HTTP GET and an HTTP POST request. In practice, it's possible to use HTTP GET for requests for processing and HTTP POST for view requests, but it's generally not a good idea. The GET request is a request to view a page and possibly to retrieve dynamic information.

The introduction of processing (POST) requests is the origin of many of the complexities of web programming. It's why MVC has been introduced to web applications.

Why? Because if a user request does not specify what the user wants to see, the application has to figure it out. In MVC terms, it has to make decisions about which View will be displayed. The code to do that clearly belongs to the user interface; it's not business logic, so it's not part of the Model. And the decision about what View to display cannot be done in one of the Views. The logic to do it—for instance, the "Valid?" decision diamond in figure 15.3—is Controller logic. This is the point at which the View-Controller distinction becomes relevant

15.1.3 Command or action?

The terms *command* and *action* are used almost synonymously in web programming. The user requests an action; the application executes it. The user issues a command;

the application executes it. In fact, action is probably more common than command. But the word *action* in itself can mean anything the user or the application does, which is why *command* seems more appropriate. Table 15.3 illustrates the difference.

Table 15.3 The variations on the term *command*

Term	Meaning
Command	An intention-expressing message from the user to the application
Action	A user interface event (user action) or a code sequence execution by the application (system action)
Request	In HTTP, a message sent by one computer to another using the HTTP protocol

Since *action* is so ambiguous and *request* is one step removed from the user, *command* may be preferable. But *action* is fine as long as we understand the distinctions and don't become confused.

But it's not without its own problems; there is another linguistic confusion to clear up. Notice that we've defined *command* as a message. But in programming, *command* has a tendency to refer to the function, method, or class that executes the command. But the message and the receiver of the message are two different things. This is an exact parallel to a function call and a function. No one confuses a function call with a function, since the terminology distinguishes them clearly. But with commands, there is a gray area. Is a command object the message or the receiver? It can be passed around like a message, but strongly implies the code contained in the class it belongs to.

Still, it's useful to try to distinguish the two. It's reasonable to use *command* to mean the message, not the application code that responds to it, since this is what it means in plain English.

15.1.4 Web MVC is not rich-client MVC

Traditional graphical user interfaces as used in desktop applications are very different from web interfaces. These so-called rich-client interfaces communicate with the user in much more flexible ways. In particular, in a rich-client interface, a part of the user interface can be updated without updating everything. In a conventional web interface, everything must be updated for every HTTP request. (This does not apply to AJAX, which is more like a traditional rich-client interface than a traditional web interface.)

> **NOTE** Some use just the term GUI to refer to non-web graphical user interfaces, but that is misleading, since most web browsers do have a graphical user interface as defined by WIMP (windows, icons, mice, and pull-down menus).

The word processor I'm currently using is an example of the kind of situation in which rich-client MVC is useful. (Although I don't know how it's actually implemented.) The document itself is in one window, and the document's outline is in a Navigator window. If I change, add, or delete a heading in the document, the heading changes in the Navigator too.

Conventional web user interfaces don't do this. The text-editing capabilities aren't available and there is no way a server-side application can tell a client-side window to update. Rich-client MVC uses an *Observer* pattern to update all the views that need to be updated. This use of the Observer pattern in turn depends on having normal object-oriented relations between all the objects, with no HTTP requests necessary to communicate between them.

Rich-client MVC is so different from web MVC that they should probably have different names. They are not twins; they're more like second cousins. They serve entirely different purposes. The purpose of rich-client MVC is to do the kinds of real-time updates a word processor does. The purpose of web MVC is to handle the HTTP request in a consistent and orderly way.

Rich-client MVC works with multiple simultaneous views of the same data. Web MVC works with sequential views of different (or similar) data. Rich-client MVC is focused on View *instances:* In a word processor, there may be two windows with the same kind of view of the same document. The data is identical and the code for the view is identical. But since they're different instances of the same view, we can scroll them separately. Web MVC is focused on view *type* or *class:* a user list is different from a user form, but the web application never needs to handle two identical user lists.

If you take ideas from rich-client MVC—beyond the separation between the three components—and try to apply them to web applications, you will get confused. And people do get confused about web MVC. Table 15.4 summarizes some key differences.

Table 15.4   Differences between rich-client MVC and web MVC

	Rich client	**Web**
Purpose	Handle complex real-time updates	Handle the HTTP request
Views	Has multiple simultaneous Views of the same data	Normally shows only one View at a time
Observer pattern	Present	Absent
Communication	Controller talks to Model; Model talks to View.	Controller talks to both Model and View. Model is passive.

AJAX applications may be more like traditional rich-client interfaces. There are different variations and degrees; understanding both kinds of MVC may be useful if you do much AJAX work. Now that we have some understanding of what MVC is and is not, let's try to find out the most essential things we need to do to start applying it.

15.2   THE WEB COMMAND PATTERN

What, then, is the way to structure user interaction on the Web? Let's try isolating the most essential building blocks that need to be present. And let's use that to do something that will be as simple as possible while allowing us to create a consistent and solid structure. We will be looking at some of the essential building blocks that may seem obvious to some but may be misunderstood when they're not made explicit.

It may be risky to introduce an additional concept in a problem area that's already rife with inconsistent, confusing terminology, but we need a name for the combination of these elements. So let's call it the Web Command pattern.

In this section, we'll first do an overview of the pattern, and then look at its parts in turn: Command identifier, Web handler, and Command executor.

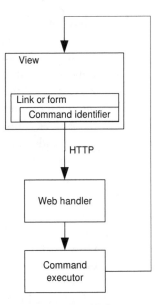

Figure 15.4 The Web Command pattern: passing a command identifier in the HTTP request and handling it

15.2.1 How it works

The Web Command pattern shows how to handle user commands in a web application. It is present in most frameworks and web pattern descriptions, but tends not to be made explicit. The reason for describing it is to make sure we have a firm grasp of the basic structure before we start to build more sophisticated designs on top of it. It is intended as a complement to other web presentation patterns, rather than an alternative.

The *View* is an HTML page that contains a link or a form. The link or form contains a command identifier. The command identifier is passed in the HTTP request. The HTTP request is handled by a web handler that extracts the command identifier and runs the command executor, which is a function method or class that's specialized for the particular command.

15.2.2 Command identifier

To make this work, the links on the web page must code the name of a command in a consistent way. One way to achieve this is to add a variable to a URL:

```
<a href="index.php?cmd=editDocument">
```

Or, if we're dealing with a form, to add a hidden input to it:

```
<form action="index.php">
  <input type="hidden" name="cmd" value="postDocument">
...
```

The other way to code the command is simply to let the file name represent the command. For example:

```
<a href="document/edit.php">
```

Now the form doesn't even need the hidden input:

```
<form action="document/post.php">
```

These two different ways of coding the command in the URL repreent the difference between the Front Controller and Page Controller patterns. These patterns have received a lot of attention. The Front Controller/Page Controller distinction is important, but less essential than the fact that the URLs should reflect commands as we've defined them: messages that represent the user's intent. This is the key to keeping the user interaction clean and well-structured, but it's not always easy to identify the proper commands. For example, is defining a new object (say, a contact in an online address book) a different command than editing an existing one? Perhaps, or perhaps not. From a database point of view, they are different (insert and update command); from a user point of view also (creating a contact or changing a contact). Only some part the forms look very alike, but the business rules differ most of the time. Yet in a simple web application, they are similar enough both technically and conceptually that combining them in one command won't cause serious problems. On the other hand, the command that causes the edit form to be displayed and the one used to submit the data afterward are definitely two different commands. So in the Page Controller version, you would need to have at least one file to handle the form (say, edit.php) and one to process the data from the form (say, post.php). And, you would probably have a list.php file as well.

This is the difference between a web application that uses the Web Command pattern and any random PHP application. You can have a PHP application that funnels everything through an index.php file (Front Controller style) or that uses a number of distinct files (Page Controller style). But if the commands are not clearly identified, the user interaction will tend to be a mess either way.

15.2.3 Web handler

The HTTP request is received by a handler. The handler is most visible in a Front Controller structure. You have a main PHP file, typically index.php. At the beginning of that file, there is some code to start the appropriate function or class to handle the command. At its simplest, it's just

```
call_user_func($_REQUEST['command']);
```

Please don't do this in a real application. It's definitely insecure, since any user can execute any function that happens to be defined. But it's an extremely simple illustration of the principle. We will cover this in more detail in the next chapter.

The Page Controller way of doing it is to leave the handler job to the web server. The web server gets a request for edit.php and executes that file, which contains the `edit` command.

15.2.4   Command executor

The command executor is the code that executes the command. (Usually, this code is just called a command, but for the purposes of this discussion, we're deliberately using the unwieldy term "command executor" to distinguish it from the command message.) In the traditional descriptions of the Front Controller, each command typically has its own class. But the command executor can be implemented in several ways. It can be

- A command class
- A method in a class that contains several command executors
- A plain function
- A plain PHP file

In the following section and the next chapter, we will see how the insights we've developed can be used to power a gentle push from procedural to object-oriented.

15.3   *KEEPING THE IMPLEMENTATION SIMPLE*

To the untrained eye, the MVC implementations that are presented in forums and articles on the Internet may seem overcrowded with objects and classes—oddly-named characters ("controllers," "dispatchers," "mappers," and so on) running around like confused chickens with little sense of purpose. And sometimes the untrained eye may be right. On the other hand, there may be good reasons for the apparent confusion. In well-factored object-oriented code, each class may be easy to read if you understand what it does, but the interaction of all the parts may be more difficult to figure out.

In this section, we'll see an example of a simple, procedural PHP web application, and then introduce the simplest possible improvements to solve its most obvious problems.

15.3.1   Example: a "naive" web application

To keep it simple, instead of starting with something that has all the bells and whistles, let's start at a place that will be more familiar to the average PHP programmer: a procedural web page that flows from top to bottom with no need to figure out what's talking to what. It may be confusing, but for other reasons. Then, let's see what we can do to improve it. We won't do anything fancy and object-oriented just to show off.

The example is a longish one: a form for submitting news articles. In a real application, there would be a news list page as well (newslist.php), which would contain links to the form for the purpose of editing news articles and submitting new ones. We're using this as an example because a form allows us to demonstrate more web programming principles than a list page would.

It's deliberately made less than perfect, but it could be made even worse. Abbreviating all the variable names to one or two characters, for instance, will obfuscate it very effectively. But that's a cheap trick, and we want to keep it readable enough to make it understandable with comments added. What the code actually does is relatively simple, straightforward, and normal, so it shouldn't be too hard. The news articles themselves are simplistic, containing only a headline and a text body.

The code is simplified in some ways to make it easier to read the listing. It actually works, but it looks ugly as sin in the browser, and everything nonessential such as error handling and validation is absent.

For demonstration purposes, the example assumes that `register_globals` is turned on. That's the directive that lets you use session variables, GET and POST variables, and others as if they were simple global variables with simple names.

As the PHP manual reminds us repeatedly, `register_globals` *should not* be turned on if you can avoid it. The manual emphasizes this as a security issue, but it is more than that. It's also critical to avoid confusion and chaos. In general, a session and request variable should never have identical names, and with `register_globals` turned off, they never will.

This point—why unmarked globals are confusing—is one of the things listing 15.1 demonstrates.

Listing 15.1 "Naive" news entry form

```
mysql_connect('localhost','kane','hok4h7');
mysql_select_db('ourapp');
if (!empty($headline)) {              ❶ Is this a form submission?
    if ($id) {                                      ❷ Existing
        $sql = "UPDATE News SET ".                     article
            "headline = '".$headline."',".
            "text = '".$text."' ".
            "WHERE id = ".$id;
    } else {                          ❸ New article
        $sql = "INSERT INTO News ".
            "(headline,text) ".
            "VALUES ('".$headline."','"
            .$text."') ";
    }
    mysql_query(mysql_real_escape_string($sql));
    header("Location: newslist.php");    ❹ Redirect to
    exit;                                   news list
} else {            ❺ Edit article
    if ($id) {
        $sql = 'SELECT text, headline '.
            'FROM News WHERE id = '.$id;
        $r = mysql_query(mysql_real_escape_string($sql));
        list($text,$headline) = mysql_fetch_row($r);
    }

  echo '<html>';
    echo '<body>';                              ❻ The news
    echo '<h1>Submit news</h1>';                   form
    echo '<form method="POST">';
    echo '<input type="hidden" name="id"';
```

```
        echo 'value="'.$id.'">';
        echo 'Headline:';
        echo '<input type="text" name="headline" ';
        echo 'value="'.$headline.'"><br>';
        echo 'text:';
        echo '<textarea name="text" cols="50" rows="20">';
        echo ''.$text.'</textarea><br>';
        echo '<input type="submit" value="Submit news">';
        echo '</form>';
        echo '</body>';
        echo '</html>';
}
```

6 The news form

❶ The `$headline` variable comes from the form. So if it is set, we assume that the user has submitted the form and that we are required to store the article. Otherwise, we will want to display the form. A slightly better way to do this would be to test for the presence of POST variables and assume that POST indicates a form submission. (For instance: `if ($_POST)...`)

❷ If the HTTP request contains a news article ID, we assume that the user is editing an existing article.

❸ If not, we assume the user wants to create a new news article.

❹ After the database has been successfully updated, we redirect to the news list page. (To keep the example simple, there's no validation and no error checking.)

❺ If there is a news article ID present when we are ready to show the news form, we assume that it came from an edit link and get the article from the database.

❻ The news form. All the HTML code is inside echo statements just to show how that looks. That doesn't mean it's a good idea, but it's fairly common.

15.3.2 Introducing command functions

The biggest problem with the example is that we're trying to guess the user's intentions based on variables that were not intended for this purpose. The primary purpose of `$headline` is to hold the value of the headline the user entered, not to decide whether there's been a form submission. Similarly, `$id` is supposed to specify which article is to be displayed in the form, not tell us whether the user wants a new article or an existing one. To make matters worse, although the variables are HTTP variables, there is no clear indication of that. If we had used `$_POST['headline']` and `$_GET['id']` instead, it would be clearer.

Just to illustrate the structure of the conditional statement, we'll replace the content of the page with comments, making the control flow more apparent:

```
if ($_POST['headline']) {
    if ($_REQUEST['id']) {
        // Run SQL UPDATE statement
```

```
    } else {
        // Run SQL INSERT statement
    }
    // Redirect to news list
} else {
    if ($_REQUEST['id']) {
        // Get news article (ID, headline, text)
    }
    // Show form
}
```

NOTE   To keep it extremely simple for now, we are using the superglobal arrays freely in these examples. In the next chapter, we will discuss Request objects and their relationship to input filtering.

The `if` tests are all intended to determine the user's intention. This intention can be coded in a way that's easier to understand and keep track of if we make sure that the HTTP request contains a `command` (or `cmd` or `action`) variable. (URLs may not be the best place for long, descriptive names.) As shown in the section on the Web Command pattern, this variable can be added as part of a link URL or as a hidden input in a form. In this case, there are four different situations representing different actions that the user is attempting to perform. This leads to the following commands:

Command	Purpose
editArticle	Show the form initialized with an existing article and ready to edit.
newArticle	Show the empty form ready to enter a new article.
insertNews	Run INSERT to save a new article.
updateNews	Run UPDATE to save changes to an existing article.

Listing 15.2 shows what the news form page looks like after we refactor it to use commands. There are two other improvements as well: The variables are changed so we can turn `register_globals` off. And instead of echoing the HTML code, there is an HTML section.

Listing 15.2   News form example refactored to use command functions

```
switch($_REQUEST['cmd']) {
    case 'updateNews': updateNews(); break;
    case 'insertNews': insertNews(); break;
    case 'editArticle': editArticle(); break;
    case 'newArticle': newArticle(); break;
    default: die("No such command: ".$_REQUEST['cmd']);
}

function insertNews() {
    $sql = mysql_real_escape_string(
        "INSERT INTO News ".
        "(headline,text) ".
        "VALUES ('".$_POST['headline']."','"
```

```
            .$_POST['text']."') "
    );
    mysql_query($sql);
    header("Location: http://localhost/newslist.php");
    exit;
}

function updateNews() {
    $sql = mysql_real_escape_string(
        "UPDATE News SET ".
        "headline = '".$_POST['headline']."',".
        "text = '".$_POST['text']."' ".
        "WHERE id = ".$_POST['id']
    );
    mysql_query($sql);
    header("Location: http://localhost/newslist.php");
    exit;
}

function editArticle() {
    $sql = mysql_real_escape_string(
        'SELECT id,text,headline '.
        'FROM News WHERE id = '.$_REQUEST['id']
    );
    $r = mysql_query($sql);
    $article = mysql_fetch_assoc($r);
    showForm('updateNews',$article);
}

function newArticle() {
    showForm('insertNews',array());
}

function showForm($command,$article) {
    ?>
<html>
<body>
<h1>Submit news</h1>
<form method="POST">
  <input type="hidden" name="cmd"
    value="<?php echo $command ?>">
  <input type="hidden" name="id"
    value="<?php echo $article['id'] ?>">
  Headline:
  <input type="text" name="headline"
  value="<?php echo $article['headline'] ?>"><br>
  Text:
  <textarea name="text"ols="50" rows="20">
    <?php echo $article['text'] ?></textarea><br>
  <input type="submit" value="Submit news">
</form>
</body>
</html>
<?php
}
?>
```

The `switch` statement calls the function that has the same name as the command variable from the HTTP request. This is a bit repetitive, and it will seem even more so if you organize other pages in the same way. It's tempting to automate the process by calling whatever function is named in the HTTP request:

```
$commands = new NewsCommands;
if (method_exists($commands,$command = $_REQUEST['command'])) {
    $commands->$command();
}
```

The problem with this is that we are not testing for unknown commands, and that's insecure. By automating it, we make it possible for any user to call any function that's available (and takes no arguments) simply by adding it to the URL (for example, `cmd=phpinfo`).

One way to overcome this is to keep the command functions in classes. Later, when we build what's known as a *Front Controller*, we will see how to do that. (Actually, this example may be considered a primitive Front Controller.)

To make sure our logic works, we use a function for the HTML output as well. We call the `showForm()` function with two arguments: the name of the command that is to be submitted by the form, and an associative array representing the news article.

Figure 15.5 shows the sequence of events that happens when the user submits the form. The POST request contains a `cmd` variable from the hidden input in the form. The `switch` statement calls the command function with the name specified by the variable. After processing, the command function redirects to the appropriate continuation page (or calls the `showForm()` function to display the form).

Since all PHP variables are global unless you put them inside a function or class, another advantage of putting all the PHP code inside command functions is that it guarantees there are no hidden global variables. As mentioned in chapter 4, global variables are generally considered harmful to your program's health, at least when used in excess.

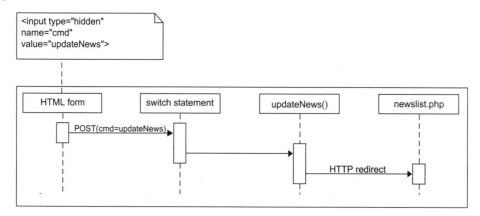

Figure 15.4 One possible sequence of events upon submitting the form in listing 15.2

15.4 SUMMARY

Everyone who's interested in advanced web programming talks about the Model-View-Controller pattern, but there is much confusion surrounding it. It is important in web programming because it helps us separate the logic of the user interface from the rest of the program and also to isolate and clarify the logic to interpret the HTTP request.

The most important key to making the pattern work is identifying a command or action that expresses the user's intent and making sure the HTTP request contains the information to identify it. We've seen the simplest way to handle a command: a procedural function. In the next chapter, we will see how it can be done using a method in a class or a separate class.

Now that we have taken a close look at the basics of web MVC, we are ready to dive into the more complex, object-oriented variations on this theme. In the next chapter, we will study the Page Controller and Front Controller patterns, discover how to encapsulate the HTTP request in an object-oriented class, and take a look at how to get controllers to work with a Composite View.

CHAPTER 16

Controllers

I've never flown a fighter aircraft, and I don't believe I want to try it. (Nor do I think they would let me. Those planes are expensive.) I know only what I've seen in documentaries: you make too sharp a turn, the G force rises steeply to 7, 8, or 9 or thereabouts, and whoops...you're out.

You come out of the turn; eventually you regain consciousness. But...you don't remember what happened. You start to ask questions. Who am I? Where am I? Ahhh...now I remember. I'm in a cockpit! What's that ahead? A mountain? The ground?

PHP does this. It forgets. When PHP runs as mod_php in an Apache process (the most common scenario), all the data gets dumped on each new HTTP request.

You can use session variables to create continuity. But even if you reconstitute your objects from session storage, message-passing between objects is interrupted. Communication is temporarily impaired, since all you have is the HTTP request. This is the background for the discussions in the previous chapter.

Some make too much of the difference between Java and PHP, attributing too much magic to the ability of a Java Servlet container to keep data in memory between requests. But the fact is that high-availability web applications have to support failover: if you pull the plug on one machine, another takes over without the user noticing. If all the session data is in RAM on one machine, pulling the plug will destroy your session data. In other words, failover requires some kind of persistent session storage on any platform and in any programming language.

This interruption makes the HTTP request resemble a leap across a chasm. The MVC pattern helps us put a bridge across, but not a very sturdy one. We want something more solid and dependable. That's what the web interaction design patterns are for. Most of them have names like Page Controller, Front Controller, or Application Controller. What they all have in common is their purpose: handling user input.

In this chapter, we'll first discuss how to encapsulate the HTTP request. Then we'll learn the simplest controller pattern, Page Controller, and solve the challenges posed by using a very simple, "naive PHP" approach to these. Finally, we implement the Front Controller pattern.

16.1   CONTROLLERS AND REQUEST OBJECTS

In the previous chapter, we discussed the parts of the Model-View-Controller architecture. The Controller receives and interprets user input. In a web application, this means processing the HTTP request.

Keeping this simple fact in mind can make life easier. If the number of different varieties of controller seem intimidating, it's good to know that their fundamental purpose is the same. It also helps us resist the temptation to use the word *controller* indiscriminately for any class that controls something.

We have a closer look at the Page Controller and Front Controller patterns later in this chapter. But before we go there, we need to make sure we know how to represent the HTTP request in a way that's useful to the controllers.

16.1.1   A basic request object

Since controllers always need to interpret the HTTP request, the request has to be available to the controllers in a form they can use. The simplest alternative is to use the plain superglobal arrays: $ _GET$ and $\_POST$. (Using $\_REQUEST$ is generally discouraged for security reasons.)

But among object-oriented PHP programmers, it's common to encapsulate the HTTP request in an object. It allows more flexible juggling of GET and POST variables and it can be helpful when implementing input filtering.

Making an object to encapsulate the HTTP request is useful when creating controllers. The superglobal arrays are easy to use, but they are not flexible enough.

A typical request class is shown in listing 16.1. It's basically just an ultra-thin wrapper for an array—a storage container for variables.

Listing 16.1 A basic Request class—is it secure?

```
class Request {
    private $request = array();

    public function __construct() {                    ❶ Initialize from
        $this->request = $this->initFromHttp();          superglobals
    }

    private function initFromHttp() {
        if (!empty($_POST)) return  $_POST;
        if (!empty($_GET)) return  $_GET;
        return array();
    }

    public function get($name) {
        if (!array_key_exists($name,$this->request)) return '';
        return $this->request[$name];
    }
                                                Get or set a
                                                   named    ❷
    public function set($name,$value) {            variable
        $this->request[$name] = $value;
    }
}
```

❶ We initialize the object from the superglobal arrays. This is set up so that $_POST overrides $_GET.

❷ get() and set() simply get or set a named variable. We could even use __get() and __set(), allowing us to access variables as $request->email and the like. We will see later why there may be a problem with using __set() this way.

This is a typical and convenient Request class. But is it secure? Hardly; there is no built-in input filtering or validation, and there is no way to do filtering except after you've retrieved a value from the Request object.

16.1.2 Security issues

In this chapter, we're using *filtering* to mean filtering and/or validation. This is meaningful from an overall security standpoint. If you validate a data item, find it wanting, send an error message back to the user, and the user submits a changed one, that whole process can be considered a kind of filtering. In the next chapter, we will use the term *validation* exclusively, since it seems to fit better into the kind of object-oriented paradigm described there.

One approach is to add filtering methods to the class. (At this writing, this is the approach taken in the Zend Framework, which is still at a preliminary stage.)

```
class Request {
    public function getAlpha($name) {
        return preg_replace('/[^[:alpha:]]/', '',
            $this->get($name));
    }
}
```

Another simple way to do it would be to remove the initialization in the constructor and require us to filter each value manually, in this manner:

```
$request = new Request;
$request->set(
    'username',
    preg_replace('/[^[:alpha:]]/',$_POST['username']);
```

This $request object is not much more advanced than a simple array for collecting filtered input.

Yet another alternative is to create a filtering mechanism that can be applied to the request from the outside:

```
$filtering = new Filtering;
$filtering->addAlphanumericFilter('username');
$filtering->addEmailFilter('email');
$filtering->filter($request);
```

This approach lets us manipulate all the HTTP variables that we've defined filtering for. But what if we've forgotten one or more of them? If we have, presumably these will pass through the filtering unscathed. We could keep track of the variables and delete the ones that haven't been filtered. We need an extra mechanism to do that, so the implementation will be more complex.

If we are going to go to such lengths, it seems more natural to use the "clean" principle (as described in the introduction to security in appendix B); having a copy of only those values we know to be filtered. Listing 16.2 shows an example of how such an API might work.

Listing 16.2 A way of filtering that's safe if you forget to add some filters

```
$filtering = new Filtering;              ←——    Create the
$filtering->addAlphanumericFilter(          ❶   filtering
    'username',                                  mechanism       ❷  Define
    'The user name must be filled in'                              filtering
);
$filtering->addEmailFilter(
    'email',
    'The email address is not valid'
);
if ($filtering->filter(new RawRequest)) {
    $clean = $filtering->getCleanRequest();     ❸  Filter and get
    $email = $clean->get('email');  ←——             clean request
    // etc. Process -- redirect            ❹  Get validated
}                                             value
```

```
else {
    $messages = $filtering->getErrors();   ◄─┐   Get error
}                                          ❺   messages
```

❶ We start by creating an instance of the filtering mechanism.

❷ We add a couple of filters specifying which input variables should be filtered according to which criteria. We also have the ability to specify error messages that will be available if the checks fail.

❸ The `filter()` method works on a raw request object. This object is not intended to be used directly. `filter()` returns TRUE if all variables match the filtering criteria. On success, we can get a new, clean request object; this object is a different class than the raw request object. The two classes have different methods, so the clean request object cannot be replaced with a raw request object by mistake.

❹ We can get the validated values from the clean request object in a convenient way.

❺ If the validation fails, we can get the error messages we need to display.

We are getting a bit ahead of ourselves here, since the next chapter deals with input validation. For now, let's just make a temporary diagram of which classes might be required to implement this design. Figure 16.1 is mostly obvious from the example. The CleanRequest and RawRequest objects are given, the Filtering object has the methods used in the example, and it's reasonable to assume that we will need separate classes for different kinds of filtering.

In the next chapter, we will go into the details of a secure request architecture, using slightly different terminology.

Representing the HTTP request in a safe way is a prerequisite to maintaining security when applying web presentation patterns. Now that we have dealt with that, we're ready to take on the first one of these patterns, Page Controller.

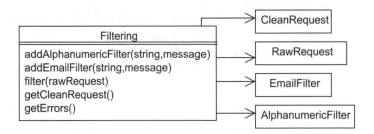

Figure 16.1   Quick sketch of a possible design for request object filtering

16.2   USING PAGE CONTROLLERS

As mentioned in the previous chapters, the two conventional web presentation patterns are called Page Controller and Front Controller. As with Composite View, these may be considered fancy names for practices that should mostly be familiar to the average PHP programmer. In fact, the Page Controller structure may seem very similar to the average naive PHP application. It may seem like just any collection of PHP pages with links to each other. There is a bit more to it than that, though. As we saw in the previous discussion, the word *page* is one of the hardest to define. In *Patterns of Enterprise Application Architecture* [P of EAA], Martin Fowler defines Page Controller as "an object that handles a request for a specific page or action on a website." To make it meaningful, we will define it in this context as a single PHP file that handles a command.

In this section, we'll first try out a simple Page Controller structure for our commands. Then we'll discuss the most important challenges that arise from this design. The first one is choosing which View to display depending on validation results or other criteria. We also want to unit test the page controllers. When we try that, it will become clear that we need to avoid HTML output, and using templates is a good way to achieve that. Finally, we'll discover how to unit test redirects as well.

16.2.1   A simple example

Let's start with the edit form. When we left off in the previous chapter, we had created two commands for this: `editArticle` and `newArticle`. For the sake of the Page Controller, it's a good idea to make the command structure a little more coarse-grained, so we'll put both commands in an edit.php file.

In addition to merging the two commands, we'll modernize the code by using an object-oriented approach to getting the data from the database. How to build the objects that retrieve the data is the subject of chapters 19-21; here, we're just using the relatively simple APIs provided by these objects.

We'll also use a Composite View template as described in chapter 14. This is not necessary for the Page Controller to work. It's entirely possible to do the Page Controller in the same style as the previous examples in this chapter, with MySQL functions and an HTML section containing the form. There are advantages to object-oriented data access and templates, but this example doesn't strictly need them.

Listing 16.3 shows the edit.php file.

Listing 16.3   news/edit.php with templates and object-oriented data access

```php
$mapper = new NewsMapper;
if (is_int($request->get('id'))) {
    $article = $mapper->find($request->get('id'));
}
else {
    $article = new NewsArticle('','');
}
$template = new Smarty;
```

❶ Create object to retrieve news

❷ If ID, get news article

❸ If not, create

```
$template->assign('content','newsform.tpl');
$template->assign('article',$article);
echo $template->fetch('normal.tpl');
```
4 Plug news form
into content area

❶ We retrieve the news article as an object from the database by using a separate object called a News Mapper.

❷ Since we've merged the `edit` and `new` commands, we're back to testing for the presence of an ID to check which one the user wants. If the ID is set, we get the article with that ID.

❸ If the ID is not set, we assume that the user wants to write a new article. We instantiate a NewsArticle object with an empty headline and an empty body text. These show up as empty fields in the form. For example, if we had wanted to display a default value for the headline, we could have used that as the first argument to the constructor:

```
$article = new NewsArticle('Man bites dog','');
```

❹ We plug the news form template into the content area as described in chapter 14.

We also merge the `update` and `insert` commands to make a post.php as shown in listing 16.4.

Listing 16.4   news/post.php using object-oriented data access

```
$mapper = new NewsMapper;
$article = new NewsArticle(                    ❶ Create
        $request->get('headline'),               NewsArticle
        $request->get('text'));

if ($request->get('id')) {
    $article->setID($request->get('id'));      ❷ Update if ID is
    $mapper->update($article);                    present
}
else {
    $mapper->insert($article);       ←──❸  Insert if ID is not present
}

header("Location: news/list.php");
exit;
```

❶ This time we create a NewsArticle object using the headline and text entered in the form.

❷ If there is an ID in the POST request, we assume that we want to update an existing article. To do that, we have to set the ID in the NewsArticle object and let the mapper run the update.

       CHAPTER 16 CONTROLLERS

❸ If the article is a new one, we run the `insert()` method on the mapper. The mapper or the database takes care of generating an ID for the article.

The Page Controller structure has some advantages. It's intuitive and uses the web server to do part of the job. You can organize and sort the commands in a natural way using the file system, even if there are lots of them. You can have news/edit.php and contacts/edit.php. It's easy to avoid loading any more code than what you need in each case.

On the other hand, it's less flexible than the Front Controller structure. It's harder to pre- and post-process and harder to test. And it's harder to let one command call another command, which is one reason why we chose to make coarser-grained commands.

16.2.2   Choosing Views from a Page Controller

The previous examples have no input validation. That weakness hides a deeper problem. The problem is that if validation fails, we want to redisplay the form with the values the user already entered. Keeping the values means having a NewsArticle object on hand, and we do. When the user submits the form, we start by constructing the object, so that part of it is taken care of.

But how do we redisplay the form? The classic solution in naive PHP is to include the edit.php file when that happens. So let's do a super-simple validation just to find out how that works. We test whether the headline is empty, and if it is, we include the edit.php file.

```
$article = new NewsArticle(
        $request->get('headline'),
        $request->get('text')
);

$article->setID($request->get('id'));

if (empty($request->get('headline'))) {
    include('news/edit.php');
    exit;
}
// Save the article to the database and redirect to list.php
```

The problem with this is that the edit.php file starts by establishing the NewsArticle object, either by getting it from the database or making an empty one. So to keep that from happening, we have to add an extra `if` test:

```
if (!$article) {
  if (!empty($request->get('id'))) {
    $article = $mapper->find($request->get('id'));
  }
  else {
    $article = NewsArticle::createEmpty();
  }
}
```

The conditional logic is getting uncomfortably complex, and this way of doing it is artificial anyway. We are letting the edit.php file serve both as a web page and as an include file, and that's fundamentally unsound. A better solution is to isolate the template display code in a separate file, say view_form.php:

```
$template = new Smarty;
$template->assign('content','newsform.tpl');
$template->assign('article',$article);
echo $template->fetch('normal.tpl');
```

This allows us to remove that extra `if` test. And what we have done is, in MVC terms, separate the View from the Controllers. edit.php and post.php are both Controllers, while view_form.php is a View.

But there is still another problem. When we use `include` this way, we are passing variables implicitly from one file to another. The application depends on the `$article` object being created in post.php and then being passed silently into edit.php through the include mechanism. If instead we enclose the contents of view_form.php in a function, include it at the beginning, and run the function where it's needed, we can pass those variables explicitly.

```
function viewForm($article) { }
```

It's clear that this makes the code clearer and more reusable. But it's easy to forget that when using includes in PHP. In these simple examples, using a plain `include` is relatively innocuous. But as complexity increases, including script code (as opposed to functions and classes) can lead to a great deal of confusion.

We can go further along this path by encapsulating the View code in a class. For example, the class could be a template child class or a specialized form class.

16.2.3 Making commands unit-testable

One of the downsides to the naive PHP page controllers is that they're harder to test. It's not impossible, but awkward: you can include the file and use output buffering to catch the HTML output and test its contents.

If the commands are functions or classes instead, they're easier to test separately. In general, making code testable tends to help improve its design. It requires modularity. So if we solve the problems that occur when we try to unit test our web application, it will help us make the code more reusable and easier to maintain. This is test-driven design in practice.

When we want to test our commands, there are at least two clear problems that need to be solved:

- When there's HTML output, we have to catch that output or make some changes so we can get the output more easily.

- Some commands do a redirect. There is no simple way to detect the fact that a redirect has been sent, and it's customary to exit unceremoniously after a redirect. Exiting causes the test script to stop executing before it reports any test results.

16.2.4 Avoiding HTML output

The next problem is avoiding output. If we want to test an `editArticle()` command, we should make sure the headline and the text of the existing article are displayed in the input boxes in the form. To check this, we must be able to get the HTML code in a variable for testing instead of having it output all the time. One way to achieve this is to use output buffering:

```
function testEditCommand() {
    // Pretend there's been an HTTP request
    $_REQUEST = array('id' => 1);
    ob_start();
    editArticle();
    $form = ob_get_contents();
    ob_end_clean();
    $this->assertPattern('!input\ type="text"\ name="headline"
            .*Fire\ in\ Silven\ Valley!six',$form);
}
```

(The x pattern modifier is there just to enable us to break the regular expression into two lines. That means we have to escape all the spaces.)

This way of using output buffering certainly works, but it's a bit cumbersome. It does enable us to check precisely what HTML output the PHP page produces. On the other hand, do we really need to wade through the HTML code using regular expressions? Perhaps it would be enough to test that the variables inserted into the HTML code are correct. We can do that, and avoid output buffering, if we keep the HTML in a template and check that the template object has been fed the correct variables.

16.2.5 Using templates

We can let the command return a template and the client (the web page) can display it. Now we can redesign our tests so that we will be able to test the commands effectively. If we let the command function return a template object, we can get the variables from the returned template and test that they are correct:

```
$template = someCommand();
$this->assertEqual(
        'Man bites dog',
        $template->get_template_vars('headline'));
```

In the application itself, we display the result of template processing instead.

What are called *template objects* here are objects that have all the information they need to display themselves. With some template engines, the template object can do that. A Smarty object, on the other hand, is not able to display itself, since it's not a template. To generate the HTML result, you need to pass a template resource as a parameter to the Smarty object:

```
$smarty->display('newslist.tpl');
```

We want the command to be able to make the decision about which template to display, so the object returned from the command must have the name of the template file built in. Alternatively, we might let the command return an array containing the Smarty object and the template resource. Then we could do this:

```
list($smarty,$template) = someCommand();
$smarty->display($template);
```

But this makes the implementation unnecessarily dependent on Smarty. Better to have a generic template interface.

While we're at it, we might as well gather the command functions in a class. That will eliminate the risk that someone will execute a function that was not intended as a command.

In the Page Controller example, we had edit.php include view_form.php. Doing something similar with methods in a NewsCommands class, we can let the view-Form() method return a Template object:

```
class NewsCommands {

    function editCommand() {
        $mapper = new NewsMapper;
        $article = $mapper->find($request->get('id'));
        return $this->viewForm($article);
    }

    function viewForm($article) {
        $template = new Template_Smarty('normal');
        $template->set('content','newsform.tpl');
        $template->set('article',$article);
        return $template;
    }
}
```

To run this in a real application, we'll need to build a Web Handler, which is part of the Front Controller pattern. But, for now, just to show how it works, here is some concrete code to run it:

```
$commands = new NewsCommands;
$template = $commands->editCommand();
$template->display();
```

This gets the news article from the database and displays it in the editing form.

16.2.6   The redirect problem

Now we've solved one of the problems that make testing awkward. One remains: the fact that commands sometimes need to issue redirects. Redirects are typically used after successful form submissions. In fact, it's good practice to redirect after a POST request and then use GET to show the next page.

It's hard to test whether the code has done a redirect. If we could return a value instead, testing would be easy. But we want to do different things depending on circumstances: Some commands will return a template so that we can redisplay the form. Others will return something to tell us to do a redirect so that we can display the news list. So if we return something that is not a template (say, a string representing a URL to redirect to), we may need to start adding conditional logic like this:

```
if ($template instanceof Template) {
    $template->display();
}
else { //The template is actually a URL for redirect?
    header("Location: $template");
    exit;
```

One solution: avoiding redirects

It's not elegant. One opportunity that opened up when we started using templates is to drop the redirect. If we make the news list available as a template, we can get that template, fill it with data, and display it. In fact, if we have a command to show the news list, we can use that both here and to display the news list in the first place.

The approach works, but there is one snag: the news list page is displayed, but we started out processing a POST request on to newsform.php. The address bar in the browser will display `newsform.php` in the URL. When we redirected to newslist.php, that was the URL shown in the address bar. And here's the real problem: if you click the Reload button in the browser, it decides it's been asked to rerun the POST request and displays the message in figure 16.2. This is the main reason why you should (almost) always redirect after a POST request in traditional, non-AJAX web programming.

In some cases, this may be only a minor nuisance. On the other hand, there is another way to handle it.

Another solution: redirecting transparently

We can do a redirect via a sort of "degenerate template": a Redirect object that performs the redirect when you call a display method on it. Listing 16.5 shows how an object like this can be defined.

Figure 16.2 Annoying message on clicking Reload

Listing 16.5   Class to make Redirect objects that imitate a template

```
class Redirect {
    var $url;
    function __construct($url) {
        $this->url = $url;
    }

    function display() {
        header("Location: ".$this->url);
        exit;
    }
}
```

So now, instead of calling the showNewslist command, we can return a Redirect object instead:

```
return new Redirect('newslist.php');
```

The Redirect class is an example of a design pattern Fowler calls *Special Case*—or something very similar. You can use Special Case to avoid having to write conditional statements to take care of special cases. Polymorphism does the job instead: the cases are handled differently depending on what kind of object is handling them.

Since PHP does not normally check the types of objects, we can use duck typing as described in chapter 4. We can execute a method call on an object and it will work even if the objects have no relationship beyond the fact that both their classes have that one particular method implemented. Alternatively, we can formalize the resemblance by using the interface keyword. This gives us an interface like the one in the section on type hints in chapter 3. The interface has fewer methods than the template, since it doesn't have the ability to set or get variables or return HTML code:

```
interface Response {
    public function display();
    public function execute();
}
```

Now the Redirect class can implement the Response interface:

```
class Redirect implements Response { }
```

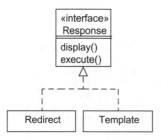

Figure 16.3   Redirect and Template as Response objects

Figure 16.3 shows the relationship between the classes. As mentioned, whether the Redirect and Template objects formally implement the Response interface is of little practical importance.

Again using code similar to the Page Controller example, we can now implement a `post` command that will return a redirect to the news list on success, the form template on failure:

```
class NewsCommands {

    function postCommand($request) {
        $mapper = new NewsMapper;
        $article = new NewsArticle(
                $request->get('headline'),
                $request->get('text'),
                );

        $article->setID($request->get('id'));

        if (empty($request->get('headline'))) {
            return $this->viewForm($article);
        }
        if ($request->get('id')) {
            $mapper->update($article);
        }
        else {
            $mapper->insert($article);
        }

        return new Redirect('list.php');
    }
}
```

We are getting closer to being able to build a Front Controller. In fact, we have all the building blocks we need for a Front Controller except for the main controller component, the Web Handler.

16.3 BUILDING A FRONT CONTROLLER

A *Front Controller* is a mechanism that handles all requests for a web site or application. PHP applications frequently achieve this by having a single file—more often than not called index.php—that is used for all requests and handles them by including other files.

In different applications, index.php may contain different things depending on the structure of the application: links, templates, redirects, and includes. But to simplify all this, we can distinguish between two fundamentally different ways of using it:

- As a start page that contains links to other pages.
- As the page representing the *only* URL used in the application. There are links, but all the links go back to index.php and are distinguished only by the query string.

Complex web applications tend to end up using the second strategy, because page navigation is more flexible: in principle at least, all resources are available at all times.

Using index.php in this way is an example (or approximation) of the Front Controller pattern. The principle is that all requests from the user are funneled through the same control logic to sort out which component can deal with it. This control logic is called the Web Handler.

There is some terminological confusion about the Front Controller as well. It's common to call the component that first gets the HTTP request the Front Controller. I'm sticking with Fowler, who calls this piece a Web Handler or just Handler in the UML diagrams in [P of EAA]. (On the other hand, in his Java example, it's called a Front Servlet.)

The alternative is *Page Controller*, which we've already covered.

In this section, we'll start by dealing with the parts of the Front Controller in turn. We'll look at the Web Handler and the commands, using two approaches to commands: one class per command, or multiple commands per class. Then we'll look at some specific challenges that can occur with forms: multiple submit buttons and submits that are generated in JavaScript.

16.3.1 Web Handler with single-command classes

As Fowler describes it ([P of EAA]), a *Front Controller* has one command class per command. This is what the Gang of Four [Gang of Four] calls the *Command* design pattern.

To use this for a Front Controller, we want to take the command variable from the HTTP request and use that to run the command directly. That's easy if we have a class for each command. We make our index.php file do something like this:

```
$class = "Command_".$request->get('cmd');
$command = new $class;
$command->execute($request);
```

This tiny piece of code is the part of the Front Controller that is known as the Web Handler. The Front Controller consists of the Handler, the commands, and any other classes that serve these. The command class need not have any other methods except execute().

We pass the Request object to the execute() method to make the HTTP request variables available to it. Assuming that $request has filtered and validated, we want the command method to use it rather than $_POST and $_GET directly.

Sometimes the command objects for a Front Controller are called Page Controllers. Instead of discussing what terminology is the best or "correct," we will just keep in mind the fact that the terminology differs, but the meaning is the same.

The alternative to having one command per class is to group several commands together as methods in one class. We will take a closer look at command groups shortly. Figure 16.4 shows how the same two commands can be implemented in these two ways.

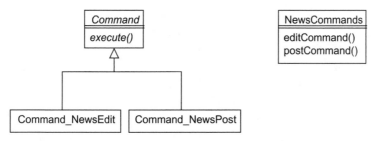

Figure 16.4 **Commands as single classes versus a command group class**

16.3.2   What more does the command need?

There are many features that may be added to the Front Controller. The most urgent priority is simply to give it whatever resources it might need to do its job. It may be able to create the objects it needs, such as finders to get data from a database. On the other hand, creating such objects inside the method makes mock testing more difficult. And there may be other global resources that are needed.

With the average object, we can pass whatever it needs into the constructor. But with commands created by the Front Controller, there is no way to hard-code this construction. We need a standardized way to make the required resources available.

One possibility is to pass a configuration or context object (as it's frequently called) to the constructor of the command or command group objects, or to the `execute()` method. Fowler uses an `init()` method for this purpose. Or you can introduce extra objects as optional arguments to the constructor:

```
public function __construct($menu=FALSE) {
    $this->menu = $menu ? $menu : new Menu;
```

There seems to be no clear reason why one of these approaches should be better than the other.

Alternatively, you can make a configuration object globally available. This is discussed in the context of database connections in chapter 19. A Service Locator similar to the one in chapter 19 could be used like this:

```
class EditMessageCommand {
    public function __construct() {
        $this->menu = ServiceLocator::instance()->menu();
    }
    public function execute($request) {
        // command code
    }
}
```

16.3.3   Using command groups

It is that easy to implement a Web Handler. On the other hand, it could be even simpler. Instead of a class with just one method, we could have a plain function for each command and call that. But in any application that has more than a few commands,

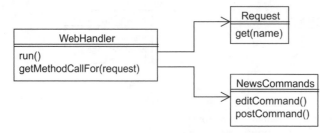

Figure 16.5　A front controller with a command group class

it's an alternative to group them into classes, each of them having several related commands. For instance, we might have a NewsCommands class for all news-related commands and a UserCommands class for all user-related commands.

The simplest way to make a handler to execute a command that is in one of several possible classes is to add both the name of the group and the name of the command to the HTTP requests. So a link might look like this:

```
<a href="index.php?group=news&cmd=new">New</a>
```

Or if we leave it to the handler to separate the group and the command, we could do something like this.

```
<a href="index.php?cmd=news.new">New</a>
```

Now we could just let index.php contain the handler, but testable code is better, so let's make a class out of it. It is extremely simple; all it does is split the cmd variable from the HTTP request, generate a class and method name based on that, and run the method.

```
class WebHandler {
    function run() {
        list($class, $method) = $this->getMethodCallFor($_REQUEST);
        require_once $class.'.php';
        $commands = new $class;
        $template = $commands->$method($request);
        return $template->execute();
    }

    function getMethodCallFor($request) {
        list($group,$command) = explode('.',$request->get('cmd'));
        return array(ucfirst($group).'Commands',$command.'Command');
    }
}
```

We pass the Request object to the command method to make the HTTP request variables available to it. Assuming that $request has been through input filtering, we want the command method to use it rather than $_POST and $_GET directly.

Figure 16.5 is a class diagram of the design.

The handler executes the template and returns the HTML result, so it doesn't output anything. We'll do that in the index.php file. We've stripped it of everything interesting, so by now it is minuscule:

```
require_once 'WebHandler.php';
$handler = new WebHandler;
echo $handler->run();
```

Several PHP MVC frameworks use this kind of approach (what I've called a command group). The Zend Framework is one of these, with several actions (commands) in one class called a Controller:

```
Zend::loadClass('Zend_Controller_Action');

class NewsController extends Zend_Controller_Action {
    public function indexAction() { }
    public function editAction() { }
    public function postAction() { }
}
```

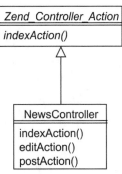

indexAction() is the default action for news.

Figure 16.6 shows this class in UML. It's the equivalent of the earlier command group except for the indexAction() method. Since this is an abstract method in Zend_Controller_Action, it *must* be implemented.

We've now covered the most important aspects of the Front Controller, but some special situations still need to be addressed. One of these is integrating forms with multiple submit buttons into the design.

Figure 16.6 The command group, Zend style

16.3.4   Forms with multiple submit buttons

Adding a command variable to an HTTP request is usually as simple as in the examples we've already seen: With a plain link, you add a command variable to the query string of the link URL. With a form, you add a hidden input called command (or anything else, as long as it's consistent).

But there are some situations that require more handling. One of these is when there is more than one submit button in a form and you need different commands for the buttons. Then you need to attach the command name to the button rather than the form. An easy way to do this is to use PHP array indexes in HTML forms:

```
<input type="submit" name="command[layout.previous]"
  value="Previous">
<input type="submit" name="command[layout.next]" value="Next">
```

To interpret this, all we need to do is to let the Web Handler check whether the command variable is an array. If it is, we use the array key as the command name:

```
function getMethodCallFor($request) {
    if (is_array($request->get('cmd')))
        $cmd
            = array_shift(array_keys($request->get('cmd')));
    list($group,$command) = explode('.',$cmd);
    return array(ucfirst($group).'Commands',$command.'Command');
}
```

Now any submit button can generate any command. Alternatively, we could achieve the same effect with JavaScript, but it's better to avoid JavaScript if we can, since some users disable it in their browsers.

16.3.5   Generating commands with JavaScript

Another variation that sometimes occurs in web applications is when non-button elements of the page have JavaScript that will cause the form to submit when the control is changed. An example would be a `<select>` menu like this one:

```
<select name="module" onChange="this.form.submit();">
  <option>News</option>
  <option>Discussion</option>
  <option>Calendar</option>
</select>
```

Since this example already uses JavaScript, it's safe to use more JavaScript. That makes it easy to add a command name to the HTTP request:

```
this.form.cmd.value='changeModule';this.form.submit();
```

This will work if the form has a hidden input called `cmd`.

The Page Controller and Front Controller patterns make the overall design much less troublesome. But there are still times when something more is needed. Complex composite views are an example, so let's take a brief look at this type of challenge.

16.3.6   Controllers for Composite Views

As pointed out in chapter 14, there are several challenges when we want to construct a web page from components. One is to construct a composite layout from component templates. Another is to create the dynamic content (composite data) needed for a composite view.

Yet another, perhaps even more difficult challenge is to get components of a Composite View to communicate through HTTP requests. Some components don't need to be involved in this. These are the components that are not interactive or contain simple links, perhaps to outside resources. Banners, ads, and text content may fall into this category. On the other hand, menus, paging components, and real interactive content such as forms—interactive calendars or the like—may make it hard for a plain web command to make the required updates to the components that may be affected. Paging is an example. When the user chooses the next page in a list of news or search results, we need to update both the news list and the links related to paging. Another example is the kind of menu used in the example of the Composite pattern in chapter 7. We want to mark the currently selected menu option. So in addition to the actual task performed by the menu option, the menu itself needs to be updated.

As yet, there are no easy, standardized solutions for this kind of complexity. We can only suggest some ways to structure code to make it cleaner.

Let's try thinking of a menu as a *widget*, a user interface element with a separate, independent existence. The user communicates with this widget by clicking on one of its links. Due to the odd nature of web interfaces, the widget has no way of responding directly. Instead, an HTTP request is sent, but it is not addressed to the widget specifically.

It's tempting to make the widget a single, monolithic class in PHP, with the ability to both generate HTML for the widget and interpret the user's response. But we're more likely to keep the code clean if we separate Model, View, and Controller. In other words, a separate component controller may save us from chaos if the code we write within the standard Front Controller setup gets too messy. Listing 16.6 is an example: a controller for a menu that handles the job of marking the currently selected menu option.

Listing 16.6   A component controller to handle a menu

```
class MenuController {
    const OPTION_ID_VAR = 'optid';            ❶ Variable names as
    const CONTROLLER_ID_VAR = 'ctrl';            class constants

    public function __construct($menu) {      ❷ The controller      Should  ❸
        $this->menu = $menu;                     needs the          this
    }                                            menu object        controller
                                                                    run?
    public function wantsToControl($request) {
        return $request->get(self::CONTROLLER_ID_VAR) == 'menu';
    }

    public function execute($request,$view) {
        $optionId = $request->get(self::OPTION_ID_VAR);
        $this->menu->markPathToMenuOption($optionId);   ❹ Mark the
    }                                                      menu path

    public function addToView($view) {        ❺ Add the menu to
        $view->set('menu',$this->menu);          the template
    }
}
```

❶ The two constants are names of variables in the HTTP request. To make these more configurable, we could have a separate class to handle all such names.

❷ The menu controller is fed a Menu object similar to the one in the Composite example in chapter 7.

❸ The wantsToControl() method checks to see whether this particular controller needs to be activated. For this example, we are assuming that there is variable in the HTTP request to indicate that a menu option has been chosen, indicating a need to run this controller. Unless there is another mechanism to maintain the state of the menu when it's unchanged, the controller may need to run every time. In that case, we might change this method to `return TRUE`.

Another possibility is to run all controllers every time. In that case, this method is unnecessary.

④ The only real task performed by `execute()` is calling the Menu object's `mark-PathToMenuOption()` method with the correct menu option ID. These two lines may seem somewhat trivial, and yet this is the point of having a separate menu controller. We have encapsulated the ability to figure out from the HTTP request which menu option needs to be marked. If we change the way the menu communicates in the HTTP request, we can change this class only.

⑤ `addToView()` is a simple trick to achieve the separation between Composite View data and a composite template as mentioned in chapter 14. The View that's passed into the method may be anything that has a `set()` method: for example, a complete PHPTAL template, an adapter, or some kind of data holder. It may represent the whole web page or just a piece of it that may be rendered and later inserted into the complete view.

16.4   SUMMARY

The classic patterns for web MVC are called Page Controller and Front Controller.

You can implement them using the plain superglobal arrays $_POST and $_GET, but most who are into object-oriented PHP choose to encapsulate the HTTP request in a separate object. One advantage of this is that input filtering can be built into the request object instead of being foreign to the general design of the application.

Page Controller is simple and close to naive PHP. Front Controller is a common pattern in most frameworks, providing a centralized point of control that handles every HTTP request. It is not as complex as its name and some implementations may lead you to think. In its most basic form, it is just a few lines of PHP code.

A Front Controller delegates processing to command or action objects or command groups. PHP frameworks often use command groups. Composite views may need composite controllers to manage the complexity of the interaction.

There is one major issue in user interaction we haven't covered yet: user input validation. This is a separate subject that is featured in the next chapter. We will deal with server-side and client-side validation, how to synchronize the two, and how to create secure request objects.

Input validation

"What could be less exciting than a company that makes retread tires in Muscatine, Iowa?" asks Peter Lynch in his investment book *Beating the Street*.

I don't know what's even less exciting, but I can think of plenty of things that are equally dull. Lots of routine, unexciting activities go on in the so-called real world. Input validation is one of them. It's not glamorous; there will never be a Hollywood movie about it. It's not even visible most of the time, so it's easy to overlook until you're actually forced to do it.

But web programmers are generally aware of the need to do it. According to Lynch, Bandag (the company that makes retread tires in Muscatine, Iowa) increased its value by a factor of 30 in 15 years. Clearly, you can be successful without doing anything superficially exciting.

Input validation is important for two reasons: *security* and *usability*.

It is essential to security, since unvalidated input leaves a web application open to all sorts of attacks, especially the dreaded SQL injection attacks.

But it's also required for usability. If a user in the process of registering gets an SQL error message instead of a suggestion to choose a user name that's not in use, it's obviously not an acceptable comfort level for the end user.

A web site is like a hotel: your guests have to be safe, of course, but that's not enough to make them enjoy their stay. Security is about keeping them safe, usability is about keeping them comfortable, and content is about getting them interested.

This chapter is not primarily about the security aspect of input validation. It focuses mostly on the design challenges while keeping the goals of security and usability in mind. We'll start by discussing how input validation fits into the overall application. Then we'll look at simple server-side validation and discuss its problems. Next, we'll try out client-side validation. Returning to server-side validation, we build an object-oriented design that solves many of the problems we outlined earlier. Finally, we'll discuss the possibility of synchronizing server-side and client-side validation so that we can avoid defining all validations twice.

17.1 *INPUT VALIDATION IN APPLICATION DESIGN*

Let's try to make validation more exciting, or at least more interesting, by investigating it and exploring some non-trivial ways to do it. Considering how simple validation is in principle, it's infuriatingly difficult to find the ideal strategy. Validation has odd properties that make it hard to conceptualize a solution. Where does it belong? On the server, on the client (using JavaScript), or both? If it's on the server, which layer does it belong to? In this section, we'll discuss these questions, look at some general strategies for validation, and define some form-related terms.

17.1.1 Validation and application architecture

Most validation is possible in JavaScript on the client. Much validation is just checking that a field is not empty. JavaScript is convenient for the user because it's fast, and a pop-up box is sure to get the user's attention. (It's sometimes called modal input: You have to do something about it to proceed. In other words, the system is in a mode in which it doesn't respond the way it would if the dialog box weren't there.)

But some validations require server-side information. For example: When somebody chooses a user name to log in, the application has to check that it's not in use already. To check that, it has to query the database. In traditional web programming, that's not possible in a client-side script. Today, with the technique known as AJAX, it *is* possible. But AJAX is an entirely different world of web programming, and entering it just to improve a few validations is probably more than what we want to do. Besides, it only improves usability, not security.

There is no validation that cannot be done on the server. But server-side validation is less convenient for a user who has to wait for an answer from the server to find out what information needs to be re-entered.

If we look at server-side validation as if that were the only option, the question that comes up is where it belongs architecturally. Should it be in the Presentation Layer, the Domain Layer, both, or neither? It's tempting to say that validation depends on the properties of the domain object(s) the user is manipulating. Therefore, we can leave the

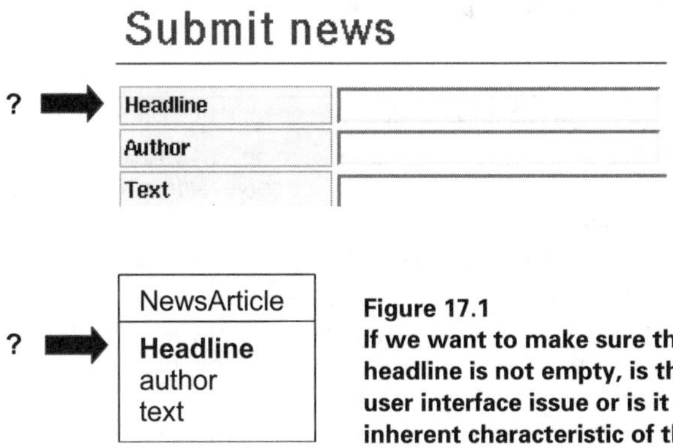

Submit news

Figure 17.1
If we want to make sure the headline is not empty, is that a user interface issue or is it an inherent characteristic of the

validation job to the domain objects. For example, we can let the news article class encapsulate the rule that all news articles need to have a headline; it can never be empty.

That seems tidy, and it means we can keep more information related to the domain object in the domain object itself. But validation can also be seen as a user interface issue. Which is it? Figure 17.1 highlights the question. The idea that it belongs to the domain object seems reasonable, yet the validation requirements are likely to change or vary more than the core domain object itself, and that is a valid reason for separating validation from the domain object. Furthermore, the rule about empty headlines is ultimately a (usually collective) user preference. It could also vary depending on the user or the situation.

To use a different example: When you first register as a user, you might only have to provide two to four different items of information about yourself. Later, you might be asked for additional information. Logically speaking, this form would be addressing the same domain object, but the information being entered would be different, and so would the demands for validation. You might be required to enter your snail mail address, but not to re-enter your password.

And if there's an administrator form for editing user accounts, the administrator may have greater liberties to include or leave out information than other users would. That means we have at least three sets of validation requirements for the same domain object.

17.1.2   Strategies for validation

Let's step back and try to find out what problem we're really trying to solve. Table 17.1 shows a list of requirements for form validation. It's hard to satisfy all these requirements at once. That is one reason why there are so many different ways to approach validation.

There are several strategies for trying to satisfy as many of these requirements as possible. Some are simple; some are more complex and ambitious. Some of the more common ones are:

Table 17.1   Requirements for form validation

Requirement	Comments
Ease of use	Client-side JavaScript validation is easier and quicker for the user.
Completeness	In traditional, AJAX-free web programming, any validation that requires access to server-side data requires full server-side involvement.
User interface consistency	If we combine client-side and server-side validation in the simplest possible way, the user interface is inconsistent: some messages are displayed as JavaScript pop-ups and some as HTML text.
Security	JavaScript validation can be bypassed simply by turning off JavaScript in the browser. Since submitting unvalidated input can cause security problems, server-side validation is essential.
Once and only once	To combine ease of use with security, it may be desirable to do the same validation both on the client and on the server. Having to code a set of standard validation procedures in both JavaScript and PHP is not a major problem. But having to specify the validation for each field in every single form in two different places is difficult and error-prone.

Server-side only. Do all the validation in PHP code on the server and display the results to the user on the HTML page. Typically, you have some functions or classes defined to do it so you don't have to repeat the same tests over and over for different fields.

Client-side mostly. Have a JavaScript for the form and run it when the user submits it. If you need server-side validation, you can add it when necessary. This strategy was common some years ago and may still be viable in an application to which only selected users have access, such as a private intranet; otherwise it is too insecure.

Form generation. This is a more ambitious strategy that involves having all the information about the form—including validation rules—in one place (typically PHP code or some kind of XML representation of the form) and using that both to generate the form and to read the information needed to validate.

Form generation with JavaScript. Frameworks and form handling packages often generate the form with JavaScript to validate it and handle server-side validation as well.

We've developed a basic understanding of what validation means and—in a general sense—what problem we want to solve. Before we get more specific about the problems of validation, let's briefly define some terms so that we know what we're talking about.

17.1.3   Naming the components of a form

In most of this chapter, we will use the term *field* to refer to the components of a web form. The use of this term in computing predates graphical user interfaces, relational databases, and object-oriented programming. To make sure we are clear about the terminology, table 17.2 defines some terms as they will be used in this chapter.

Table 17.2   Definitions of form component terms

Term	Definition
Input element	The HTML element that creates a form control.
Form control	The onscreen representation of an input component.
Form field	The abstract representation or abstract aspect of a form input component. For example, the name of a country can be input through a text input control, a select menu, or in other ways, but represents the same field in all cases.

After reviewing the overall strategies for input validation and defining the components, we are ready to examine some specific problems we are trying to solve. What makes input validation so hard that the plain PHP way falls short?

17.2   *SERVER-SIDE VALIDATION AND ITS PROBLEMS*

The typical, plain PHP way of doing validation is simple but flawed. That makes it a good place to start: we can start simple and try to eliminate the flaws while introducing as little extra complexity as possible.

If validation is only for convenience, we might think we will get away with Java-Script only. But as a general rule, we should assume that we need validation for security reasons, making server-side validation essential. Also, some validations require access to server-side data.

Server-side validation is simple and easy if our requirements are modest. It gets harder quickly if we want all the bells and whistles. Let's start with the most basic way possible, identify its shortcomings, and find the simplest possible ways to overcome them.

Let's say we have a form with a text field called `headline` that is required. This will generate a variable in the HTTP request that's translated to `$_POST('headline')` and `$_REQUEST('headline')` in the PHP script. Assuming this has been transformed to a request object as shown in the last chapter, the painless and relatively brainless way to validate this is to add the following at the beginning of the script.

```
if ($request->get('headline') == '')
    echo "'Headline' must be filled in<br>";
```

It works, but there are some problems with this approach. In this section, we'll discuss each of these problems in turn: duplication, styling, testing, and page navigation. Then we'll consider the difficult issue of how to solve all of them at the same time.

17.2.1   The duplication problem

One problem is duplication. If we just write out the code to do all the tests, we will duplicate that code on each page. This begins to be a real problem with more complex validations. We wouldn't want to copy and paste the code to validate an email address. But this problem is easily solved by using simple functions. So we would do something like this:

```
if (!valid_email($request->get('email'))
    echo "'Email address' is invalid<br>";
```

But there is another, deeper and more difficult duplication problem: the duplication between the information present in the form itself and the information in the validation code. The most obvious problem is the text in the message.

```
echo "'Email address' is invalid<br>";
```

The string email address must match the label for the input element in the HTML form. So if we want the text on the web page to read just *Email* instead of *Email address*, we need to change the message, too.

The name of the input element is also duplicated. When we change the text in the form, we might change the element name, too. If we do, we need to change that in the PHP validation code as well. On the other hand, we could leave it and ignore the fact that it doesn't quite match the user's name for it, since the user doesn't see the element name.

But the bigger problem happens when we delete an input element from the form. Now we will get an error message whenever we try to use the form. If we do any manual testing at all, we will catch this problem before it reaches the end user, but it's annoying. More likely, we will make the opposite mistake: forget to add validation and forget that we've forgotten because it's on another page.

Server-client duplication problems are relatively hard to solve. We can either live with them or use a more advanced strategy (such as the form generation strategy mentioned earlier) that coordinates the form contents with server-side validation.

17.2.2 The styling problem

Another problem with our basic validation scheme is that we are mixing PHP code and HTML markup. The echo statements contain a <br> tag. And even if they had no HTML code in them, we would need something to make sure the user notices our messages. Red color is usually a safe bet, unless there is red color present on the page already.

The minimal solution to disentangle the HTML from PHP is to keep the error messages in an array:

```
<?php
function valid_email() { ... }
if (!valid_email($request->get('email'))) {
    $GLOBALS['messages'][] = 'Email address not valid';
    }
?>
```

And then in the template or PHP section, we loop through the messages, using CSS styling to generate the conspicuous font style:

```
<html>
  <head>
    <title>User registration</title>
    <style>
```

```
      div#messages p{ color: red; font-size: 15px;
        font-weight:bold;}
    </style>
  </head>
  <body>
    <div id="messages">
      <?php foreach ($GLOBALS['messages'] as $m): ?>
      <p><?php echo $m ?></p>
      <?php endforeach; ?>
    </div>
    <!-- The rest of the HTML page goes here -->
  </body>
</html>
```

Now we have solved the styling problem by introducing a global array that is not likely to cause any trouble. The duplication problem is harder, though, and so is the testing problem.

17.2.3 Testing and page navigation problems

Another problem with the most simplistic forms of server-side validation is that there really is no way to test it in isolation from the web page itself, so the only way to be sure it works is to test the whole page. We can test simple validation functions in isolation, but there is the risk that the validation process as a whole might fail. The interaction between the validation function and the message display in the previous section is an example.

And in all of this, we have neglected to consider another aspect of server-side validation: Typically we need to show completely different pages depending on whether validation succeeded or failed. Although we have already discussed page navigation in earlier chapters, we need to keep this, too, in mind when designing validation.

17.2.4 How many problems can we solve?

The conventional approaches to validation and form handling solve many of these problems. However, none of them are perfect. Form handling and validation demand more of our ability to separate markup and program code, since building form controls using dynamic information is much more complex than showing data in a table.

For the purposes of this chapter, this is something of a dilemma. We can follow the beaten path or start exploring unknown territory. If we want to look at an apparently complete validation and form handling solution, the easiest choice is to timidly go where nearly everyone has gone before. Unfortunately, in a PHP context, this typically means generating most of the HTML markup with print or echo statements, and this is incongruent with what our goals have been so far.

The alternative is to start wandering into the unknown. The problem with that is that there is no authoritative guide to tell us what road to take. That in turn means that we need to explore different directions. For reasons of space and uncertainty, it's not wise to go too far in any of them.

What we will do is something of a compromise: we will study some basics in relative detail. For some of the more complex strategies, we will just consider the pros and cons of each option.

We'll start with a simple strategy: plain client-side validation.

17.3 CLIENT-SIDE VALIDATION

JavaScript has not been universally adored. Even though the situation has improved in recent years, it can be difficult to get JavaScript code to work in all versions of all browsers (cross-browser compatibility). And in juggling two different programming languages on two different computers to do one thing, it's hard to maintain a strong, consistent structure. Also, since JavaScript can be turned off in a browser or bypassed by using a program to send tailored HTTP requests, JavaScript validation might prevent accidental breaches of security by innocent users but does not prevent deliberate attacks.

But from a usability point of view, JavaScript is a natural choice for validation in particular. The user gets immediate feedback that is impossible to overlook. The validation code and the HTML elements that define what's being checked can all be on one page.

This means that client-side validation avoids most of the problems from the previous section. The duplication is less problematic because the input element and its validation code are closer together, so it's all there when we need to make a change. The styling problem is irrelevant because there is one standard way to present the messages. The page navigation problem is avoided by not submitting the form unless validation succeeds.

Testing, on the other hand, is not necessarily easier. And there is the security problem and the fact that there are certain validations we can't do on the client.

In this section, we'll first look at a perfectly orthodox example of JavaScript validation, validating all form fields in one fell swoop. Then we'll discuss why we can, or can't, validate the fields one-by-one instead. Finally, we'll see a complete form example using field-by-field validation.

17.3.1 Ordinary, boring client-side validation

Normal, plain JavaScript validation uses one script to validate one form. Listing 17.1 shows a small and simplistic but otherwise typical example.

Listing 17.1 Using a simple JavaScript to validate a form

```
<html>
  <head>
    <script type="text/javascript">
      function validate(form) {                    The function
        var valid = true;                     ❶ accepts a form
        if (form.elements['headline'].value == '') {
          alert("'Headline' must be filled in");         ❷ Test field,
          valid = false;                                    alert on
                                                            error
```

```
        }
        if (form.elements['text'].value == '') {
          alert("'Text' must be filled in");
          valid = false;
        }
        return valid;    ◄── ❸ Return status to prevent submit
      }
    </script>
  </head>
  <body>
    <div id="content">
      <h1>
        Post message
      </h1>
      <form method="POST"  onSubmit="return validate(this)">  ◄─
        <input type="hidden" name="command"
        value="submitMessage" />
        <table width="500">
          <tr>
            <td class="InputLabel">Headline:</td>
            <td>
              <input type="text" name="headline" size="30"/>
            </td>
          </tr>
          <tr>
            <td class="InputLabel">Text:</td>
            <td>
              <textarea name="text" rows="20" /></textarea>
            </td>
          </tr>
        </table>
        <div id="Submit">
          <input type="submit"  value="Submit" />
        </div>
      </form>
    </div>
  </body>
</html>
```

onSubmit ❹
handler runs
validation

❶ Validation is done by a JavaScript function that accepts a reference to a form object as an argument. It does all its checking on this form object. The `valid` variable holds the status of the validation process. It remains true until one of the validation tests detects a problem.

❷ We test the value of the `headline` input element, which is a text input control. If the element has not been filled in, its value is equal to an empty string, and the following statements are executed. If the element has not been filled in, we alert the user with a message that says it must be filled in. Since there's now been a validation error, we set the `valid` variable to `false`.

3 At the end of the validation function, we return the `valid` variable. This is important to prevent the form from submitting if there has been a validation error.

4 We define the validate function as an `onSubmit` handler for the form. It is essential to use the form's `onSubmit` property rather than something else such as the `onClick` property of the submit button. That's because `onSubmit` allows us to prevent the form from being submitted if validation fails. The `return` keyword is the other essential part of that process. If validation fails, the `validate` function returns `false` and `onSubmit` passes that `false` value on, causing the form submission to be aborted.

The `this` keyword refers to the form itself. So that is how we pass the form to the `validate()` function.

17.3.2   Validating field-by-field

We've validated the whole form at once when the user clicked the submit button. Now let's explore. We'll let each input box take care of its own validation. This is unorthodox, even heretical. JavaScript gurus may tell us it's the wrong thing to do entirely. But we'll try it and see where it leads us.

To validate each field separately, all we need is an `onBlur` handler that leaps into action the moment we move the cursor out of the input box. Again using the news entry form as an example, we know the headline, at least, will have to be required. We could use a `required()` function which is set up so it's run `onBlur`—in other words, when the user leaves the headline field:

```
<input type="text" name="headline"
  onblur="required('Headline',this)">
```

The `required()` function will check whether a text input field has contents and display a message if it hasn't:

```
function required(name,control) {
    if (control.value) return;
    alert('\''+name+'\' must be filled in');
    valid = false;
}
```

`control` is the object representing the input element. It's the same object that is referred to as `this` in the `onBlur` handler.

If the element has a value, we return without doing anything. If not, we display a message box using the user-oriented name supplied in the first argument to the `required()` function.

For a slightly more demanding example, let's create a user registration form. It is as simple as a user registration form can get, with input fields for an email address and a password, and one more to confirm the password. That means we need to check the email address and the length of the password and make sure the two instances of the password are identical.

For the purposes of the example, we will simplify the email address checking by just checking that the field is not empty. This may seem over-simplistic, but it's not hard to modify it so it uses a regular expression for the password.

How simple we want it is another matter. One of the better PHP books uses a regular expression of about 50 characters to validate email addresses. The regular expression in the PEAR HTML_QuickForm package has more than 500 characters. But that's still not enough for a rigorous test of a valid email address. The ultimate email validation expression may be in Jeffrey E. F. Friedl's book *Mastering Regular Expressions*; it's 6,598 bytes long.

This means that we need at least two different validators: one for checking that the password has a minimum length, and one for checking that the two inputs are equal.

Checking for equal inputs is more demanding in terms of design, since the design is based on relating each validation to a single field.

We want a message like the one in figure 17.2, and it's reasonable to display it when the user leaves the Confirm password field.

What we need, then, is to execute the validation function on leaving the confirmation field, but we need to refer to the other one. The simplest way to do that is to give its name as an argument to the function:

```
<input type="password" name="confirm"
onBlur="equalInputs(this,'Passwords','password')"/>
```

Again, the validation function is relatively simple:

```
function equalInputs(control,text,othername) {
    var othercontrol = control.form.elements[othername]
    if (control.value == othercontrol.value) return true;
    alert(text+' don\'t match');
    return false;
}
```

This is easy to keep track of and keep in order. When we edit the template file, all the information relating to one input element is inside the element itself; we only need to consider one field at a time. There's no need to make sure that a validation function outside the form has exactly the right validations.

User registration

Figure 17.2   Displaying a validation message when the user leaves the Confirm password input box

17.3.3 You can't do that!

But alas, there is a problem: It only works if the user visits the input box in the first place. Anyone can just submit the empty form before touching it.

That is why the JavaScript gurus frown upon this approach. But there *is* a way around the problem. We can make a JavaScript function that moves the cursor to all relevant input elements before submitting the form and run that `onSubmit`.

This is perfectly feasible. It's also supremely convenient for the user, since there is immediate feedback. But there is a slight and possibly annoying problem with certain browsers and operating systems: if we switch windows or desktops while the cursor is inside the field, we may be forced back to the browser.

There is another compromise to solve this: We can keep the `onBlur` functions, and let those functions store the messages they generate. Then we can display the messages on submit. That lets us keep the advantages of specifying validation in the input element itself—all the information relevant to one field lumped together for convenient maintenance—while removing any problems with `onBlur`.

On the other hand, there is no final verdict on which approach is preferable: the user might prefer to get immediate validation feedback rather than wait until the form is completed. To make it easy to switch between the two strategies, we can use a bit of object-oriented JavaScript programming to isolate this single element of variation. Instead of calling the JavaScript `alert()` function (or the `alert()` method of the current Window object), the validation functions can call an Alerter object. Listing 17.2 shows how an Alerter object can be used in our three validator functions.

Listing 17.2   Using an Alerter object in place of the JavaScript alert() function

```
function minLength(control,text,minlength) {
    if (control.value.length >= minlength) return true;
    alerter.alert(control,
        '\''+text+'\' must be at least '+minlength+' characters');
    return false;
}

function required(control,text) {
    if (control.value) return true;
    alerter.alert(control,'\''+text+'\' must be filled in');
    return false;
}

function equalInputs(control,text,othername) {
    var othercontrol = control.form.elements[othername]
    if (control.value == othercontrol.value) return true;
    alerter.alert(control,text+' don\'t match');
    return false;
}
```

But what does an Alerter class look like? Let's look at the most complex one first (see listing 17.3), the one that stores the messages so that we can show them after the user has visited all the fields in the form. Although this is called a function, it is a class, since a JavaScript class is defined as a function. This, then, is the DelayedAlerter class.

Listing 17.3 An Alerter class that stores messages instead of alerting the user immediately

```
function DelayedAlerter() {                    ❶ Variables to keep
    this.messages = new Array();                  track of validation
    this.valid = true;
    this.alert = function(element,text) {      ❷ Function for
        this.messages[element.name] = text;       delayed alert
        this.valid = false;
    }

    this.showMessages = function() {           ❸ Show
        for (var name in this.messages) {         messages at
            alert(this.messages[name]);           the end
        }
    }
}
```

❶ We need two member variables to keep track of validation: an Array object that we will use to store the validation error messages and a variable to store the validation status.

❷ The alert() method is defined as a function that is explicitly assigned to a member of the object (this).

When the method is run, the messages array, which is indexed with the field name, stores the message. Since the alert() method is called only when there has been a validation error, we can set the validation status to false.

❸ Finally, we have a showMessages() method to display the messages when we submit the form.

In contrast to this class, the Alerter class that gives immediate feedback to the user is simpler (see listing 17.4). It just displays the message and remembers the fact that there's been a validation error in the form. The showMessages() method does nothing, since there is no need to display all the messages together at the end.

Listing 17.4 ImmediateAlerter: a simpler alerter that displays the alert immediately

```
function ImmediateAlerter() {
    this.valid = true;
    this.alert = function(element,text) {
        alert(text);
        this.valid = false;
    }

    this.showMessages = function() {}
}
```

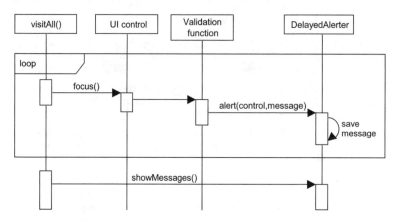

Figure 17.3 The visitAll() function loops through the form controls, using a DelayedAlerter object to save the messages

To use either alerter class, we need to have an alerter object handy. The simplest way to do this is to keep it in a global variable. One global variable won't hurt us, since the whole JavaScript is relatively simple. And with the alerter object, we can at least keep all the global information in one object. So we can start the JavaScript with this:

```
var alerter = new DelayedAlerter();
```

What if we want to change the behavior? If we want immediate instead of deferred alerts for a specific form, all we have to do is replace the global variable with the other alerter. We can do this in the `<head>` section of the HTML file:

```
<script type="text/javascript" src="validation.js"></script>
<script>var alerter = new ImmediateAlerter();</script>
```

But what actually happens when the user submits the form? Although it is a plain function, it is the centerpiece, the most important and complex component of the machinery.

The sequence diagram in figure 17.3 and the code in listing 17.5 show how this function loops through all of the input fields in the form by positioning the cursor physically in all of them in turn.

Listing 17.5 `visitAll()` function to trigger validation for all input and textarea elements

```
function visitAll(form) {
    var lastControl;
    alerter = new DelayedAlerter();        ❶ Create an
                                              alerter
    for (var i = 0; i < form.elements.length; ++i) {   ❷ Loop through
        var control = form.elements[i];                   all elements
        if ( control.type != 'text'
          && control.type != 'textarea'    ❸ Check only checkable
          && control.type != 'password' )      elements
            continue;
```

```
        control.focus();        ◄──④  Visit element, blur the previous one
        lastControl = control;
    }
                                       Blur the
    lastControl.blur();            ⑤  last element
    alerter.showMessages();
    return alerter.valid;       ◄──────⑥  Return validation status
}
```

❶ We are about to visit all the elements of the form automatically. Even if we are using the ImmediateAlerter when the user is navigating the form manually, the automatic visit carries different requirements. In this case, we want to keep the messages and display them after we're finished visiting all the fields. This is exactly what our DelayedAlerter does. So in case the existing Alerter is an ImmediateAlerter, we replace the global ImmediateAlerter object.

❷ We iterate through all the elements in the form.

❸ If the element is not of a type we need to check, we continue to the next one. Other input controls, such as select elements, normally need no validation since the choices are already restricted, but the function can easily be extended to include these.

❹ Now for the actual visit to the input control. Giving focus to the input control automatically blurs the previous one. If the previous input control has a validation function, the blur event triggers it.

❺ Now we blur the final element. All the others have been blurred when focus was given to the next one. Then we call the Alerter to show any messages that have been registered.

❻ Finally, we return the validation status of the form. If none of the validations of individual input controls failed, the global valid variable has its initial value, true, and the form is submitted. If some failure occurred, the alerter.valid variable has been set to false, and the form is not submitted.

17.3.4 The form

To make our adventure in client-side validation complete, listing 17.6 is the complete form for simple user registration. Since no dynamic content is needed for client-side validation, this is a plain HTML file, not a PHP file or a template.

Listing 17.6 Using onBlur on each input element

```
<html>
  <head>
    <link rel="STYLESHEET" href="app.css"/>
    <script type="text/javascript" src="validation.js"></script>
  </head>
  <body>
    <div id="content">
```

```
<h1>
  User registration
</h1>
<form method="POST" name="newsForm"
  onSubmit="return visitAll(this)">
  <input type="hidden" name="command" value="submitMessage"/>
  <table width="500">
    <tr>
      <td class="InputLabel">Email address</td>
      <td>
        <input type="text" name="email"
        onBlur="required(this,'Email address')"/>
      </td>
    </tr>
    <tr>
      <td class="InputLabel">Password</td>
      <td>
        <input type="password" name="password"
        onBlur="minLength(this,'Password','6')"/>
      </td>
    </tr>
    <tr>
      <td class="InputLabel">Confirm password</td>
      <td>
        <input type="password" name="confirm"
        onBlur="equalInputs(this,'Passwords','password')"/>
      </td>
    </tr>
  </table>
  <div id="Submit">
    <input type="submit" value="Submit"/>
  </div>
</form>
</div>
</body>
</html>
```

One important feature that is not clear from the example is the fact that we can attach any number of validation functions to a single field. All we need to do is to use several JavaScript statements separated by semicolons.

The arguments to the JavaScript functions are a user-oriented name for the input element (for displaying in the alert box), the object representing the input element (this), and an optional comparison argument that represents string length in one case and the name of another element in another case. The visitAll() function is supplied with an object representing the form.

As mentioned previously, there are certain things we can't do on the client. The kind of validation we've seen can be deliberately bypassed. This is a gaping security hole for any application with public access. Furthermore, client-side validation has no access to server-side data. So let's start improving our server-side validation design.

17.4 OBJECT-ORIENTED SERVER-SIDE VALIDATION

As usual, one of our main considerations is to get the HTML markup out of our PHP code, which means sorting and collecting the similar pieces of the puzzle. What is server-side validation all about? We typically want to validate an HTTP request consisting of several variables stemming from a single form.

If we want to be flexible about how we display error messages, we can keep them in some kind of error message collection; the simplest example of such a collection would be a simple array of message strings. Similarly, we want to collect the validation code in one place and to be able to change the validation data in a single location, such as a configuration file.

Your average framework keeps the validators in some kind of object representing the form we want to validate. A relatively procedural approach for the validation process would be to have an array of arrays representing validation data (field name, validation type, and so on) and to loop through this data, letting the data drive the validation. (The validation data is a kind of metadata: data about data. It defines some of the pre-existing knowledge we have about the data in the HTTP request.) Some publicly available form-handling packages do this. A more readable and object-oriented approach has separate validator objects for each field.

In this section, we'll go deeply into the design of server-side validation. We'll start by discussing a possible, fairly typical design that uses objects to represent rules and validators. Then we'll finish the secure request object architecture we started on in the previous chapter. The request object makes validation for a single field easy, but we still need a class to put everything together, so we'll implement that. We'll continue by introducing the Specification design pattern to make the design more abstract and reusable. After that, we'll discuss how the design we've arrived at expresses our knowledge about validation, and add some finishing touches.

17.4.1 Rules and validators

To get some idea of how object-oriented validation might be done, let's look at one possible design, which is similar to the one used by WACT (http://www.phpwact.org/).

Figure 17.4 is a UML class diagram of this design. The request object contains the data to be validated. A *rule* is an object that is capable of doing a specific validation on a specific field. It has the field name stored inside it, so it knows how to get the value from the data source. What kind of validation it performs depends on what child class of the Rule object we use.

> **NOTE** WACT's Rule objects validate something more abstract known as a *data space*. Here, we'll just call it an HTTP request to make it easier to understand how it works.

The Validator object holds multiple Rule objects, typically representing all the rules necessary to validate all the fields in a single form. When we ask the Validator object to validate a request, it activates each of the Rule objects in turn.

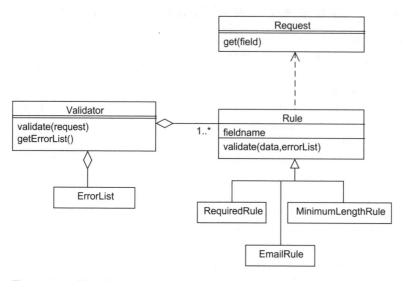

Figure 17.4 Class diagram of a possible object-oriented design for validation

The trickiest part of this is remembering and keeping the error messages that are generated. In JavaScript validation, we can get away with displaying only the first error we detect, since there is not much time lost in validating the form repeatedly. In server-side validation, we don't want to handle the errors one by one, since that would require the user to resubmit the form and wait for the response. Therefore, we want to inform the user about all the errors at once.

If we write procedural code, or if all the validation is handled by a single object, we can just keep an array of errors handy and add to it. But when we delegate the validation tasks to a series of individual validators, collecting the errors becomes a nontrivial challenge. An error list that is available to the Rule object is not automatically available to the Validator object.

We could keep the error list in a global variable, but it's better to avoid using a global object if we can. The design in figure 17.4 solves the problem by keeping an Error-List object inside the Validator and passing it to each Rule in turn. The ErrorList object acts as a *collecting parameter* that grows as the Rule objects adds error messages to it. (In PHP 4, we would have to be careful to pass the ErrorList to the Rule object by reference. In PHP 5, that is no longer necessary.)

But we have one more requirement: we want to be able to get a clean, secure request object as demonstrated in the previous chapter. Let's put the design under the microscope, turn it inside out, and see what else we can do with it.

17.4.2 A secure request object architecture

As hinted in the previous chapter, we want a request object architecture that will prevent us from forgetting to validate some values. We want any unvalidated values to be unavailable to the application. As we saw, one way to do this is to have two different request objects: one raw (insecure) and one filtered or validated (secure).

We want to develop something like the architecture we sketched in the last chapter (see figure 16.1). Let's start with the component objects that we know we'll need.

The raw request object

The RawRequest class can be made very simple, as shown in listing 17.7.

Listing 17.7   A raw request object that is to be used only as raw material for the validation process

```
class RawRequest {
    private $data = array();

    public function __construct($data=FALSE) {          ❶ Construct with
        $this->data = $data                                optional data
                    ? $data
                    : $this->initFromHttp();
        unset($_REQUEST);                       ❷ Destroy the
        unset($_POST);                            superglobals
        unset($_GET);
    }
    private function initFromHttp() {           ❸ POST
        if (!empty($_POST)) return  $_POST;       overrides
        if (!empty($_GET)) return  $_GET;         GET
        return array();
    }
    public  function getForValidation($var) {   ❹ Intended for
        return $this->data[$var];                 validators only
    }
}
```

❶ We construct the object in a way that allows us to pass the source data into the constructor if we want to. In other words, we can construct in either of these ways:

```
$raw = new RawRequest;
$raw = new RawRequest($_POST);
```

❷ After constructing the object, we destroy the superglobal request variables. This may seem brutal, but again, the idea is to prevent nonvalidated input from being used inadvertently.

❸ As in the earlier example, `initFromHttp()` runs if we haven't entered any data into the constructor. This is set up so that `$_POST` overrides `$_GET`.

❹ Finally, there is a getter method—`getForValidation()`—named thus to prevent the RawRequest object from being used inadvertently instead of the clean request object. The clean request object has a plain `get()` method instead, so the chance of confusing the two is minimal. If we do pass the RawRequest object into the application by mistake, trying to use `get()` on it will cause a fatal error that should be hard to ignore. Another way to prevent that would be by using type hints requiring us to use a CleanRequest object.

The clean request object

The CleanRequest (see listing 17.8) class is even simpler than the RawRequest class. We have split the responsibilities that would normally be in a single class, making the resulting classes even simpler and smaller.

Listing 17.8   A CleanRequest class to be used as a container for validated data

```
class CleanRequest {
    private $data = array();

    public function get($var) {
        if (!array_key_exists($var,$this->data)) return '';
        return $this->data[$var];
    }

    public function set($var,$value) {
        $clone = clone $this;
        $clone->data[$var] = $value;
        return $clone;
    }
}
```

There is only one slightly unusual thing here: the `set` method, instead of changing the object it's called on, returns a changed clone. Why? Because a request object is a value object as described in chapter 8. It is an object whose identity is unimportant. But the test of whether an object should be represented as a value object is really its practical use. In the case of this simple CleanRequest object, it is not yet necessary. We want to set all the values in one validation run and be finished with it. It's basically a read-only object when seen from the application. In other words, the application really doesn't care how the `set()` method works.

And yet, if we extend our use of the CleanRequest object a little further, the issue comes up. Imagine that we want to use it to generate link URLs. If there is information in the URL that we want to propagate, that is a relevant possibility.

For example, if we have several paged news lists, we may want the link to the next and previous page to contain the ID for the news list. Something like this,

```
index.php?subject=world&page=3
```

If the `subject` variable is present in the request, we might do something like this to generate the link to the next page:

```
$nextrequest = $request->set('page', $request->get('page') + 1);
```

If we add a simple method to generate a URL query string from the request object, we're practically in business propagating the data:

```
class CleanRequest...
    public function toQueryString() {
        if (count($this->data) == 0) return '';
        $vars = array();
        foreach ($this->data as $var => $val) {
            $vars[] = "$var=$val";
        }
        return "?".join('&',$vars);
    }
}
```

This small example makes it clear why it's reasonable for the request object to be implemented as a Value Object. If we do change the contents of the request as we've just seen, we don't want the change to show up unexpectedly in other parts of the application, so having a changed clone is the better option.

Juggling the two request objects

We want the basic API for validation to be very simple and logical, as in this sketchy example:

```
$validation = new Validation;
$validation->addAlphanumericValidation();
$ok = $validation->validate($request);
```

The problem is how to deal with the results. If we want to have both a RawRequest object and a CleanRequest object, as suggested in the previous chapter, there has to be some logic for copying values from the raw request to the clean request when they've been validated. Also, and this is true even if we don't want two different request classes, we have to keep the error messages somewhere.

Instead of giving the individual validators (*rules* according to figure 17.4) these additional responsibilities in addition to validation, we can wrap the two request objects and the error list in another class that lets the validators get values from the raw request, add errors to the list, and tell it what values have been validated. We'll call this a ValidationCoordinator. A UML class diagram is shown in figure 17.5.

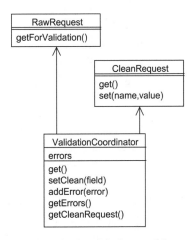

Figure 17.5 A validation coordinator to keep track of validation results while acting as a wrapper for the original RawRequest object

The first three methods, get(), setClean(), and addError(), are intended for use by the validators. getErrors() and getCleanRequest() are for getting information out after the validation process is finished.

Listing 17.9 shows how the coordinator class can be implemented.

Listing 17.9   The validation coordinator

```
class ValidationCoordinator {
    private $raw;
    private $clean;
    private $errors = array();

    public function __construct($raw,$clean) {        ❶ Construct with
        $this->raw = $raw;                               both request
        $this->clean = $clean;                           objects
    }

    public function get($name) {                      ❷ Get value from
        return $this->raw->getForValidation($name);      raw request
    }

    public function setClean($name=FALSE) {           ❸ Copy validated
        if (!$name) return FALSE;                        value to clean
        $this->clean = $this->clean->set(               request
            $name,
            $this->raw->getForValidation($name));
    }

    public function addError($error) {                ❹ Add message
        $this->errors[] = $error;                        on failure
    }

    public function getErrors() {                     ❺ Get the
        return $this->errors;                            results
    }

    public function getCleanRequest() {
        return $this->clean;
    }
}
```

❶ We construct the coordinator object with the two request objects. The clean request is likely to be empty.

❷ The get() method gets a value to be validated from the raw request.

❸ setClean() copies a validated value from the raw request to the clean request. This means that the validator can tell the coordinator that the value is clean, but does not have to know what the coordinator does about it.

If setClean() gets a NULL or FALSE value, it does nothing. This is a simple way to make it possible for some validations to run but not cause the copying to happen. We will use and discuss it later.

❹ When validation fails, the validator can use addError() to add an error message to the error list.

❺ After validation is finished, we need getErrors() and getCleanRequest() to get the results from the coordinator.

It may seem like a lot to have three classes for doing something so relatively simple. But each class is simple and clean, and details can be hidden from view when programming the application.

17.4.3   Now validation is simple

With the coordinator, we've made the job relatively easy for the validator. All the validator has to do is check the value itself and report the results to the coordinator. On success, it uses setClean(); on failure addError(). Listing 17.10 is a specific validator to ensure that a field is alphanumeric. Again, this validator corresponds to a rule in figure 17.4. We are using the term *validator* since the concept of a "rule" will become shakier when we decompose this class in a while.

Listing 17.10   A validator to check whether a field is alphanumeric

```php
class AlphanumericFieldValidator {
    private $fieldname;
    private $message;

    public function __construct($fieldname,$message) {        ❶ The validator
        $this->fieldname = $fieldname;                           needs field and
        $this->message = $message;                              message
    }

    public function validate($coordinator) {                  ❷ The value comes from
        if (ctype_alnum(                                         the coordinator
            $coordinator->get($this->fieldname)))
        {                                                         Call setClean()
            $coordinator->setClean($this->fieldname);        ❸ if OK
            return TRUE;
        } else {
            $coordinator->addError($this->message);          ❹ Add error message
            return FALSE;                                       if not OK
        }
    }
}
```

❶ The validator must know the field to validate and the message to report when validation fails.

❷ We get the value to validate from the coordinator. The actual checking is done by a built-in function that tells us whether the value is alphanumeric.

❸ If the value is alphanumeric, the validator calls `setClean()`, which makes the coordinator copy the value to the clean request object.

❹ If the value is not alphanumeric, the validator adds its error message to the list kept by the coordinator.

There is one problem here, perhaps glaringly obvious: This particular validator is tailored to one specific type of validation, and we want to be able to do all sorts of validations. If we copy the entire class and change the small part that actually checks validity, we have some bothersome duplication.

Let's return to that later. This one example illustrates how the process works, and that's all we need to move on.

By now we could perform validation by creating all the objects involved, in this way:

```
$coordinator = new ValidationCoordinator(
    new RawRequest,
    new CleanRequest
);
$validator = new AlnumFieldValidator(
    'username',
    'The name must consist of letter and numbers only!'
);
if($validator->validate($coordinator)) {
    $clean = $coordinator->getCleanRequest();
    //...
} else {
    $errors = $coordinator->getErrors();
    //...
}
```

But we've validated only a single field, and the code is much more complex than we intended.

Well, we need another class to hide the complexity.

17.4.4 A class to make it simple

We're not comfortable yet; we have too many objects floating around. We still haven't created the class that corresponds to the one called Filtering in the previous chapter (see figure 16.1). This is a case for a simple version of the design pattern known as Facade [Gang of Four]. Its goal is to "provide a unified interface to a set of interfaces in a subsystem."

Let's do that. Figure 17.6 shows how a ValidationFacade class can relate to the others. The facade will act as the visible validation component in the application. The request classes aren't even shown in the diagram, underlining the fact that the facade need not deal with them directly.

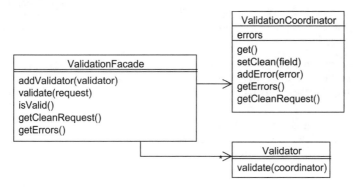

Figure 17.6 ValidationFacade and its neighbors

Validating a coordinator may seem unnaturally abstract, but the idea is that the facade sees the coordinator (after it's been created) as if it were a simple request object that can be validated by passing it to the validator(s).

The code for the ValidationFacade class is given in listing 17.11. We might call it something else; just Validation perhaps. Or we could call it the Validator and call the small validation classes something else. The naming may seem cosmetic, but since it will have a high profile, it's good to have a name that will work well in practical programming. For this example, ValidationFacade may be the name that best expresses how it relates to the rest of the classes, so let's keep it for now.

Listing 17.11 A ValidationFacade class to tie together all the small classes

```
class ValidationFacade {
    private $coordinator;                               ❶ Handle all
    private $validators = array();                        components
    private $hasValidated = FALSE;

    public function addValidator($validator) {         ❷ Add validator to
        $this->validators[] = $validator;                validate value(s)
    }

    public function validate($request) {
        $this->coordinator = $this->createCoordinator(  ❸ Create the
            $request,                                        coordiator
            new CleanRequest);
        foreach ($this->validators as $validator) {     ❹ Run validators
            $validator->validate($this->coordinator);
        }
        $this->hasValidated = TRUE;
        return $this->isValid();
    }                                            Returns TRUE ❺
                                                 if no errors
    public function isValid() {
        if (!$this->hasValidated) return FALSE;
        return count($this->coordinator->getErrors()) == 0;
    }
}
```

```
                                                              ❻  Separate
    public function createCoordinator($raw,$clean) {             creation method
        return new ValidationCoordinator($raw,$clean);           for testing
    }

    public function getCleanRequest() {                       ❼  Get
        if (!$this->isValid()) return FALSE;                     the
        return $this->coordinator->getCleanRequest();           results
    }

    public function getErrors() {
        if ($this->isValid()) return FALSE;
        return $this->coordinator->getErrors();
    }
}
```

❶ The Facade class needs to handle all the components that go into validation. The coordinator is one of them.

Another responsibility of the Facade is to let us run several validators without having to call `validate()` on each manually. We use a simple array to hold the validators. Another possibility is to use a Composite validator.

In addition to all these objects, we also need a simple Boolean flag (TRUE/FALSE) variable keep track of the state of the validation: has validation been performed yet or not? This is mainly to avoid a fatal error if you happen to try to get the clean request object or the error list before validating.

❷ To define what we want to validate, we can add validators. In principle, a validator can validate one or more values, and a single value can be validated by one or more validators.

❸ We start validation by creating the coordinator. We create it here rather than in the constructor because we want to make sure that validation starts with an empty Clean-Request object.

Using a separate creation method to create the coordinator may seem odd. It's actually for the sake of testing. A facade is difficult to test, since we want a simple interface. In that context, creating several objects explicitly is clutter. So we need a way to inject mock objects that doesn't affect the normal interface. This is one way to do that. We can extend the class and override the creation method with a method that creates a mock object. (SimpleTest has a "partial mock" capability to simplify this.)

❹ We run each validator in turn. The coordinator acts as a so-called Collecting Parameter, soaking up error messages and copying values into the CleanRequest object in the process. When validation has finished, we can set the $hasValidated flag to TRUE. Finally we return the validation status so that the `validate()` method can be used as a test in a conditional statement.

❺ To discover the validation status, we start by checking whether validation has been run. If not, we don't really know whether it's OK, and for security purposes, that's not good enough. Therefore, the validation status is still red, and we return FALSE. If validation has been run, the absence of error messages is the criterion for success.

❻ The `createCoordinator()` method is extremely simple. As mentioned, it's only there so that we can override it for testing.

❼ `getCleanRequest()` and `getErrors()` are used to get the results from validation. The clean request is only available on success; the error list is only available on failure. Instead of returning FALSE when one of these is not available, we might want to return an empty CleanRequest object or an empty error array.

The interface for the Facade remains somewhat more complex than we want it, since we have to add the validators as instantiated objects:

```
$validationFacade->add(new AlnumFieldValidator(
    'username',
    'The name must consist of letter and numbers only!'
    )
);
```

Since it's not yet as simple as we want it, we need to add special methods to the facade to handle each type of validation. But to get that exactly right, we must first handle the problem of how to structure the actual validators in a way that's logical and avoids duplication.

17.4.5 Using Specification objects

Evans describes a design pattern called Specification that can be used to do the actual checking. A Specification is an object that checks whether another object satisfies a given criterion. In our context, it may be considered simply wrapping a test in a class:

```
class AlphanumericValueSpecification {
    public function isSatisfiedBy($candidate) {
        return ctype_alnum($candidate);
    }
}
```

That was simple. But is it trivial? Not quite. We want the specification to be a separate object in order to insert it into a validator. That will make the validation criterion pluggable in a validator like the one in listing 17.10.

The interesting thing about a Specification is that it can test any object, in principle. What we really want to do is to check a Request object—or the ValidationCoordinator, which is a stand-in for the Request object in this context.

Listing 17.12 shows how we can do this. The SingleFieldSpecification class is a thin wrapper around the value specification. It just knows what field it's after; the other classes have all the other knowledge.

```
class SingleFieldSpecification {
    private $fieldname;
    private $valueSpecification;

    public function __construct($fieldname,$specification) {
        $this->fieldname = $fieldname;
        $this->valueSpecification = $specification;
    }

    function getValidatedField() {
        return $this->fieldname;
    }

    function isSatisfiedBy($candidate) {
        return $this->valueSpecification->isSatisfiedBy(
            $candidate->get($this->fieldname));
    }
}
```

The $candidate that's being tested is a plain Request object or a stand-in for a Request object, such as the ValidationCoordinator object. The coordinator delivers values by means of a get() method. If we want it more abstract, we can use a more generic name for an interface that has methods such as get() and set():

```
interface Keyed {
    public function get($key);
    public function set($key,$value);
}

class ValidationCoordinator implements Keyed...

class SingleKeySpecification...
    function isSatisfiedBy(Keyed $candidate) {
        return $this->valueSpecification->isSatisfiedBy(
            $candidate->get($this->fieldname));
    }
}
```

But why one class just to check the validity of the request/coordinator? Why not let the validator do this along with the task of reporting the results back?

The advantage of this approach is that it keeps the validator blissfully ignorant of what kinds of tests are performed on the request/coordinator object.

That makes it easy to add tests on multiple values. Sometimes validation concerns the relationship between different values, as when we want to check that a password and a confirm password field have been filled in with identical values.

Listing 17.13 is a class that can be used in place of the SingleFieldSpecification in listing 17.12.

```php
class EqualFieldsSpecification {
    private $field1;
    private $field2;

    public function __construct($field1,$field2) {
        $this->field1 = $field1;
        $this->field2 = $field2;
    }

    public function isSatisfiedBy($candidate) {
        return $candidate ->get($this->field1)
            == $candidate ->get($this->field2);
    }

    public function getFieldname() {
        return FALSE;
    }
}
```

The slightly mysterious thing in listing 17.13 is getFieldName(). Returning FALSE is simply a signal that we don't want this particular validation to cause the values to be accepted as clean. If we used it for checking password confirmation, the password must be subjected to additional individual validation before we let it pass.

Now we can implement a single validator class (see listing 17.14) that can be responsible for any kind of validation, since the actual validity checking is farmed out to a Specification object.

```php
class BasicValidator {
    private $specification;
    private $message;

    public function __construct($specification,$message) {
        $this->specification = $specification;
        $this->message = $message;
    }
    public function validate($request) {
        if ($this->specification->isSatisfiedBy($coordinator)) {
            $coordinator->setClean(
                $this->specification->getValidatedField());
            return TRUE;
        }
        else {
```

❶ The validator knows what to check

❷ Report OK field to coordinator

```
            $coordinator->addError($this->message);        | ❸ Report
            return FALSE;                                   |    error to
        }                                                   |    coordinator
    }
}
```

❶ The responsibility of the validator itself is to talk back; to report to the coordinator what's OK and what isn't. In the constructor, we supply it with an error message that it can use for that purpose. It also needs the Specification object that encapsulates the nature of the check being performed.

❷ If the Specification object is satisfied, the validator uses `setClean()` to report that fact to the coordinator. The coordinator then copies the value to the CleanRequest object.

Returning TRUE is not strictly necessary in the context, but it's logical.

❸ If the Specification object is not satisfied, the validator adds the error message to the coordinator's error list.

Figure 17.7 is a class diagram of this design. The interfaces have not been made explicit in the code we've seen, but they are implied. It illustrates how the design implements the dependency-inversion principle ("depend on abstractions" in its simplified form), or the related idea of programming to an interface, not an implementation.

But abstractions are not just a way of achieving flexibility. They can also express conceptual knowledge.

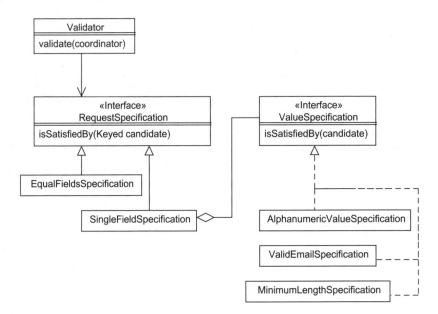

Figure 17.7   Validation using Specification objects

17.4.6 Knowledge-rich design

We've developed a working, fine-grained implementation of validation. It cleanly separates the general (single-value specifications) from more specialized classes (validation in this specific architecture). The single-value specifications—unlike the validation facade—can be reused in any number of contexts.

On the other hand, what good is our ability to reuse these classes? The specifications—the ones we've seen, anyway—are so simple that you might argue that it's just as well to reimplement them.

That's true. On the other hand, we have separated the responsibilities. And beyond making it easier to make localized changes, it's logical. It's easy to understand once you've understood the concepts. We now have what Evans calls a *knowledge-rich design*. We have named and distilled the concepts. We have made clear the conceptual difference between using a criterion (a Specification) on a single value and using it on a request object. We can see that keeping track of errors is a fundamentally different task than finding out whether a criterion is met.

There is still something missing. The object model still doesn't reflect the fact that we sometimes—but not always—want validation on a value to lead us to accept it as properly validated and therefore clean. This difference is hidden in the code, represented by the second line in this excerpt from listing 17.9,

```
public function setClean($name=FALSE) {
    if (!$name) return FALSE;
}
```

and this degenerate method in the EqualFieldsSpecification class:

```
public function getfieldname() {
    return false;
}
```

It's simple, but its meaning is not immediately clear. The code isn't telling that story. The alternative would probably involve at least one extra class. It would be more complex, but at the same time it would move this particular issue to the foreground and make it visible on reading the code.

17.4.7 Adding validations to the facade

Our finishing touch is making it easier to set up validation in the application. This is all the more pressing since the complexity of the design makes construction more complex.

```
class ValidationFacade...
    public function addAlnumValidation($fieldname,$message) {
        $this->addValidator(
            new BasicValidator(
                new SingleFieldSpecification(
                    $fieldname,
                    new AlnumValueSpecification
```

```
        ),
        $message
      )
    );
  }
}
```

It should be clear from the example why we're doing this. The complexity of building the object in the constructor gives us flexibility, but is also far too elaborate for everyday application programming. Now we can do it as simply as this:

```
$facade->addAlnumValidation(
    'username',
    'The name must consist of letters and numbers only!'
    )
);
```

To simplify further, we should probably make the error message optional and let the validator generate it. But let's have some fun instead. Let's give this method a fluent interface:

```
$facade->addAlnumValidation()
    ->forField('username')
    ->withMessage(
        'The name must consist of letters and numbers only!');
```

To accomplish this, we need to do something similar to what we did in the Composite example in chapter 7.

Studying the example piece by piece, what does the first method call have to return? It has to return either the validator or the SingleFieldSpecification object. We choose the validator because it is highest on the food chain. We return it first from the addValidator() method and then from addAlnumValidation(). We also need to make the arguments to addAlnumValidation() optional or remove them altogether:

```
class ValidationFacade...
    public function addValidator($validator) {
        return $this->validators[] = $validator;
    }

    //...

    public function addAlnumValidation($fieldname='',$message='')
    {
        return $this->addValidator(
            new BasicValidator(
                new SingleFieldSpecification(
                    $fieldname,
                    new AlnumValueSpecification
                ),
                $message
            )
        );
    }
}
```

Now that we have the validator object available, all we need to do is implement `withMessage()` and `forField()` as setter methods in the validator and Specification classes:

```
class BasicValidator...
    public function withMessage($message) {
        $this->message = $message;
        return $this;
    }

    public function forField($fieldname) {
        $this->specification->forField($fieldname);
        return $this;
    }
}

class SingleFieldSpecification...
    function forField($fieldname) {
        $this->fieldname = $fieldname;
    }
}
```

Now that we've covered both client-side and server-side validation, it's time to discuss how to synchronize the two.

17.5 SYNCHRONIZING SERVER-SIDE AND CLIENT-SIDE VALIDATION

We've been discussing server-side and client-side validation separately. That's fine if we can make do with one of them, but if we want both, we're looking at the prospect of defining each validation twice in different ways. There are ways to solve that problem, but some of them involve reintroducing some of the limitations we've been discussing.

A complete solution to all these problems is beyond the scope of this book. But the least we can do is outline some possible ways to synchronize server-side and client-side validation. We'll start with the most common solution in PHP applications, generating the HTML form code piecemeal from field and validation data. Then we'll look into generating both types of validation code from a separate configuration file. Finally, we'll consider a possibility that is experimental, but interesting: starting with the client-side validation and generating the server-side validation definitions from that.

17.5.1 Form generator

The most common strategy in PHP is to generate all the HTML from data in the PHP code with no template handling whatsoever. Form-handling packages such as HTML_Quickform do this: they generate all the HTML code piecemeal from a form object containing form element objects and validation data. Figure 17.8 shows how this works in principle.

This approach is convenient and supported by easily available open-source software. It is possibly the easiest way to create forms in a PHP web application. Something like the following sets everything up and displays a form:

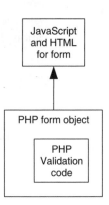

```
$form = new HTML_QuickForm('postMessage');
$form->addElement('text', 'headline', 'Headline:');
$form->addElement('textarea', 'text', 'Text:');
$form->addElement('submit');
$form->addRule('headline', 'Please enter a headline',
    'required', null, 'client');
$form->display();
```

Figure 17.8 The form-generator approach to synchronized validation

Then we can rerun the same code when processing the form submission.

But, even if this is an extremely easy way to *create* it, it will not necessarily make maintenance easy. As always, the web designer's work requires us to use a template instead.

17.5.2 Configuration file

Another approach, one that's common in frameworks, is to generate both server-side and client-side validation from a configuration file (see figure 17.9).

The configuration file is typically XML. From that we can generate server-side validation objects and JavaScript. The JavaScript is typically of the ordinary, boring variety, but it would be even easier to generate the kind of validation function calls per field shown earlier in this chapter.

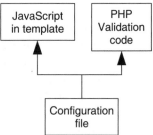

Figure 17.9 Synchronizing validation from a configuration file

17.5.3 Generating server-side validation from client-side validation

A configuration file may contain exactly the information we need to perform validation. But so does the template if it contains JavaScript validation code. That means it can be used in place of the configuration file—theoretically, that is. Of course, if that code is in the form of a manually-hacked script, it will be almost impossible to extract the validation information from it. But if it's systematic enough, it is possible to use the JavaScript in the template as the source of information for server-side validation, as shown in figure 17.10.

This works if the validation information in the template is structured for easy retrieval, as in listing 17.6. This input element is an example:

```
<input type="text" name="email"
  onBlur="required(this,'Email address')"/>
```

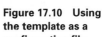

Figure 17.10 Using the template as a configuration file

There is nothing to prevent us from using PHP and its XML handling, including XPath, to read the function name and the field name to be used for server-side validation. Listing 17.15 is a simplistic procedural example.

Listing 17.15 Getting form elements from a template using XPath

```
$formName = 'registration-form';                     ❶ SimpleXML
$sxml = simplexml_load_file('regform.html');  ◁        representation of form
$elements = $sxml->xpath(
    "//form[@name='".$formName."']".                      ❷ Filter using
    "//*[name()='input' or name()='textarea'][@onBlur]");    XPath
foreach($elements as $element) {           ❸ Get
    print $element['name']."\n";              attributes
    print $element['onBlur']."\n";
}
```

❶ We start by generating a SimpleXML object from the file containing the form.

❷ To locate the elements we need in the template file, we run an XPath query. The query locates the `<form>` element that has an `id` attribute corresponding to the given form name. Within the form, it finds all `<input>` or `<textarea>` elements that have an `onBlur` attribute.

We've used the double slash twice in the XPath expression. The effect is that the query finds the `<form>` element wherever it might be located; there are no restrictions on what or how many levels of markup may exist before and after the form. Similarly, the `<input>` and `<textarea>` elements may be located anywhere inside the form. This is extremely convenient, but it's not considered efficient. This shows that there may be some real-world challenges to overcome before using this approach in practice.

❸ We now have the input elements represented by an array of SimpleXML objects. Now we can get the attributes of these elements, including the JavaScript validation functions. They're available as if they were elements of an associative array.

17.6 SUMMARY

Input validation and form handling may not be glamorous, but they are complex and challenging enough to be interesting. Security and usability are the two high-level requirements. We want to meet both of these in a client-server environment using two distinct programming languages. This creates a level of complexity that makes the ultimate solution hard to find. Still, there are some helpful strategies. Client-side validation can be done in the normal fashion or using a more unorthodox approach, validating each field individually. Server-side validation can be done cleanly with object-oriented techniques. Combining and synchronizing both is hard, but there are several ways to do it.

It's possible to create a request object architecture that is both convenient to use and ensures that we don't forget to validate anything. The internal implementation of this architecture, though, is rather complex.

Validation is primarily needed for handling form input. It is perhaps the most complex aspect of form handing. In the next chapter, we'll begin to see how more complete form handling can be achieved.

C H A P T E R   1 8

Form handling

There was a system administrator at a university once who claimed that his job would be perfect if it weren't for those pesky students. Except, obviously, the job wouldn't exist if there were no students.

That's what the real world is like. There are users, and they have to enter their personal data and all sorts of other information. Form handling is complex and tricky, but there's no use in complaining about it.

Well, we could try blaming the HTTP protocol. From the point of view of a web programmer, the default behavior of an HTML form is inconvenient. The user enters some text into a form, clicks the submit button, and frequently returns to the same form. Ninety-nine percent of the time, the user wants the data in the form to stay there, but it doesn't unless we program it to do so.

Making it simple and intuitive takes work. So much work that it's hard to do the subject justice in one chapter.

Every self-respecting web development framework has a form class. On the other hand, if we're trying to solve practical problems rather than develop a self-respecting web development framework, our priorities will be different. We want to keep it as simple as possible, at least in the beginning. We want to avoid trying to satisfy requirements that may seem logical if everyone were to use the software, but are not actually needed for a basic implementation.

In this chapter, we'll first go over the requirements and design for form handling, using the PEAR package HTML_QuickForm to make the amount of work manageable. Then we'll implement the solution, using wrappers for input elements and for the form itself.

18.1 DESIGNING A SOLUTION USING HTML_QUICKFORM

The PEAR package HTML_QuickForm is one of many available packages that make form handling easier. It's easily available and has the features we need. Above all, it has a relatively complete set of validation capabilities for normal use. They're not all implemented as flexibly as we might want them, but let's see how far we can go with it. It will be an interesting learning experience.

In this section, we'll first take an overall view of the need to keep requirements and design simple. Then we'll discuss how to integrate the results from our PHP code into the HTML form. We'll study the conceptual aspects of form handling to come up with some meaningful abstractions. With those in hand, we'll be ready to make the requirements more specific. Finally, we'll look at one particular stumbling block: the difficulty of setting the value of a `<select>` menu.

18.1.1 Minimalistic requirements and design

As mentioned earlier, frameworks typically have one or more separate classes representing a form. When handling forms, validation is by far the most complex task. The rest, relatively speaking, is a piece of cake. In fact, we might ask whether we need a separate form class at all. Validator objects, one for each field, should suffice.

Still, there are a couple of reasons to have a form class. One is to have a single place to access everything we need for form handling. The other reason is that when we populate the form with the values that were entered previously, it makes sense to use the one object to represent all the information about a field.

We want to take the drudgery out of form handling—to make it more convenient when there are real productivity gains to be had from that convenience.

- *Template handling.* For the reasons discussed in chapter 13, we want to separate program code from HTML markup. We want web designers to do their work in an environment that's as close to pure HTML as possible. This requires some kind of template handling.

- *Validation.* Obviously, we want to be able to validate the form contents, preferably both server-side and client-side.

- *Populating the contents of the form.* We could live without a system that automatically updates the values in the form for redisplay—setting the values manually is nowhere near as much work as validation—but populating the form with values will save us a bit of time and eliminate a bit of duplication.

- *Feature-revealing code.* To make the code as readable as possible, let's try to avoid making it *too* convenient. Hiding as much of the mechanics of the process as possible is tempting, but the code will be more self-documenting if important steps in the process are explicit—validating the form, populating it, and passing values into the template.

- *Testable.* A by-product of making the code more explicit is making it testable. We want to be able to replace important objects with mock objects. Typically, this involves passing them into a constructor or other method.

18.1.2 Putting generated elements into the HTML form

Perhaps the greatest challenge of all in form handling is getting the form contents and the HTML markup to work together as a team. This is, of course, the same challenge as in other dynamic web pages, but a typical form has a particularly high density of individual values to be inserted, especially if there is client-side validation. Also, the form speaks to a mixed audience, since some of it is intended for the human user and some is not. We'll see what we can do using the simplest possible strategy, and consider whether we need the HTML_QuickForm Renderer class.

Manual template building

The simplest way to insert elements of the form object into the template is the direct route. That means something like this, using PHPTAL syntax:

```
<span tal:content="form/elements/headline/getLabel">
  Headline (this is sample text that PHPTAL removes)
</span>
<input type="text"
  name="${form/elements/headline/getName}"
  value="${form/elements/headline/getValue}" />
```

We can avoid making the paths this long if we want; the example is just intended to illustrate the principle.

Having a template, getting the values from the form object, and inserting them into the template is the basic way to do it. The alternative is passing the form object to the template.

Do we need the renderer?

Given the popularity of HTML_QuickForm, it's not surprising that we're not the only ones who have wanted to use it with a template engine. The developers of HTML_QuickForm have responded rather appropriately by letting a separate Renderer object do the job of generating the HTML for the form. That means we can produce something else by using a different Renderer. There are already other Renderers, including one that is specialized for Smarty.

So if we want some other template engine, one thing we could do is to make our own Renderer. But is it necessary? The Renderer is an abstraction that comes out of a more complex and ambitious design than we're after right now—one that's capable of generating the full HTML code for a form. We can achieve the same thing more simply by calling the components of the form object directly in the template, as shown earlier.

We may or may not want to include the label in the form object. When the approach is this simple, it's easy to make the label a fixed string in the template if we want the template designer to be able to change it.

18.1.3 Finding abstractions

As mentioned earlier, we can get more mileage out of our code by identifying some appropriate abstractions. When dealing with forms, it's easy to make the abstractions too dependent on the technical implementation in HTML. A better way to define the abstractions is by starting out with how different input controls work. That will help decide what we need to do with them in code. And since these are user interface elements, "how they work" is mostly synonymous with what the user is able to do with them. This does not map exactly to the HTML implementation. A plain `<select>` drop-down menu does the same thing for the user as a set of radio buttons: it allows him or her to select one out of a fixed set of alternatives, as shown in figure 18.1.[1]

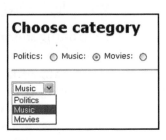

Figure 18.1   A plain drop-down menu is functionally equivalent to a set of radio buttons

A `<select multiple>` box does the same thing as a set of check boxes, allowing the user to choose more than one item (see figure 18.2).

Table 18.1 summarizes these two abstractions and text input as well.

Now that we have the abstractions and the basic guidelines, we're ready to get more specific about what we need and don't.

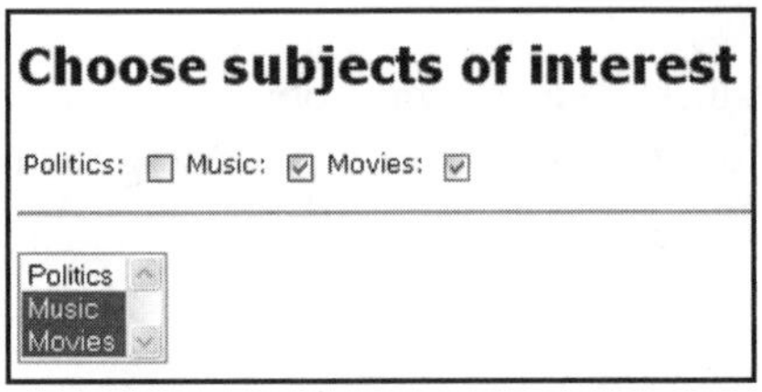

**Figure 18.2
A multi-select box is functionally equivalent to a set of checkboxes**

---

[1] The W3C XForms recommendation recognizes this similarity.

Table 18.1   An abstract, user-oriented way of looking at form input controls

User task	Examples	HTML implementation
Text input	Single-line text input field Multi-line text area	`<input type="text"...>` `<textarea>`
Select one option from a fixed list of alternatives	Drop-down menu Set of radio buttons	`<select>` repeated `<input type="radio"..>`
Select one or more options from a fixed list of alternatives	Multi-select box Set of check boxes	`<select multiple="multiple">` repeated `<input type="checkbox"...>`

18.1.4   More specific requirements

Since we're using an existing package, we want to use the parts of it that we need, and only those. There are some features we don't need and some we do need.

We don't need this

If we use HTML_QuickForm in the default way—generating all the HTML piece by piece from the form element objects—we have to add all form controls to the form. With a template approach, this is not necessary. Even though generating everything may seem convenient, there are some things that become easier and more straightforward when we use templates. All the elements that are not actually used to input values can just be written as HTML in the template. This includes buttons, images, "hidden inputs,"[2] and anything else we need except text and selection input controls. In fact, if we were to decide to populate the form manually with values from the HTTP request, we would only need to represent the ones that have to be validated.

We will have support for text inputs, select menus, and radio buttons. We won't deal with multi-select controls. This leaves our form handling incomplete, but even moderately complex web applications sometimes don't have multi-select controls, and our simple approach doesn't burn any bridges or close any doors. We can always do it the old-fashioned way if we need to.

We do need this

If we want to support only the most basic elements of a form, the element objects we will need are the following:

- *A text input object.* We don't need to distinguish between single-line text input controls and text areas at all in our PHP code, although we will, of course, do so in the HTML markup. Both can be validated in the same way and have their values set in the same way.

- *A select menu object.*

---

[2] Again, thinking abstractly, it's not really an input control even though it's represented as one (`<input type="hidden"...>`) in HTML.

- *A radio button group object.* This should work as similarly to the select menu object as possible. Usability considerations should dictate the choice between radio buttons and a menu. To the PHP application, they will look the same.

Although we don't want to generate all HTML code piecemeal, there is something to be said for generating some elements. For example, a `<select>` element with a dynamic number of options doesn't resemble pure HTML much in a template, whatever we do with it.

18.1.5 The select problem

It would be easier if we had a way to set the <select> element's value similar to the value attributes of the <input> element. There is no value attribute on a <select> element, so we can't do this:[3]

```
<select value="Warm">
  <option>Cold</option>
  <option>Warm</option>
  <option>Hot</option>
</select>
```

Except, actually we *can* do it, or something similar.

One way is to use some extra JavaScript. But is it really worth the possible complications of using JavaScript just to make the template more readable?

Another is to post-process the template, replacing the previous example with this:

```
<select>
  <option>Cold</option>
  <option selected="selected">Warm</option>
  <option>Hot</option>
</select>
```

But post-processing is also extra work and complexity, and we are trying hard to keep it simple. So we're back to adding a conditional `selected` attribute to each and every menu `<option>` element.

The alternative is to generate the entire select element. It's not a major liability. The only thing the template designer loses is the ability to style the individual select element differently from the others. And generating the element is not hard to do; in fact, we can use the existing capability in HTML_QuickForm.

Let's have both options: generate the entire element or just variables so all the HTML code can be in the template.

Now it turns out that we need the Renderer after all, to generate HTML for the single elements. Listing 18.1 shows how this works.

---

[3] The XForms recommendation solves the problem by keeping all the existing values—for all form controls—in a separate *model* section instead of having value attributes on the controls themselves.

Listing 18.1   Using a QuickForm Renderer for a single element

```
require_once 'HTML/QuickForm.php';
require_once 'HTML/QuickForm/Renderer/Default.php';
require_once 'HTML/QuickForm/text.php';
$element = new HTML_QuickForm_text('headline');
$renderer = new HTML_QuickForm_Renderer_Default;
$renderer->setElementTemplate("{element}");
$element->accept($renderer);
print $renderer->toHtml();
```

All of the files—the main QuickForm file, Renderer, and text input element—have to be included separately.

QuickForm elements can be created and used independently of an actual form. That is what we do in this example. We use the default Renderer; the one that generates HTML. When we use the form object itself, we don't need to think about the Renderer, since the form object will create it for us to generate HTML. But with an element, we have to create the Renderer.

By default, the Renderer generates HTML table row and cell tags around the element. We want to prevent that, since we want to mix the element freely with other HTML markup. Fortunately, HTML_QuickForm has the ability to set a template for a single element. For our purposes, we reduce the template to just the element itself.

The element object receives the Renderer in the `accept()` method and makes the Renderer do the job of generating HTML. Finally, we get the generated HTML code from the Renderer.

Now that we know in a general sense what we need to implement, let's see how we can do it.

18.2   IMPLEMENTING THE SOLUTION

We are using an existing library package to implement something similar on top of it. This will typically involve design patterns like Decorator, Adapter, Facade, and the various factory patterns. These patterns are noninvasive: they can be used to provide the interface and behavior we want without altering the underlying libraries.

In this section, we'll start by designing a general way to wrap the HTML_QuickForm input elements. Then we'll study how the various input controls can be implemented in this way. These elements have to be created, so we'll look into that next. Validation also needs to be taken care of, and we need to know how to use the form object when defining a form in a template. Since there is not enough space to make everything complete, we end the chapter by discussing some ideas on further development.

18.2.1 Wrapping the HTML_QuickForm elements

We want the form element objects to have the features we need from HTML_QuickForm and yet be easy to use in a template. That means we have to both use some methods from the QuickForm element and add some methods of our own. That's a job for one of those undignified Decorators that cannot be redecorated because they change the interface too much. Figure 18.3 shows the structure we're looking for. We have to be able to set and get the value of the element, but the implementation will vary depending on the type of element. We also want to be able to get the name of the element and to generate complete HTML in case we need it. And we will use the QuickForm default renderer even though it might seem like overkill for just a single element.

Listing 18.2 shows the code for the abstract input control. The `asHtml()` method is basically the same code as in listing 18.1.

> **Listing 18.2** The input control parent class acts as a Decorator for the HTML_QuickForm element and also uses a default Renderer to generate HTML for the element

```
abstract class AbstractInputControl {
    protected $quickFormElement;

    abstract public function setValue($value);
    abstract public function getValue();

    public function asHtml() {
        $renderer = new HTML_QuickForm_Renderer_Default;
        $renderer->setElementTemplate("{element}");
        $this->quickFormElement->accept($renderer);
        return $renderer->toHtml();
    }
    public function getName() {
        return $this->quickFormElement->getName();
    }
}
```

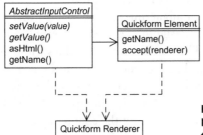

Figure 18.3
How our input control wraps the Quickfom element

We want to be able to get both the value and the name of the element. The get-Name() method is the same for all element types, but getValue() needs to be in the child classes, since there are minor differences in how they work.

18.2.2 Input controls

The input controls are different in principle; this fact is what our abstractions express. This means that they have to be handled differently. Text input elements (text areas and text input boxes) are relatively simple, but need validation. Select menus come in two flavors: single and multiple selection. Radio buttons are especially difficult, since HTML_QuickForm has no explicit support for such features as setting the value of a radio button group.

Text input elements

Text input fields need validation. So do select fields, but not in quite the same way. (Menus and the like cannot be filled in incorrectly by the user, but this can be bypassed by sending an HTTP request by some other means than the form that's intended for it. But to simplify our job for now, we'll assume that we're doing validation for usability only, which means that text input elements are the only ones on our radar screen.) We must be able to specify the validation type and the message to be displayed if validation fails. We'll look at how to make HTML_QuickForm do the actual validation later; for now, we'll do the basic part, using the QuickForm object as a data container whose values can be accessed in a template.

Listing 18.3 is a TextInput class that does this somewhat basic job.

> **Listing 18.3   A TextInput class that contains an HTML_QuickForm_text object**

```
class TextInput extends AbstractInputControl
{
    protected $quickFormElement;        ①  The element we're decorating
    private $validation;            ②  Validation type and
    private $message;                   message

    public function __construct(
        $quickFormElement,$validation,$message) {      ③  Pass everything
        $this->validation = $validation;                   in the
        $this->message = $message;                         constructor
        $this->quickFormElement = $quickFormElement;
    }

    public function setValue($value) {            ④  Simple
        $this->quickFormElement->setValue($value);       delegation
    }

    public function getValue() {
        return $this->quickFormElement->getValue();
    }
```

```
public function getLabel() {
    return $this->quickFormElement->getLabel();
}

}
```

④ Simple delegation

① `$quickFormElement` is the element we're decorating. It contains the name, label, value, and potentially other information, but no validation information thus far.

② `$validation` is the validation type; `$message` is the message to display if validation fails.

③ All the member variables are set by passing them as arguments to the constructor. One of these arguments is the QuickForm element object. As we've seen in several cases before, this is a way to create flexibility. We can configure the QuickForm element object before inserting it into our own object.

④ `setValue()`, `getValue()`, and `getLabel()` just call the decorated Quick-Form element object in the simplest possible way.

Select menus

Since it has no validation to do, the select menu class is even simpler than the text input class. But just to make the design clearer, let's have an abstract class to represent the similarity between a select menu and a radio button group. We'll call it Select-One. That gets us the class design shown in figure 18.4.

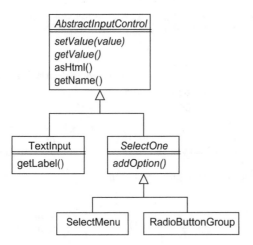

**Figure 18.4
The inheritance hierarchy for the elements illustrates abstract similarities and differences**

The abstract class is simple:

```
abstract class SelectOne extends AbstractInputControl
{
    protected $quickFormElement;
```

```
    public function __construct($quickFormElement) {
        $this->quickFormElement = $quickFormElement;
    }

    abstract public function addOption($text,$value);
}
```

The SelectMenu class (see listing 18.4) is not much larger, mainly because the HTML_QuickForm_select object does so much of the job for us.

```
class SelectMenu extends SelectOne{
    protected $quickFormElement;
    public function addOption($text,$value) {               ❶ Adding
                                                              options is
        $this->quickFormElement->addOption($text,$value);     easy
    }

    public function setValue($value) {
        $this->quickFormElement->setValue($value);
    }

    public function getValue() {                            ❷ Single select
        $values = $this->quickFormElement->getValue();        returns
        return $values[0];                                    single value
    }
}
```

❶ A select menu is more complex than a text input field in one respect: we need to add options. But since the QuickForm has this feature already, it's not hard to implement.

❷ getValue() in the QuickForm element is based on a different concept than ours. QuickForm sees all <select> elements—single-input and multi-input—as two different variations on the same object. We are taking a different and more user-oriented perspective: A single-select and a multi-select are different, while the single-select is basically the same as a group of radio buttons.

Because of this mismatch, we won't use the getValue() of the QuickForm element directly. It returns an array of selected values. Since our class represents an element that can have only one value, it's natural to return only the first element in this array.

Radio buttons

Representing a group of radio buttons is somewhat more complex, because there is no direct support for it in HTML_QuickForm. There is a class representing a group of elements and one representing a radio button. But there is no implementation of the actual workings of a group of radio buttons. Therefore, we need some more code in this case (see listing 18.5).

Listing 18.5 A RadioButtonGroup class

```
class RadioButtonGroup extends SelectOne
{
    private $value;                              ❶ Keep value and
    private $options = array();                    options separately

    protected $quickFormElement;

    public function addOption($text,$value) {
        $elements = $this->quickFormElement->getElements();   ❷ Add by
        $element = new HTML_QuickForm_radio(                     replacing
            NULL,$text,NULL,$value);                            all
        $elements[] = $element;
        $this->quickFormElement->setElements($elements);
        $this->options[$value] = $element;
    }

    public function setValue($value) {
        $this->value = $value;                               ❸ Set
        if (!array_key_exists($value,$this->options)) return;   value
        $this->options[$value]->setChecked(TRUE);              in
    }                                                          both
                                                               places
    public function getValue() {
        return $this->value;
    }

    public function options() {
        return $this->options;
    }
}
```

❶ Since HTML_QuickForm does not have a representation of how radio buttons work, we need to handle more of it ourselves. To make this possible, we keep both the value and the button objects themselves in instance variables.

❷ For some reason, there is no way to add an element to a QuickForm group. Instead, we have to get all the elements as an array, add a new one to the array, and put the whole array back.

❸ To set the value of a radio button group, we set the checked property of the radio button representing that value. We also store the value separately to make it easy to retrieve.

setValue() for the QuickForm group does something different, which is not what we need here.

18.2.3 Which class creates the form controls?

We haven't started on the form class yet. Doing the form class requires us to think about how to create the form elements. It might seem simple to do something similar to what HTML_QuickForm does:

```
$form->addElement('text', 'headline', 'Headline:');
```

HTML_QuickForm gets this to work even for elements such as `<select>`, the menu options being given as an array of data.

But let's start first with a way to add element objects to a form. We can add the other, convenient method later if we want to. So this is what we're going for:

```
$form->add($element);
```

Where does `$element` come from? Since we're using decorators, construction becomes complex, with nested constructor calls. This makes it too cumbersome to use the constructors in client code. We need some creation methods. They could be in a separate factory class, but let's keep them in a form class for the time being:

```
class Form {
    public function createTextinput(
        $name,$validation,$message,$label='')
    {
        return new TextInput(
            new HTML_QuickForm_text(
                $name,$label),$validation,$message);
    }

    public function createSelect($name) {
        return new SelectMenu(
            new HTML_QuickForm_select($name));
    }
    public function createRadioButtons($name) {
        return new RadioButtonGroup(
            new HTML_QuickForm_group($name));
    }
}
```

The select and radio button groups are created without options, so we'll have to add the options manually in the client code:

```
$radiogroup = $form->createRadioButtons('time');
$radiogroup->addOption('Morning','morning');
$radiogroup->addOption('Now','now');
$form->add($radiogroup);
```

We're using the HTML_QuickForm object the same way we did with the elements. And the method to add the element to the form is simple:

```
class Form {
    public function __construct() {
        $this->quickForm = new HTML_QuickForm;
    }
```

```
public function add($control) {
    $this->quickForm->addElement($control->getQuickFormElement());
    $this->elements[$control->getName()] = $control;
}
}
```

The QuickForm object gets its QuickForm element, and we're adding it to our own array, too. This allows us to get the best of both worlds: we can let QuickForm take care of validation, while we have control of the element objects we will use in the template.

18.2.4 Validation

But oops, we forgot to add the code to use the validation feature of the QuickForm object. The way to do that in HTML_QuickForm is with a method called add-Rule(). But since we're only doing it for text elements, we need to do an if test to find out what kind of element it is, right?

```
if ($element instanceof textInput)
    $this->getQuickForm->addRule(...)
```

But doing if tests on the types of objects is not recommended by the gurus. It violates the Liskov substitution principle and the open-closed principle. In plainer terms, the problem is that every time we add another element type, we need to change the conditional statement in the Form class. If we keep the behavior in the element instead, a new element type can handle this by itself with no need to modify the Form class. The way to achieve that is to pass the form object to the element object and let it do the following:

```
class TextField {
    public function addQuickFormRuleToForm($form) {
        if (!$this->validation) return;
        $form->getQuickForm()->addRule(
            $this->getName(),
            $this->message,
            $this->validation,
            null,
            'client'
        );
    }
}
```

Now we can call the method while adding the element to the form:

```
class Form {
    public function add($control) {
        $this->quickForm->addElement($control->getQuickFormElement());
        $this->elements[$control->getName()] = $control;
        $control->addQuickFormRuleToForm($this);
    }
}
```

That's all we need to use HTML_QuickForm's validation capabilities. We've set up everything HTML_QuickForm needs, and now all we need to do is call it:

```
class Form {
    public function getValidationScript() {
        return $this->quickForm->getValidationScript();
    }

    public function validate() {
        return $this->quickForm->validate();
    }
}
```

It's a weakness of the HTML_QuickForm package that it does not let us specify explicitly what we want to validate. Replacing it with the object-oriented validation code we developed earlier in this chapter is one way to remedy that weakness. Another is to do further manipulation to make the HTML_QuickForm object do our bidding. It's not easy, though.

We could try manipulating the inside of the HTML_QuickForm object to set the values we want to validate, but there is a high risk that in new versions of HTML_QuickForm, they would be represented differently, and that might break our code. The alternative is setting the $_POST variable and re-creating the QuickForm object, but it's odd. It's not quite like the tail wagging the dog; it's more like putting a new tail on the dog with a remote control so that we'll be able to wag it ourselves.

This illustrates the problems of using a package that has components baked into it in a way that makes them hard to separate. We do get something for free, but beyond a certain point, there are diminishing returns: trying to make it bend over backward to serve our needs becomes less and less productive.

Figure 18.5 summarizes the Form object and its related objects. As mentioned, the QuickForm elements are used both directly and indirectly, by way of the QuickForm object.

18.2.5   Using the form object in a template

Now all we need in order to be able to use the Form object to fill in a template is a simple accessor to get the elements we stashed away in an array outside the HTML_QuickForm object:

```
class Form {
    public function getElements() {
        return $this->elements;
    }
}
```

That is all we need to plug the data into a template. Listing 18.6 shows how.

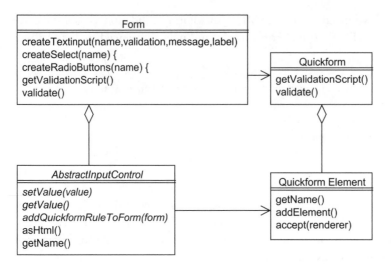

Figure 18.5   The form object and its related components

Listing 18.6   Plugging form data into a PHPTAL template

```html
<html>
  <head>
    <div tal:replace="structure form/getValidationScript" />
  </head>

  <body>
    <span tal:define="draft elements/status/options/draft"/>
    <span tal:define="published
      elements/status/options/published"/>
    <form method="post" onsubmit="return validate_(this);">

<table>
        <tr>
          <td tal:content="elements/headline/getLabel">
              Headline (this is sample text that PHPTAL removes)
          </td>
          <td>
            <input type="text"
              name="${elements/headline/getName}"
              value="${elements/headline/getValue}" />
          </td>
        </tr>
        <tr>
          <td tal:content="elements/category/getLabel">
              Category (this is sample text that PHPTAL removes)
          </td>
          <td tal:content="structure elements/category/asHtml">
            <select>
            </select>
          </td>
        </tr>
```

JavaScript generated by HTML_QuickForm ❶

Abbreviating long paths ❷

Default HTML_QuickForm function name ❸

Simple text element ❹

Let HTML_QuickForm generate HTML ❺

```
            <tr>
              <td>
                <span tal:content="published/getLabel"/>:
                <input type="radio" name="${elements/status/getName}"
                  value="${published/getValue}"
                  tal:attributes="checked published/getChecked" />
                <span tal:content="draft/getLabel"/>:
                <input type="radio" name="${elements/status/getName}"
                  value="${draft/getValue}"
                  tal:attributes="checked draft/getChecked" />      ❻
              </td>
            </tr>
            <tr>
              <td tal:content="elements/body/getLabel">
                  Body (this is sample text that PHPTAL removes)
              </td>
              <td>
                <textarea tal:content="elements/body/getValue"
                  name="${elements/body/getName}">
                </textarea>
              </td>
            </tr>
          </table>
          <input type="submit" />
        </form>
      </body>
    </html>
```

Explicit HTML for radio buttons

❶ The JavaScript generated by the HTML_QuickForm package comes complete with `<script>` tags, and PHPTAL replaces the `<script>` tag here with all of that.

❷ We add these two `tal:define` elements for convenience to avoid having to enter the long paths of the radio buttons repeatedly. If we avoid cluttering the template with this, we can define the paths when we set the variables in the template instead.

❸ The odd-looking JavaScript function name is what we get from HTML_QuickForm when we don't name the form. That will have to be improved if we want more than one form on a page.

❹ The typical text input element is simple: just use the label, name, and value from the form element object.

❺ We generate the select menu as HTML from the form object. There are `<select>` tags as documentation to indicate that there will be a `<select>` element here. PHP-TAL removes them and adds the actual `<select>` element that is generated and returned from the `asHtml()` method of the element object.

❻ Unlike the `<select>` element, we represent the radio buttons with explicit HTML. `elements/status` is the object representing the set of radio buttons. `published` and `draft` are the objects representing each radio button.

18.2.6 What next?

We've used a mixture of techniques to come up with form handling that does what it's supposed to do. It's transparent: with some knowledge of PHP and HTML, it's relatively easy to understand what it does. But it's still somewhat cumbersome if we want to do complex groups of radio buttons with actual markup. How can we simplify this still further? We can use ideas similar to those we saw in the section on synchronizing server-side and client-side validation.

Our current way of inserting values into to the template file adds little actual information to the HTML markup. Take this excerpt from listing 18.6:

```
<td tal:content="elements/headline/getLabel">
    Headline (this is sample text that PHPTAL removes)
</td>
<td>
  <input type="text"
    name="${elements/headline/getName}"
    value="${elements/headline/getValue}" />
```

Repeating the `elements/headline` path is just a way of making this intelligible to the template engine. It's a text input field called `headline`; that's the gist of it.

If we simplify the task by ignoring the label at first, we could generate the above from this basic markup:

```
<input type="text" name="headline">
```

All we would need to do is to pre-process the template using our Form object to generate the version that can be read by the template engine. The label could be generated if we use the HTML `<label>` tag:

```
<td>
  <label for="headline">Headline</label>
</td>
<td>
  <input type="text" name="headline">
```

We might even try to generate all the form handling code from the HTML form itself (the pre-template) if we have some way of specifying validation. This is the opposite of the HTML_QuickForm approach.

18.3 SUMMARY

The bigger challenges of input validation arise when we want to synchronize server-side and client-side validation or to handle all aspects of form interaction. The easy way out in the short term is to use one of the available packages that generate all the HTML for a form from an object-oriented representation in PHP code. But to allow us to maintain the separation between markup and program code, more advanced strategies are required. Although a complete solution is likely to be a heavyweight package, we've explored some approaches, discovered a more abstract way of describing form fields, and seen how a standard form-handling package such as HTML_QuickForm can be used with other tools for this purpose.

Form handling is the last part of our investigation of the complexities of user interaction. In the next chapter, we will start learning about the Data Source Layer of the application. The first topics are database connection, abstraction, and configuration.

C H A P T E R   1 9

Database connection, abstraction, and configuration

Databases are a major component of any programmer's diet. PHP programmers eat databases for breakfast, not to mention lunch, dinner, and late-night snacks. With MySQL in particular (and more recently SimpleSQL), databases have been fast food for many years: easy to install, deploy, and use.

But as any health fanatic will tell you, frivolous eating is dangerous. The first risk we run when consuming food is indigestion. The digestive process is supposed to work painlessly, but sometimes it doesn't. In programming, we call these bugs. We're inured to them, though. We're not like the people who scream and tear their hair out whenever the printer stops working. Those people probably are constitutionally incapable of working in computer programming.

The next possible obstacle in food consumption is constipation. Something similar happens in software development when the development process slows down due to the need for increasingly complex queries. If the application is complex and needs to store complex data, that's partly unavoidable. But the more we understand about the relationship between data and code, the better equipped we will be to make it work and keep it working.

Then there's the more demanding question of how food affects your health in the long term, or, in our world, of what eventually happens to a project that has no consistent strategy for managing objects, data, and databases. Just as health-care professionals need to know how foods reduce your risk of heart disease, we want to know what strategies are most effective for preventing serious trouble in the project.

In this chapter, we will start with the most basic parts. Thinking about fast food again, we at least want to safeguard delivery and try to eat without littering. Let's make sure we know where we keep the phone number for the pizza delivery service. And let's not leave our code in a state that resembles the floor of a chimpanzee cage at lunchtime.

In this chapter, we'll first introduce database abstraction: the ability to treat different kinds of databases as if they were the same. Then we'll discuss how we can adjust and add to database resources by using adapters and decorators. Finally, we'll discover how to make a database connection available wherever it is needed in the application. Database connections are typical of the need for configuration information in the application, so we will learn some techniques that are also useful for other data and objects that need to be globally available.

19.1 DATABASE ABSTRACTION

All relational database management systems (RDBMSes) are basically the same. They store data in tables and let you manipulate the data using SQL, a standardized language for querying, inserting, and modifying data.

But anyone who has used at least two RDBMSes knows that there are also differences. Although most of them support a minimum standard syntax for SQL, if you want to do anything not-quite-standard, you might have to do completely different things for different databases.

For example, most experienced PHP programmers know the MySQL LIMIT clause. To get just the first 10 rows, we can do this:

```
SELECT * FROM Users LIMIT 10;
```

This is not standard SQL. PostgreSQL has a very similar syntax; other databases generally don't. In Transact-SQL (Sybase and Microsoft), we can use TOP or SET ROW-COUNT to limit the number of rows. The equivalent syntax for DB2 is the following:

```
SELECT * FROM Users FETCH FIRST 10 ROWS ONLY;
```

This kind of difference may be hard to deal with if you want to switch from one RDBMS to another, and that is the point of database abstraction. Database abstraction is a way to make different databases look the same to the application programmer by making them available through a similar interface. For example, the Creole database abstraction package lets you do this:

```
$stmt = $conn->createStatement();
$stmt->setLimit(10);
$rs = $stmt->executeQuery("SELECT * FROM Users");
```

NOTE   This example shows the principle, but beware of the fact that Creole and similar packages may not support a given database.

You might not think you will ever have to switch databases, but it's easy to underestimate the likelihood of having to switch. As Joe Celko says in the article *I Will Never Have To Port This Code*:

> *... unless you throw out a program within a year of writing it, it's either going to be ported [to another RDBMS] or so seriously maintained it might as well be a port; and I don't mean that it's necessarily going to be moved to a totally different database product. Moving to another release of the same product is enough to cause problems* [Celko].

As always, we don't want to spend too much time preparing for future events, even if they're likely to happen, but using database abstraction is usually not much of a burden. And it will be increasingly convenient as abstraction layers mature.

19.1.1 Prepared statements

A naive PHP application may contain unescaped SQL statements with embedded variables:

```
$result = mysql_query("SELECT name from Products where id = $id");
```

This is insecure, at least on its face, because variables may come from the user. If the input is not filtered properly, it leaves the door open to SQL injection attacks.

The secure principle is to always filter input and escape output. And when you send a database query from a PHP program, that is considered output. The basic MySQL way to solve this is to use `mysql_real_escape_string()` on all variables:

```
$result = mysql_query(
    "SELECT name from Products where id = ".
    mysql_real_escape_string($id));
```

But it's better yet to use prepared statements. There are several different implementations of these; fortunately, they are sufficiently similar that if you've learned to use one, using another is mostly a matter of changing the syntax a bit. Listing 19.1 shows how to use prepared statements in the Mysqli extension. Mysqli has the advantage of being widely available, although it is tied to one specific database management system.

Listing 19.1 Prepared statement example using Mysqli

```
$mysqli = new Mysqli(                              ❶ Create Mysqli
    'localhost','user','password','newsdb');           connection
$stmt = $mysqli->prepare(                          ❷ Prepare the
    "SELECT name from Products where id = ?");          statement
```

```
$stmt->bind_param("i",$id);          ❸  Add data and
$stmt->execute();                        execute
$stmt->bind_result($name);
$stmt->fetch();                      ❹  Get result in
$stmt->close();                          $name variable
```

❶ Using the object-oriented Mysqli syntax, we start by creating a Mysqli connection object.

❷ Then we prepare the statement. The `prepare()` method returns a prepared statement. This is an object representing a slightly abstracted SQL statement, with slots or placeholders that can be filled with values. It can be reused, setting different values in the slots every time.

In the Mysqli extension, we represent the placeholders with question marks when we define the prepared statement. This is the most common technique in database abstraction.

❸ To specify a value for the parameter, we use `bind_param()`. The first argument to the method is the data type (*i* for integer). The second argument is the value. `execute()` runs the SQL query using the prepared statement.

❹ Using `bind_result()` tells Mysqli that retrieved values are to be assigned to the `$name` variable. `fetch()` makes Mysqli actually assign the variable. Now the product name is in the `$name` variable.

This way of getting the variables may seem odd. It would probably be more practical if the `fetch()` method just returned the data instead of assigning it to variables. But for some reason, this is not the way the Mysqli extension works.

The PHP Data Objects extension (PDO) is superior in several ways, primarily due to the fact that it allows you to access several different RDBMSes through the same API.

The PDO way (or rather one of them; PDO is comfortably flexible) is illustrated in listing 19.2. It is the same in principle, but many details differ.

Listing 19.2   Prepared statement example using PDO

```
try {                                         ❶  Create connection,
    $conn = new PDO(                              handle exceptions
        'mysql:dbname=newsdb;host=localhost',
        'user',
        'password');
}
catch (Exception $e) {                        ❷  Throw new, more
    throw new Exception($e->getMessage());        secure exception
}
$conn->setAttribute(                          ❸  Set PDO to throw
    PDO::ATTR_ERRMODE,                            more exceptions
    PDO::ERRMODE_EXCEPTION);
$stmt = $conn->prepare(                       ❹  Named placeholder
    "SELECT name from Products where id = :id");
```

```
$stmt->bindParam(':id',$id);
$stmt->execute();
$row = $stmt->fetch();
```
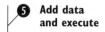

⑤ Add data and execute

---

❶ Since PDO throws an exception when it fails to connect to the database, we have to use `try` and `catch` if we want to handle the error. Creating the database connection object is the same as in the previous example with slightly different syntax.

❷ Catching the exception is particularly important in this case, since the backtrace that's displayed by default shows both the name and the password of the database user. To handle it, we throw a new exception. That may seem futile, but the difference is that we avoid the risk of displaying the password. However, the exception will still display a backtrace including the MySQL error message that contains the name of the database user.

This means that we need to catch the exception at a higher level of the application and not show the full backtrace to the user. The advantage of an exception in this case is that we don't have to worry about how many levels exist in between. We can catch the exception somewhere in the code that handles navigation and presentation, and redirect to an error page.

❸ Subsequent errors can be handled in the same way if we set up PDO to throw exceptions when other errors (such as SQL syntax errors) occur. Therefore, we set the error mode. The first argument just tells PDO that we want to set the error mode; the second argument tells PDO what we want it set to.

❹ Preparing the statement is the same as in the Mysqli example except that we're allowed to use a named placeholder instead of a question mark.

❺ `bindParam()` is also similar in that it specifies the value to be inserted into the slot. `execute()` executes the SQL query, and `fetch()` returns the database row as an array.

Besides improving security, prepared statements can make query execution more efficient if we reuse a statement object. And although prepared statements may seem inconvenient (they do require a few extra lines of code), they relieve you of the chore of having to quote and escape all variables properly. Even if we were to disregard security and go back to the naive PHP style, we might find ourselves doing something like this:

```
$result = mysql_query("SELECT * from Products where name = $name");
```

This generates an SQL syntax error, since we've neglected to put quotes around `$name`. And with a long list of variables, the error message may be hard to read. This is not terribly problematic, but it is inconvenient, and can we avoid it by using prepared statements.

19.1.2 Object-oriented database querying

Database querying in PHP abounds with simple and complex abstraction layers. There is not one single, unified package that supports all different databases and database features. That's why we often need to implement some glue of our own to make the existing packages do our bidding smoothly. To that purpose, it helps to have a good conceptual understanding of how the existing packages are designed.

Listing 19.3 shows yet another version of the prepared statement package, this time using Creole, which is inspired by (and very similar to) Java's JDBC.

Listing 19.3   Prepared statement example using Creole

```
try {
    $conn = Creole::getConnection(
        "mysql://user:password@localhost/newsdb");
}
catch (Exception $e) {
    throw new Exception($e->getMessage());
}
$stmt = $conn->prepareStatement(
    "SELECT name from Products where id = ?");
$stmt->setInt(1,$id);
$resultset = $stmt->executeQuery();
$resultset->first();
$name = $resultset->getString('name');
```

Compared to the earlier examples, the only news here is that there is a separate ResultSet object. This is a conceptually clean way to think about it. Figure 19.1 is a slightly abstracted class diagram of this structure. The methods of the ResultSet class may have any number of different names, often starting with `fetch` or `get`. That's why only the responsibilities are noted in the figure.

What PDO does (see listing 19.2) is merge the prepared statement and the result set into a single object, although the query and the results from that query are

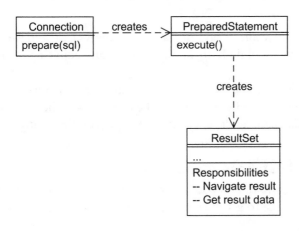

Figure 19.1
Typical conceptual structure for object-oriented database querying

conceptually very different things. That's not necessarily a practical problem, but making the distinction helps us understand it better.

On the other hand, this is an example of the fact that sometimes we need something slightly different from what the available database objects have to offer. To solve that problem, we can use decorators and adapters.

19.2 DECORATING AND ADAPTING DATABASE RESOURCE OBJECTS

What if we want to add something to one of the classes in the design shown in the previous example? One way is to create child classes, if possible, but the inheritance relationship involves a degree of coupling that is not ideal when we don't control the classes we are inheriting from. The alternative, then, is to use Decorators. We jumped the gun in chapter 7 by looking at a couple of examples of what Nock calls the Resource Decorator pattern, decorating a PEAR DB object to log calls and generate exceptions.

One thing to be aware of when decorating the components shown in figure 19.1 is that if you decorate one of the classes, you have to decorate the class that creates it as well. If we want to decorate the prepared statement, we must decorate the connection as well, since obviously the standard connection is not capable of returning our decorated prepared statement. A similar relationship exists between the statement and the result set.

There are several reasons why we may want to do this:

- Simply to add configuration data to the connection.
- To guard against changes in the underlying layer. For example, if we are using the Mysqli extension and want to switch to PDO, we can keep our own classes and change the way they access the connection, statement, and result set. If it was a decorator, it's now an adapter.
- To add features. For example, PDO has no way of handling dates; we can add that by using a decorator. Or we could use a Decorator to log queries as in the example in chapter 7.

The dividing line between Decorator and Adapter is not always clear and we need not worry about it. A class may well do both, adding features and adjusting the interface somewhat.

In this section, we'll do a simple example first: a database connection that reads the connection parameters from a configuration file. Then we'll look at the more advanced challenge of making a database result set act as an SPL-compatible Iterator so that we can use it like an array in a `foreach` loop.

19.2.1 A simple configured database connection

One of the simplest things we can do is decorate the database connection with a class that reads a configuration file to get the connection parameters. The basic way to do this is to let the configuration file contain PHP code that sets variables. That works OK for a configuration file if it's only to be used by administrators who know what they're doing, and won't leave the file with a syntax error that kills the entire application. This kind of thing is fairly typical:

```
$config["db_host"] = "localhost";
$config["db_username"] = "developer";
$config["db_password"] = "secret";
$config["db_database"] = "newsdb";
```

To make it a little more interesting, we'll wrap the variables in a function and return them. Our simple configuration file looks like this, then:

```
function dbConfig() {
    $db = 'newsdb';
    $host = 'localhost';
    $user = 'developer';
    $password = 'secret';
    return compact('db','host','user','password');
}
```

The connection class does little except create a database connection as specified in the configuration file:

```
class NewsDatabaseConnection {
    private $mysqli;

    public function __construct() {
        require_once(CONFIG_DIR.'dbconfig.php');
        extract(dbConfig());
        $this->mysqli = new mysqli($db,$host,$user,$password);
    }

    public function prepare($sql) {
        $this->mysqli->prepare($sql);
    }

    // Etc., more methods belonging to the connection
}
```

extract() takes the array created by compact() and turns it back into single variables. extract() is interesting, but can cause problems if used indiscriminately. Used this way, it's safe. The data we're extracting does not come from the user, and we're releasing the variables into a limited local scope.

CONFIG_DIR is a constant that should contain a directory outside the web root to protect the configuration file optimally.

The normal procedure for a Decorator is to accept the object it's decorating as an argument to the constructor. This one is different in that respect, but otherwise resembles a regular Decorator.

19.2.2 Making an SPL-compatible iterator from a result set

Any iterator can be used with `foreach` if it implements the SPL Iterator interface. For a more realistic example, let's make our own database result set object that will work in a `foreach` loop. This is primarily an Adapter rather than a Decorator.

We will implement a class that is slightly more complex than the minimum needed to support basic iteration with `foreach`, because we want to support the `rewind()` and `key()` methods in the SPL Iterator interface. The iterator would work with null implementations of these. But without a real implementation of `rewind()`, we would lose the ability to run `foreach` more than once on the same result set. Normally, we wouldn't need to do that, but since you can run `foreach` repeatedly on an array, not being able to do it is counterintuitive and might lead us to make mistakes. Something similar applies to the `key()` method. Implementing it allows us to say

```
foreach ($result as $key => $row) {}
```

Although `$key` is not strictly needed for a database result, this is the intuitive behavior for `foreach`.

The design is illustrated in figure 19.2. The complete interface of the MySql-ResultIterator class is given by the SPL Iterator interface, which is built into PHP.

Listing 19.4 shows the result iterator class.

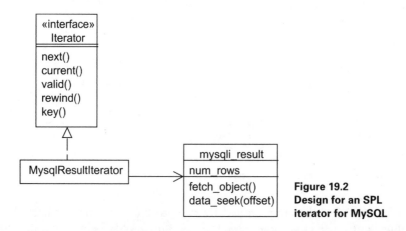

**Figure 19.2
Design for an SPL
iterator for MySQL**

Listing 19.4 Database result iterator class that implements the SPL Iterator interface so that it can be used in a `foreach` loop

```
class MysqlResultIterator implements Iterator {          ⟵  Iterator
                                                             ("foreachable")
    private $mysqliResult;                               ❶   interface
    private $current;
    private $rowNum = 0;

    public function __construct($mysqliResult) {
        $this->mysqliResult = $mysqliResult;             ❷  Initialize
        $this->rewind();
```

```
    }

    public function rewind() {
        $this->mysqliResult->data_seek(0);          ❸  Start from first row
        $this->next();
        $this->rowNum = 0;          ◀──┐  Keep track of          Return false  ❺
    }                                ❹  current row             beyond last row
    public function valid() {
        return $this->rowNum < $this->mysqliResult->num_rows;  ┐
    }                                                          │
                                                               │
    public function next() {
        $this->current = $this->mysqliResult->fetch_object();  ┐
        ++$this->rowNum;
    }                                                 Advance the
                                                       iterator  ❻
    public function current() {        ❼  Return
        return $this->current;             current row
    }

    public function key() {            ❽  Analogous to
        return $this->rowNum;              array key
    }
}
```

❶ To work in a `foreach` loop, the class must implement the Iterator interface.

❷ Our MysqlResultIterator object wraps a mysqli_result object. We run the `rewind()` method to initialize the iterator correctly so that the first call to `current()` returns the first row. This is not strictly necessary when we use the iterator with `foreach`, since a `foreach` loop causes `rewind()` to be called before looping. But just in case someone wants to use the iterator without using a `foreach` loop, it's a good idea to make sure it is properly initialized.

❸ To start the iterator from the beginning, we first position the mysqli_result object on the first row. Then we call `next()` to make the first row available the first time we call `current()`.

  Technically, it would have been easier to implement an iterator that required the client to call `next()` before getting anything from the iterator. (The JDBC ResultSet object works this way.) But from the client's point of view, it may seem more logical to have a current element available once you create the iterator. Anyway, this is the way the SPL Iterator interface works.

❹ The $rowNum instance variable keeps track of the current row.

❺ The `valid()` method returns FALSE if the current row is after the last row. Alternatively, we could use a flag that starts out as TRUE and is set to FALSE when the mysqli_result object returns FALSE. But we need the $rowNum variable in any case for the key() method. Having one variable rather than two to keep track of the state of the iteration is a slightly more robust way to do it.

❻ The next() method fetches a row into the $current variable so that the next call to current() will return that row. We are using fetch_object(), which gets us the row as a primitive object rather than as an array. It's mostly a matter of taste which we want to use; the advantage of the object is that—whatever error-reporting state—we will get an error message if we try to use the name of a database table column that does not exist.

❼ The current() method returns the $current variable that is set by the next() method.

❽ The key() method returns the current row number for use as a key in the foreach statement.

Now we can use the iterator in a foreach loop with keys if we want to:

```
$result = new MysqlResultIterator($mysqliResult);
foreach ($result as $n => $row) {
    echo "Row number: $n\n";
    echo "Name: ".$row->name;
}
```

The $n variable will contain the row number starting from 0, and the $row variable will contain the row as a primitive object returned by the mysqli_result object. In most cases, we won't need the row number, and we can do this instead:

```
foreach ($result as $row) { }
```

In the previous subsection, we saw how to make a database connection read from a configuration file. This is somewhat primitive, and sooner or later you may have to resort to a more flexible strategy for making the connection available.

19.3   MAKING THE DATABASE CONNECTION AVAILABLE

Having one preconfigured database connection and creating a new instance every time we need one is perfectly workable for many applications. Most PHP applications just have one way of connecting to a single database, and the risk of creating a large number of connections is slight.

And even if we want to switch to a different RDBMS, we might be OK just changing the classes to work with it. In theory, that is. But what about while you're making the change? What if you want to make the change gradually, starting with some parts of the code while keeping the rest constant?

Agile principles are pulling us in both directions here. On the one hand, we want to keep our design as simple as possible. On the other, to make refactoring and testing easier, more decoupling is helpful, even if we have to add a couple of extra classes.

Another consideration, which is too big an issue to cover in depth here, is the issue of how many connections you want—limiting the number of connections or making sure you have different connections. What we can say is that using a more flexible design for handling connections also makes it easier to control how many connections are created.

Nock lists three strategies for making a database connection available to domain objects:

- Active domain objects manage their own connections, creating new ones as needed.
- The calling code passes the connection to the domain objects.
- Connections are created by a globally accessible connection factory.

How to make a connection factory globally accessible is a fascinating question in itself that will be answered in this section.

We'll start by looking at the Singleton pattern, which is the classic object-oriented version of global data. Then we'll see a couple of patterns that help avoid some of the problems of Singleton: Service Locator and Registry.

19.3.1 Singleton and similar patterns

The issue of how to access globally available data and services is remarkably difficult considering the simple nature of the problem to be solved. There are a large number of object-oriented ways to do it, many of them variations on the Singleton design pattern. But in general, there are three levels of sophistication in the approaches used:

- Plain PHP globals
- Singleton and related approaches
- More sophisticated strategies such as Registry, Service Locator, and Dependency Injection

In general, it's more important to make sure we don't lose track of globals than to encapsulate them in an object-oriented way.

The Singleton pattern is popular, but is also the subject of endless discussions about how often and when it is appropriate. In essence, a Singleton is just a glorified global object.

Let's start simple and build gradually and try to discover what we may gain by using the Singleton pattern. If we want a single database connection available anywhere in our application, we can always use a plain global variable:

```
$GLOBALS['newsDbConnection'] = new NewsDatabaseConnection;
```

What's wrong with that? Perhaps nothing, especially if the variable is only set at the beginning of the script and not changed later. (There's plenty wrong with it in Java, though. In fact, it's impossible, since Java has no global variables.) The real headache only starts when using global variables becomes a habit. As discussed in chapter 4, this can cause a great deal of confusion.

Also, there is a risk that someone will overwrite the variable with something completely inappropriate purely by mistake.

A slightly more sophisticated way to do the same thing would be to make it a public class variable:

```
class DatabaseConnections {
    public static $newsDb;
}
DatabaseConnections::$newsDb = new NewsDatabaseConnection;
```

Now we've provided a home for the connection, solidifying its claim to existence and perhaps making our intention easier to understand for someone who is unfamiliar with the application.

There is also less risk that the variable will be overwritten by someone who didn't know it existed in the first place. Anyone overwriting it is probably doing some deliberate hacking.

To prevent even this, we could make the class variable private and have a method in the class to initialize it:

```
class DatabaseConnections {
    private static $newsDb;

    public static function newsDb() {
        return self::$newsDb;
    }

    public static function init() {
        self::$newsDb = new NewsDatabaseConnection;
    }
}

DatabaseConnections::init();
```

It may seem odd that we have to run some code just to get the class set up. On the other hand, the configurable Service Locator in the next section also requires us to do something to make it useful.

We've also lost something: the ability to replace the connection with a mock object for testing.

The oddity of initialization disappears if we make the class a full Singleton. To make it a conventional Singleton, we need to do two things: make the class initialize automatically when we ask for an instance and make the two classes (DatabaseConnections and NewsDatabaseConnection) become one class.

```
class SingleDatabaseConnection {
    private static $soleInstance = FALSE;
    // Other instance variables for the connection

    public static function instance() {
        if (!self::$soleInstance)
```

```
            self::$soleInstance = new SingleDatabaseConnection;
        return self::$soleInstance;
    }

    public function prepare($sql) {}

    // Further methods for the connection
}
```

To merge two classes, we've had to introduce all the methods from the connection class itself. This highlights one of the recurrent criticisms against the Singleton pattern: it violates the single-responsibility principle by mixing the responsibility of singleness with the other responsibilities of the class.

We also need to be aware that a Singleton, when implemented in this way in PHP, only lasts for one HTTP request-response cycle.

And while we've effectively prevented the connection from being overwritten, it's also impossible to replace with a mock object. We can get around that by making the connection an instance variable of the Singleton instead of the Singleton itself. That's what the Registry and Service Locator patterns do.

19.3.2   Service Locator and Registry

Although we've only scratched the surface of access to global resources, let's look at an idea which may seem advanced, but becomes reasonable once you start to decouple objects from their global dependencies. If you consider the problem of making classes reusable outside the application, the surest bet is for a class to use only what it's fed, for example,

```
class NewsFinder {
    public function __construct($db) {
        $this->db = $db;
    }
}
```

Now we can have a NewsFinder class that does not depend on anything except the database connection it gets passed as an argument to the constructor. Of course, the actual interface of the class the connection object belongs to is crucial. If we want to use type hints, we may do the following to ensure that the needed methods are available in the passed-in connection.

```
interface DatabaseConnection {
    public function query($sql);
    public function prepare($sql);
}

class NewsDbConnection implements DatabaseConnection { }

class NewsFinder {
    public function __construct(DatabaseConnection $db) {
        $this->db = $db;
    }
}
```

This makes the NewsFinder class eminently reusable; at least as far as class dependencies are concerned.

But how do we achieve this in a real application? Without some additional tricks, we are left with the need to pass a database connection down through several levels.

The currently popular solutions for handling this are called Dependency Injection and Service Locator. This is popular with frameworks, since it keeps the application classes from depending on particular implementations of services. For instance, the framework can provide a template mechanism that can easily be replaced with another that has the same interface.

Using a Service Locator makes this

```
class NewsFinder {
    public function __construct($db) {
        $this->db = ServiceLocator::databaseConnection();
    }
}
```

This makes the Service Locator look like a connection factory, but there are differences:

- The Service Locator can provide other services, not just database connections.

- The Service Locator can be configured with a database connection instead of just creating it.

A simple Service Locator may be implemented as in listing 19.5.

Listing 19.5   Service Locator for a database connection

```
class ServiceLocator {
    private static $soleInstance;
    private $connection;

    public function __construct($connection) {
        $this->connection = $connection;
    }
    public static function load($locator) {
        self::$soleInstance = $locator;
    }
    public static function databaseconnection() {
        return self::$soleInstance->connection;
    }
}
```

The design of this class is almost identical to the example in Martin Fowler's article on Dependency Injection [Fowler DI]. This variation on the Singleton pattern is interesting. Unlike the standard Singleton pattern, the instance is hidden inside the class and there is no way to return it. And we can set the single instance:

```
ServiceLocator::load(
    new ServiceLocator(new NewsDbConnection));
```

It's odd, but it works, and it enables us to configure the Service Locator with the database connection we need. It also makes the instance (and the connection) replaceable for testing. On the other hand, there's no longer any guarantee that the connection cannot be overwritten. That is simply the price we have to pay.

In a real Service Locator, of course, we may put any other kind of service needed by application classes, for example, factories, templates, classes containing pure configuration data or options, or user interface components such as a global menu.

What exactly to place in the Service Locator is worth thinking long and hard about. If we stay with the database connection idea, there are some alternatives. In fact, a raw database connection might not be what we want.

If we let the Service Locator return a connection factory instead, we could easily replace a MysqlConnectionFactory with a PgsqlConnectionFactory, and (in theory, or if we're really clever) the application would not know the difference. This is a simple case of the Abstract Factory pattern from the Gang of Four. Figure 19.3 depicts the overall structure.

Another possibility is to have the Service Locator return a data access class such as the NewsFinder from the beginning of this section. Now we could (in theory, or if we're really clever) replace the NewsFinder with another class that gets the news from an RSS feed instead of a database.

In other words, it depends on what and how much you want or need to be able to configure.

The Service Locator resembles the Registry pattern from Fowler's *Patterns of Enterprise Application Architecture* [P of EAA]. In fact, Fowler says that his Service Locator example is used as a Singleton Registry, whatever that means.

Registry is possibly more general than Service Locator in terms of the kind of information it's able to return (in other words, it's not limited to services). But the idea of a Service Locator is a good one because it makes it easier to keep track of all the pieces. All the stuff that's supposed to be globally available can be accessed via a single class. And in addition, by defining the objects that are available as services, we may avoid stuffing a plethora of tiny objects into the Service Locator. If we want a small object or piece of data, we can consider whether it should be returned by one of the services.

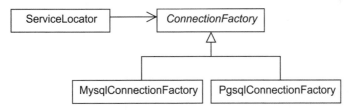

Figure 19.3 Simple Abstract Factory pattern for using connection factories with a Service Locator

19.4 SUMMARY

Database abstraction is a well-established way of making database management systems replaceable. Typical database abstraction layers let you query the database without depending too much on database-specific syntax and features. They also have the ability to prepare statements for quicker and more secure execution.

There are several database abstraction packages for PHP, but DBO is likely to become more prevalent with time.

The Decorator and Adapter design patterns, or more simply, wrapping a class with another class, is particularly useful for database connections and the resources provided by database abstraction layers. It's a universal way to add missing features and change the API of an abstraction package.

Database connections provide the classic example of the need to make global resources available to an application. There are various ways to create and supply connections, from the simplest to the more complex, using progressively more advanced design patterns including Singleton, Registry, and Service Locator.

In the next chapter, we continue our journey into the world of object-oriented data access, looking closely at the challenges of encapsulating, hiding, generating, and generalizing SQL.

PART 4

Databases and infrastructure

In the last part of this book, we will take on the challenges of databases and persistence. Trying to store objects in a relational database is a lot like shoving round pegs into square holes. Once we've gone down the object-oriented path, we need to know how to deal with this problem, and the way to deal with it is to use more objects to solve it. We will study database connections and abstraction layers. We will take a look at various ways to handle configuration data such as database names and database user names. And we will use design patterns to ease the difficulty of transforming and translating objects to database data and vice versa.

C H A P T E R   2 0

Objects and SQL

I've never designed physical products, only software. But I've noticed that physical objects, no matter what their shapes, tend to be packaged in rectangular boxes and crates. An example would be the broadband router I received in the mail a while ago. There was the router itself, neatly box-shaped, an AC adapter, which is much more irregular, a cable folded and packaged with a clip, and an installation guide. All of this was safely ensconced in an unsurprisingly rectangular cardboard box with the aid of some extra packaging materials.

Although I'm anything but an expert on this kind of packaging, I can guess one reason the outermost box is rectangular: it's easy to stash on storage shelves. I can just imagine what would happen if they were irregularly shaped: put package number 500 in place, and it topples the 499 previous ones.

Something similar happens in object-oriented programming. It's a bit like trying to put a round peg into a square hole. Object-oriented programming and relational databases don't go well together because the way data is represented and handled is fundamentally different in the two worlds.

In this chapter, we'll first go a little deeper into this problem. Then we'll discuss encapsulating and hiding SQL so that we won't have to deal with SQL except in specialized data access classes. Finally, we'll find out how and how much to generalize the way we generate SQL so that we can reduce duplication.

20.1 *THE OBJECT-RELATIONAL IMPEDANCE MISMATCH*

The lack of compatibility between object-oriented programs and relational databases is sometimes referred to as the *object-relational impedance mismatch.* There are many differences between objects and databases. OOP packages data and behavior together; database tables are pure data. Objects are handled individually; a database table represents a collection of objects. Relational databases have no precise equivalents for object inheritance, association, and composition. And to make it work, you need two different types of languages: SQL and an object-oriented programming language.

Overcoming the mismatch involves two fundamentally different kinds of challenges. One is repackaging and rebuilding the data to make relational data out of PHP objects and vice versa. The other challenge is talking to the database in its native language, SQL.

Building a little further on the packaging metaphor, imagine that you run a small company that builds electronic equipment. To make it simple, let's say you have to deal with two people: one person who takes care of building the components (the objects) and another person whose job is to place the components in the warehouse (the database). Let's call them the production manager and the warehouse manager. Together they know how to make the product and store it. But the process in between, to package it so it doesn't fall off the shelves, is not in anyone's job description. So what do you do? Do you, the CEO, take the job yourself? Do you hire another person to do it? Or do you let one of the two existing employees do it? If so, which one?

As programmers, we face similar choices. One way to move data to and from the database is to do it in the main program of the application itself. This may be the most straightforward approach, but it's as if the CEO were sitting at his desk, packing components into boxes. A CEO might actually do that for a while in a startup company, but it might not be the optimal way of organizing the work. An alternative is to let the objects store themselves by giving them methods that can access the database. Or we can leave the work to classes that are separate from both the domain objects and the database, classes that are specialized for the work of packaging and re-packaging the data.

The other challenge in our electronics company is the fact that the production manager and the warehouse manager speak different languages. The production manager speaks only PHP and the warehouse manager speaks only SQL. These two languages are even more different than English and Chinese. Fortunately, they are also simpler. But we need someone to translate. Do you, the CEO, speak both languages? Of course you do; you're smarter than everyone. But again, it might be wise to delegate some of the work. A professional interpreter will make life easier.

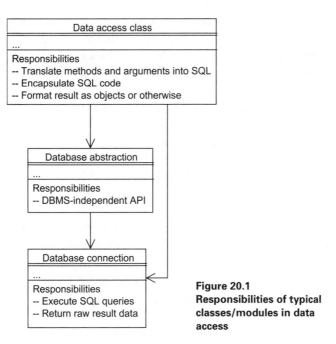

Figure 20.1
Responsibilities of typical classes/modules in data access

In figure 20.1, the data access class is the one that has this interpreter role. It may or may not have other responsibilities as well. The data access class may use the connection directly or indirectly via the database abstraction layer. It may also use both, reserving the direct route for RDBMS-specific features that are not handled by the abstraction layer.

Let's start looking at the language translation challenge. How can we create a PHP API that generates the SQL we need to query the database?

20.2   ENCAPSULATING AND HIDING SQL

It's common practice in PHP programming to put in an SQL statement wherever it seems to be needed in the code: in other words, wherever the need to access the database arises. This may work for very simple applications, but when complexity increases, it degenerates into a tangled mixture of PHP and SQL code not unlike the mixtures of PHP code and HTML markup we discussed earlier. This leads to duplication: SQL statements that are strewn across the code tend to be similar in ways that are not obvious because you never see them together. So the approach breeds duplication. Subtle duplication, that is. If you have 5 or 10 different SQL statements in different places that use the same database table, you will have a hard time spotting duplication both in the SQL statements themselves and in the surrounding code. That is why we want to concentrate related SQL code together. A natural way to do this is to use object-oriented classes.

Classes let us extract the database access code into separate files. SQL is a very different programming language than PHP, and there are some developers as well as DBAs that have specialized knowledge of it. So it can be a good idea to isolate SQL statements together.

Another reason to separate SQL from PHP code is because even with the best structure imaginable, it's hard to avoid duplication in SQL queries while keeping the queries relatively readable. If we accept some duplication, it's easier to deal with that duplication if similar SQL statements are kept close together. If three different SQL statements share the same list of columns and you need to add a column to the list, keeping the statements in close proximity keeps the challenge manageable.

Also, unit testing becomes easier, since separate classes for database access are easier to test in isolation.

There is a bewildering variety of design patterns for handling database access. They tend to be rather elaborate and contain a number of different elements: they generate SQL statements, perform the query, and prepare the result in some form that's palatable to the application (typically associative arrays or objects). Fowler [P of EAA] and Nock both describe a number of patterns for object-oriented database access. Their patterns overlap one another in interesting ways, and I've found it educational and revealing to analyze them and compare their various aspects and properties to find similarities and differences.

So instead of diving into the patterns, we will look at the steps in the process one-by-one and study the alternatives.

In this section, we'll start with a basic example of how to encapsulate an SQL query inside a method. Then, since we need to insert data into the queries, we'll look at some different ways—beyond those offered by prepared statements—to substitute strings in SQL queries.

20.2.1 A basic example

The fundamental principle of object-oriented database access is to encapsulate a query inside a method call. So you have a method to find all news articles, another method to find one with a specific ID, one to insert a new article, and so on. If you need to do something substantially different from what you've done before, you write another method.

This way of working makes the program code more readable. Instead of SQL statements, we use method calls with relatively simple, intuitive names like `Article-Finder::findAll()`.

If you're used to SQL, a statement like

```
SELECT headline, summary, body FROM Articles
```

might be just as easy to understand or perhaps even easier. But once you start adding complex WHERE clauses or joins, the intent of the SQL statement is not likely to be clear to anyone at first glance.

Encapsulating SQL inside methods also limits the amount of duplication of SQL code. If you embed SQL statements wherever they're used in the program, you're likely to repeat yourself without realizing it. If you need a user's login name and password for authentication, and the user's full name to display a "hello" message, you might write two different SQL statements for that, when in fact you only need one. (Admittedly, having two different statements may be slightly faster. But programmer efficiency should be a higher priority than program efficiency when you write the program. You can optimize later, if necessary.)

So for our first, most basic example, we have a TopicFinder class to get discussion topics from the database. The example has only one method, `find()`, which retrieves a topic with a given ID.

```
class TopicFinder {
    function find($id) {
        $connection = ConnectionFactory::getConnection();
        $sql = "select * from Topics where topic_id = $id";
        $result = $connection->query($sql);
        return $result->fetchRow(DB_FETCHMODE_ASSOC);
    }
}
```

NOTE   I'm using Fowler's naming conventions most of the time. `find()` is a method that finds an object by ID. There's no reason why you have to call it `find()`, but it's a good idea to name methods consistently.

To get the connection, we use a connection factory as described in the previous chapter. The connection is a PEAR DB connection. We use the connection to run a simple query to get the data. By using `DB_FETCHMODE_ASSOC`, we get the result as a plain associative array and return that from the method.

20.2.2 Substituting strings in SQL statements

String substitution in PHP is relatively basic, and using it to generate SQL statements is not hard, but since we will be doing so much of it, we want to be able do it in a way that will be as flexible and readable as possible. So let's review and evaluate some language features, functions, and strategies.

Database abstraction layers usually have placeholders that help you with this, but they don't handle just any conceivable substitutions you might want to do. They will let you substitute single data items, but not larger pieces of SQL code such as a complete WHERE clause. So with an abstraction layer that uses question marks as placeholders, this will work:

```
INSERT INTO Topics (name) VALUES (?)
```

This, on the other hand, won't work:

```
SELECT ? FROM Topics WHERE ?
```

Variable interpolation

The simplest way to place data from variables in an SQL statement is to use variable interpolation with double quotes:

```
$id = 100;
$name = 'Trains';
$sql = "INSERT INTO Topics (id, name) VALUES ($id,'$name')";
```

This requires that the `$id` and `$name` variables are set before this statement; so if what you want to do is set up an "SQL template" in a string and substitute the variables into it later, you need to do something else.

Concatenation

Another elementary way to achieve the same effect is to use string concatenation:

```
$sql = "INSERT INTO Topics (id, name) ".
    "VALUES (".$id.",'".$name."')";
```

This is less readable, but it allows you to use any expression in place of the variables: method calls, for instance,

```
$sql = "INSERT INTO Topics (id, name) ".
    "VALUES (".$article->getID().",'".$article->getName()."')";
```

sprintf()

Yet another technique, sometimes ignored in PHP, is to use `sprintf()`:

```
$sql = sprintf("INSERT INTO Topics (id, name) ".
       "VALUES (%s,'%s')",$id,$name);
```

This is more elaborate, but has its advantages. The SQL statement itself is relatively readable, and you can define the SQL statement first and add the values later:

```
$template = "INSERT INTO Topics (id, name) VALUES (%s,'%s')";
//...
list($id,$name) = array(1,'Trains');
$sql = sprintf($template,$id,$name);
```

This is more similar to what the database abstraction layers do, since they let you prepare a statement with placeholders first and then add the data later:

```
// (Creole syntax)
$template = "INSERT INTO Topics (id, name) VALUES (?,?)";
$stmt = $this->connection->prepareStatement($template);
//...
$stmt->set(1,1);
$stmt->set(2,'Trains');
$rs = $stmt->executeQuery();
```

This example illustrates another benefit of placeholders: you don't have to worry about quoting, because the database abstraction package takes care of that automatically. In the `sprintf()` example, the second value needs quotes around it because it's a string. In the Creole example, no quotes are needed.

Multiline queries

Complex SQL statements are more readable if you divide them across several lines. But there is no simple, straightforward way of embedding these multiline statements in PHP code without causing side effects. Perhaps the simplest way to do it is to just place a quotation mark before and after the SQL lines and indent the SQL appropriately:

```
public function insert() {
    $sql = "
        INSERT (id,name)
        INTO Topics
        VALUES (%s,%s)
        ";
//...
}
```

The problem is that this adds a large amount of whitespace. An SQL parser will happily ignore it, but you might not like the fact that all the whitespace appears when, for instance, you want to print the statement. Besides, it's not easy to edit if you want to merge or split lines.

Another common way of embedding multiline queries is to concatenate lines:

```
$sql =
    "INSERT (id,name) " .
    "INTO Topics " .
    "VALUES (%s,%s)";
```

`$sql` will now contain one single long string with only the spaces required by the SQL syntax. But it is even harder to edit than the previous example.

Another possibility is to keep the SQL code flush to the left margin. This looks terrible if you do it inside a function or method which is already indented, but it could work if you keep the SQL statements in separate classes, at the beginning of a class, or even between methods in a class. Here is a class that only acts as a container for SQL statement strings:

```
class TopicsSqlStatements {

const INSERT = "
INSERT (id,name)
INTO Topics
VALUES (%s,%s)
";

const FIND_ALL = "
SELECT id, name
FROM Topics
";

}
```

Now these statements can be accessed globally as `TopicsSqlState-ments::INSERT` and `TopicsSqlStatements::FIND_ALL`, for example,

```
$sql = sprintf(TopicsSqlStatements::INSERT,1,'Trains');
$result = $connection->query($sql);
```

Yet another alternative is the so-called "here document" syntax. This is actually a rather readable alternative to quotes, but it's barely documented in the PHP manual. And you can't combine it with the previous strategy, since PHP won't let you define a class constant with a here document. The closest thing to a class constant is a method that returns a string, so you *could* do this:

```
public function INSERT() {
return <<< SQL
INSERT (id,name)
INTO Topics
VALUES (%s,%s)
SQL;
}
```

But what do you gain by that? Only redundant syntax, it seems.

Two-step replacement

The previous example could have been done with abstraction layer placeholders instead of `sprintf()`. But the placeholders in a prepared statement are specialized for representing single data items. If what you want to replace is larger—for example, the entire WHERE clause of a SELECT statement—placeholders won't work, but `sprintf()` will.

Listing 20.1 shows how we can start out with a generic SELECT statement, adding first the WHERE clause itself and then the data for the WHERE clause.

Listing 20.1   TopicFinder with two-step string replacement

```
class TopicFinder {
    const SELECT_STMT =                           ❶ Generic select
        "SELECT id,name from Topics WHERE %s";        statement

    function __construct() {
        $this->connection =
            CreoleConnectionFactory::getConnection();
    }                                             ❷ WHERE
                                                     clause
    function findWithName($name) {                   specifies
        $stmt = $this->connection->prepareStatement(  name
            sprintf(self::SELECT_STMT,"name = ?"));
        $stmt->setString(1,$name);        ◄──────── ❸ The name itself
        $rs = $stmt->executeQuery();   ❹ Run and
        $rs->first();                     get results
        return $rs->getRow();
    }
}
```

```
function findWithIdLargerThan($id) {
    $stmt = $this->connection->prepareStatement(
        sprintf(self::SELECT_STMT,"id > ?"));        ⑤  Different
    $stmt->set(1,$id);                                   column and
    $rs = $stmt->executeQuery();          ⑥  Run and get operator
    $rs->first();                             results
    return $rs->getRow();
}

}
```

◼

❶ We start out with a generic SELECT statement, making this a class constant so it's available whenever we need it.

❷ In the findWithName() method, we replace the unspecified WHERE clause with one that selects all topics that have a name that matches the placeholder.

❸ Then we insert the name into the query.

❹ Finally, we run the query and return the result.

❺ In the other method, findWithIdLargerThan(), we make the generic SELECT statement into a statement that selects all topics with an ID larger than the value represented by the placeholder.

❻ These three lines—to execute the query and get the data—are duplicated in the two methods and might be extracted into a separate method. Alternatively, we could make our own prepared statement object and put the method there. We'll try that out when we discuss how to write a Finder class.

By the way, this particular example could have been done by simply attaching the WHERE clause by concatenation at the end of the generic SQL statement. But that approach will fail as soon as we add anything more (such as an ORDER BY) at the end of the statement.

Simple string substitution may be just a less-secure alternative to placeholders in prepared statements. The need to piece together SQL queries becomes urgent only when we start thinking of our queries in more general terms. That's what we'll do in the next section.

20.3 GENERALIZING SQL

It's tempting to generalize the SQL in our applications to the point where as little as possible is duplicated. For instance, the comma-separated columns in a table may appear identically in several different SELECT statements. Why not reuse it? And if you do that, it may occur to you that the column names appear in INSERT and UPDATE statements as well.

This line of development leads in the direction of generating all queries from metadata—primarily table and column names. This is what Fowler calls *Metadata Mapping*. One problem with this strategy is that you have to sacrifice the immediate readability of SQL statements for programmers who are familiar with it. Halfway solutions resemble and extend what we've done so far, generating SQL by using a mixture of recognizable, literal SQL code, and variable substitutions. It's not as obvious to the SQL-trained eye as complete literal SQL statements. In the previous listing (20.1), you have to read at least three lines of code to figure out what the simple SQL end result will be.

Generating all queries from metadata solves that problem by completely removing the need to use explicit SQL syntax. But SQL is so complex, multifaceted, and flexible that being able to generate any conceivable query is next to impossible, and even generating everything you need in most practical situations is a lot of work. That's why ready-made object-relational mapping tools are popular.

On the other hand, even without full Metadata Mapping, you can make the majority of data access code generic. This will greatly reduce the effort required to implement new objects and database tables. The halfway measures sacrifice some SQL readability to help us remove duplication and keep the PHP code clean.

In this section, we'll first look at how we substitute column lists and table names in SELECT queries. After a quick reminder of SQL aliases, we'll see how we can generalize INSERT, UPDATE, and DELETE statements. Then we'll have a quick look at the idea of query objects. Finally, we'll do an overview of the design patterns that can be used to describe some of what we've done.

20.3.1   Column lists and table names

We'll start out with a couple of simple substitutions and see how that works. One of the simplest is to have a string containing the comma-separated list of columns for a table and use that for different SELECT statements. Another substitution is to make the table name replaceable. The example in listing 20.2 shows how to use this to implement an oversimplified generic Finder class.

> **Listing 20.2   Generic Finder class that needs only constant strings to function as a specific Finder**

```
abstract class Finder {
    private $connection;
    public function __construct() {
        $this->connection = ConnectionFactory::getConnection();
    }
    public function findAll() {
        $result = $this->connection->query(sprintf(
                "SELECT %s FROM %s",
                constant(get_class($this)."::COLUMN_LIST"),
                constant(get_class($this)."::TABLE")
                ));
```

```
        return $result->fetchRow();
    }
}
```

Now all we need is for the column list and table name to function as a specific Finder:

```
class TopicFinder extends Finder {
    const TABLE = 'Topics';
    const COLUMN_LIST = 'id,name';
}

class NewsFinder extends Finder {
    const TABLE = 'News';
    const COLUMN_LIST = 'headline,introduction,text';
}
```

When the findAll() method constructs the SQL statement, it uses the constant from the class the instance belongs to. For instance, let us say we are running a TopicFinder:

```
$finder = new TopicFinder;
$topic = $finder->findAll();
```

Inside the findAll() method, $this represents the TopicFinder instance, so get_class($this) returns the string "TopicFinder." The constant() function returns the constants belonging to that class. Figure 20.2 is a class diagram of this structure.

The child classes only contain metadata. Now the Inheritance Police are after us, though. We have used inheritance to just add a couple of configuration values to the class. Why not just specify them when creating the Finder object?

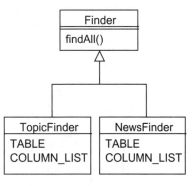

Figure 20.2   Finder hierarchy

```
$finder = new Finder('News','headline,introduction,text');
```

If this is too big and ugly, we can use a factory class to encapsulate the metadata, so that we can say this instead:

```
$finder = FinderFactory::newTopicFinder();
```

This leads to the design in figure 20.3.

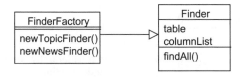

Figure 20.3
Getting rid of the Finder hierarchy

So why did I even come up with the idea of using inheritance? Probably because Fowler does that in his Finder examples. He has a better excuse, though, since there are real behavioral differences between his Finder classes. In other words, once we need two methods that are specific to each type of finder, we need the hierarchy again, as shown in figure 20.4.

Now if we want to get rid of the hierarchy once more, we will have to abstract the idea of finding an object using a specific criterion. The simple way to do that would be a method such as

```
public function findWithColumnValue($columnName,$value) {}
```

However, this will prove insufficient as soon as we need to select by more complex criteria such as *larger than*. There is no way to make this reasonably flexible without resorting to query objects. (These are briefly described later in this chapter.)

Another annoying feature of the Finder class is the ugliness of the expression to generate the column list and the table name:

```
constant(get_class($this)."::TABLE")
```

And why? Just to get at one simple value that's stored in the class. The limitations of PHP 5 class constants are starting to bother us again.

There are other alternatives, though. There are other places to represent the table name and column list strings. The simplest way may be to make them instance variables:

```
private $TABLE = 'Topics';
private $COLUMN_LIST = 'id,name';
```

NOTE   If they are in the base Finder, it's natural to make them `private`. If we use inheritance, they would have to be `protected` instead.

This makes it possible to generate the SQL statement in a more palatable way:

```
$result = $this->connection->query(sprintf(
        "SELECT %s FROM %s",
        $this->COLUMN_LIST,
        $this->TABLE
        ));
```

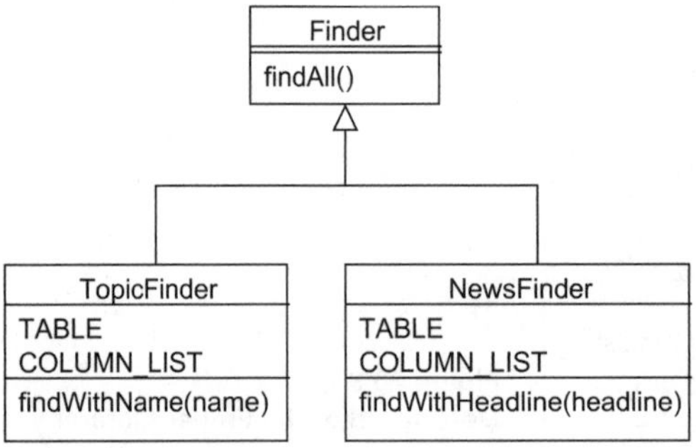

**Figure 20.4
We may need the hierarchy anyway
for specific finder methods**

20.3.2   Using SQL aliases

If you use SQL regularly, this may be elementary, but don't forget that you can use AS in the column list to make the names that are returned easier to work with. This counts if you use any database function or abstraction that returns named column values, typically an associative array. AS can be used to create a meaningful name for something that's the result of a function:

```
SELECT concat(firstname, ' ',lastname) AS name from Persons
```

Sometimes it's also useful to avoid having to change the PHP code if the database changes. So if you have a column called `lastname` and, during a psychotic break, someone changes it to `surname`, you can replace `lastname` with `surname  AS lastname` , and the PHP code will work as before.

20.3.3   Generating INSERT, UPDATE and DELETE statements

As soon as we have the list of columns, why not use it to generate INSERT and UPDATE statements as well? It seems straightforward: take a list of column names and a list of values, concatenate some strings, and you've saved yourself the trouble of typing the same column names all over again.

But alas, there is one complication: quoting. If we had an array of values, we might try to generate a value list this way:

```
$valuestring = 'VALUES ('.join(',',$values).')';
```

This will almost certainly give you an SQL syntax error, since string values won't be quoted:

```
VALUES (1,Trains)
```

Instead, since string values in INSERT and UPDATE statements must be inside single quotes, we need to generate this:

```
VALUES (1,'Trains')
```

The problem is that there is no failsafe way to distinguish between a number and a string in a dynamically typed language such as PHP. We can use the is_numeric() function and add quotes if it returns FALSE. But if someone names their dog "42" or enters "747" as their preferred means of transportation, our application is at risk of crashing.

We now have three options. We can

- Ignore the problem, assuming either it's too rare to be a real issue or that it will be prevented by checking the user's input. The existing PHP database abstraction layers seem not too-concerned with it. In any case, to avoid database errors, we have to make sure numbers entered are clean—that they contain no non-numeric characters. So perhaps we should do the converse: make sure all strings are unequivocally recognizable as strings by making sure they contain at least one non-numeric character.

- Make sure that we know the column types of all the data and use that to make sure all strings are quoted correctly. This adds complexity. It starts getting us deep into the issues of how to deal with metadata.

- Do the quoting manually by adding quotes to each string value before generating the SQL statements.

How might we do the quoting manually? It's easy when we enter the SQL statements explicitly in the PHP code and just add the data. When we want to generate an INSERT statement from the row data, it's less obvious, but not difficult. We just add the quotes—in quotes—at the end and the beginning of the value, as in `"'$value'"` or `"'".$value."'"`. In context, it would appear something like this:

```
$rowData = array(
    'id' => $topic->getID(),
    'name' => "'".$topic->getName()."'"
    );
```

This makes it possible to write code for generating SQL statements while ignoring the quoting problem. Now we can create a simple class that generates INSERT and UPDATE statements. Using array functions, it's relatively short and sweet.

```
class SqlGenerator {

    public static function makeInsertStatement($table,$rowData) {
        $columns = join(',',array_keys($rowData));
        $values = join(',',array_values($rowData));
        return "INSERT INTO $table ($columns) VALUES ($values)";
    }

    public static function makeUpdateStatement($table,$rowData) {
        foreach ($rowData as $key => $value) {
            $entries[] = "$key = $value";
        }
        return "UPDATE $table SET ".join(', ',$entries).
            " WHERE id = ".$rowData['id'];
    }
}
```

We have made a somewhat shaky assumption here: that the ID column in the database table is always called id, pure and simple. More likely, it will be called something else, and we will have to specify that as an argument to the methods. (Or we could make it an instance variable of an SqlGenerator object. That would mean changing the methods so they're no longer static.)

If we want to add quotes automatically, we can use a separate method that tests whether the value is numeric and adds quotes if it isn't:

```
class SqlGenerator {
    public static function prepareValue($value) {
        if (is_numeric($value)) return $value;
        return "'$value'";
    }
    public static function makeInsertStatement($table,$rowData) {
        $columns = join(',',array_keys($rowData));
        foreach ($rowData as $value) {
            $values[] = self::prepareValue($value);
        }
        return "INSERT INTO $table ($columns) VALUES (".
            join(',',$values).")";
    }
    public static function makeUpdateStatement($table,$rowData) {
        foreach ($rowData as $key => $value) {
            $entries[] = "$key = ".self::prepareValue($value);
        }
        return "UPDATE $table SET ".join(', ',$entries).
            " WHERE id = ".$rowData['id'];    }
}
```

As mentioned, this will fail if there is a dog named "1053," but it will work in nearly all cases.

But what if we're working with objects and want to store the objects? What if we want methods that will accept an object—instead of an array-based data structure—and generate the INSERT or UPDATE statements based on that? The code to pull the data out of the object will be specific to the class of object. So this will be different for, say, topics and customers. But the SqlGenerator can be used for any table and any set of columns, so we can't simply add code to it that's specific to a table. One solution would be to make child classes of the SqlGenerator to handle the specifics. But remembering the Inheritance Police, let's try it first without inheritance this time. Give the SqlGenerator an object it can call upon to do the specific parts of the job. This object is actually a strategy object, so we could call it something like SqlGeneratorStrategy, but since its job for the time being will be to convert a domain object into an array, we'll call it a converter. So the generator remains independent of the class of domain object we're working with—it stays aloof from the details of the domain object, as it were—but it takes a Converter into its household that does know how to deal with those details.

```
$generator = new SqlGenerator(new TopicConverter);
$sql = $generator->makeUpdateStatement($topic);
```

The Converter object is not just converting the object; we'll also move those two crucial bits of metadata into it, the table name and the ID column name. So we have a new solution to the problem of where to keep them: instead of using inheritance or storing the two values directly in the SqlGenerator, we keep them in the Converter, since this is an object that depends on the domain object.

```
abstract class ObjectToArrayConverter {
    abstract public function convert($object);
    abstract public function TABLE_NAME();
    abstract public function ID_COLUMN();
}

class TopicConverter extends ObjectToArrayConverter {
    public function convert($topic) {
        return array(
                'id' => $topic->getID(),
                'name' => "'".$topic->getName()."'"
                );
    }
    public function TABLE_NAME() { return 'Topics'; }
    public function ID_COLUMN() { return 'id'; }
}
```

As in some of the earlier examples, the abstract class is the equivalent of an interface when it has no concrete methods.

What we now have is just enough to enable the SqlGenerator to accept an object and generate SQL from it.

```
class SqlGenerator {
    private $converter;

    public function __construct($converter) {
        $this->converter = $converter;
    }

    public function makeInsertStatement($object) {
        $rowData = $this->converter->convert($object);
        $columns = join(',',array_keys($rowData));
        $values = join(',',array_values($rowData));
        return "INSERT INTO ".$this->converter->TABLE_NAME().
            " ($columns) VALUES ($values)";
    }
    public function makeUpdateStatement($object) {
        $rowData = $this->converter->convert($object);
        foreach ($rowData as $key => $value) {
            $entries[] = "$key = $value";
        }
        return "UPDATE ".$this->converter->TABLE_NAME().
            " SET ".join(', ',$entries).
            " WHERE ".$this->converter->ID_COLUMN().
            " = ".$rowData['id'];
    }
}
```

The methods are no longer static, since this design is based on having the SqlGenerator object contain the Converter object.

There is a fairly obvious way to make the client API even simpler: we can let the converter find out what converter is needed based on the class of domain object. We can let a factory method return the appropriate converter for the domain object:

```
class SqlGenerator {
    public static function getConverterFor(DomainObject $object) {
        if ($object instanceof Topic) return new TopicConverter;
        if ($object instanceof Customer)
            return new CustomerConverter;
        // etc...
    }

    public static function makeInsertStatement($object) {
        $converter = self::getConverterFor($object);
        $rowData = $converter->convert($object);
        $columns = join(',',array_keys($rowData));
        $values = join(',',array_values($rowData));
        return "INSERT INTO ".$converter->TABLE_NAME().
            " ($columns) VALUES ($values)";
    }
}
```

I've shown only the `makeInsertStatement()` method. The others need to be changed in a similar way, accepting only the domain object and getting the converter using the `getConverterFor()` method. I've also made the methods static again, since we're now instantiating a new converter every time we call one of the methods. Figure 20.5 is a class diagram of the design of the SQL generator with converters for domain objects. The two concrete converter classes, TopicConverter and Document-Converter, are just two examples. There could be converters for any number of domain object classes.

You can see from the diagram that there is no implementation inheritance involved. The ObjectToArrayConverter class functions as a pure interface.

The alternative using implementation inheritance is shown in figure 20.6. This is a somewhat simpler structure, and the code will be simpler, but it's less flexible. Also, what the concrete classes actually do is not as clear. The TopicSqlGenerator class *is* a converter, but it's not named as such.

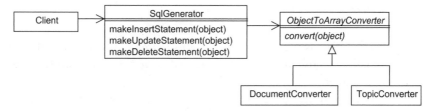

Figure 20.5 The SqlGenerator with converters

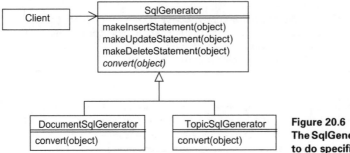

Figure 20.6
The SqlGenerator with subclasses to do specific object conversions

20.3.4 Query objects

The SqlGenerator is capable of generating most of the INSERT, DELETE, and UPDATE statements needed in an object-oriented context. It won't allow you to delete, insert, or update more than one object at a time, but that's not usually a problem. Doing several updates in a loop is slow, but that won't hurt you unless you do it frequently.

SELECT statements, on the other hand, are much more difficult, since WHERE clauses can get complex, especially if you want to select based on more than one criterion.

The way to handle this is either to hand-code specialized methods for all complex SELECT statements or to use query objects that can generate WHERE clauses from criteria that are specified in a way that doesn't depend on SQL.

Object/relational mapping tools do this all the time. The following example—taken directly from the Propel user guide—shows the principle:

```
$c = new Criteria();
$c->add(BookPeer::TITLE, "War%", Criteria::LIKE);
$c->setLimit(10);

$books = BookPeer::doSelect($c);

foreach($books as $book) {
  print "<br/>" . $book->getTitle();
}
```

The Criteria object is the query object in this example. It's an object that can contain several criteria, representing the data needed to generate the WHERE clause of the SELECT statement.

An advantage of this design is that the application always uses an abstract interface to get data. If instead there were a method called findWithTitle(), that method would only be applicable to objects that have titles. When we use query objects, all method names are independent of the type of object we're finding.

20.3.5 Applicable design patterns

The SqlGenerator is related to the *Update Factory* pattern [Nock]. But actually, Update Factory does only what the Converter does: it generates a Java HashMap—corresponding to the PHP associative array—from the domain object. Nock's use of the term factory is unusual, since factories usually produce full-fledged objects. The HashMap produced by Nock's factory is technically an object but conceptually just a data structure.

Query Object is described by Fowler in [P of EAA].

20.4 SUMMARY

Object-oriented programming languages and relational databases are in some ways fundamentally incompatible. This creates challenges for programmers: we need to represent SQL queries in some form that at least makes duplication manageable, and we need to package and repackage data when moving it to and from the database.

A completely literal SQL query is easy to execute from a PHP script. As soon as we start to generalize queries, we need some tools and techniques we can use to make it easier. The simpler approaches involve various, relatively plain forms of string handling. For doing it in a more general and systematic way, it helps to use an object-oriented approach. This gives us enough flexibility to create most of what we need.

In the next and final chapter, we wrap up the subject of data access by discussing the design considerations and design patterns for data access classes such as DAO, Data Accessor, Finders, Row Data Gateway, and Active Record. We will also study the relationships, similarities, and differences between them to make each of them as sharply defined as possible.

C H A P T E R   2 1

Data class design

As we've seen, the marriage of a database and an object-oriented program is usually not a match made in heaven. It's more of an arranged marriage, although casual relationships are also possible.

Some ceremony is helpful in getting the liaison started. The patterns presented by Martin Fowler in *Patterns of Enterprise Application Architecture* [P of EAA] are a good rough guide to the alternative ways of creating a systematic and lasting bond between data storage and program code. In this chapter, we will approach these patterns from a slightly different perspective, trying to create some shortcuts along the way.

And, of course, we would like the classes and the database to live happily ever after, but like it or not, we are likely to find ourselves having to work on the relationship. Refactoring is as important here as in other parts of the application.

In this chapter, we'll start with the simplest object-oriented approaches to retrieving data from a database and writing it back. Then we'll see how to build persistence into the objects themselves. We'll also discover the approach of keeping persistence out of the objects to avoid making them dependent on the persistence mechanism. Finally, we'll take a look at these patterns from the point of view of using them rather than implementing them.

21.1 THE SIMPLEST APPROACHES

A database is like a piggy bank: putting something into it and taking something out of it are distinct challenges. They require mostly different procedures and skills. The SqlGenerator object we created previously has methods to generate INSERT, UPDATE, and DELETE statements, but none for SELECTs. A SELECT statement is much more complex, and other information is needed to generate it. When a database is used for object storage, we need to convert and repackage the data in different ways depending on whether we're reading from or writing to the database.

So why not have one class to find and one to save data? You get more classes, obviously. You may not necessarily want to do that in real life. But it is a clean solution both conceptually and technically. And it is instructive: studying the two separately helps elucidate the differences and similarities between the various approaches and design patterns.

Therefore, we'll start this section by studying how to retrieve data with Finder classes. Then we'll add a way to insert and update data, and discover that this approach has been named the Table Data Gateway pattern.

21.1.1 Retrieving data with Finder classes

To find data in a database, it's tempting to use a query object class. But a query object that handles complex queries and joins can be quite complex. So, for a realistic example that's relatively hard to generalize, let's try one that requires a join. The example is a Finder class for News articles with author data that is stored in a separate User table. We can handle this using a less generalized approach to SQL. Listing 21.1 shows such a class, using the Creole library and prepared statements to get the data.

Listing 21.1 News Finder class using a Creole database connection

```
class NewsFinder {
    public function __construct() {
        $this->connection =
            CreoleConnectionFactory::getConnection();
    }

    public function find($id) {
        $stmt = $this->connection->prepareStatement(       ❶ Concatenate
            "SELECT headline,introduction,text, ".            the names
            "concat(Users.firstname,' ',Users.lastname) ".   in SQL
            "AS author, ".
            "UNIX_TIMESTAMP(created) AS created,id ".       ❷ Easy but
            "FROM Documents, Users ".                          MySQL-
            "WHERE Documents.author_id = Users.user_id ".      specific
            "AND id = ?");
        $stmt->setInt(1,$id);            ❸ Using placeholders
        $rs = $stmt->executeQuery();     ❹ Return first
        $rs->first();                      row as array
        return $rs->getRow();
    }
}
```

```
    public function findWithHeadline($headline) {
        $stmt = $this->connection->prepareStatement(
            "SELECT headline,introduction,text, ".
            "concat(Users.firstname,' ',Users.lastname) ".
            "AS author, ".
            "UNIX_TIMESTAMP(created) AS created,id ".
            "FROM Documents, Users ".
            "WHERE Documents.author_id = Users.user_id ".
            "AND headline = ?");
        $stmt->setString(1,$headline);
        $rs = $stmt->executeQuery();
        $rs->first();
        return $rs->getRow();
    }
    public function findAll() {
        return $this->connection->executeQuery(
            "SELECT headline,introduction,text, ".
            "concat(Users.firstname,' ',Users.lastname) ".
            "AS author, ".
            "UNIX_TIMESTAMP(created) AS created,id ".
            "FROM Documents, Users ".
            "WHERE Documents.author_id = Users.user_id ".
            "ORDER BY created DESC");
    }
```

❺ Return the result set iterator

❶ We're using SQL to generate the full name from the first and last names. If we wanted to make an object out of the row, it might be better to do this job inside the object instead of in SQL. That would mean storing the names in separate variables in the object and having a method that would generate the full name.

❷ Assuming that `created` is a MySQL `datetime` or `timestamp` column, using `UNIX_TIMESTAMP()` is an easy MySQL-specific way of getting the date and time in a format that is convenient to use in PHP.

❸ In this situation, using placeholders is almost equivalent to interpolating (or concatenating) the ID directly in the SQL statement. The most important difference is that Creole will escape the value if it's a string.

❹ In this and the following method, we use the Creole result set to return an array representing the first row.

❺ In the `findAll()` method, we return the Creole result set iterator. This is interesting, since it will work as an SPL iterator, allowing us to do this:

```
$rs = $this->finder->findAll();
foreach ($rs as $row) {
    print $row['headline']."\n";
}
```

In other words, the iterator acts as if it's an array of associative arrays. On the other hand, it will also work like a JDBC-style iterator:

```
while($rs->next()) {
    $row = $rs->getRow();
    print $row['headline']."\n";
}
```

This is really only useful to those who are used to JDBC. What *is* useful is the ability to get specific data types. For example, if we want to get rid of the MySQL-specific `UNIX_TIMESTAMP()` function, we can remove it from the SQL statement and use the result set's `getTimestamp()` method as follows:

```
foreach ($rs as $row) {
    print $row['headline']."\n"; // or: $rs->getString('headline');
    print $rs->getTimestamp('created','U')."\n";
}
```

This is an odd hybrid approach, using the result set and the $row array interchangeably, but it works.

In listing 21.1, there is a lot of duplicated SQL code. As mentioned, that can be a good idea, since it leaves SQL statements relatively intact, and that may make them more readable. The duplication creates a risk of making inconsistent changes. But when the statements are concentrated in one class as they are here, it's possible to avoid that.

On the other hand, the amount of duplication is so large in this case, and the differences between the statements so small, that it's tempting to eliminate it. We can do that by having a separate method to prepare the statement, as in listing 21.2.

Listing 21.2   News Finder class with SQL duplication eliminated

```
class NewsFinder {
    public function find($id) {
        $stmt = $this->prepare("AND id = ?");
        $stmt->setInt(1,$id);
        return $stmt->executeQuery();
    }

    public function findWithHeadline($headline) {
        $stmt = $this->prepare("AND headline = ?");
        $stmt->setString(1,$headline);
        return $stmt->executeQuery();
    }

    public function findAll() {
        $stmt = $this->prepare ("ORDER BY created DESC");
        return $stmt->executeQuery();
        return $result;
    }

    private function prepare($criteria) {
        return $this->connection->prepareStatement(
                sprintf("SELECT headline,introduction,text, ".
```

```
                        "concat(Users.firstname,' ',Users.lastname) ".
                        "AS author, ".
                        "UNIX_TIMESTAMP(created) AS created,id ".
                        "FROM Documents, Users ".
                        "WHERE Documents.author_id = Users.user_id %s",
                        $criteria));
    }
}
```

To my eyes, that makes the code more, rather than less, readable, although the `pre-pare()` method requires a rather odd-looking SQL fragment representing an addition to the existing WHERE clause.

Figure 21.1 is a simple UML representation of the class. We will use this as a building block for the Table Data Gateway in the next section.

There is more duplication here, though. To get the results in the form of arrays of associative arrays, we're repeating the code to get the data from the Creole result set. This is not much of an issue for this one class. But if we want to write more Finder classes, we need to do something about it.

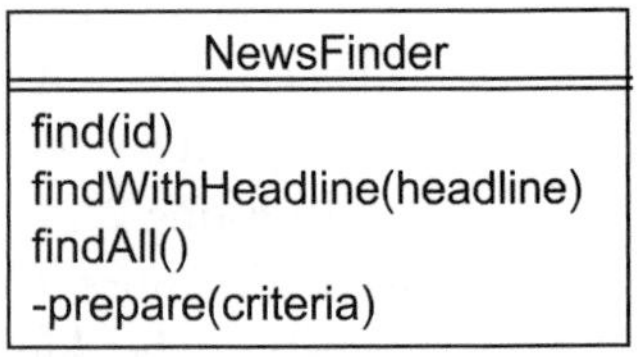

NewsFinder
find(id)
findWithHeadline(headline)
findAll()
-prepare(criteria)

Figure 21.1   NewsFinder class

21.1.2   Mostly procedural: Table Data Gateway

Fowler's Table Data Gateway pattern is a class that—in its simplest form—handles access to a single database table. The principle is to have a class that finds and saves plain data in the database. The data that's retrieved and saved is typically not in the form of objects, or if it is, the objects tend to be rather simple data containers.

The Finder we just built is half a Table Data Gateway. In other words, the methods in a Table Data Gateway that retrieve data from a database are like the Finder methods in the previous examples. The methods that are missing are methods to insert, update, and delete data.

Building a Table Data Gateway

To insert and update data we use `insert()` and `update()` methods and specify all the data for the row as arguments to the method:

```
$gateway->insert($headline,$introduction,$text,$author);
```

A Table Data Gateway is not very object-oriented. It's more like a collection of procedural code in a class. Although with a Table Data Gateway we do create an instance of the class, the resulting object is primarily an engine for executing procedural code.

Instead of building a complete Table Data Gateway, let's do the part that we're missing: update, insert, and delete. We can have a separate class called NewsSaver to do this, as in listing 21.3. In the listing, we're using Creole with prepared statements and a connection factory as discussed in the previous chapter.

Listing 21.3 A NewsSaver class to complement the NewsFinder

```
class NewsSaver {

    private $connection;
    public function __construct() {
        $this->connection
            = CreoleConnectionFactory::getConnection();
    }

    public function delete($id) {
        $sql = "DELETE FROM News where id =".$id;
        $this->connection->executeQuery($sql);
    }

    public function insert($headline,$intro,$text,$author_id) {
        $sql = "INSERT INTO News ".
        "(headline,author_id,introduction,text,created) ".
        "VALUES (?,?,?,?,?)";
        $stmt = $this->connection->prepareStatement($sql);
        $stmt->setString(1,$headline);
        $stmt->setInt(2,$author_id);
        $stmt->setString(3,$intro);
        $stmt->setString(4,$text);
        $stmt->setTimestamp(5,time());
        $stmt->executeUpdate();
        $rs = $this->connection->executeQuery(
                "SELECT LAST_INSERT_ID() AS id");
        $rs->first();
        return $rs->getInt('id');
    }

    public function update($id,$headline,$intro,$text,$author_id)
    {
        $sql = "UPDATE News SET ".
            "headline = ?, ".
            "author_id = ?, ".
            "introduction = ?, ".
            "text = ? ".
            "WHERE id = ?";
        $stmt = $this->connection->prepareStatement($sql);
        $stmt->setString(1,$headline);
        $stmt->setInt(2,$author_id);
        $stmt->setString(3,$intro);
        $stmt->setString(4,$text);
        $stmt->setInt(5,$id);
        $stmt->executeUpdate();
    }
}
```

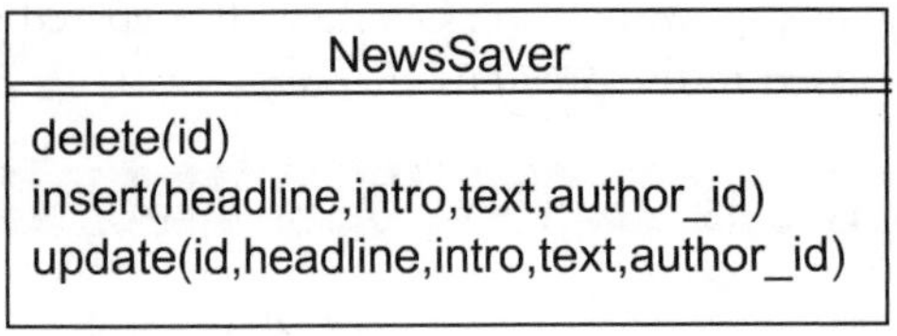

```
                  NewsSaver
─────────────────────────────────────
delete(id)
insert(headline,intro,text,author_id)
update(id,headline,intro,text,author_id)
```

**Figure 21.2
NewsSaver class**

The approach to generating and executing SQL in this example is so similar to earlier examples that the details should be self-explanatory. The argument lists are shown in bold, since they are the distinguishing feature of this particular approach. The data to be stored is introduced as single values rather than arrays or objects. Summarizing the class in UML, we get figure 21.2.

If you want a complete Table Data Gateway, you can simply merge the NewsFinder and the NewsSaver classes, as shown in figure 21.3.

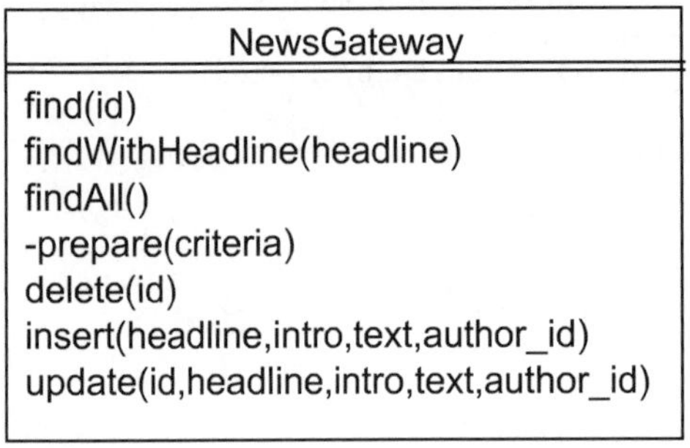

```
                  NewsGateway
─────────────────────────────────────
find(id)
findWithHeadline(headline)
findAll()
-prepare(criteria)
delete(id)
insert(headline,intro,text,author_id)
update(id,headline,intro,text,author_id)
```

**Figure 21.3
Merging the NewsFinder
and NewsSaver classes
into a Table Data Gate-**

Alternatively, you can keep the NewsFinder and NewsSaver classes and use delegation to make NewsGateway a simple facade for those two classes. Listing 21.4 shows just two methods as an example.

Listing 21.4 A partial implementation of a NewsGateway as a Facade for the NewsSaver and NewsFinder classes

```php
class NewsGateway {
    private $finder;
    private $saver;
    public function __construct() {
        $this->finder = new NewsFinder;
        $this->saver = new NewsSaver;
    }

    public function find($id) {
        return $this->finder->find($id);
    }

    public function delete($id) {
        $this->saver->delete($id);
    }
}
```

CHAPTER 21 DATA CLASS DESIGN

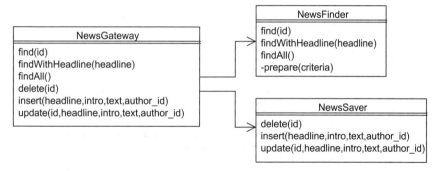

Figure 21.4 Instead of merging the NewsFinder and NewsSaver classes, we can combine them by having the NewsGateway delegate work to the other two

Figure 21.4 is a UML representation of the complete structure. In UML, each class is identical to the ones shown before, except that the NewsGateway class no longer has the private `prepare()` method. In actual implementation, the NewsGateway class is completely different from the merged NewsGateway class, since the methods delegate all the work to the NewsFinder or NewsSaver classes instead of doing it themselves.

This alternative may be considered a cleaner separation of responsibilities; on the other hand, having three classes instead of one may seem unnecessarily complex if you find the merged version easy to understand. The main point is to show how easily you can juggle and combine these classes.

Finding and formatting data using Table Data Gateway

According to Fowler, what to return from Finder methods is tricky in a Table Data Gateway. What should the table row look like when you use it in the application? Should it be an array or an object? What kind of array or object? And what happens when you need to return a number of rows from the database?

The path of least resistance in PHP is to let a row be represented by an associative array and to return an array of these. Listing 21.5 is a dump of two rows in this kind of data structure.

Using an SPL-compatible iterator is a variation on this. From the client code's point of view, it looks very similar.

Listing 21.5 Return data from a Table Data Gateway as arrays

```
Array
(
    [0] => Array
        (
            [user_id] => 1
            [username] => victor
            [firstname] => Victor
            [lastname] => Ploctor
            [password] => 5d009bfda017b80dd1ce08c7e68458be
```

```
            [email] => victor@example.com
            [usertype] => regular
    )

    [1] => Array
        (
            [user_id] => 2
            [username] => elietta
            [firstname] => Elietta
            [lastname] => Floon
            [password] => 7db7c42a13bd7e3202fbbc94435fb85a
            [email] => elietta@example.com
            [usertype] => regular
        )
```

Another possibility is to return each row as a simplified object. This would typically not be a full domain object with all capabilities, but rather an object that acts primarily as a data holder. This kind of object is what Fowler calls a Data Transfer Object (sometimes abbreviated as DTO), since it's an object that's easy to serialize and send across a network connection.

PEAR DB has a feature that makes this easy, since you can return objects from the fetchRow() method. Listing 21.6 shows a dump of this kind of return data.

Listing 21.6   Return data from a Table Data Gateway as objects

```
Array
(
    [0] => User Object
        (
            [user_id] => 1
            [username] => victor
            [firstname] => Victor
            [lastname] => Ploctor
            [password] => c7e72687ddc69340814e3c1bdbf3e2bc
            [email] => victor@example.com
            [usertype] => regular
        )

    [1] => User Object
        (
            [user_id] => 2
            [username] => elietta
            [firstname] => Elietta
            [lastname] => Floon
            [password] => 053fbca71905178df74c507637966e02
            [email] => elietta@example.com
            [usertype] => regular
        )
```

CHAPTER 21 DATA CLASS DESIGN

The example in the PEAR DB manual shows how to get PEAR DB to return DB_row objects, but it's also possible to return objects belonging to other classes if they inherit from DB_row. That means you can add other methods to the objects if you want:

```
class User extends DB_Row {
    function getName() {
        return $this->firstname." ".$this->lastname;
    }
}
```

To make PEAR DB return the objects, do the following:

```
$db = DB::Connect("mysql://$dbuser:$dbpassword@$dbhost/$dbname");
if (DB::isError($db)) die ($db->getMessage());
$db->setFetchMode(DB_FETCHMODE_OBJECT, 'User');
$res =$db->query('SELECT * FROM Users');
while ($row = $res->fetchRow()) {
    $rows[] = $row;
}
print_r($rows);
```

But is there a good reason to prefer objects over arrays to represent database rows? In many programming languages, using objects would help you by making sure there was a clear error message if you tried to use a nonexistent member variable. But in PHP, the basic error checking for arrays and objects is similar. If you use

```
error_reporting(E_ALL)
```

you will get a Notice if you try to use an undefined index of an array or an undefined member variable of an object. In either case, there is no danger that mistyping a name will cause a bug, unless you start modifying the array or object after it's been retrieved from the database. If you do want to modify it, you'll be safer by making it an object and modifying it only through method calls. For example, if you want to remember the fact that a user has read news article X during the current session, you might want to add that information to the news article object by having a method in the news article object to register that fact. And if you want to display the age of a news article, you could have a method that calculates and returns the age.

The real advantage of using objects lies in being able to do this kind of processing. If you need to get the date and time in a certain format, you can add the capability to the object without changing the way the data is stored in or retrieved from the database. Another advantage is that we can let the objects themselves handle persistence.

21.2 *LETTING OBJECTS PERSIST THEMSELVES*

Bringing up children becomes less work when they start to be able to go to bed in the evening without the help of adults: when they can brush their teeth, put on their pajamas, and go to sleep on their own. This is like the idea of letting objects store themselves in a database. Plain, non-object-oriented data is like a baby that has to be carried around, dressed, and put to bed. An object that has the ability to do things on its own is something quite different.

The Table Data Gateway pattern works with "babies": plain data that has few capabilities of its own. We use specialized objects to do the job of storing and getting data from the database, but the data itself does not have to be—and has mostly not been—in the form of objects.

If we do represent data as objects, we gain the ability to add behaviors to these objects. That means we can make them responsible. It's a relatively simple and intuitive way to implement object persistence: letting the objects store themselves in the database. The application code creates an object, and then calls an `insert()` method (or alternatively, a `save()` method) on the object to keep it in the database: something like this

```
$topic = new Topic('Trains');
$topic->insert();
```

This approach is used in several of Fowler's and Nock's data storage patterns. Fowler has Row Data Gateway and Active Record; Nock has Active Domain Object. They are all similar in principle, but there are some interesting differences, especially in retrieving objects from the database.

This section has the same structure as the previous one: we'll first look at finding data and then see how objects can insert themselves to the database.

21.2.1 Finders for self-persistent objects

You can retrieve objects from the database in an explicit or implicit way. Implicit retrieval gets the data from the object from the database behind the scenes when the object is constructed. So all you need to do is specify the object's ID, and the object is retrieved from the database without any need to tell it to do that.

```
$newsArticle = new NewsArticle(31);
$newsArticle->setHeadline('Woman bites dog');
$newsArticle->save();
```

This is the approach taken by Nock. From the application's point of view, it is the prettiest and most consistent way of implementing self-persistent objects. The code does not mention anything but the persistent object itself and the class it belongs to.

Explicit data retrieval is more like what we've done earlier. So to get an object with a specific ID, we can use a finder class as before:

```
$finder = new NewsFinder;
$newsArticle = $finder->find(31);
$newsArticle->setHeadline('Woman bites dog');
$newsArticle->save();
```

This may look less appealing. On the other hand, since it's more explicit, it could be easier to understand. We want our code to be as readable as possible, and concealing what is actually going on (a database read) may cause misunderstandings. Method names should generally describe the intention of the method. What about constructors, then? Constructors usually just instantiate and initialize the object; reading data from a database is more than we normally expect. Perhaps it's better to have a method such as find() that tells us more precisely what is going on.

There is another problem with the implicit approach. The first time we create an object, it's not in the database yet. So obviously, we need to construct the object without reading it from the database. In other words, we need a constructor that just does basic initialization. In Java, this is solved by having different constructors that do different things depending on the list of arguments. Yet I find it confusing that one constructor reads from the database and one doesn't. I have to remember that the one that reads from the database is the one that accepts only the ID as an argument.

In PHP, this problem is even worse, since you can have only one constructor. So we need conditional logic based on the number and/or types of arguments, and that's not pretty. But there is a way around PHP's inability to have more than one constructor: using creation methods. If one of those methods finds an object by ID in the database, we might as well call it find(). So we've just taken a detour, and now we're back to the explicit approach.

Yet another factor is the fact that we will likely need to get objects from the database by other criteria than just the ID. In other words, we need other finder methods. If one of the finder methods is implemented as a constructor and the others aren't, that's yet another inconsistency. Nock solves this problem by having a separate collection object: there is a Customer object that's found by using the constructor, and a CustomerList object whose constructor gets all the customers from the database. In addition, you can have other constructors that represent customer lists returned by other queries.

Let's try Fowler's strategy of doing all reading from the database explicitly by finder methods.

How do we implement it? We've already developed finder classes that do everything except actually instantiate the objects. All we need to do is to add that last step.

The easiest way to do this is to add a load() method to the finder to do the job of creating the object from the array (or object) representing the row:

```
class NewsFinder {
    public function load($row) {
        if (!$row) return FALSE;
        extract($row);
        $object = new NewsArticle(
            $headline,
            $introduction,
            $text,
            $author_id,
            new DateAndTime($created)
        );
        $object->setID($id);
        return $object;
    }
```

```
public function fetchObjects($stmt) {
    $rs = $stmt->executeQuery();
    $result = array();
    while($rs->next()) {
        $result[] = $this->load($rs->getRow());
    }
    return $result;
}
}
```

The `load()` function is mostly code that's specific to the NewsFinder. The `fetchObjects()` method, on the other hand, could be used in Finders for other objects as well.

To deal with this, the path of least resistance is to extract `fetchObjects()` into a parent class. The alternative is to decorate the prepared statement class and keep the code there. This may be somewhat more logical, since returning results in a generic way is already part of the statement's responsibility.

But the kind of object to be returned depends on which specific finder we are using. How do we get the right class of object? There is an elegant solution: we can pass the fetch method(s) an object that creates the output objects we want. This object will be a kind of factory object: it takes a database row (or possibly a result object returned from the database abstraction layer) and generates the output object from that. We can call it a loader to distinguish it from other kinds of factories.

Since we want to pass the loader to the statement object, let's have an interface (or an abstract class). That allows us to use type hints.

```
interface Loader {
    public function load($row);
}
```

The loader itself does nothing but instantiate the object, set its data, and return it:

```
class NewsLoader implements Loader {
    public function load($row) {
        if (!$row) return FALSE;
        extract($row);
        $object = new NewsArticle(
            $headline,
            $introduction,
            $text,
            $author_id,
            new DateAndTime($created)
        );
        $object->setID($id);
        return $object;
    }
}
```

We've used the opportunity to convert the timestamp into an object as well. So the NewsArticle object will contain a DateAndTime object rather than a plain timestamp.

But this means the SQL statement must return a UNIX timestamp. As mentioned earlier, this means that we either have to store the timestamp as an integer in the database or use RDBMS-specific functions to convert it. Instead of relying on the database to return the timestamp, we can use a date conversion class:

```
$dbComponentFactory = new MysqlComponentFactory;
extract($row)
$converter = $dbComponentFactory->getDateConverter();
$dateandtime = new DateAndTime($converter->toUnixTimestamp($created));
```

Without going into it deeply, let us just note that this is another example of the Abstract Factory pattern [Gang of Four]. Once we've created the component factory that's appropriate for the current RDBMS, we might use it to create objects for doing other RDBMS-specific tasks such as limiting queries or ID generation.

Now let us get back to our original goal—letting a decorator for the prepared statement class generate domain objects while remaining independent of the specific domain object class. The structure in figure 21.5 is what we need. It may seem complex, but the important roles are played by the NewsLoader and CreoleStatement classes. We've isolated the knowledge about the particular domain object, the NewsArticle, putting it in the NewsLoader class. To reuse this with another kind of domain object, the NewsLoader class is the only one we have to replace.

Let's look at the implementation of the `fetchFirst()` and `fetchAll()` methods that have the ability to generate objects without knowing their type. Listing 21.7 shows how the CreoleStatement class accepts a Loader object and uses it to generate domain objects.

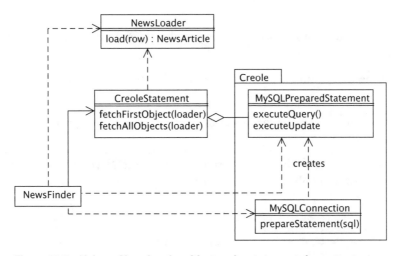

Figure 21.5   Using a NewsLoader object and a statement decorator to generate objects from retrieved data

```
class CreoleStatement {
    private $statement;
    public function __construct($statement) {          ❶ Decorate the original
        $this->statement = $statement;                   statement object
    }

    public function executeQuery() {                   ❷ Two sample
        return $this->statement->executeQuery();         methods
    }

    public function executeUpdate() {
        return $this->statement->executeUpdate();
    }

    public function fetchFirstObject(Loader $loader) {  ❸ Use the loader
        $rs = $this->executeQuery();                       to create
        $rs->first();                                      objects
        return $loader->load($rs->getRow());
    }

    public function fetchAllObjects(Loader $loader) {
        $rs = $this->executeQuery();
        $result = array();
        while($rs->next()) {
            $result[] = $loader->load($rs->getRow());
        }
        return $result;
    }
}
```

❶ We create the decorator as usual by passing the object to be decorated into the constructor.

❷ We will need methods from the decorated object. Only two are shown here, but many more may be relevant.

❸ Methods to get objects use the loader to create an object from an array representation of a database row.

Now all we need to do is to use these methods in the NewsFinder, passing a newly created NewsLoader object to the statement object.

```
class NewsFinder {

    public function find($id) {
        $stmt = $this->prepare("AND id = ?");
        $stmt->setInt(1,$id);
        return $stmt->fetchFirstObject(new NewsLoader);
    }

    public function findAll() {
```

```
        $stmt = $this->prepare("ORDER BY created DESC");
        return $stmt->fetchAllObjects(new NewsLoader);
    }
}
```

Passing an object this way is standard object-oriented procedure for passing some code for execution, but it *could* be achieved by passing anonymous functions or just a function or method name instead.

21.2.2   Letting objects store themselves

Now we can write the insert(), update(), and delete() methods. These methods are suspiciously similar to their equivalents in the Table Data Gateway—that is, our NewsSaver as shown in listing 21.4. The main difference is that the values to be saved are taken from the object itself. Listing 21.8 shows how this works. This is a Row Data Gateway pattern in Fowler's terminology. If we add domain logic to it, it will be an Active Record. It's tempting to drop the distinction and call this an Active Record.

Listing 21.8   A NewsArticle class for objects that can insert, update, and delete themselves

```
class NewsArticle implements DomainObject {
    public function insert() {
        $sql = "INSERT INTO News ".
        "(headline,author_id,introduction,text,created) ".
        "VALUES (?,?,?,?,?)";
        $stmt = $this->connection->prepareStatement($sql);
        $stmt->setString(1,$this->getHeadline());
        $stmt->setInt(2,$this->getAuthorID());
        $stmt->setString(3,$this->getIntroduction());
        $stmt->setString(4,$this->getText());
        $stmt->setTimestamp(5,time());
        $stmt->executeUpdate();
        $rs = $this->connection->executeQuery(
                "SELECT LAST_INSERT_ID() AS id");
        $rs->first();
        return $rs->getInt('id');
    }

    public function update() {
        $sql = "UPDATE News SET ".
            "headline = ?, ".
            "author_id = ?, ".
            "introduction = ?, ".
            "text = ? ".
            "WHERE id = ?";
        $stmt = $this->connection->prepareStatement($sql);
        $stmt->setString(1,$this->getHeadline());
        $stmt->setInt(2,$this->getAuthorID());
        $stmt->setString(3,$this->getIntroduction());
        $stmt->setString(4,$this->getText());
        $stmt->setInt(5,$this->getID());
        $stmt->executeUpdate();
```

```
    }
    public function delete() {
        $sql = "DELETE FROM News where id =".$this->getID();
        $this->connection->executeQuery($sql);
    }
}
```

Figure 21.6 is a simplified UML representation that illustrates the principle. The NewsArticle class has the attributes of a news article (id, author, headline, text) and methods to delete, insert, and update itself. Compared to the NewsSaver in figure 21.2, the main difference is that the class has all the data that needs to be stored in the database, so there is no need for the method arguments.

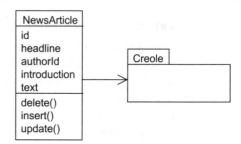

Figure 21.6   NewsArticle class as Row Data Gateway/Active Object

There are several ways to reduce the amount of duplication between the class in listing 21.8 and other persistent objects. One is to use the SqlGenerator from the previous chapter. Another approach, which is the one Fowler takes, is to extract as much generic code as possible into a parent class. The code to generate the ID is the most obvious candidate to be extracted in this way.

We've seen how to delegate the persistence work to the object we're persisting. As ideal as this may seem, we may get rid of some difficult dependencies by doing the exact opposite. This is the point of Fowler's Data Mapper pattern.

21.3   THE DATA MAPPER PATTERN

Having the object itself take care of persistence is convenient, but it's no guarantee of eternal bliss, since it makes the domain objects dependent on the persistence mechanism. The problem shows up if you want to transplant your objects to another application. Suddenly the close tie to the persistence mechanism and the database becomes a liability. There may be no easy way to use them without bringing the entire database along. That's why it may be a good idea to do something completely different: leave persistence to classes that only handle the objects temporarily instead of having a permanent relationship with them.

In this section, we'll first do a slight variation of an earlier example, making it compatible with the idea of a Data Mapper. Then we'll look at the similarities and differences between the data access patterns we've seen so far.

21.3.1 Data Mappers and DAOs

In Fowler's terminology, a Data Mapper is an object that gets objects from and stores objects to a database. The pattern differs from Active Record in using a completely separate mapper object to do the job, rather than the domain object itself.

The J2EE pattern Data Access Object [Alur et al.] is similar in principle, although the description of the pattern is concerned with retrieving and storing so-called Transfer Objects rather than real domain objects. But DAO is frequently used as a more general term encompassing more data access strategies than Data Mapper.

NOTE   In the book, Transfer Objects are called Value Objects, but this is inconsistent with the usage by several gurus. In the online description of the pattern, they are called Transfer Objects.

Again, finding and saving are rather different. The part of a Data Mapper that gets objects from a database is identical to a Finder for an Active Record as described earlier in this chapter. Saving the objects is slightly different. Figure 21.7 shows the principle. This is similar to figure 21.2; the difference is that the NewsArticle object has replaced the list of single data values.

Listing 21.9 shows the implementation.

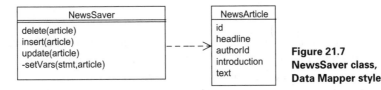

Figure 21.7
NewsSaver class,
Data Mapper style

Listing 21.9   A NewsSaver class that is half of a Data Mapper

```php
class NewsSaver {
    private $connection;
    public function __construct() {
        $this->connection
            = CreoleConnectionFactory::getConnection();
    }

    public function insert($article) {
        $sql = "INSERT INTO News ".
        "(headline,author_id,introduction,text,created) ".
        "VALUES (?,?,?,?,?)";
        $stmt = $this->connection->prepareStatement($sql);
        $this->setVars($stmt,$article);
        $stmt->setTimestamp(5,time());
        $stmt->executeUpdate();
        $rs = $this->connection->executeQuery(
                "SELECT LAST_INSERT_ID() AS id");
        $rs->first();
        return $rs->getInt('id');
    }
```

```
public function update($article) {
    $sql = "UPDATE News SET ".
        "headline = ?, ".
        "author_id = ?, ".
        "introduction = ?, ".
        "text = ? ".
        "WHERE id = ?";
    $stmt = $this->connection->prepareStatement($sql);
    $this->setVars($stmt,$article);
    $stmt->setInt(5,$article->getId());
    $stmt->executeUpdate();
}

private function setVars($stmt,$article) {
    $stmt->setString(1,$article->getHeadline());
    $stmt->setInt(2,$article->getAuthorId());
    $stmt->setString(3,$article->getIntroduction());
    $stmt->setString(4,$article->getText());
}

public function delete($article) {
    $sql = "DELETE FROM News where id = ".$article->getId();
    $this->connection->executeQuery($sql);
}
}
```

The setVars() method contains the code that's needed by both the update() and the insert() methods. In fact, looking back at the previous listing (21.8), we can see that a similar method might be extracted there.

A full Data Mapper can be achieved simply be merging this class with the Finder for the active record.

21.3.2   These patterns are all the same

Fowler's data source patterns look different in UML, but are very similar in implementation.

An Active Record is a Row Data Gateway with domain logic

Although many details and variations differ in Fowler's descriptions of these two patterns, the bottom line is that a Row Data Gateway is transformed into an Active Record if you move domain logic into it.

Fowler says, "If you use Transaction Script with Row Data Gateway, you may notice that you have business logic that's repeated across multiple scripts...Moving that logic will gradually turn your Row Data Gateway into an Active Record."

An Active Record is an object with a built-in Data Mapper

The Active Record pattern just means introducing data access code into a domain object. From the client's perspective, this is equivalent to having a Data Mapper inside the object and using it to do INSERT, UPDATE, and DELETE operations, as in the following fragment of a class:

```
class NewsArticle {
    public function __construct() {
        $this->mapper = new NewsMapper;
    }
    public function insert() {
        $this->mapper->insert($this);
    }
}
```

In fact, we can use the NewsSaver in Data Mapper style to achieve this. Starting out with the previous figure (21.7), adding the methods to the NewsArticle object and changing the places of the two objects, we have figure 21.8 which shows this design.

A Data Mapper is a Table Data Gateway that deconstructs an object

The Table Data Gateway and Data Mapper patterns are also very similar. The Table Data Gateway accepts the data as single values; the Data Mapper accepts it in the form of objects. In a simple Table Data Gateway, the insert() method may have this signature:

```
public function insert($subject,$text) { }
```

Then we use $subject and $text as input to the SQL INSERT statement. In the corresponding Data Mapper, it will be like this instead:

```
public function insert($message) { }
```

Now, instead of $subject and $text, we can use $message->getSubject() and $message->getText(). There's no obvious reason why there should be more of a difference.

Fowler refers to Data Mappers as complex, but the fact is that the complexity is in the mapping process rather than the Data Mapper pattern itself. Mappings that involve multiple class and table relationships are complex to program.

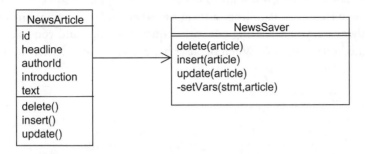

Figure 21.8   Active Record that delegates data storage to a separate Data Mapper (NewsSaver) class

21.3.3 Pattern summary

As mentioned, the principle of self-persistent objects is the theme of Nock's Active Domain Object pattern and of Fowler's Row Data Gateway and Active Record patterns.

The NewsLoader is an instance of Nock's Domain Object Factory pattern.

Reconstituting a DateAndTime object from the database is an example of Fowler's Embedded Value pattern. Entity objects usually need a separate table for storage; value objects such as dates can be represented by one or more columns in a table that stores objects belonging to another class, in this case news articles.

So far we've looked mostly at how we can implement data classes. Now it's time to compare how they work in actual use.

21.4 FACING THE REAL WORLD

We've discussed many of the pros and cons of different patterns, approaches, and techniques. What we haven't considered yet is the way they work in an actual web application. One good reason to do that is the fact that PHP objects don't survive from one HTTP request to the next unless you specifically store them in a session. Using an object-oriented approach can sometimes mean creating objects only to save the data inside them, and that may seem cumbersome.

Starting from that, we'll see how the patterns compare when we try to use them in a typical web application. Then we'll take a look at another challenge that the real world sometimes throws at us: optimizing queries.

21.4.1 How the patterns work in a typical web application

The different data storage patterns have different APIs that affect the programming of the web application. For a simple web application, the interface needs to be simple and comfortable.

Finders are easy to use. Whether they return arrays or objects, there's no problem putting the data out on the web page. Most template engines have ways of getting data from objects by running getter methods.

For saving data, it's a bit more complex. The Table Data Gateway API is practical in web applications. When you want to insert, update, or delete something, you typically have a collection of data from a form or (when you're deleting) an ID from a URL. In either case, you're starting out with request variables, and you can use these directly as method arguments. When the user has entered a new article, you might be doing this:

```
// Table data gateway insert
$gateway = new NewsGateway;
$gateway->insert(
        $request->get('headline'),$request->get('intro'),
        $request->get('text'),$request->get('author_id'));
```

Compared to this, a more object-oriented approach might seem cumbersome. You have to create an object before you can store the data. This is not so bad when you insert a new object:

```
// Row Data Gateway insert
$article = new NewsArticle(
        $request->get('headline'),$request->get('intro'),
        $request->get('text'),$request->get('author_id'));
$article->insert();
```

But when you need to update an existing article, you have to get the object from the database first and set all the data:

```
//Row Data Gateway update
$article = NewsFinder::find($request->get('id'));
$article->setHeadline($request->get('headline'));
$article->setIntro($request->get('intro'));
$article->setText($request->get('text'));
$article->setAuthorId($request->get('author_id'));
$article->update();
```

The Table Data Gateway approach is somewhat simpler:

```
// Table Data Gateway update
$gateway = new NewsGateway;
$gateway->update($request->get('id'),$request->get('headline'),
        $request->get('intro'),$request->get('text'),
        $request->get('author_id'));
```

Also, there's one less database query, since we're just doing the UPDATE without doing a SELECT to get the row first.

But the more object-oriented approach *is* more flexible. As long as we're only doing one or two things with an object, its virtues are less apparent. But what if we want to make different kinds of changes in different circumstances? For example, what if we had a separate form just for changing the headline? Or, perhaps more likely, what if we have one form for users to change their password, and another to change their preferences? If the information is represented as an object, we just change the data in the object that we need to change and update the object. With the Table Data Gateway approach, we need an extra method in the Gateway to handle a similar situation. We need one method to update the user's preferences and another method to update the user's password. If we don't, if we make one method to update all of them at once, the problem is how to find the data that the user hasn't specified in the form. We will have to either read it from the database or keep it in session variables. Both of these alternatives are neater if we use an object to represent the data.

We've covered most of the basic design patterns for data access and some more advanced ones. To go beyond those, you may start on the road leading to a full Object-Relational Mapping tool (ORM), using such patterns as Metadata Mapping and Query Object (mentioned in the previous chapter). Even if you don't, you may run into another source of complexity: the need to optimize queries.

21.4.2 Optimizing queries

Object-oriented approaches to database access emphasize programmer efficiency over program efficiency. For example, you may not need all the columns every time you use a find() method to retrieve an object. It's more efficient to have a query that asks only for the columns you need. What should you do?

Similarly, here's a question that was asked in a discussion forum: what if you need to delete 100 objects in one go? Deleting one at a time is obviously inefficient.

The answer to these questions is simple, and the principle is the same: if you need an extra query for performance, make an extra method in the data access class to run that query. Just make sure you really need it. If you need to delete 100 objects often, and it really is slow to do it one by one, this could be worth it. But don't optimize just to optimize. Don't optimize a query that obviously doesn't need it, such as one that gets only a single row from the database. (There might be exceptions to that. For example, there are column types in MySQL that are capable of storing 4GB of data. But the average database row is relatively small.)

21.5 SUMMARY

The simplest approaches to storing objects in a database sidestep the problems of mismatch between objects and relational data by dealing with data in the form of plain, non-object-oriented variables and arrays. This reduces the need to package the data. Fowler's Table Data Gateway pattern uses an object-oriented, or at least encapsulated, mechanism to store and retrieve the data, but keeps the data representations simple and similar to those in the database.

A slightly more advanced alternative—of which Active Record is the most popular example—is to let objects store themselves in the database by adding methods to the object classes to handle insert, update, and delete operations. The methods take the data from the object, insert it into SQL queries, and run the queries.

It's also possible to handle object persistence with objects that are specialized for the purpose, as in Fowler's Data Mapper pattern. This goes a long way toward making object persistence transparent to the application.

A P P E N D I X   A

Tools and tips for testing

The testing chapters in this book primarily deal with the process, principles, and logic of testing. Therefore, we've saved some juicy details for dessert, focusing on how to do specific things in the two most popular unit testing frameworks, SimpleTest and PHPUnit.

A.1 THE BASICS

Basic examples of how to use SimpleTest and PHPUnit are available elsewhere, but just to make sure we get the mechanical aspects right and don't get bogged down in some stupid error situation, we'll do an ultra-simple example that is neither conceptually challenging nor useful. We'll do this in SimpleTest first and then in PHPUnit.

Brain-dead SimpleTest example

We'll test the workings of the PHP `date()` function with a couple of simple assertions. Listing A.1 shows how this is done. Most of what is going on in it has already been explained in chapter 9. The example is included here for the sake of comparison with PHPUnit and to provide a test that can be run exactly the way it is, since it contains the code to be tested as well.

```php
<?php
require_once 'simpletest/unit_tester.php';
require_once 'simpletest/reporter.php';
error_reporting(E_ALL);

class BrainDeadTest extends UnitTestCase {
    function testDate() {
        $this->assertEqual('January 1, 1970',date('F j, Y',0));
        $this->assertPattern(
            '!\w+ \d+, \d+!',
            date('F j, Y'));
    }
}

$test = new  BrainDeadTest();
$test->run(new HtmlReporter());
```

We are testing the date() function, matching first the literal string of a date corresponding to time 0. For the second test, we want to check that the current date is also OK. Since this will vary between test runs, we use a regular expression.

Brain-dead PHPUnit example

A good way to get started with PHPUnit is to use its "skeleton" feature. To use it, you need a class file: a file that contains a class and has a file name corresponding to the class. For example, we can create a file called Foo.php containing the following:

```php
<?php
class Foo {}
```

And then we generate the "skeleton":

```
phpunit -skeleton Foo
```

This generates a file FooTest.php that contains a complete test class from which we can glean lots of interesting information about the mechanics of running PHPUnit.

Since the Foo class has no methods, no test methods are added to FooTest.php. But if we add our brain-dead test, it will work. The said test looks like this in PHPUnit:

```php
function testDate() {
    $this->assertEquals('January 1, 1970',date('F j, Y',0));
    $this->assertRegexp('!\w+ \d+, \d+!',date('F j, Y'));
}
```

This may be a somewhat perverse way of doing it, since FooTest is not doing what it's meant to do—testing the Foo class—but it works.

Now we can run FooTest.php directly:

```
php FooTest.php
```

Or we can use the `phpunit` script:

```
phpunit FooTest.php
```

Running it the first way depends on a fancy trick using a `main()` method in the test class. The `phpunit` script just needs the test class.

A.2 ORGANIZING TESTS IN A DIRECTORY STRUCTURE

There are many ways of organizing unit tests in directories. How you will want to do it will depend on how the application is organized. The most basic way is to keep the test files in the same directories as the code under test. Another fairly simple approach, used by SimpleTest for its own unit tests, is to keep all the test files in one directory.

Whatever way we organize the tests, the trick to make it work is to set the include path appropriately in all test files and then include the files the same way it's done in the application itself. If the application itself is in a single directory, you may not need to do this, but if there's some directory organization, doing it this way will prevent confusion.

The goal is to make sure the includes work and that we test the code we're developing rather than some deployed version.

The include path should always start with the root of the directory structure we're working with.

More specifically, it should start with the directory that *corresponds* to the include directory for the deployed version of the project. If the project is installed in /usr/local/lib/php/myproject and the system include path for PHP contains /usr/local/lib/php/myproject, the include path for the test file should start with the myproject development directory. If the system include path only has /usr/local/lib/php/, the include path for the test file should use the parent directory of the myproject development directory instead.

For example, if the test file is two levels down from the project root, we can do as shown in listing A.2.

Listing A.2   Setting the include path in test files

```
set_include_path(                       ❶
    dirname(__FILE__).
    '../..'.
    PATH_SEPARATOR.                     ❷
    get_include_path());

require_once 'DataSource/QueryBuilder/Query.php';   ❸
```

❶ To change the include path, we use `set_include_path()`. The path starts with the root of the directory structure for the project, in this case the grandparent directory of the current directory. We use `dirname(__FILE__)` to make this dependent on the file's location, not the current working directory when running the test.

The addition to the include path must come first; otherwise the test cases will use the deployed version of the project, if there is one. The path can be relative or absolute, whichever makes more sense for the project.

❷ Then we add PATH_SEPARATOR, which gives us the correct path separator for the current operating system (colon in Linux/Unix, semicolon in Windows). We add the existing include path at the end.

❸ We include the code we want to test by using the path from the project root. In this case, it might be that both files are in the same directory. If so, we could use just the file name. But adding the path from the project root allows us to move the test file independently of the file we're testing.

A.3   PHPUNIT AND SIMPLETEST ASSERTIONS

The basics of writing a test class are similar in SimpleTest and PHPUnit: the way to structure the test case classes is the same, and the most-commonly used assertions are almost identical.

Beyond the basics, the gap widens. Some less-commonly used assertions are subtly or grossly different. Mock objects, in particular, are called in different ways.

Table A.1 shows the assertions that have equivalent meanings in SimpleTest and PHPUnit.

In addition to the arguments shown, all assertions take a $message argument. Rather than bloat the tables by repeating it for every single assertion, we will look at an example of how it works.

If $created is a date and time object representing when something was created, you could use the following assertion to make sure the reason for failure is clear:

```
$this->assertTrue(
    $created->before($now),
    "Create time is not in the past: ".$created->isoformat()
);
```

Table A.1   Assertions that are equivalent in PHPUnit and SimpleTest

Meaning	SimpleTest	PHPUnit
Two variables, arrays, or objects have the same value or content.	assertEqual($expected, $actual)	assertEquals($expected, $actual)
The inverse of the above.	assertNotEqual($unexpected, $actual)	assertNotEquals($unexpected, $actual)
$condition evaluates to TRUE.	assertTrue($condition)	assertTrue($condition)
$condition evaluates to FALSE.	assertFalse($condition)	assertFalse($condition)
$string matches $pattern, a Perl-compatible regular expression.	assertPattern($pattern, $string)	assertRegExp($pattern, $string)

continued on next page

Table A.1 Assertions that are equivalent in PHPUnit and SimpleTest *(continued)*

Meaning	SimpleTest	PHPUnit
`$string` does not match `$pattern`.	assertNoPattern($pattern, $string)	assertNotRegExp($pattern, $string)
`$variable` belongs to `$class_or_type` or a child class of it.	assertIsA($variable, $class_or_type)	assertType($class_or_type, $variable)
`$variable` does not belong to `$class_or_type` or a child class of it.	assertNotA($variable, $class_or_type)	assertNotType($class_or_type, $variable)
`$variable` is null.	assertNull($variable)	assertNull($variable)
`$variable` is not null.	assertNotNull($variable)	assertNotNull($variable)

In addition, there are assertions in SimpleTest that have no equivalent in PHPUnit and vice versa. Generally, these are less-commonly used, but you may need some of them occasionally. Table A.2 shows the assertions that are present in PHPUnit but not in SimpleTest.

Table A.2 Assertions that are specific to PHPUnit

Meaning	PHPUnit
`$array_or_iterator` contains the element `$element`.	assertContains($element, $array_or_iterator)
`$array_or_iterator` does not contain the element `$element`.	assertNotContains($element, $array_or_iterator)
If `$expected` and `$actual` represent objects, they must be references to the same object. If not, they must be the same type and value/content.	assertSame($expected, $actual)
The inverse of `assertSame()`.	assertNotSame($expected, $actual)

Table A.3 presents the assertions that are specific to SimpleTest. `assertIdentical()` in SimpleTest may seem similar to `assertSame()` in PHPUnit. But ironically, the two assertions are not quite the same—not identical.

The table also lists two methods that can be used when there is no simple way to use assertions to verify the success of a test—when the expected behavior is an error or an exception.

Table A.3 Assertions (and two addtional methods) that are specific to SimpleTest

Meaning	SimpleTest
Usually used to compare floating-point numbers with a bit of leeway, this method allows a margin of error in comparisons.	assertWithinMargin($first, $second, $margin)

continued on next page

Table A.3 Assertions (and two addtional methods) that are specific to SimpleTest _(continued)_

Meaning	SimpleTest
Simple inversion of `assertWithinMargin()`.	`assertOutsideMargin($first, $second, $margin)`:
`$first` and `$second` are the same, but not necessarily references to the same object or value. This compares types as well as values. This means that different classes will trigger a failure, as will a comparison between the string "1" and the integer 1. Array key order is also considered important.	assertIdentical($first, $second)
Inversion of `assertIdentical()` The items can differ by type, value or hash key order.	assertNotIdentical($first, $second)
The two variables are references to the same object or value.	assertReference($first, $second)
Two objects are identical, but are not the same object. This asserts that a shallow copy was created.	assertClone($first, $second)
Will send a failure if a matching error is not detected by the end of the test.	expectError($expectation)
Will send a failure if the test does not end with the exception being thrown.	expectException($expectation)

In addition to these assertions, The SimpleTest web test has specific assertions for—among other things—checking the content of web pages. These are presented in context in the next section.

A.4 SIMPLETEST WEB TEST API

In normal unit testing, you can get away with using few of the available methods. `setup()`, `assertTrue()`, and `assertFalse()` cover most of what you need for everyday testing.

Web testing requires a richer set of methods. Therefore, we will show the API for the SimpleTest web tester in more detail.

As before, all assertions have an optional message as the last argument.

Sending and checking HTTP requests

Table A.4 SimpleTest methods for sending HTTP requests and checking the non-content parts of the result

Medhod	Action
get($url, $parameters = false)	Fetches the page given by `$url`. The first request in a test must be an absolute URL, but after that relative paths are fine. `$parameters` can contain extra parameters to add to the query string of the URL.
post($url, $parameters = false)	Does a conventional form encoded POST request straight to a URL.

continued on next page

Table A.4 SimpleTest methods for sending HTTP requests and checking the non-content parts of the result *(continued)*

Medhod	Action
head($url, $parameters = false)	Sends a HEAD request without changing the current base URL. This can be handy for fetching CSS or image files that have side effects.
assertResponse($responses)	Will fail if the HTTP response code of the last page fetch does not match the expected value, or array of expected values.
assertMime($types)	Will fail if the MIME type of the last fetch does not match the expected value.
assertHeader($header, $value = false)	Tests to see that a header was received in the last fetch. If just the header name was specified then the mere existence of the header will pass. When testing against a value, either an exact string or an expectation object can be tested against.
assertNoHeader()	Will issue a failure if that header was sent on the last page fetch regardless of the header content.
getUrl()	The current URL.
ignoreErrors()	When SimpleTest gets any kind of socket error, it will trigger a fail. This suppresses that behavior so that you can assert a page does not exist or send an expected error.
addHeader($header)	Adds a header to every request from now on.
setMaximumRedirects($max)	Limits the number of times SimpleTest will redirect. If you wish to make an assertion about the redirect page itself, you must set this value to zero or SimpleTest will skip straight past it.
setConnectionTimeout($time-out)	Limits the number of seconds SimpleTest will wait if there has been no socket activity.
useProxy($proxy, $username = false, $password = false)	For this test, use the URL in $proxy as a proxy server. This is necessary if testing from behind a firewall.

Assertions about page content

Table A.5 SimpleTest assertions for checking the text and HTML content of an HTTP response

Method	Action
assertTitle($title = false)	The page title will be compared with $title. $title can be an expectation object for a looser or negative match.
assertText($text)	Confirms that the visible text is present in the page, including frames. The comparison is space normalized, but case sensitive unless an expectation object is used instead.
assertNoText($text)	Inversion of assertText().
assertPattern($pattern)	Tests to see whether the Perl regex matches any part of the HTML content. This test is performed against the raw source.
assertNoPattern($pattern)	Inversion of assertPattern().

Links

Table A.6 SimpleTest methods for checking for the presence of links and clicking them

Method	Action
clickLink($label, $index = 0)	Will click on the link text specified. If several links have the same text then an index can tell SimpleTest how many to skip before clicking.
clickLinkById($id)	Click a link using the `id` attribute.
assertLink($label)	Tests to see whether a link is present. Space is normalized, but text is case sensitive.
assertNoLink($label)	Inversion of `assertLInk()`.
assertLinkById($id)	Use the `id` attribute to find the link.
assertNoLinkById($id)	Use the `id` attribute to find the link.

Forms and buttons

Table A.7 SimpleTest methods for checking forms, filling them in, and submitting them

Method	Action
click()	The most-used method in the whole of the SimpleTest web tester. Will try to find a button to click on, failing that a link, or failing that image "alt" or title text. All text is space normalized (all space is compressed to a single space), but is case sensitive. Any HTML entities are automatically encoded so that you can use the visible text in the comparison.
clickSubmit($label = 'Submit', $additional = false)	Will click on a submit button or button tag only. Additional parameters may be added to the form request for debugging purposes. Either to vary hidden fields or to simulate additional JavaScript behavior.
clickSubmitByName($name, $additional = false)	Will click on a submit button or button tag only. Additional parameters may be added to the form request for debugging purposes. Either to vary hidden fields or to simulate additional JavaScript behavior.
clickSubmitById($id, $additional = false)	Will click on a submit button or button tag only. Additional parameters may be added to the form request for debugging purposes. Either to vary hidden fields or to simulate additional JavaScript behavior.
clickImage($label, $x = 1, $y = 1, $additional = false)	Searches for image "alt" or title text to click on. Additional parameters will be added.
clickImageByName($name, $x = 1, $y = 1, $additional = false)	Searches for image "alt" or title text to click on. Additional parameters will be added.
clickImageById($id, $x = 1, $y = 1, $additional = false)	Searches for image "alt" or title text to click on. Additional parameters will be added.

continued on next page

Table A.7 SimpleTest methods for checking forms, filling them in, and submitting them *(continued)*

Method	Action
submitFormById($id)	Submits a form without bothering with the submit button. This can be used to simulate automatic submits by JavaScript.
setField($label, $value)	Sets a form field before clicking the submit button or image. `label` is the value of the label tag surrounding the field, or the name attribute if there is no label. For a file upload, the field must be set to the path of the uploaded file.
setFieldByName($name, $value)	This is the same as `setField()`, but the label tag is ignored.
setFieldById($id, $value)	Uses the `id` attribute instead of the label tag or name attribute.
assertField($label, $expected = true)	Issues a failure if the current setting of the form field does not match the expected value.
assertFieldByName($name, $expected = true)	Issues a failure if the current setting of the form field does not match the expected value.
assertFieldById($id, $expected = true)	Issues a failure if the current setting of the form field does not match the expected value.

Displaying content and information

Table A.8 SimpleTest methods for showing (rather than testing) the HTML and text content of an HTTP response

Method	Action
showRequest()	Dumps of the last page request sent by SimpleTest.
showHeaders()	Shows the incoming headers from the last page event.
showSource()	Dumps of the current HTML content including all subframes.
showText()	Dumps just the visible text as a string. All whitespace is compressed. Although not useful in itself, it does make it easy to search for content.

HTTP authentication

Table A.9 SimpleTest methods for checking and performing HTTP authentication

Method	Action
authenticate($username, $password)	Gets past a 401 challenge header. You normally issue this method straight after the `get()` or `click()` call. SimpleTest handles simple authentication only.
assertAuthentication($authentication = false)	Tests that the browser is currently in an authenticated site and tests for the authentication type. Only simple authentication is currently supported.
assertNoAuthentication()	Tests that we are not in a simple authentication realm.
assertRealm($realm)	Issues a failure if $realm does not match the authentication realm description. An expectation can be used instead of exact text.

Browser navigation

Table A.10 SimpleTest methods for emulating brower restart, reload, back, and forward

Method	Action
restart()	Equivalent to closing the browser and then opening it again.
retry()	Equivalent to the retry or reload button on the browser. Handy for testing vulnerable forms.
back()	Equivalent to the back button on the browser.
forward()	Equivalent to clicking the forward button after clicking the back button.

Cookies

Table A.11 SimpleTest methods for checking, setting, modifying, and ignoring cookies

Method	Action
getCookie($name)	Reads a cookie value for the current domain.
setCookie($name, $value, $host = false, $path = '/', $expiry = false)	Sets an arbitrary cookie.
assertCookie($name, $expected = false)	Tests the named cookie value against exact text, or an expectation object.
assertNoCookie($name)	Tests that no cookie exists by that name in the current domain.
ageCookies($interval)	Moves cookie expiry forward in time. This allows us to simulate a long gap between closing and opening the browser to expire long-lived cookies. Used with `restart()`.
ignoreCookies()	Do not read any cookies and ignore the ones we have.

Frames

Table A.12 SimpleTest methods for frame navigation

Method	Action
ignoreFrames()	Do not load frames.
setFrameFocus($name)	Focus on a named frame only, ignoring all other content. This can sometimes be necessary for navigating complex framed displays with similar content.
setFrameFocusByIndex($choice)	The frames are numbered from 1 onward in case they don't have names.
getFrameFocus()	The current frame.
clearFrameFocus()	This returns SimpleTest to the default top level view.

APPENDIX B

Security

Security is an incredibly important topic in the field of web application development. As a PHP developer, you're going to be responsible for the security of your PHP code, and your applications are sure to be the target of frequent attacks. This appendix tries to give a basic introduction to get you started on the right foot, so that you can learn strategies and techniques for secure PHP programming.

It also shows a few of the most common and dangerous attacks currently facing PHP developers, such as cross-site scripting (XSS) and SQL injection. You'll see how these attacks are initiated and what steps you can take to protect your PHP applications.

B.1   FILTER INPUT

Terminology is a necessary evil for computer programmers. What does *filter* mean? Is it the same thing as *validate*? What is *input*?

Filtering is a somewhat formal term with aliases that include validating, sanitizing, and cleaning. Interpretations vary, but security experts agree that a best practice is to consider filtering to be an inspection process. The purpose of the inspection is to determine whether the data being inspected is valid, thus why some people call this validation. Regardless of what you call it, this is a cornerstone of web application security.

Input is data that is not generated within your application. All input is tainted and should be considered suspect until you can be absolutely sure it is valid. An example of data generated within your application is hard-coded data, such as the email address in the following example:

```
$email = 'chris@example.org';
```

Clearly, you're providing the data assigned to $email, so you can trust it (unless you cannot trust yourself!). An email address that originates from any remote source is input:

```
$email = $_POST['email'];
```

Common sources of input include form data, URLs, cookies, HTTP headers, and RSS feeds. Even data from databases and session data stores should be considered input, although you can opt to consider these sources to be an integral part of your application instead of remote sources of data. (Just keep in mind that this ties the security of your application to the security of these systems.) Figure B.1 illustrates the principle.

This means every single time you use data that is provided by a remote source, your first step should be to inspect it to make sure it is exactly the type of data you expect. Filter input.

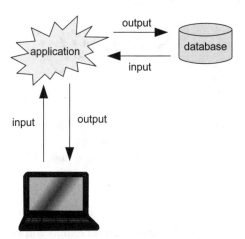

Figure B.1   Interaction with databases and similar sources should be considered input and output.

In order to safely keep up with what has been filtered and what hasn't, you can employ a simple naming convention such as the use of a separate array of filtered data called $clean:

```
$clean = array();

if (ctype_alpha($_POST['username'])) {
    $clean['username'] = $_POST['username'];
} else {
    /* Error */
}
```

If you prefer an object-oriented approach, there are many similar solutions, and you should adopt a practice that fits your own personal preferences. Just try to make it easy to reliably distinguish between filtered and tainted (not filtered) data, and you'll be on the right track. A failure to safely make this distinction can be as dangerous as not filtering input at all.

Since security vulnerabilities are caused by an application's interaction with attackers and other users, output as well as input can be used maliciously. The counterpart of filtering input is escaping output.

B.2 ESCAPE OUTPUT

Many common security vulnerabilities in PHP applications can be attributed to a failure to escape output. In fact, many security vulnerabilities commonly attributed to a lack of input filtering are really output escaping problems. For example, Nitesh Dhanjani, a web application security expert, noted in his blog that cross-site scripting (XSS) vulnerabilities are due to a lack of output escaping, despite the common belief that they are an input filtering problem.

Like filtering, *escaping* is a term that is sometimes interpreted differently by different people. Escaping is any process where you represent data in such a way that it can be preserved—rather than interpreted—in another context. Common examples of escaping functions include `htmlentities()` for preserving data in HTML and `urlencode()` for preserving data in URLs.

Understanding when and why to escape something depends entirely upon your ability to understand context. A simple example is escaping something to be used in a URL:

```
$url = array();
$url['name'] = urlencode($clean['name']);
$link = "http://host/path/to/script.php?name={$url['name']}";
```

This example demonstrates a few new concepts. First, the use of $url is identical in concept to the use of $clean. It's an array that is always initialized to an empty array, and only data that has been escaped for use in a URL is stored therein. Also worth noting is that the data being escaped has already been filtered, because it is $clean['name'].

Depending on the filtering rules, $clean['name'] might not actually require escaping. Its value might already be safe to use in this context. For example,

```
$clean['name'] = 'chris';
```

Resist the temptation to depend on such assumptions to determine whether the escaping is necessary. Escaping can safely be used on any value; if it's unnecessary, no change is made:

```
$clean['name'] = 'chris';
$url['name'] = urlencode($clean['name']);
/* $url['name'] = 'chris'; */
```

The fundamental purpose of escaping is to preserve data in a different context. This can be difficult to appreciate, because the process of escaping typically modifies it:

```
/* $clean['name'] = "O'Neill"; */

$mysql = array();
$mysql['name'] = mysql_real_escape_string($clean['name']);

/* $mysql['name'] = "O\'Neill"; */
```

It's important to realize that the modification is temporary and is only necessary to keep the data from being misinterpreted. For example, the single quote in O'Neill can potentially mangle the format of an SQL query. If you use the escaped version (O\'Neill) in the SQL query, the original, unescaped data (O'Neill) is what is actually stored in the database. For this reason, you should never need to remove the escaping of anything. If you do, it likely indicates a problem in your programming logic.

Understanding context can be especially difficult when combined. For example, consider the following link:

```
<a href="http://host/path/to/script.php?name=chris">Link</a>
```

The name in this URL (chris) initially exists only in the context of HTML. However, when this link is clicked, it exists in the context of a URL. This particular example uses a value that is safe in both contexts without escaping, but what if the value is dynamic? What if it can legitimately contain data that is unsafe in one or both of these contexts? In this case, you must escape for both, and order is important:

```
/* $clean['name'] = "Eugene O'Neill"; */
$url = array();
$html = array();

$url['name'] = urlencode($clean['name']);
$html['name'] = htmlentities($url['name'], ENT_QUOTES, 'UTF-8');

$link = "http://host/path/to/script.php?name={$html['name']}";

/* $link = 'http://host/path/to/script.php?name=Eugene+O%27Neill'; */
```

If this link is followed with a web browser, script.php can use $_GET['name'], and its value is simply Eugene O'Neill. Thus, although the name is escaped twice, the escaping is only used to preserve the name in different contexts.

Now that you understand the important topics of filtering and escaping, you can learn about a few of the most-common and dangerous attacks.

B.3   CROSS-SITE SCRIPTING

Cross-site scripting (XSS) continues to be one of the most-common web application vulnerabilities. XSS vulnerabilities exist when tainted data is not escaped properly when being output to the client: for example, whenever you are generating dynamic HTML, and some of it is suspect, such as in the following example:

```
$username = $_COOKIE['username'];

echo "<p>Welcome back, $username!</p>";
```

Because all values in `$_COOKIE` constitute input, they should be filtered before being used. Worse, all data being used in the context of HTML should first be escaped. Escaping alone prevents this vulnerability:

```
$html = array();

$html['username'] = htmlentities(
    $_COOKIE['username'], ENT_QUOTES, 'UTF-8');

echo "<p>Welcome back, {$html['username']}!</p>";
```

A better practice is to always filter input and escape output:

```
$clean = array();
$html = array();

if (ctype_alnum($_COOKIE['username'])) {
    $clean['username'] = $_COOKIE['username'];
} else {
    /* Error */
}
$html['username'] = htmlentities(
    $clean['username'], ENT_QUOTES, 'UTF-8');
echo "<p>Welcome back, {$html['username']}!</p>";
```

In addition to ensuring that you also use valid data in your important business logic, this combination also provides redundant protection against XSS. This approach is called Defense in Depth, a popular security principle that stresses the value in redundant safeguards.

While XSS occurs on output, there are other attacks that happen inside the application if input data is not filtered. SQL injection is one of these.

B.4 SQL INJECTION

As is the case with cross-site scripting (XSS), SQL injection is a result of using tainted, unescaped data in a different context. Rather than the context being HTML, SQL injection attacks target SQL queries. Consider the following example:

```
/* $password = hash($_POST['password']); */

$sql = "SELECT count(*)
        FROM   users
        WHERE  username = '{$_POST['username']}'
        AND    password = '$password'";
```

Although this example doesn't show the execution of the SQL query, it demonstrates the vulnerability. Because data supplied by the user is used to construct the SQL query, a clever user can supply data that modifies the intended behavior of the query. Consider the following:

```
$_POST['username'] = "chris' /*";

/* $password = hash($_POST['password']); */
```

```
$sql = "SELECT count(*)
        FROM    users
        WHERE   username = '{$_POST['username']}'
        AND     password = '$password'";
```

In this example, $sql is the following (an arbitrary hash is used to represent the hashed password, because it's unrelated to the topic at hand):

```
SELECT count(*)
FROM    users
WHERE   username = 'chris' /*'
AND     password = '412e11d5317627e48a4b0615c84b9a8f'";
```

Because /* denotes the beginning of a comment, the SQL query is effectively

```
SELECT count(*)
FROM    users
WHERE   username = 'chris'
```

If the count is being used to determine whether authentication is successful, which is often the case, a user who supplies such a username can log in as the user chris without knowing the password.

Protecting against SQL injection is pretty simple. If you filter input and escape output, there is no practical risk of a successful attack:

```
$clean = array();
$mysql = array();

/* $password = hash($_POST['password']); */

if (ctype_alnum($_POST['username'])) {
    $clean['username'] = $_POST['username'];
} else {
    /* Error */
}

if (ctype_xdigit($password)) {
    $clean['password'] = $password;
} else {
    /* Error */
}

$mysql['username'] = mysql_real_escape_string($clean['username']);
$mysql['password'] = mysql_real_escape_string($clean['password']);

$sql = "SELECT count(*)
        FROM    users
        WHERE   username = '{$mysql['username']}'
        AND     password = '{$mysql['password']}'";

/* mysql_query($sql); */
```

NOTE   This example uses an escaping function specific to MySQL. There are native escaping functions for most popular databases, and you should always choose the native escaping function over a generic one such as addslashes().

As with XSS, escaping alone prevents the vulnerability, but you should never rely on a single safeguard for protection.

If you use a database library with support for prepared statements and bound parameters, you can enjoy the strongest protection against SQL injection:

```
$statement = $db->prepare("SELECT count(*)
                          FROM    users
                          WHERE   username = :username
                          AND     password = :password");

$statement->bindParam(':username', $clean['username']);
$statement->bindParam(':password', $clean['password']);

$statement->execute();
```

Because this approach ensures your data never enters a context where it can be considered anything but raw data, there is no risk of SQL injection.

We've seen how two of the most important attacks can be prevented by filtering input and escaping output. But there are times when these measures fall short. One example is session fixation.

B.5 SESSION FIXATION

Fully understanding session fixation requires that you fully understand sessions, but the basic idea is that for sessions to work, each request from the client must include a session identifier. By default, PHP uses a cookie to propagate the session identifier, but it can also be passed in $_GET. Because of this, an attacker can try to trick a victim into using a specific session identifier by embedding it in a link:

```
<a href="http://host/path/to/script.php?PHPSESSID=1234">
  Click Here!
</a>
```

A user who follows this link will effectively pass a session identifier of 1234 to the target site. If session_start() is called on the receiving page, the user's session will be assigned the session identifier chosen by the attacker. This is a very dangerous and common scenario.

Luckily, it's easy to defeat session fixation attacks. The root cause of the problem is that an attacker can potentially know the session identifier of a user who is logged in. As long as the user is anonymous, there is no risk. Therefore, simply regenerate the session identifier when a user logs in to be sure you're using a fresh, PHP-generated session identifier:

```
if (auth($_POST['username'], $_POST['password'])) {
    session_regenerate_id();
    $_SESSION['auth'] = TRUE;
}
```

PHP handles regenerating the session identifier, preserving all of the old session data, and propagating the new session identifier. All you have to do is call this one function whenever there is a change in the user's privilege level, and you're protected.

B.6 MORE INFORMATION

It is impossible to adequately cover web application security in a short appendix, and you should continue to educate yourself on the topic to be sure that you're well-prepared.

The following resources can help get you started:

- The PHP Security Consortium at http://phpsec.org/
- The Web Application Security Consortium at http://webappsec.org/
- The Open Web Application Security Project at http://owasp.org/
- *Essential PHP Security*, by Chris Shiflett [Shiflett], and its companion web site at http://phpsecurity.org/
- *php|architect's Guide to PHP security* by Ilia Alshanetsky [Alshanetsky]

B.7 SUMMARY

We've seen three of the most-common security threats: cross-site scripting (XSS), SQL injection and session fixation.

We've also seen three ways to prevent these attacks. The first two—escaping output and filtering input—are general security mechanisms that can prevent several different attacks, including ones that have not been mentioned here. What kind of output escaping to apply depends on the nature of the output medium. How to filter input varies with the kind of data being input. We've also seen how to apply a specific remedy for session fixation by regenerating the session identifier.

If we forget to use these safeguards even once, security may be compromised. Using simple conventions—such as keeping filtered input in a separate array called $clean—helps us to remember and keep track of what has been filtered.

resources

All URLs listed here were valid at the time of publishing.

WORKS CITED

In print

[Alur et al.] Alur, Deepak, et al. *Core J2EE Patterns.* Sun Microsystems Press, 2001.

[Alshanetsky] Alshanetsky, Ilia. *php/architect's Guide to PHP Security.* Marco Tabini & Associates, 2005.

[Beck] Beck, Kent. *Test-Driven Development by Example.* Addison-Wesley, 2003.

[Evans] Evans, Eric. *Domain-Driven Design.* Addison-Wesley, 2004.

[Feathers] Feathers, Michael. *Working Effectively with Legacy Code.* Prentice Hall, 2005.

[Fowler Refactoring] Fowler, Martin, et al. *Refactoring: Improving the Design of Existing Code.* Addison-Wesley, 1999.

[Gang of Four] Erich Gamma, Richard Helm, Ralph Johnson, John Vlissides. *Design Patterns.* Addison-Wesley, 1995.

[Larman] Larman, Craig. *Applying UML and Patterns.* Prentice Hall, 2005.

[Nock] Nock, Clifton. *Data Access Patterns.* Addison-Wesley, 2004.

[P of EAA] Fowler, Martin. *Patterns of Enterprise Application Architecture.* Addison-Wesley, 2003.

[POSA] Bushman, Frank, et al. *Pattern-Oriented Software Architecture.* John Wiley & Sons, 1996.

[Shiflett] Shiflett, Chris. *Essential PHP Security.* O'Reilly, 2006.

[Uncle Bob] Martin, Robert C. *Agile Software Development. Principles, Patterns, and Practice.* Prentice Hall, 2003.

Online

[Celko] Celko, Joe. *I Will Never Have To Port This Code.* 2003. http://www.intelligententer-prise.com/030422/607celko1_1.jhtml

[Fowler DI] Fowler, Martin. *Inversion of Control Containers and the Dependency Injection Pattern.* 2004. http://www.martinfowler.com/articles/injection.html

[Fowler Time Point] Fowler, Martin. *Time Point.* http://www.martinfowler.com/ap2/time-Point.html

index

MANNING EBOOK PROGRAM

All ebooks are 50% off the price of the print edition!

In the spring of 2000 Manning became the first publisher to offer ebook versions of all our new titles as a way to get customers the information they need quickly and easily. We continue to publish ebook versions of all our new releases, and every ebook is priced at 50% off the print version!

Go to www.manning.com/payette to download the ebook version of this book and have the information at your fingertips wherever you might be.

MANNING EARLY ACCESS PROGRAM

Get Early Chapters Now!

In 2003 we launched MEAP, our groundbreaking Early Access Program, to give customers who can't wait the opportunity to read chapters as they are written and receive the book when it is released. Because these are "early" chapters, your feedback will also help shape the final manuscript.

Our entire MEAP title list is always changing and you can find the current titles at www.manning.com